Secularization and the Working Class

Secularization and the Working Class

The Czech Lands and Central Europe in the Nineteenth Century

Edited by
Lukáš Fasora, Jiří Hanuš,
and Jiří Malíř

PICKWICK *Publications* · Eugene, Oregon

SECULARIZATION AND THE WORKING CLASS
The Czech Lands and Central Europe in the Nineteenth Century

Pickwick Publications
An Imprint of Wipf and Stock Publishers
199 W. 8th Ave., Suite 3
Eugene, OR 97401

www.wipfandstock.com

ISBN 13: 978-1-61097-014-3

Cataloging-in-Publication data:

    Secularization and the working class : the Czech lands and Central Europe in the nineteenth century / edited by Lukáš Fasora, Jiří Hanuš, Jiří Malíř.

    xiv + 242 p. ; 23 cm. Includes bibliographical references and index.

    ISBN 13: 978-1-61097-014-3

    1. Working class—Europe—Religious life. 2. Europe—Religion—19th century. 3. Secularization Europe. I. Title. II. Fasora, Lukáš, III. Hanuš, Jiří. IV. Malíř, Jiří.

HC59.15 S25 2011

Manufactured in the U.S.A.

Published within GAČR project entitled Social Interaction between Aristocracy, Bourgeoisie and Working Class: The Case of Moravia in 1873–1918, no 409/08/0591, and within Centre for Studies in Central European History: Sources, Countries, Culture—no MU MSM 0021622426.

Translators: Graeme Dibble, Michaela Kapušová, and John McKenna

Reviewers: Ivana Noble (Prague) and Pavel Kladiwa (Ostrava)

Contents

Contents

Contributors

Lukáš Fasora, Filozofická fakulta Masarykovy univerzity, Brno
fasora@phil.muni.cz

Jiří Hanuš, Filozofická fakulta Masarykovy univerzity, Brno
jirh1963@gmail.com

Miloš Havelka, Fakulta humanitních studií Univerzity Karlovy, Praha
milos.havelka@googlemail.com

Roman Holec, Filozofická fakulta Univerzity Komenského v Bratislavě, Bratislava
rh1918@yahoo.com

Martin Jemelka, Katedra historie FF Ostravské univerzity v Ostravě, Ostrava
Jemelka.Martin@seznam.cz

Kristina Kaiserová, Filozofická fakulta Univerzity Jana Evangelisty Purkyně, Ústí nad Labem
kaiserova@albis-int.cz

Jiří Kořalka, Praha
jiri.koralka@volny.cz

Marie Macková, Ústav historických věd Filozofické fakulty Univerzity Pardubice, Pardubice
mackova.marie@tiscali.cz

Jiří Malíř, Filozofická fakulta Masarykovy univerzity, Brno
malir@phil.muni.cz

Pavel Marek, Katedra historie Filozofické fakulty Univerzity Palackého, Olomouc
marekpa@tiscali.cz

Jiří Matějček, CLEO, pracoviště historické sociologie, Kutná Hora

Juergen Schmidt, Humboldt-Universität zu Berlin, Berlin
juergen.schmidt@asa.hu-berlin.de

Josef Šebesta, Praha
josef.sebesta@raz-dva.cz

Preface

"At first sight it would appear that the issue of religion has lost its former importance and is more of a secondary concern in the workers' movement. If religion and faith in God are discussed, everyone contemptuously dismisses them, and the smile and disdain are natural signs of intelligence. But beneath the surface of this contempt, beneath this apparent calm, there is widespread ignorance as to the causes of both the great religious struggles of the old world and manifestations of religion in modern life."[1]

THESE DELIBERATIONS BY THE editor of the leading socialist paper *Hlas lidu* from 1908 sum up very precisely the issues which the organizers put forward at the symposium "Secularization of the working class in the 19th Century," which was held by the history department of Masaryk University in Brno in 2009 and which forms the basis of this publication.

When contemplating the notion of secularization we are aware of the ambivalence of this cultural and social phenomenon which manifests itself primarily through a decline in the importance of the Church and religion in both individual and public life, while at the same time there is a search for new identities and moral codes, which might be, for example, the nation, class, or even a new relationship towards religion, redefined according to the criteria that are most suited to the modern age. In this respect the so-called "religion of humanity" plays a significant role.

There emerge three aspects to the historical analysis of secularization: firstly an analysis of the revolutionary events of the modern age, particularly where there is an impact on the relationship between the state and the Church—this research looks at the French Revolution and its influence on Central Europe, the revolutions from 1848–1849, as well as revolution "from above," which applies in particular to the *Kulturkampf* during the Bismarck era. The second crucial trend in the basic research involves the development of science in the modern age and the relationship between science, progress and politics.[2] Here historians were interested in the expansion of science in various social groups and its application in schools and other educational institutions. The third trend which also influenced our research concerned modernization and an analysis of sociocultural realities—European development was described as a transition from an agricultural, hierarchical society to an urbanized, democratic society, a society which was both industrialized and secularized. The work of the British historian Hugh McLeod shows in a (West) European comparison the difference in the speed and course of seculariza-

---

1. "Dělnictvo a náboženství," *Hlas lidu*, September 30, 1908.
2. See Loewenstein, *Víra v pokrok. Dějiny jedné evropské ideje.*

tion that can be seen in a relatively small area in the modern era, how the variety of conditions linking socio-economic and cultural matters are almost unlimited from the viewpoint of various social levels and formations, from the viewpoint of gender, genera-tions, etc.[3] To express this variety in a Central European context would seem to be an exceptionally difficult task. Nevertheless, the formulation of research questions must be based on these realities.

The aim of this publication is certainly not to be, nor can it be, a comprehensive picture of religion and faith within the lower levels of society and the working class in particular, but rather a collection of several interesting features and connections within a Czech and Central European context which up until now have escaped the attention of historians who have concentrated mainly on Western European and American events. The Czech lands present an interesting area for research into secularization for at least two main reasons—firstly due to the manner in which, until recently, the subject had been addressed by Marxist historiography, and secondly, the specific character of the social formation called the working class.

Whether historians only paid lip service to Marxist approaches or whether they were actually ideologically attached to them, the ideological pressure from the Communist regime led them to interpret religion and faith as obstacles to workers forming a class consciousness. The inexorable progress of history and the realization of the historical role of this social class was to gradually lead the workers towards a repudiation of the religious concept of the world, and the task for historians was to support this journey through an interpretation of past events. During the era of the Communist regime this highly ideological concept proved extremely restrictive for the more capable historians and only a few of them were able to look at the theme from a different perspective—which did not, of course, prevent them from protecting themselves in their texts with quotations from the acknowledged classics and leading lights of Marxist ideology. Within a Marxist-Leninist ideological framework in the Czech lands and the countries of the socialist bloc there was room for creative study of the cultural changes affecting the working class when this was placed within the context of the national-emancipation process, which—even though it was mainly carried out by members of the bourgeoisie—also affected the working class. Anti-clericalism as an important element of the Czech national revival presented a significant platform for co-operation between the bourgeois parties and working-class organisations, and this theme could not be ignored even by Marxist historiography in the search for "progressive" national traditions. Opportunities also arose for the application of non-dogmatic approaches to the theme in microhis-torical research and ethnographic studies, which—often very carefully and only by implication—demonstrated in their results the incompatability of the ideological clichés with reality. The microhistorical research mentioned often provides valuable material for the second issue—the socio-economic and cultural restrictions on the concept of the "working class," an issue which goes hand in hand with the question of the profiles of the so-called bourgeoisie, petite bourgeoisie, middle class, etc. Although British and German

---

3. McLeod, *Secularisation in Western Europe 1848–1914.*

historians started to examine this problem in the 1960s, it was not until the 1980s that Austrian historians published works in this area, with Czechs following approximately ten years after that. A major reason was the significant variety in the living conditions of the lower and middle levels of society in Central European countries and the existence of several transitory social forms, resulting in a lack of methodological clarity. The industrialization of the Czech lands and the Habsburg Empire not only occurred much more slowly than in Western Europe, but was also somewhat half-hearted. Those industrial centres with large numbers of workers consisted geographically and socially of sparse islands surrounded by agricultural areas; in Moravia they were concentrated around Brno and Ostrava, while in Bohemia they were situated around Prague, Pilsen, and smaller industrial areas in the foothills to the north and east of the country. In comparison with Western Europe the important industrial centers in the Czech lands had numerous links to agriculture, whether it was the widespread use of the working class for domestic labor, the phenomenon of subsistence farmers dividing their living and identity between the countryside and the city, or the typical form of Czech industrialization where a factory was built right in the middle of the countryside and orientated towards the use of unqualified but very cheap labor from the ranks of the lower classes of rural society.

The Czech worker in the second half of the nineteenth century had much stronger links to rural life than his British or German counterpart and was less affected by modern trends in science and education, and therefore more integrated into traditional society with its authorities and religious dogmas and ideas. Nevertheless, during the second half of the nineteenth century even the Czech working class underwent significant changes which had earlier affected the German-speaking population and later also the Czech-speaking population. Around 1900 the technological and general economic changes also manifested themselves in the character profile of the typical worker. He gradually moved away from his former life due to the possibility of education and professional development, which contributed to a solid financial basis and even raised the living standards of the working class. From the 1890s the acquisition of basic necessities and social security for a greater number of workers, though of course with large differences across trades, regions and gender, paved the way for an intellectual transformation of the workers. A generation now firmly connected to the city had an education, even at the most basic level, which provided a scientific interpretation of the world, so that by around 1900 religion and faith were being pushed further out of people's minds, though only a very small minority would consider faith internally or externally to be a fallacy. This was also connected to the rise in political Catholicism, which by the end of the 19th century had led to the establishment of several institutions in the form of associations transforming into modern political parties[4] and which provided effective competition to the Social Democrats and leftist thinking. Whilst in the industrial regions of Western Europe the most serious contenders for the "new religion" were the socialist movements with their supposedly scientific view of the world as the most coherent substitute for the religious

---

4. Malíř, *Od spolků k moderním politickým stranám.*

view, in the Czech lands the expansion of Marxist socialism was obstructed by weighty ideological opponents.

In the second half of the nineteenth century the Czech lands were the setting for a fierce national struggle which by the end of the nineteenth century had directly affected the working class. During the period in the 1880s when the workers' movement was being suppressed by the conservative Austrian government of Viscount Eduard Taaffe, the differences between the individual nationalities of the working class within the Austrian "Small International" had still not clearly emerged. However, even in the 1870s it was obvious that having German speakers as the leading figures of the Social Democratic movement in Vienna was going to be an issue for the Czech working class. The leaders of the Social Democratic party tried to address this problem by granting some autonomy to the Czech branch of the political party, though at the same time they played down the serious problems which arose from the complicated situation of having workers of differing nationalities. The more qualified German workforce watched with resentment and unease as a tide of unqualified workers from the Czech countryside swept into the hitherto purely German towns and regions, and within the workers' movement national identity became a far more important homogenizing factor than the Marxist identification with class. The end of state repression of the workers' movement after 1890 and the concurrent rise of more liberal and more radically nationalist political forces in the Czech and German camps brought social issues more into the sphere of national rivalry and also brought some of the workers' concerns closer to the radical nationalists. In place of a religious view of the world was a so-called progressive interpretation, though of course without the underpinning of Karl Marx and Friedrich Engels, but with the central idea being the "national interest." With a view to the national interest, forces from both the German and Czech camps attempted, with great success, to address the working class. They portrayed religion and the Catholic Church as being anathema to the interests of the nation and the workers, and attacked the stereotyped Austrian alliance of throne and altar. In the Czech lands this was seen in the fierce anti-clericalism of the Young Czech party and the so-called national workers, and in a German context there was the Deutsche Arbeiterpartei with its pan-German view of the world, though with a more realistic social policy, and its hostility towards Catholic ultramontanism.

Competition from nationalist forces, but also from the modernized Christian-Social movement, weakened the influence of Social Democracy on wide sections of the working class. Even so, the Social Democrats maintained a clear predominance among the urban working class; apart from "red" strongholds such as Brno, Pilsen or Liberec, this also involved many small towns where Social Democracy found itself on the defensive, coming under pressure from nationalist political forces. The core of Social Democratic sympathizers was undoubtedly made up of factory workers, mainly qualified workers—the influence of the socialists sharply declined among men in sectors with a higher representation of unqualified and especially female workers (the textile, clothing and tobacco industries).

Women, present mainly in sectors with low qualification requirements, represented a thorny problem for the socialists because of their persistent adherence to traditional values (and thus also to certain traditional forms of religion). Although the party based its campaigning on the principles of August Bebel's famous book *Women and Socialism* and formally declared its support for the idea of full emancipation of women, the Social Democrats still had to approach this matter very circumspectly in the predominantly Catholic environment of the Habsburg monarchy. The majority of the party's male backers frowned upon the fact that the female workforce had become a significant part of the labor market in the late nineteenth century and posed more of a threat to the econo-mic position of qualified workers than disputes with employers. However, this was surely about more than just a conflict of economic interests. Because of their lack of education, women were more attached to traditional values and represented an imaginary cultural bridge to the rural world, where the first two generations of workers continued to maintain extensive family ties which would provide assistance in case of unemployment or industrial action. We find only a few exceptional cases of politically active women, mainly in the very core of the Social Democratic movement, i.e. in political associations, while in other satellite organizations the proportion of women was low. Women in the numerous socialist satellite organizations, especially consumer cooperatives and educational societies, also preferred to move anti-religious propaganda into the background and concentrate on other issues. It was not even unheard of for Social Democratic organizations to publish calendars with religious themes and lists of saints' days for commercial reasons. Not even in the case of the socialist movement can one speak of the disruption of the traditional image of the family, firmly linked with religion, in which the woman's main responsibility was looking after the household and the children.

The situation was very different within small-scale industry as here the socialists were only marginally influential. The problem for the Social Democratic movement was that when confronted by their opponents they were unable to carry out *revolutions of the mind*. The workers' attachment to the rural way of life, traditional society, religion and faith was, for the time being, stronger than the power of the Social Democrats. The workers' education gave way to primitive propaganda which overlapped with tradition rather than uprooting it. The Social Democrats made little headway in achieving the movement's important goal, whereby "from the fire of new ideas, thought through to their conclusion, the workers will throw out the old ideas and cast off the remnants of bourgeois culture which enshroud the core of their proletarian being."[5] In 1902, Viktor Adler, the leader of the Austrian Social Democrats, also expressed his doubts about the true Marxist content of the workers' education: "The task of workers' education is not to learn how to write properly, to speak properly, to eat properly or to behave properly. We do not demand from you any kind of correct (i.e., bourgeois) behaviour, we demand self-consciousness."[6] However, the relationship of a large majority of the working class and party functionaries towards Marxism remained extremely limited, restricted to propaganda slogans: it was certainly not strongly rooted in a Marxist world view and therefore a repudiation of a religious understanding of the world.

---

5. "Vzdělávejme se!" *Hlas lidu* June 3, 1908.

6. Pepper, *Die frühe österreichische Sozialdemokratie*, 98.

Our knowledge of the cultural profile of Czech workers at the start of the modern era therefore gives rise to a series of questions. The wide variety and ambivalence of many economic, social and cultural processes and influences, together with the state of research after the Communist era, mean that further questioning using a more modern methodological approach is required.

L. Fasora,

J. Hanuš,

and

J. Malíř

PART ONE

Methods and International Inspiration

1

Two Trends in the Process of Secularization in the Nineteenth and Twentieth Centuries[1]

Miloš Havelka

"They plow'd in tears, the trumpets sounded before the golden plow, and the voices of the living creatures were heard in the clouds of heaven . . ."

—William Blake

"However, Austrian Catholicism was never completely authentic. After the collapse of the Reformation, especially in the Czech Lands, it never had a challenger and became the comfortable official religion"

—Tomáš G. Masaryk

IT IS IMPOSSIBLE TO ignore the extent to which in the last two decades of the twentieth century an interest in religion once more came to the forefront of the humanities, in particular history, sociology and culturology. At the turn of the millennium this interest was deepened by political developments, not least because of the connection with global terrorism. The French scholar of Arabic studies and religion Gilles Kepel described this situation as *God's revenge* to express his belief that an often simplified or fundamentalist form of religion had returned to the public and political life of nations in the case of all three of the Abrahamic religions—Christianity, Judaism and Islam.[2] According to Kepel, *God's revenge* symbolically began in the second half of the 1970s with three important religious events—the return of the Ayatollah Khomeini to Iran, the election of Karol Wojtyla as Pope and the political support of Menachem Begin by the previously restrained Israeli fundamentalist parties, which enabled his ascent to power. Over time these events began to exert wide-ranging influences on religious attitudes in other aspects of social life. For example, the German systematic theologian Friedrich Wilhelm Graf warned in his book *Die Wiederkehr der Gotter: Religion in moderner Kultur* [The

---

1. This paper was made possible by grant no. P405/10/J060 from the Czech Republic Grant Agency.
2. Kepel, *Boží pomsta.*

Return of the Gods: Religion in Modern Culture][3] of the hitherto neglected or underesti-mated effect of religion in several central areas of modernity and points out, for example, the thematization of religious pluralism in market models (religious economics) and in a denominationally based comparison of development (shared history).

The function of religion and its position within the structure of modern society also began to occupy authors whose works had previously been concerned with the more widespread influence of the Enlightenment, such as Niklas Luhman, Jürgen Habermas, and Ulrich Beck.[4] A longer-term interest in religiosity is also encountered in the phenom-enologically oriented sociology of Thomas Luckmann and Peter L. Berger.[5] The work of Raymond Aron on the specific aims of "secularized" religions has been developed by the Munich-based Hans Maier and the Rome-based Emilio Gentile.[6]

In the Czech Republic there has been a bias towards the translation of French politi-cal works over German studies: alongside the previously cited Gilles Kepel, one can also mention Marcel Gauchet[7] as well as René Rémond's historical overview *Náboženství a společnost v Evropě* [Religion and Society in Europe], which places a somewhat one-dimensional emphasis on the interpretation of the development of political power in the relationship between the state and religion.[8]

These and other attempts to analyze the position and function of religion in contem-porary society are complemented by the compensation-oriented renewed interest in the older theme of *secularization*. In individual works this concept can often be significantly over-worked and obfuscatory in its content, as well as frequently being oversimplified.[9]

---

3. Graf, *Die Wiederkehr der Gotter.*

4. Luhmann, *Die Religion der Gesellschaft*; Habermas, *Zwischen Naturalismus und Religion*; Beck, *Der eigene Gott.* The extensive literature on the sociology of religion in Germany (Max Weber, Ernst Troeltsch, Ernst Simmel, Joachim Wach, and others from the first decades of the last century; it could even be somewhat provocatively said that modern German sociology emerged from the sociology of religion) created a strong tradition in sociological religious studies, to which we can also add these modern studies: Fürstenberg, *Religionssoziologie*; Matthes, *Einführung in Die Religionssoziologie*; Helle, *Religionssoziologie*; Knoblauch, *Reigionssoziologie*, etc., then the important and internationally recognized collections such as Faber and Hager, *Rückkehr der Religion oder sekuläre Kultur?* and Gärdner et al., *Atheismus und religiöse Indifferenz.* Attention was also given to the collection Greyerz and Siebenhüner, *Religion und Gewalt. Konflikte Rituale, Deutungen*, etc. In connection with this, the Egyptologist Jan Assman has a unique position with his work on the connection between religion and cultural memory.

5. Berger and Luckmann, *Sociální konstrukce reality*; Thomas and Luckmann, "Sociology of Religion and Sociology of Knowledge"; Luckmann, *Invisible Religion*; Berger, *The Rumor of Angels*; Berger, *Vzdálená sláva.*

6. See Maier, *Politická náboženství*; Gentile, *Politická náboženství.*

7. See also Gauchet, *Odkouzlení světa.*

8. Publikation *Religion et société en Europe* (1998) was published in Czech in 2003.

9. For example, the above-mentioned René Rémond views the issue of secularization solely as the transfer of political power from a religious state to a neutral state. He understands secularization purely in descriptive terms, as a more or less progressive separation of the church from the state and a division of religion and society. There is no mention of the "wissen-sociological" dimension promoting modernity and the rationalization of life, religious tolerance is not analysed—neither in its economic dimension nor in the context of the wider civilizing conditions of individual freedom, etc.

Therefore, within the more general perspective of historical semantics[10] and the history of thought, this paper aims to focus attention on certain specific connections in the approaches of historical sociology to the issue of secularization.

The setting[11] of this contribution is a thesis on the ambiguous and multidimensional process of secularization in the nineteenth and twentieth centuries, which corresponds to the plurality of its research specification. This has arguably manifested itself in the "de-churching" of the public realm as well as the transfer of religious convictions into the private realm, or even the "de-spiritualization" of subjectivity, which means freeing views on life, experience and knowledge from their religious moorings, something which Max Weber analysed with his concept of the "disenchantment of the world" (*Entzauberung der Welt*).[12]

From the viewpoint of historical semantics it is also necessary to stress that the concept of secularization changed its content significantly approximately halfway through the nineteenth century.

As is shown in theological compendia,[13] the use of this concept was originally connected with the transference of church property into secular hands and it is most often encountered in legal and economic religious history. Secularization was characterized therein as a one-sided appropriation of church property against the will of the church, in particular church ownership of land and its use for non-religious purposes. (Even today we come across similar attempts at laicizing property that originally belonged to the church, and the property-rights view should not, of course, disguise any wider anti-church, anti-religious, or even general cultural consequences such as have been seen with the wrangling over St. Vitus' Cathedral.) Viewed in this way, which specifically thematizes the duality of the "spiritual" and the "worldly" (economic) dimensions of religious life, the concept of "secularization" supposedly appeared for the first time in the arguments of the French ambassador during the preliminary negotiations of the Peace of Westphalia (April 8, 1646).[14]

10. Compare here Kosseleck, "Einleitung," XIII–XXII.

11. The notion of "setting", (sometimes also "backdrop" or the broader "background") comes from literary science, and in its most general sense it indicates a relationship between two levels of meaning. The setting as the *actively functioning backdrop* (knowledge) identifies and makes intelligible the objects which appear before it, so that it unambiguously locates them and gives particular significance to them. For example, a vague and, due to its use of formal devices, ambiguous literary text such as *Utrpení knížete Sternenhocha* by Ladislav Klíma can be interpreted within the setting of Czech literary expressionism. In philosophical-methodological discourse it was linked to discussions on Foucault's notions of discursion, episteme, the dispositive, etc.

12. Probably the most complete list of research fields in the secularization process is that given by the English religious historian Hugh McLeod. According to him, secularization can be viewed in connection with (1) personal faith, (2) participation in religious practices, (3) the role of religion in public institutions, (4) its significance in the public realm, (5) its part in creating individual and collective identities, and finally (6) in connecting people's beliefs with mass culture (see McLeod, *Secularisation in Western Europe 1848–1914*; see also McLeod, *Náboženství a lidé západní Evropy 1789–1989*).

13. See, e.g., the watchword "Säkularisation," in *Religion in Geschichte und Gegenwart*, 1280–88.

14. Meiern, "Acta Pacis Westphalicae publica," vol. II, 15, paragraph 14, cited in *Religion in Geschichte und Gegenwart*, vol. 5, 1280.

This is therefore a historical phenomenon which has not only been present throughout various periods of time—as can be seen in ancient Rome with the confiscation of property from various Christian communities at the time of the persecution of the first Christians, thus removing the basis for their existence. The secularization of property should not be considered to be solely concerned with power-grabbing or anti-religious tendencies. We also encounter similar phenomena in Christian countries in different periods and in different areas—Austria, Prussia, Würtenberg, Spain, Portugal, and Latin America[15]—while after the French Revolution, which here almost serves as a paradigm, the confiscation of property was significantly linked to anti-church and anti-religious ideological arguments.

In the latter half of the nineteenth century the concept of secularization was used almost exclusively to describe the waning influence of religion on man's way of thinking, on the organization of society and on the policies of the state. What links, in the broadest sense, both the above-mentioned meanings of this long-term, non-linear and multi-dimensional historical process is the "laicization" of religious assets (in a material or spiritual sense) and their surrender to temporal objectives. The application of this concept could thus denote more than just changes in religiosity and the worldly position of the church. In this way, the historico-sociological view of the process of secularization began to take in a rapid expansion (complementary to secularization) of "world views," supported in various ways by an intense if "secular faith" in their own universal validity, as in the case of the growing rationalization and modernization of European society and accompanying changes in specific areas in the development of the legal, economic and social life of European society, in which it is not easy to say what was the cause and what was the effect. The change in the accepted notion of secularization naturally led to a historical search for its new components and also to a new interpretation of certain issues.

The Reformation's and later the Enlightenment's anti-ecclesiastical purging of faith—not to mention Max Weber's famous thesis on the relationship between Protestant ethics and capitalism, which can be interpreted not only conceptually in its significance for an understanding of the origin and "uniqueness of Occidental capitalism," but also in a secularizing sense with regard to the subsequent process of divesting economic activity of its former religious character (with its resultant simplified patterns of success)—could be seen as being as formative a force as were the attempts to change the view of socio-historical events and their structural power. As an example, Jean Bodin's *Methodus ad faciem historiarum cognitionis*, from 1560, aspires to replace the previous "theology of history" with its own "philosophy." The orientation of the book towards secular causes, for example the motive of power or the various "national characters," began to establish the basis for a new schematization of historical development, independent of a consecrated plan of providence. Similarly, the "new anthropology"[16] of Thomas Hobbes did not explain man as part of a created, predetermined order of the world (as in Aristotle's theory of "natural places"), but in terms of his instinctive structures, orientated towards

15. See *Religion in Geschichte und Gegenwart*, vol. 5, 1280.

16. See in particular Henrich, "Die Grundstruktur der modernen Philosophie," 83–109.

self-preservation (*conservatio sui*); the basic "social contract" then became the framework for people's political lives, which allowed a part of their self-preservation energies to be delegated to the state (to the army and police in particular). Therefore the future began to open up as a strange and uncertain sphere occupied only by individual interests, a sphere of self-affirmation and emancipation, independent to a considerable degree from the order of creation and the goal of redemption.

The general desire of modern philosophy and science for objectivity in their functioning, based on the search for a supposedly unshakeable foundation of knowledge and the essential principles of our thought, reached its peak in the Enlightenment and in its objectifying "philosophy of reflection," where the cognizant individual is transformed into the subject and things become conceptions and objects, constructed by our understanding (though with the help of the universal principles of mathematical science or Kant's transcendentally elucidating reflection) and manipulated by our will. In the name of reason and nature, the Enlightenment then became critical of all supposed preconceptions, incomplete experiences and unsatisfactory concepts, and finally helped to completely remove the original, religious-based, universalizing and wisdom-seeking connection of reason, truth, being and the world, an all-justifying basis that could naturally link the questions concerning the reason for a person's existence, for the existence of individual things and events as a whole. In place of the older principles of *hierarchy, uniformity,* and *order,* which made it possible to enquire about the true nature of being and God, appeared *equilibrium, equality*, and an *orientation* towards the individual; the world became only a horizon whose appearance and distance were dependent on the position of the observer.

Therefore, in the basis of Enlightenment thought and in its entire orientation was hidden a tendency—as a rule disruptive—towards a rational arrangement of each whole into individual, equally accessible components, and also towards a complementary attempt to interpret a totality through the objective reconstruction of its supposedly relevant, independently controlled, though in reality simplifying (and depleting) elements. Here meaning stops being a complex category[17] anchored in reality itself and necessarily changes into a merely subjective (mental) construct, whether it has a rational character or is something which we wish to believe.

The most characteristic premise of the Enlightenment's rational reflection, and at the same time also its conclusion, is the general division of man and the world, of subjectivity and objectivity, reason and the inner life, the public and the private, which form the basis of the development of post-Kantian philosophy[18] and which became the

17. Analogously, we can here employ the metaphor which Max Planck once used to characterize the connections of the individual areas of physical science: "If we look more thoroughly then . . . the system of physics does not amount only to one individual picture, but rather to a whole collection of pictures; for in every category of natural phenomena we had a particular painting. And these various pictures were not interconnected. It was possible to remove one of them without disturbing the others . . ." (Cited in Cassirer, *Substanzbegriff und Funktionsbegriff*, 409).

18. The supposedly inevitable division of man and the world not only became the starting point for the critics of the existing philosophy, such as the young Schelling and Hegel, who tried to supersede it with their unifying program of *the philosophy of the absolute*, but over a longer period also for the further

cultural principle of modern civilization, and in this sense a new dimension to the issue of secularization. On one side of the division we have to deal with an objective approach to the world, emerging from the conviction that, despite the chaos on the surface, everything is in fact rational and in principle accessible via a structure,[19] and on the other side we find subjectivity and the inner life of individuals, in which is preserved everything which the experience-related reason of modern science has gradually displaced from its objectively material concept of reality and abandoned to individual existence: secondary qualities and values, faith and wisdom, goodness and beauty, desire and dreams, memory and hope, and also God and (originally generally binding) humanity.[20] However, the

------

development of philosophical thought. (For more detail see Havelka, "Byl Herbart filosofem biedermeieru," 25–38).

19. During the Enlightenment the integrity of the world was governed by the principles of reason and had the character of a system: the Enlightenment only recognizes as knowledge that which can be understood through subsumption into the principles of unified reason and that which can be integrated into a system of knowledge, and in this sense it is restrictive. These Enlightenment motifs were then expanded upon during the German classical period. An understanding of the whole (of integrity and of order), which is the origin and the end and, as such, more than the sum of its parts, can and must overcome the inevitable division of Enlightenment reason. As is known through Hegel (see his *Introduction to Lectures on the Philosophy of History*), the historiography of his age, specifically that of Niebuhr and Ranke, was not a science, but only a (particularizing) narration in the style of a chronicle concerning the consequences of events. According to Hegel, it was unable to perceive the universality of the process which yields events, and had abandoned in advance the search for its inner necessity and regularity (see Hegel, *Vorlesungen*, 53). The knowledge of these historians is arguably unscientific because they are contenting themselves with it and not trying to reach beyond it to the whole, they are not attempting a (philosophical) system, they are not trying to discover universal principles, the guiding process of the world's development. On the contrary, this science of the necessity of development and the laws of historical events was for him a philosophy of history which supposedly knows that the world is governed by reason and that therefore the history of the world is also accessible through reason (ibid). The same also applied to the natural sciences and the position of the philosophy of nature, which should similarly have predominated within them. Hegel believed that only philosophy could understand the entirety of the world, nature, science and history, and that it was therefore the highest form of learning. History and the natural sciences began to free themselves programmatically from this subjugation to entirety and dependence on philosophy in the 1830s in the processes of the "scientization of science" and "historicization of history." This emancipation was brought about by the ethos of experience and the inductionist ideas of Mill's positivism, by an orientation towards fact and a belief that unambiguousness of interpretation is inherently and exclusively contained in the data (or even in the sources) themselves, or rather in causality, already constructing the events to which the sources testify. The unwanted side effect was the one-sided emphasis on "individual causality" (i.e. the various means and various directions of chains of events) and the conviction that historical knowledge has nothing to do with collective social phenomena and general processes, the appreciation of which requires abstract analytical concepts (e.g., "feudalism," "civic society," "industrialization," "modernization," etc), but exclusively with individual phenomena which we are able to understand, whether that be through "empathy" (Ranke), "submersion" (Droysen), or "experience" (Dilthey), etc. (See Schnadelbach, *Philosophie in Deutschland 1831–1933*, 89–94.)

20. The division of man and the world had profound repercussions in cultural, intellectual and social life as well as for the human psyche and later Max Horkheimer and Theodor W. Adorno analytically challenged the Enlightenment concept of reason. Their book *Dialectic of the Enlightenment* asserted that the further development of the human race which led to the horrors of the twentieth century was partly a result of the split (division) of Enlightenment rationality. Its original emancipatory and critical potential and the power of its scientific objectivity were unable to prevent the dangerous descent of reason into irrationality solely through the manipulation of science and oppressive ideologies: "Enlightenment degenerates into myth . . . The Enlightened form of rationality then becomes more formalising and deplenishing: . . . every

objectivity, transparency and repeatability of the cognition of subjects acquired in this way lost their ability to appeal to man and offer him solutions to questions concerning his place in the entirety of being, which then culminated in the idea of a completely dehumanized, positivist knowledge. Science paid for its objectivity through the loss of its original effort to be "the way to true being" (as in antiquity), "the way to true art" (as in the Renaissance), "the way to true nature" (as in the ideas of the modern age), "the way to true God" (as in the Reformed religions) and "the way to true happiness" (as in the socialist movement) as Max Weber emphasized in connection with his interpretation of the principles of the objectivity of modern science, continuing with a variation on Tolstoy's assertion:

> [S]cience is meaningless for it is unable to provide us with the answer to the only question which is important for us: "What should we do and how should we live?" The fact that science cannot answer this question is irrefutable. The question is then in what sense it cannot answer this question and whether it might not offer some help to the person who could phrase the question correctly.[21]

The search for answers to the meaning of history and the questioning of the character of the entire world, originally the realm of religion, were somewhat lost in the bias of the division and the different perspectives it established for the viewing of subject and object, and as those grew, so the critical potential of the Enlightenment dwindled even further into the pure manipulation of knowledge for ideological purposes, ensuring the inner integration of society in an "alienated" form.[22] The critical faculties of Enlightenment reason ended up in the service of individual and group interests.

The phenomenon of secularization should not be restricted solely to the "long 19th century,"[23] nor should it be viewed solely in its "intellectual" or power-politics component.

With regard to what has already been said, it is therefore important to distinguish between *(a) de-churching (Entkirchlichung),* i.e., the process of politically restricting, institutionally weakening, and socially isolating the church; the similarly oriented *(b)* secularization in the older sense of the word, discussed above, as the *expropriation* of church property; *(c)* secularization in its most commonly used sense, i.e. the secularization of *spiritual* and *intellectual* aspects; and finally *(d)* the *de-religiousification* of forms of public and private life.

---

substantial goal which men might adduce as an alleged rational insight is, in the strict Enlightenment sense, delusion, lies, 'rationalization.'" (Horkheimer and Adorno, *Dialectic of the Enlightenment*, 5)

21. See Weber, "Věda jako povolání," 122.

22. For the young Marx, the ideology of "false consciousness" was something that had to be overcome, and not, as for his followers, an organisational tool of power politics, i.e., a "scientific" and therefore definitive ideology.

23. See Bauer, *Das "lange" Jahrhundert.* The Central European and especially Czech nineteenth century was somewhat "shorter" and different in character. It starts with the definitive dissolution of the "Holy Roman Empire of the German nation" in 1806, or even later, at the Congress of Vienna, which has often been designated as the last frontier of the early modern period (see, e.g., Hroch, *Encyklopedie novověku.*) and the start of the late modern period.

A similar methodological separation of the various forms of secularization can lead us to Niklas Luhmann's concept of system "segmentation." He understood this segmentation as the process of differentiation of structurally similar units having a similar function. As a rule, these units are not very specialized, they do not co-operate or interact with each other, and so they are relatively autonomous. The stability of the overall framework is not threatened by the imperceptible functioning of segmentation, and the possible failure of one segmental unit does not lead to a general breakdown, merely to a reduction in the system.

(a) "De-churching" was linked with the disappearance of the church's influence in religious and non-religious spheres. Of course, this was more a matter of secular and spiritual *power* rather than faith, or more precisely the institutional manipulation of church life, even if it manifested itself in the removal of ceremonial members of the church from specific church offices, or the growing non-participation of the population in various church activities (which, of course, does not necessarily mean a reduction in the requirements and functions of religion in the public sphere). "De-churching" is also frequently associated with "laicism" as an ideological movement which demanded the radical separation of church and state.

The question still remains to what extent de-churching can be seen as a reaction to attempts by the majority of religions to maintain a long-term influence over domestic and, in many cases, also world-power polity. In connection with this we can mention Masaryk's *Světová revoluce* [World Revolution] from 1925, where in his interpretation of the First World War he emphasises the dissolution of the European "absolutist theocracies" of the nineteenth century as being one of its most important consequences.[24]

(b) The cause of the "secularization of property" was, and still is, the requirements of the state (e.g., the Theresa-Josephine reforms with their closure of monasteries and submission of religion to "state supervision") and the "absolutist" reach of the state into all areas; later there was also a weakening of the original functions of church property, sometimes as a result of the market organization of the economy (e.g., tourist access and music concerts in secularized church spaces).

(c) Secularization, as it is most commonly understood today, that is as an intellectual separation from religion as a result of scientific, secular and pragmatic arguments, as the description of an internal process whereby public life takes on a strictly secular character and becomes "religiously neutral," began to be used as a concept (secularization) in England from the start of the second half of the nineteenth century,[25] undoubtedly also on the basis of intellectual reflection on the growing industrialization, urbanization and modernization of English society. A role was no doubt played by the expanding "positivistic" notions of man and society, the first practical successes of natural science and the growing potential for the technological management of the world.

24. See Masaryk, *Světová revoluce*, 24–30; 37–40.

25. *Religion in Geschichte und Gegenwart*, vol. 5, p. 1281. See also chapter XIII (*Die Religion*) in the great synthesis of nineteenth century history by Jürgren Osterhammel (*Die Verwandlung der Welt*).

The enduring setting for this concept of secularization was the assumption of a strong world order and an original (natural) unity and spiritual connection of all areas of the social and cultural world in religion, precisely that from which we are supposedly diverging in secularization, and at the same time also the idea that this separation is something negative, that through secularization something is happening which from the nature of things should not happen. In order to illustrate further, let us turn once more to T. G. Masaryk and his first major themes in sociology—*alcoholism, prostitution* and *suicide*—which he explained by the growth of *atheism* in modern man:

> The collective phenomenon of suicide to which we are witness in today's society is the result of the demise of the unified view of the world which Christianity consistently brought to people of all educated nations. The struggle between free thought and positive religion leads to the atheism of the masses; this atheism then means intellectual and moral anarchy—and death . . . [26]

The belief that religion was a force for social and cultural integration and that in its absence destruction prevailed was linked to Masaryk's concept of the crisis of modern man. In his book on suicide Masaryk attempted to show that the ultimate reasons for this new social phenomenon of the modern age could not be attributed purely to external (natural and social) causes, but were mainly due to the influence of modern currents of thought, which replaced the firm world view uniting the moral order with belief in God, which caused the centuries-old, sacred and generally respected morality to disappear, and which, according to Masaryk, had not been replaced by anything. Suicide is therefore one manifestation of the crisis of modern man, which, together with the social and political crises, constitutes one of the main elements of the crisis of the modern age. [27]

26. Masaryk, *Sebevražda*, 143. Also in Masaryk, *Vboji o náboženstvíi*, 41–42: . . . *However, the crisis in religion manifests itself more intensively during times of unease, of spiritual anxiety, of nervousness, psychosis, pessimism, suicide. It is a profound crisis, a crisis that obsesses the entire soul—a genuine break with the old world. Religion or nihilism—that is the bloody disjunction of our age* . . . Masaryk's work on suicide was not a great success amongst Czech intellectuals even after its first Czech publication in 1904 (under the shortened title of *Sebevražda* with several alterations to the text). It did not correspond with the immediate needs of the nation and was unusual for its *empirical basis*, comparing statistics and situations in various countries and various religions. Moreover, Masaryk soon became recognized by the Czech people as a public figure and politician (and later as the founder of the state) and less as a philosopher and scientist. One of the consequences of this was that all of his work underwent attempts to "ethically stylize" its contents. Due to this tendency, this "most scientific" of Masaryk's works (Masaryk himself reputedly held it in the highest regard) may have appeared the least interesting and most complex. It should not be overlooked that in the Czech translation of *Sebevražda* there was a certain shift in some meanings: the more general notion of "civilization", which was replaced in the habilitation manuscript by "přítomnost" [the present] (Gegenwart) in the original German title of the book (. . . Massenerscheinung der Gegenwart), was further weakened using the word "osvěta" [enlightenment or education], in spite of several smaller alterations to the text which were to neutralize for a Czech readership the more conservative wording of the original book which appeared to be a criticism of the intelligentsia.

27. As Jan Patočka noted in the 1950s, when it comes to suicide Masaryk . . . *does not regard it as an illness as befits a sociologist, diagnostician and hygienist of social health, but rather . . . as a disturbance of the religious ontological order, as a revolution* . . . (Patočka, *Péče o duši*, 160). In this context we should not overlook the conservative character of Masaryk's analysis of the crisis of the modern age in *Sebevražda*, linked to the atheism of the masses, the social emancipation of the new classes and modern forms of education, which *leads to a rational and moral compromise, then producing a deathly indifference . . . corrosive scepti-*

In the third, and undoubtedly most commonly used concept of secularization, there is an emphasis on moving away from the original religious solutions to the meaning of life and the world to an exclusively secular ("earthly") solution. This does not mean, however, that the questions are being completely negated, just that different answers are being found.

(d) Max Weber was probably the first to systematically consider "de-religiousification" in its public and private forms under the title of *disenchantment of the world* (*Entzauberung*). Although this is closely related to the process of secularization of religion and faith in the 19th century, it should not be confused with it,[28] amongst other reasons because it does not mean—as is often believed—some kind of simple and straightforward "de-spiritualization" in the sense of the promotion of universal atheism, which on the contrary seems to dominate sociologist Daniel Bell's concept of *the end of ideology*, influential in the '60s and '70s, whereby modern industrial societies are characterized by the *clash between culture and production* and do not require any special legitimization either through ideology or religion. These are replaced by the moderate rationalism and transparency of the system, linked to a diversity in consumption as well as various values.[29]

Max Weber used the concept of "disenchantment" to label and interpret the unavoidable (unwanted) "side effects" of social and cultural phenomena within the more general processes of the Occidental rationalization of the world and the intellectualization of life through the power of science and science-based technology, and also as a consequence of the inevitable submission of individual and social life to the general and long-term pressure of economic rationality. In connection with this, Weber used the expression "the iron cage of submission" (*stahlhartes Gehäuse der Hörigkeit*) to express his ideas concerning the inevitable pressure historically incurred on the subjective aims

---

cism and horrible cynicism (Masaryk, *Sebevražda*, 123 and 140); it would also be possible to reconstruct the traditionalist component of Masaryk's view of his time, made obvious in his relationship to the values of the old world. According to the theologian J. L. Hromádka, Masaryk even tried to *show that Russian Orthodoxy and the spirit of the Russian aristocracy and Russian education were far more useful bulkheads against the breakdown of modern society than Western (Roman) Catholicism and Protestantism . . . Eastern Orthodox Christianity apparently preserved the mystical, submissive relationship of the human soul to eternal, untransmutable truths . . .* , it made the individual an organic part of church society and prevented him from losing *his reason or personal moral consciousness* (see Hromádka, *Masaryk mezi včerejškem a zítřkem*, 15). In this regard it is then possible to see Masaryk's Platonism as an emphasis on the *rule of the spirit over the world* (22) and at the same time to interpret Masaryk's efforts at formulating a religious dimension to Czech history as a weapon against modern subjectivism as well as liberalism and "unshakeable" positivism (21).

28. This can be seen in the title of the contextually rich and intensive study: Tinková, "Profanace posvátna a odkouzlení světa," 13–49. The individual concepts used by the author clearly connect with the issue of religion, its transformation and development, particularly in the nineteenth century; originally, however, they were aimed in various directions and belonged to various intellectual relationships. Their weak definition begs the question to what extent the author's important and original interpretations of changes in the perception and punishment of blasphemy and sacrilege between—roughly speaking—the Enlightenment and Biedermeier, were applicable even without the use of the ambitious framing/horizontal concepts of "profanity" and "disenchantment", and this also applies to the concept of "magic," for it is not clear when it means attempts at the magical manipulation of divinity and when it is only a synonym for any type of religious activity.

29. *The End of Ideology*; also in: Bell, *Kulturní rozpory kapitalismu*.

orientated and calculated by scientific-technological rationality on the structured organization of society and the economy, and particularly on man and his inner world: "... but fate decreed," writes Weber,

> that the cloak should become an iron cage. Since asceticism undertook to remodel the world and to work out its ideals in the world, material goods have gained an increasing and finally an inexorable power over the lives of men as in no previous period of history. Today the spirit of religious asceticism—whether finally, who knows?—has escaped from the cage. But victorious capitalism, since it rests on mechanical foundations, needs its support no longer ...[30]

Weber went on to analyze this idea in various contexts

> Particularly the person who is "empirically" free, that is who acts after giving thought to things, is in actuality bound to the attainment of his aims teleologically by quite different and recognisable means. "Free will" can only very rarely help the factory owner in the competitive struggle or the broker in the stock exchange. He chooses between economic collapse and following the specific maxims of economic behaviour ...[31]

It is significant that the strongest emotional characteristic of Weber's "disenchantment of the world" comes from an analysis of historical changes in the meaning of science and the consequences of the separation of faith and knowledge, science and religion as two distinct historical approaches to the world. The search for a "meaning" for modern science was therefore carried out through comparisons of science and religion in everyday life and came to the conclusion that it was a different but culturally analogous approach to the world and, in fact, another form of "faith."

Therefore, the "disenchantment of the world" was not originally connected with the process of secularization or the transformation of faith and was certainly not, as Marcel Gauchet asserts, "about the elimination of the magical as a means of salvation,"[32] but only about the limiting of magical practices which usually lay outwith religion and which endeavored to influence the course of the world and people's lives (as in the interpretation of cards, horoscopes, astrology, etc.). Magic as an attempt to manipulate the divine was, according to Weber's interpretation, replaced by scientific-technical approaches and technological means. That which may have appeared to the French Catholic Gauchet as "the elimination of the magical" could not have been a determinant for the German Protestant Max Weber, brought up in the evangelical environment of the "theology of the word" and educated in Kant's anchorage of faith in the sphere of practical reason and Kant's interpretation of *moral imperatives*.

According to Weber, the rejection of magic is a constituent element of monotheistic religions, because its acceptance would mean the limitation of God's absolute power (in which Weber follows Augustine's criticism of Pelagianism), and this manifests itself,

---

30. Weber, *Gesammelte Aufsätze zur Religionssoziologie*, 203.

31. Weber, *Gesammelte Aufsätze*, 133.

32. See Gauchet, *Odkouzlení světa*, 5. It is not possible to ascribe this statement to Max Weber as it completely contradicts his interpretation of magical operations.

for example, through iconoclasm, the prohibition of the depiction of God (in Judaism even the prohibition of the uttering of God's name) as a pre-condition of such forms of manipulation.

For Weber magic was therefore always a characteristic of pre-monotheistic religions, a particular means by which they approached the world. Its practice is linked to the idea that deities (and the laws created by them) can be influenced, with the help of certain techniques, for one's own benefit and private purposes. In that it resembles modern technology, enabling us to approach the world in a special way, to control its dangers and thus, as it were, "humanize" it.

In my view, it is in precisely this way that we should interpret the famous quotation from Weber's lecture, "Science as a Vocation":

> growing intellectualization and rationalization therefore *does not mean* an increase in our knowledge of the conditions in which we live. It means something else: the knowledge or belief that, if one *only wants to*, one can learn it at any time, that in principle there are therefore no mysterious and incalculable forces which could intervene, that on the contrary it is possible in principle to *control* all things by calculation. . . . No longer must we have recourse to magical means, like the savages for whom such forces existed, in order to control or placate the spirits. Today the task is performed by technical means and by calculation . . .[33]

These ideas of Weber's were taken to the extreme by his indirect pupil, the political decisionist Carl Schmitt, in a paper from 1929 entitled *Das Zeitalter der Neutralisierungen und Entpolitisierungen* [The Age of Neutralizations and Depoliticizations],[34] in which he elaborated his concept of the present as an *age of neutralizations and depoliticizations*. According to him, after theology, science, the absolutist state, etc. the new *centres* of social life became economics and ultimately technology, whose *immanence*, the fact that it is wholly *neutral* and *only a tool and weapon*, that it *serves everyone* and is *culturally blind*,[35] enables one to connect with and control everything, though at the cost of a particular method of simplification. In Schmitt's view, the technology of power thus begins to replace politics, or more precisely: *decentralizes* and *neutralizes* it, allowing the instrumentalization of transcendence and replacing religious faith with a process of choosing between values.

For Weber the comparison of science and religion in everyday life thus opened the way for a reformulation of Comte's theory about the religious character of science: that is, that science represents a distinct, but in its social functions culturally analogous, approach to the world, linked with a different purpose which is secularized and connected to the idea of progress.

According to Weber the result is, of course, that today "precisely the highest and most sublime values have retreated from public life into the background, either into the transcendental realm of mystic life or into the brotherliness of direct and personal hu-

33. Ibid., 118.

34. Schmitt, "Das Zeitalter," 120–33.

35. Ibid., 127.

man relations. It is not accidental that . . . today only in the smallest human contacts, from one person to another, in pianissimo, something is pulsing that corresponds to the prophetic pneuma which in former times swept through the great societies like a firebrand, welding them together . . ."[36]

Therefore, "disenchantment" does not even, as Gauchet asserts, mean an "end to the reign of the invisible,"[37] because, after all, for the ordinary person the laws of nature are just as abstract and invisible as deities.

The progressive scientism and technological mastery of the world do not therefore in themselves necessarily lead to its de-religiousification, since, as Weber emphasizes, "all of the natural sciences give us the answer only to the question of what we should do *if* we wish to master life *technically*. But *whether* we should or wish to master it technically, and whether it makes any sense to do so—this they either leave aside or assume for their purposes."[38] Therefore, although the contents of religion and faith are pushed out into the sphere of the scientifically unverifiable, i.e., to the private sphere or directly to the irratio-nal (which can but does not necessarily mean the return of magic), through the concept of "disenchantment" their different position and distinct functions are clarified. However, this in no way alters the need for faith, the manifestations of "religious" banding together by groups and classes, and certainly not the modern growth of "pseudoreligions," world religions or even fundamentalism.

The newly argumentative and self-assertive (teleological) *rationality of behavior and decision-making,* based on the principles of modern mathematical natural science, with its ability to calculate the relationship between aims and means, with its impartial judgments and its strict forming of concepts, with its "rating" of its degree of success and its clear orientation towards continuous modernization and "progress," was thus glimpsed in Weber's work as a contraposition to the person as an individual who only in his *core* can necessarily and inevitably carry all that which the scientific longing for objectivity (basically since the time of the Enlightenment) has pushed out of reach of its (methodologically based) competence into the private sphere; that which exists in some way, yet at the same time cannot be scientifically resolved: freedom and hope, love and faith, subjectivity and tradition, origin and future, beauty and values, etc.[39] This sort of "internalizing" of religion and values, however, ultimately leads to its antithesis and causes a situation in which "many of the old gods are divested of their magic and hence

36. Weber, *Metodologie, sociologie, politika*, 118 and 133.

37. Ibid.

38. Weber Max, "Věda jako povolání," 123.

39. Compare, e.g., Weber's Munich lecture "Science as a Vocation" from the turn of 1918/19: "Redemption from the rationalism and intellectualism of science is the fundamental presupposition of living in union with the divine . . ." (Weber, "Věda jako povolání," 121). This inherent contradiction was for a long time perceived and interpreted as predestined. It was thematized for the first time by Schelling and Hegel in their critiques of the supposed Kantian *division of man and the world*, concealed within the distinction between "things in themselves" and "things for us," which later, under the heading "the division of man and the world." became an important motif of culturally critical deliberations, persisting until the end of the 1960s.

rise from their graves in the form of impersonal forces, striving to gain power over our lives and resuming their age-long struggle with one another."[40]

Therefore, disenchantment does not even denote the total loss of the divine and transcendence, but rather the ability to access the world through new means, the surrender of the world to science and technology, with the sacred altering and clarifying its new position and its changed functions in society, personal life and moral behavior. (Genetic engineering still does not necessarily mean anything antireligious, even though it may seem to be probing into the secrets of creation, as this very thing has been happening since the discovery of cells, and is only a dogmatic problem.)

Implied ambiguities in the interpretation and evaluation of the process of secularization in general and in the nineteenth century in particular seem to be rooted in the ambiguity of the concept of religion on which they are based. That is to say, since the Enlightenment it has been possible to come across two quite different interpretations of it.

On the one hand, the *compensation* concept considered religion to be the consequence of human powerlessness in the face of nature and in the interpretation of life and death. At the same time it referred, whether positively or critically, to the ability of religion to placate human frustrations with the world, although in the face of modern rationalism this was shown to be something inadequate or immature. This concept had its origin in the Enlightenment's empiricism, sensualism and phenomenism, in *the rooting of the soul in the biological or social sphere*, for which modern philosophy and science then supplied further arguments.[41] The consequences of similar extrapolations of the general development of empirically based knowledge were then condensed by John Stuart Mill in the spirit of the Enlightenment into the finding still repeated to this day: "If we proceed from pure experience, we necessarily arrive at polytheism,"[42] that is at a relativism of values and inability to determine the basic principles of the life of individuals and societies. The natural consequence was then a rejection of the *theological heteronomy* of the world. John Stuart Mill expressed this most clearly in his *Autobiography* around the middle of the nineteenth century: "The old opinions in religion, morals and politics have been so much discredited among intellectuals as to have lost the greater part of their efficacy for good."[43]

The way was thus cleared for the declaration that *morality is convention and therefore fiction*—this situation is summarized by Panajotis Kondylis in his book *The Enlightenment within the Framework of Modern Rationality*.[44] In his view, morality primarily represents "a means for interests to be asserted over that which, through human coexistence, for good or ill, became social reality. The fact that even evil can behave virtuously, as long as it is in its interests," according to Kondylis served the Enlightenment "as proof of the

40. Ibid., 127.

41. See previous interpretations and notes 5/ and 6/.

42. Cited from Weber, "Věda jako povolání," 126. Also compare, e.g., Marquard, "Lob des Polytheismus," 91–117.

43. Mill, *Autobiography*, 60.

44. Kondylis, *Die Aufklärung im Rahmen des neuzeitlichen Rationalismus*, 52.

origin of morality not in nature but in the orientation of the rigorously reflective intellect towards utility . . ."[45] Similar findings by others, for example La Mettrie, de Sade, or later Nietzsche, led to the nihilistic construction of the "evil god" (*fantome abominable*).

The development of the compensation concept then continued through Ludwig Feuerbach (1804–1872) and David Friedrich Strauss (1808–1874), to Marx (and his famous maxim about religion as the *opium of the people*), and then on to Karl Kautský (1854–1939), with his comparison between early Christianity and communism,[46] to later critiques of religion in the socialist movement in general, and also to the previously mentioned Friedrich Nietzsche (1844–1900) with his genealogization of Christianity as slave morality, and in some aspects even up to Sigmund Freud (1856–1939).

In spite of it all, the secularizing power of the compensation concept, especially perceived in Catholicism and its institutions, was predominantly reflective (and later ideologically doctrinal), and in the West and in Central Europe it had a different influence at various levels of society and in various areas.[47] However, it never succeeded in problematizing Christianity to the extent that it could be more fundamentally ousted or substituted with a new world view. Moreover, the promotion of compensatory interpretations of religion, which began during the Enlightenment and was conspicuous in the twentieth century, was for a time slowed down or even suspended by romanticism[48] and Biedermeier.[49]

At the same time, this was not only about a rejection of the Enlightenment's unification of life in the name of science, a criticism of revolutionary excesses, or even a wider criticism of the lack of religion and morals among certain levels of society, but rather about the creation of a new bourgeois habit, to which belonged—at least in Protestant

45. Ibid., 513.

46. Compare, e.g., Kautský, *Původ křesťanství*, where he speaks of the "communism of original Christianity," (3) and emphasizes that "Christianity in its infancy was . . . a movement of unpropertied classes of all sorts, which we can sum up under the name proletarians, if we do not understand by this expression only wage earners," (6) whence "the proletarian point of view enables those features of original Christianity which are shared with the modern movement of the proletariat to be understood more easily than is possible for bourgeois scholars . . . (8).

47. In his deliberations on reason and the problem of theodicy Max Weber, referring to a sociological survey from 1906, pointed out, "It is not scientific arguments, but the difficulty of reconciling the idea of providence with the injustice and imperfection of the social order, which in recent years has motivated thousands of German workers to reject the idea of God" (Weber, *Wirtschaft und Gesellschaft*, 315).

48. Romanticism was primarily concerned with an interest in the Middle Ages, a respect for religiousness and the idea of an inner life and personal form of subjectivity. In many respects this period saw the post-Enlightenment re-emergence of religion in the wider circles of the European intelligentsia, whether it manifested itself in philosophy (Schelling), literature (Milton, Chateaubriand) or in the visual arts.

49. The Biedermeier "majesty of law" (Vojtěch Jirát), as we know it, for example, from the work of Karel Jaromír Erben, ultimately arose from resistance to the disruption of the natural order of the world, the sanctity of family relationships, traditional social duties and obligations, and also from a rejection of the radical Enlightenment criticism of religion. The force and creative power of Biedermeier are inconceivable without reference to Christian values, even in historicism as the "most scientific" product of the Biedermeier "spirit." It seemed that rational solutions to the problems of life and society could be institutionalized only in terms of continuity and in accordance with tradition and Christian values. Cp. Havelka, "Byl Herbart filosofem biedermeieru," 25–38.

countries—a new culture of piety and Christian moralizing. As Jürgen Osterhammel demonstrated, one of the by-products of this trend was not only the special position of religion in the public and political life of the U.S., but also, for example . . . *the successful anti-slavery movement.*[50]

It would appear that the promotion of worldviews based on forms of nationalism, which came about in the 1830s and increased in the second half of the nineteenth century, also had a smaller impact on secularization. They gained ground especially as a concomitant to the gradual industrialization and urbanization of society. Although unifying nationalist ideologies can therefore be linked with the weakening or actual collapse of *minor structures of social life*[51] which had previously been important focal points of traditional religious life, their orientation and activity were not, however, directly and immediately targeted against religion, and in some of their manifestations they could even touch upon it (although from a different basis). Something similar also applies to the incipient workers' movement, or even the promotion of socialist ideas. Although it might not be possible in this context to deny the compensatory view of religion among ideologues and activists of the workers' movement, the perception of religion among the grassroots was characterized by a certain distance from the church, socially founded and connected with the change in the workforce from a class "about itself" to a class "for itself," which could be described as a special "class consciousness" or—as Hugh McLeod terms it, "a strong consciousness of its separate identity."[52] The ideological criticism of religion was here only a function of the perception of social differences:

> The clergy continued to adhere to the principle of social hierarchy, which earned them public dislike, and it seems that under conditions of cultural division the very presence of better dressed individuals from the upper and middle classes gave sufficient reason for poorer people to prefer to avoid the church. In accordance with this, class-conscious workers stopped attending Sunday services and going to communion, since in practice they would inevitably come into contact with "their betters." However, for the most part, they did not stop celebrating weddings in the church and and they still had their children baptized, because it was usually only family members and neighbours who took part in these ceremonies . . .[53]

This was accompanied by a perception of the (unilaterally) politico-manipulative role of the church (the "alliance of throne and altar," promotion of a "national reli-

---

50. See Osterhammel, *Die Verwandlung der Welt*, 1251.

51. Compare Urban, *Kapitalismus a česká společnost*, 46–50.

52. McLeod, *Náboženství a lidé západní Evropy 1789–1989*, 155.

53. Ibid., 155–56. That this was not a case of some early form of break with religion is indicated by the observation about the church cycle of family events. The church's ties to the ruling and aristocratic classes undoubtedly also had an influence on this "estrangement" of the church and the working classes. Stendhal indicates this for the early nineteenth century in his unfinished novel *Lucien Leuwen*: ". . . Lucien saw the sacristan offering a sou to some woman of the people, not badly dressed, who had seen the open church and wanted to enter. 'Go elsewhere, mother,' said the sacristan, 'this is a private chapel.' His offer was clearly insulting; the townswoman blushed to the roots of her hair and dropped the coin on the ground. The sacristan looked around to see whether anyone was watching him and picked up the money again . . ." (ibid., 100)

gion," etc.), which was to a large extent independent of its ideological unacceptability. As is illustrated from the middle of the nineteenth century by the emergence of all sorts of Catholic or evangelical workers' associations (in Germany, for example, the Reichsverband der katholischer Arbeiter- und Arbeiterinnenverbände [The Association of Catholic Male and Female Workers] or the interdenominational Christlich-sozialer Verband [Christian-Social Association]), at that time Christianity was not, as it later was, just one of the elements of culture in wider society, but rather the natural formative and integrative principle of social and individual life.[54]

In the case of the compensation concept of religion, the central position seems to belong to none other than Ludwig Feuerbach, who in his lesser-known work on the issue of religion from 1846, entitled *The Essence of Religion* (the German title of the book *Das Wesen der Religion* might of course be more precisely translated as On the essential determination of religion) further elaborated his basic thesis from the older work *The Essence of Christianity* (1841), that the secret of theology is *anthropology*, which—simply put—means that we should read theology as if it were anthropology, or in other words: there is actually no difference between studying man and studying God. According to Feuerbach, religion is the dream of the human mind, but a dream in which we find ourselves not in the vacuum of the heavens, but on earth and immersed in its problems, especially in the contradiction between human desires and the possibilities of fulfilling them. In Feuerbach's interpretation of religion as human self-projection onto a divine being and as a particular means of isolating human ideals (which in Feuerbach's view are ultimately nothing more than an alienation of human nature) two motifs come into play: on the one hand, a belief in the human *need for dependence*, which is an idea that Feuerbach borrowed from the evangelical theologian and translator Friedrich Schleiermacher (1768–1834), and also the human *longing for perfection* and fulfillment. Nevertheless, in religion man supposedly frees himself from dependence on nature, which is a more general thesis of the time: for Feuerbach polytheism is thus only faith in the naturalness of the human essence, while monotheism is only faith in the human essence as the essence of everything (in nature), and Christ is only the individual embodiment (the "representation" of perfection) of the human race.

In addition to the compensation concept, however, the "integration" concept was developed in association with comparative linguistics, the historical legal school, and ethnological research. As already stated, its origin also lies in the Enlightenment, this time of course rooted in the attempts of some Enlightenment figures to purge faith, to

---

54. As Jürgen Osterhammel demonstrated in his monumental synthesis, in spite of the French Revolution, in spite of the theological weakness of Catholicism in the nineteenth century and in spite of the real and ideological successes of the natural sciences, Christianity in the nineteenth century (unlike later periods) remained a power of the first order, manifesting itself as (1) a source of guidance in life, (2) a focal point for the maintenance of communities and a force of social cohesion, (3) a principle for shaping collective identities, (4) a structural principle for social hierarchization, (5) a driving force of political struggles, and last but not least as (6) a field of challenging intellectual debate. (Osterhammel, *Die Verwandlung der Welt*, 1239ff.)

strip away its institutional trappings and to see in it an important guarantee of moral values, even as a "socio-formed bond" of inter-human relations.[55]

The integration concept of religion was undoubtedly also influenced by the idea of natural religion. It is, however, older. Natural religion—unlike positive religion, did not try to appeal to visions, to the church, the authority of the Word etc., but only to universal human reason. Here the source of religious understanding and the natural truths of religion is sought in the needs and abilities of humanity itself, in its natural instincts, and in reason. Historically it is connected with the search for basic truths, which must ultimately be recognized, as Herbert of Cherbury (1581–1648) claimed, by every right-thinking person and which, as Jean Bodin (1530–1596) maintained, are common to all religions.

The content and function of the integration concept was indicated by Voltaire in his well-known aphorism: "although I myself don't believe in God, I am glad when my tailor believes in him . . ." A similar conviction, even if more seriously formulated with respect to the national *raison d'etre*, also appeared explicitly in the time of Josephinism. One of the key representatives of the culture of the latter part of the 18th century, the economist, liberal reformer of criminal law, theatre critic and censor, privy councillor, rector of the University of Vienna, and president of the Academy of Fine Arts Josef von Sonnenfels, wrote around 1784 that "religion is . . . the most convenient social bond and the monarch must not relinquish such an advantageous means and must keep a careful watch to ensure that every citizen has religion." "For this reason," continues Sonnenfels, "atheism is to date a political crime, because it deprives the ruler of the means to safely control his subjects . . ."[56]

According to the integration concept, religion establishes order and justifies "law" through co-existence in the community, and at the same time ensures its universal validity. It shows the individual what will help his life to develop, but also what threatens his life ("sin," "taboo," etc.). In this perspective, the basic hallmarks of religiousness—deity, faith, prayer, ceremony, celebration, sacrifice, holiness itself, prophets and priests, and also death and the hereafter, etc.—all have significance not so much as expressions of the relationship between the worldly and the sacred, the visible and the invisible, the conditional and the unconditional, but as Montesquieu knew and G. W. F. Hegel developed after him, for their ability to give this organizing, universal "law" a culturally and historically unique form.[57]

---

55. Compare, e.g., Cassirer, *Die Philosophie der Aufklärung*: "And yet it is doubtful if, on the basis of similar declarations by its pioneers and spokesmen, the Enlightenment can be regarded as an age which is basically irreligious and hostile to faith. Such views are after all exposed to the danger that they neglect its most positive achievements . . . The strongest intellectual impulses of the Enlightenment and its truest spiritual strengths do not lie in a rejection of faith, but on the new ideal of faith which it proclaims and in the new form of religiousness which is embodied by the Enlightenment itself . . ." (180)

56. Quoted in Magris, *Habsburský mýtus*, 35.

57. The emergence and promotion of the integration concept of religion were brought about by the experiments of ethnologists like Lewis H. Morgan (1818–1852) or Sir James G. Frazer (1854–1941) and also the "pre-sociological" works of Herbert Spencer (1820–1903), Lucien Lévy-Bruhl (1857–1939) and others. The integration concept of religion was fully developed in the "founding" sociologies of Émile Durkheim

A similar centralizing role to that which Feuerbach had in the case of the compensation concept, Auguste Comte (1798–1857) had in the integration concept of religion. However, much more important in our context than Comte's attempt at a genetic explanation of human advancement (progress)[58] is Comte's analysis of the role of religion in the early scientific stage, i.e., in the *critical era* as Comte sometimes termed his *positive stage* of the development of the human race. When in 1852 Comte published his *Catéchisme positiviste* (full title: *Catechism of Positivity or Summary Interpretation of Universal Religion in Eleven Systematic Interviews between a Woman and a Preacher of Humanity*) it could have a paradoxical effect on the basic thesis of his philosophy of history. Here Comte not only set out systematically and in substantial theses his idea of the "religion of humanity," but at the same time he elaborated his conviction that modern society cannot actually exist without religion, because for its internal cohesion it requires something—in modern terminology—structurally and functionally analogous, which is the idea which has survived to this day in various forms of "secularized" or "political"

(1858–1917), Max Weber (1864–1920), Georg Simmel (1858–1918), Ernst Troeltsch (1865–1923), and others. For sociology this second concept proved to be more fruitful; in a certain sense one could even say, simplifying somewhat, that modern sociology—with its searching for the basic social bond—was actually born of the spirit of integrationally conceived religion. That is to say, what came to the fore was the issue of the social, or rather cultural origin of moral behavior and human experience in general, with their founding significance for society. This exposed the socializing function of religion as a normative value system. Religion could be interpreted as the basic social sanctioning of certain ways of behaving and certain ways of life.

58. Comte's philosophy of the history of human progress considered its three basic stages (theological, philosophical and scientific or positive) to be distinguished by a special form of culture, by the social structure and dominating social group, but primarily by various resources for developing an understanding of nature, observing it without bias and making calculations about it, i.e., in the last instance the divergence of forms of rationality. According to Comte, the "theological" or "religious" stage, which at the beginning of human history overcomes the earlier "cannibalism" and chaos in inter-human relations, develops in three levels (fetishism, polytheism, and monotheism), in which the transition from fetishism to polytheism, with its necessity of abstracting ideas and rationalizing relationships, seemed to Comte a greater cultural revolution than the transition from polytheism to monotheism: although things are still subject to the will of numerous deities, they are no longer the whim of one's own inner forces (spirits); the idea of a common fate for individuals and of a universalizing law plays a greater role, and apparently this ultimately opens the way for monotheism. The idea of "the birth of reason" from the spirit of religion is not only—as is illustrated, for example, by the work of Max Weber, Ernst Troeltsch, or Hermann Cohen—an important component of the first phase of development of the sociology of religion, but is actually one of the most widespread ideas of the nineteenth century. In connection with this, it is possible to mention as an aside the work of someone who came from and was active in Bohemia, writing in German, and yet today has unfortunately been forgotten there, the cultural historian and provocative social anthropologist Julius Lippert (1839–1909), who was regarded by American sociology as one of its forefathers (see Leyburn, "Sumner, William Graham," *International Encyclopedia*, 407). Among other things, Lippert concerned himself with "the priesthood as a social institution." At the same time he attempted to reveal the common basis of all religions in *soul worship*, in which humanity for the first time is shown "the invisible as visible." This supposedly then leads to the idea of a "personally conceived soul," from which finally "also develops the idea of the human soul." According to Lippert, its particular significance is heavily underlined by "the fact of death." In his view, this is also the origin of the principles of all "cult behaviour," which creates not only the "principles and unity of human logic, but also the most basic network of social forms of life" (Lippert, *Allgemeine Geschichte des Priestertums*, vol. I–II, 13).

religion, analyzed, and criticized from the time of Nikolaj Berdijaew through Raymond Aron right up to Hans Maier.[59]

Comte's starting point became the conviction that the necessity of unifying humankind on a democratic and industrial basis[60] can be fulfilled only on the condition that all people yield to the supreme being, that is to humankind as a whole, if humanity becomes the guideline for all behavior. Comte termed this commitment to humanity altruism, and it then became the core of his *religion of humanity*, inevitably unifying humankind in the positive stage of its development. Altruism also had an eschatological dimension for Comte; it was supposed to be the means for a historically definitive overcoming of individual, but especially group and national egoisms. This utopia of the end of egoisms was thus based on a supposedly scientific understanding of how human society works. Comte was also convinced that altruism should also be reinforced by ritual, i.e., meeting the need for order as well as emotion.

To summarize, I would emphasize the following:

1. The broad concept of "secularization" can be narrowed either with respect to the nature of the problem it is intended to analyze, or

2. with respect to the different—integration and compensation—concepts of religiosity from which it emerges. In the case of the compensation concept, its relative independence from growing social criticism of religion and the church can be perceived.

3. The notion of secularization can be distinguished from the concept of "de-churching" (*Entkirchlichung*) and also

4. from the frequently used concept of "disenchantment" (*Entzauberung*), which is connected with secularizing phenomena but should not be considered interchangeable with them.

5. The essence of "disenchantment" for Max Weber, who introduced this concept, lay not in changes in faith, the position of the church and the relationship between religion and society, but in the cultural consequences of the unique Occidental process of the rationalization of human life, the ability to calculate benefit and the ability to technically manipulate the natural world and human society in general.

6. In keeping with the intentions of Weber's viewpoint, "disenchantment of the world" should be understood as indicative of a post-Enlightenment, or more precisely post-Kantian transfer of faith and religion into the private sphere of life, similar to the way in which ideas of good, beauty, hope or love, for whose solution Weber believed science had nothing to offer, became a private and personal matter. The consequence is the relativization of values, which become an exclusively subjective project consecrated only by one's own personality.

59. See Berdiajew, *Der Sinn und Schicksal des russischen Komunismus*; Raymond, *Opium intelektuálů*; Maier, *Politická náboženství*.

60. This was called for in Comte's previous works, especially in the four-volume *Système de politique positive ou Traité de sociologie* (no print date, Paris, 1851–1854).

2

Secularization of the Working Class—The Czech Model

A Hypothesis and Methodical Contemplation[1]

JiŘí MatĚJČek

1. Recently in the historiography of Bohemia, Moravia and Silesia there seems to have been a renewal of interest in the working class,[2] which in the second half of the nineteenth and first half of the twentieth century formed a very significant part of society and in 1947 still represented 40 percent of the economically active population of the Czech lands,[3] but after 1989 was almost entirely neglected in historiography—aside from the occasional "digressions" of some badly informed "central" historians (who perhaps read only what is written by their acquaintances) and some epigones, both of them without reflection and often unconsciously repeating ideological myths from socialist times, especially the assertion that under capitalism the working class "lived in destitution."[4]

Even under socialism, of course, there did not come into being any collected work on the working class, analyzing all its characteristics—its status and patterns of behaviour, as a Marxist historian observed in 1991. Nor could such a work come into being, because to "the working class" was ascribed only the aforementioned destitution, only successful strikes, campaigns, ideas and leaders' disputes, heavenly perfection and a worldwide mission, while the "day-to-day existence" of the worker and the working-class community was not given sufficient, systematic attention, not even in the edition *Etnografie dělnictva* [Ethnography of the Working Class].[5]

1 For a number of important additions, my thanks go to Dr. J. Machačová, CSc.

2. See comment in the *Slezský sborník* (2008), no 4.

3. Maňák, "Početnost a struktura české inteligence," 398–409.

4. For the most part the workforce of centralized large-scale production, along with the majority of the trading workforce, never lived permanently in a state of destitution, if we define "destitution" as the non-fulfilment of basic biological needs. At times some of the workers lived in a state of deprivation and the workforce as a whole in poverty, which was of course only relative, and in some manufacturing branches they had a standard of living approaching that of the lower middle classes. See the quite plentiful literature cited in the aforementioned comment. The clarification of the actual status of the workforce right at the beginning of this study is not merely an end in itself—it will have significance for the overall argument.

5. Ústav etnografie a folkloristiky ČSAV (the Institute of Ethnography and Folklore of the Czechoslovak Academy of Sciences) of course came about mainly at the initiative of Antonín Robek.

23

To some extent this renewed interest yields findings about "day-to-day existence," and for this reason is highly desirable; however, at the same time it also frequently delivers petrified fallacies of Marxist propaganda.[6]

2. One of the forbidden historical themes under socialism was religion in general, and the church was outwardly ignored, so that even the "cursed historians" of the '60s did not dare to write about any possible piety of the working class. In fact, it obviously never even occurred to them because neither sources of socialistic provenance (within the purview of the prescribed socialist doctrine), nor even official documents of the nineteenth and twentieth century mentioned any possible piety of the working class. The socialist press, of course (again within the framework of ideology), fought quite fiercely against the church and (we) historians did not fully appreciate why: it was about the weakening, perhaps even the liquidation of religious influence, which above all was inconsistent with the basic focusing of socialist ideology on its own social activities (self-efficacy) and the emancipation of the working class, especially the industrial workforce.

The common flaw (one of the common flaws) of the socialist historiography of the working class, a natural consequence of its necessary "partisanship," was that it only made use of sources of socialist origin, and sources opposing socialism were either ignored or (occasionally, or perhaps often, rightly) denigrated as biased. This was also the case with the official reports of functionaries of the "bourgeois" state, who were mainly objective and sometimes even "reasonable," with a sympathy for the situation of the working class. In socialist ideology and historiography "if you weren't with us, you were against us." Intolerance, of course, also had its origin in the antagonistic situation which developed in the 1860s through the influence of the "master—servant" attitude of industrialists towards the workers. At the same time, even the working-class press did not reflect the actual characteristics or attitudes of the workforce, but was primarily a means of ideological influence and thus had a strong ethnocentric tendency (through an inadequate defense of the interests of groups). Only occasionally was there a hint of complaints by functionaries, for example about "the spinelessness of the masses, who wait while the trade unions fight for them and then live off the advantages gained," or about the lack of awareness among members of workers' associations, who "instead of listening to a lecture in the back room of the pub, prefer to sit in the bar-room with a beer and play cards."

These were some aspects of "day-to-day existence," which filtered only through oversight into socialist propaganda, never into socialist historiography and only quite exceptionally into the recollections recorded under socialism of former working-class functionaries or "self-manipulated" workers.[7] In this type of source, even in memoirs

6. See note 1 and further comment in the *Slezský sborník* (2009).

7. This applies particularly to ideologized workers' memoirs collected in the 1950s in the Archiv Národního technického muzea [Archives of National Technical Museum] in Prague. By contrast "day-to-day existence" is captured quite admirably by a record which "slipped past" the censors of a unique memoir from the period around 1900, when the tide of "new miners" from Galicia and other less developed areas reached its peak: Rohel, "Život dělnické rodiny v kolonii na Ostravsku," 7–8. The deprivation which the eyewitness describes, not material—miners were one of the best paid categories of workers—but cultural, was the same as that which Ignát Herrmann, for example, reports in the poor districts of Prague or in the

published in book form, we of course find nothing about the piety of the workers. This part of day-to-day working-class existence is entirely submerged—even more so than other elements of "mentality" (patterns of behaviour and living): there is very little source material which would show these patterns without distortion, i.e., originating before the period of socialist falsification, just as there are very few "pre-socialist" working-class memoirs at all. Equally scarce are "pre-socialist" treatments of the history of the working-class movement (which naturally deal with "day-to-day existence" just as little as history from the time of socialism).[8]

In any case it would be necessary during the study of the secularization of the working class to make use of all available sources, including the Catholic press and journalism, and to re-evaluate the official sources, which under socialism were studied without attention being paid to the question of the piety of the working class. This would primarily call for a diligent researcher(s).[9]

3. In studying the theme of secularization we must of course concern ourselves with a) the sphere of social actions and interactions which would indicate the relationships (attitudes) towards religion, b) the sphere of "mentality," "way of thinking," attitudes and other isolated patterns of behaviour and living, which are the source of these actions and interactions, and with whose help we also interpret these actions and interactions.[10] "Piety" is however very much a matter of "mentality" and "way of thinking," which does not necessarily manifest itself in "plain form" in actions and interactions, but is usually mixed in them with "social" emotions, stereotypes and attitudes. Attitudes, the immedi-

---

ghetto—Josefov. The "new authors" do not even exploit Doctor Wlassak's less than appropriate observations about alcoholism in Ostravsko for a fictitious picture of the working class.

8. Among the "pre-socialist" memoirs of the working-class (or perhaps rather laboring and socialist) environment belong Wenzl Holek's unquestionably outstanding recollections *Lebensgang eines deutsch-tschechischen Handarbeiters* and *Vom Handarbeiter zum Jugenderzieher* both edited by Göhre and František Halas senior's only slightly ideologically manipulated recollections, *Kemka. Vzpomínky bývalého textilního dělníka*. The editor was the writer Václav Kaplický and the analyzer of memoirs Jana Machačová writes that they have not been manipulated by the editor and also offer facts about the working class which from the 50s were not allowed to come to light. (Machačová, "Prostředí továrního dělnictva," 63–100.) Halas's memoirs are very rich in content and equal Holek's memoirs in their value as testification. Of course they are written from the viewpoint of a socialist trade-union official. The North Bohemian workers' leader Seff Schiller makes no mention of religion in his memoirs, most likely therefore it was not of pivotal importance to him. There might be cause for a new evaluation of the book by Tomáš Jiroušek *Dějiny sociálního hnutí v zemích Koruny české*. Jiroušek wrote from the viewpoint of Christian socialism and as a later historians also tracks the "movement" rather than patterns and "day-to-day existence." Literature from the period after 1989 as well as some older works concern themselves more with political parties than with the (Catholic) workers' movement, i.e., again with "ideas" and organizational development rather than normal life—just like the socialist literature.

9. While there can be no doubt about the diligence of professional researchers, the main flaw (of all our historiography) is the small number of researchers, which stands out in comparison with larger nations, where research in the humanities usually receives greater attention and support than in our country.

10. In this example can be seen the unsuitability—lack of structure—of the concept of "mentality," which is generally employed in our historiography. It describes "everything and nothing," largely without a system, while behaviour and actions have a complicated structure with many interconnected elements, such as needs, values, goals, attitudes, opportunities, resources (know-how) and so on.

ate "cause" or rather "basis" of behaviour, involve a relationship to an object (a person, group, thing, or event) formed rationally, but at the same time also emotionally—within the significance of the object is combined its rational and emotional (but often also ideological) appraisal. The attitude towards religion demonstrates its significance (more or less its value) for an individual or group.

On the whole it is a matter of the study of "spirituality," of the psychological and socio-psychological basis of behaviour, founded mainly on the use of memoirs, autobiographies, correspondence and other sources of a so-called personal nature.[11] For our theme the main problem is the aforementioned lack of sources of information from the working-class environment.

4. What is secularization? Catholic ideologists and propagandists, and it seems even some historians, try to pretend that secularization means only a separation of the church and the state, which is basically unrelated to the population's way of thinking, which thus remains pious (even if they themselves don't realize it), faithful, and more or less Catholic (and to this should therefore also be adapted the position of the church within society). The author of this study, however, understands "secularization" in its usual sense, as a movement away from a religious, i.e., mythical, mystical and magical "supernatural" conception of the world (existence), as it is perhaps usually understood these days in the rational humanities.[12] For that matter, if we were to interpret secularization only as a separation of the church and state, what meaning (sense) would the compound term "secularization of the working class" have? It seems that the only possibility then becomes precisely the meaning of a movement away from mystery, the loss of religious faith, which in the Habsburg monarchy took place during and after the transition from an agrarian to an industrial society in the second half of the nineteenth century, partly through the anticlerical activities of liberals and socialists and with advances in the natural sciences, the process continuing under the First Czechoslovak Republic. Already in the last quarter of the nineteenth century there arose especially among the middle classes a quite generally observed "religion of progress," which can also be understood as a substitute for religion, for faith in a better afterlife, for which one no longer had to wait. One of the significant results of this process, firmly linked with industrialization, was the formation of "nominal Catholicism," formal religious affiliation, which gained control of a large majority of the population and exists even in the present day, when Christian moral principles are applied only very selectively.[13]

11. For the study of patterns of behaviour and living we have managed to develop quite a well-considered and well-tested methodology: Machačová and Matějček, Jiří, "Vzory chování v českých zemích," 399–482. Some of the empirical material was collected in: *Studie k sociálním dějinám 19. století* 5 (1995).

12. We attempted to clarify this concept, the causes and course of secularization in the study Machačová and Matějček "Náboženství, církev, sekularizace," 1–13.

13. It is debatable whether the contemporary ethics of the "western world," albeit continually breached to a greater or lesser extent or even completely negated, arose through the activity of the church, which brought together spiritual and other elites, or through the gradual adjustment of the population to the principles of a relatively trouble-free existence by trial and error in the historical development of mankind. Even savages and for that matter atheists have principles of "decent behaviour" adapted to their situation—be it with many prayers, or with none.

Further to this I could only repeat the thesis contained in the cited study and I therefore prefer to attempt to summarize notable manifestations of religious feeling among the working class in the nineteenth century.

5. As I have already mentioned, such knowledge is thus far very meagre, as our main sources, Wenzl Holek and František Halas, have written.

Holek was subject to a religious school education (he was born in 1864), but according to his own account he attended school on and off for a total of only around three and a half years because he had to help his parents to support their large family. His parents were, in the terminology of the time, "day-laborers with unsteady employment," which meant that they worked irregularly and his father was often without work for quite long periods while he looked for more lucrative day-labor work, as Holek himself also did later. They never went to church. His mother was superstitious, but his ambitious father was a rationalist with principles of "decent behaviour," the majority of which he passed on to his son. According to the school education which the inquisitive and sociable Václav willingly adopted, "decent behaviour" involved "being good" (moral) and of course also being pious. Hence he prayed for his family to have more money. But God did not answer his prayers and they continued to live in deprivation and occasional destitution. That is why he gave up praying. This perceptive and intelligent, but logically immature and also emotional child, must have felt let down by the ineffectiveness of religious ideas and by the indifference of God himself. At the same time it bothered Václav, perhaps also under the influence of his father's principles, that the old teacher, as well the priest, required children to kiss their hands.

The adolescent Václav—again perhaps through the influence of his father, but perhaps also of a new teacher—was roused by "injustice" and even wrote a threatening letter to the manager of the sugar factory when he had to pay an unjustified fine. He was a hard-working, but certainly not compliant and uncomplaining worker. He observed with admiration the self-confidence of the specialist metal workers from Prague, who came to the sugar factory to repair equipment and "didn't take any nonsense from anyone—not even from the clerks." Later in the brickworks he looked with contempt on the behaviour of the casual workers from the countryside, who according to him were uneducated, passive and uncomplaining, shy and religious. Around the age of eighteen, he started to read Marxist socialist literature, lecture in workers' associations and write for workers' newspapers.

The preceding paragraphs contain everything from Holek's memoirs that concerns religion, faith and the church. He does not even write whether he got married in a church or had his children baptized. He probably did, just as he married his first wife (only after living together for several years) so that his children would be legitimate. During one relocation, Holek and his family were not accepted into the community by the mayor because of his (sinful) unmarried union. Even the second volume of his memoirs does not contain anything further, although Holek, when he moved to Saxony with his family around 1900, became the organizer of educational activities for young workers in clubs founded by Christian socialists and supported by the state.[14] He doesn't write anything about religion in this volume and the place he obtained in the Christian organization was clearly the result of an effort to find permanent, non-manual work, since he never gained any specialist qualification and during his social advancement was reliant only on his natural intelligence and diligence. After finishing school he clearly lost, certainly also under the influence of socialist literature, his interest in religion, which no longer had any direct significance in his life.

Holek—with his above-average intelligence and his paternal upbringing and eagerly received school education—certainly wasn't a typical day laborer; however, at the same time situations occurred in his life which were typical for all day laborers and work-ers, which he solved with the help of patterns of behaviour typical for day laborers and workers and of their given opportunities (status). In this sphere of usual patterns he was indeed a typical representative of the vast majority of the working class in the last quarter of the nineteenth century—industrial workers and day laborers, and it is therefore quite likely that his relationship towards religion could also be typical of these large groups (as we shall go on to demonstrate).

Elements of working-class anticlericalism and irreligiousness are also present in the recollections of the second protagonist, the Brno trade union official František Halas senior. He was born in 1880 as the son of a poor home-based weaver from a village, who after several moves relocated to Brno with his family and became a factory worker, because he could earn more that way than as a home-based producer. With this he found his way into the environment of the large-scale industrial working class and at the same time the provincial capital, where the socialist movement was developing rapidly. From 1888 Halas senior was a member of a socialist club and the family read the humor-ous and satirical socialist magazine *Rašple* [The File], from which the young František, clearly by nature a distinctly confident and antiauthoritarian character, derived anticleri-cal attitudes from his childhood. The second source besides his father was his elder sister Helena, a textile worker, who also read the Brno socialist publication Rovnost (Equality) and Červánky (Red Dawn). At the same time, however, his mother instilled Christian piety in the children, and his father a general decency towards people. A predisposition towards tuberculosis ran in the family and from seven children who were born only two survived until adulthood. His father too died of tuberculosis—when he was 36. During his funeral František gained another emotional argument for his anticlericalism: for the ceremony (perhaps quite splendid, as was the custom even with poor people and was demanded by relatives) the parish priest wanted his mother to come up with nine pieces of gold, the family's income for two weeks; if she didn't have the money, she would have to sell something. In the end he contented himself with seven pieces of gold. From so-cialist magazines and from his own experience František therefore acquired two social stereotypes: the greedy priest and the wicked rich man who is without mercy. Priests also belonged among the rich. At the same time he admired (and later imitated) the

14. The publisher of his memoirs, Paul Göhre, was a pastor and Christian-socialist activist.

self-confidence of the socialist workers, among other reasons because at the funeral, as a manifestation of their anticlerical stance, they did not take off their hats.

However, the majority of Brno workers probably behaved circumspectly for a long time, as was usual in the countryside environment from which they came, where it was necessary to "respect authority," as is documented elsewhere: when it was the factory manager's birthday, the workers gave him a congratulatory certificate, for which a collection was organized. Halas himself, already a known socialist who was expected to uphold the anticlerical stance of his party, got married (for the second time) in a church—to a poor nineteen-year-old girl who worked with him in the cotton mill and was raised in a staunchly Catholic family; within two years, however, he "turned her into" a socialist, a member of the Dělnická tělovýchovná jednota (DTJ) [The Workers' Physical Education Unit] and later also a workers' delegate (i.e., an "official" functionary with specific authority recognized by the law). Halas was also a workers' delegate, and in the factory and then also in the whole of working-class Brno he gained a considerable influence over the direction of the radical youth, when in the course of the 1890s the working class's opinion of socialists, initially regarded as dangerous outcasts, gradually began to change.

Halas never actually married his first wife (just as Holek didn't for a long time)—he was not comfortable with the pre-wedding preparations at the rectory. Unmarried cohabitation was quite common, especially among "new" workers, and can also be interpreted as a break away from the influence of the church.

In all his activities as a trade union leader, Halas did not fight for some spiritual elevation of the working class (for example through the Christian faith), but for its material interests—higher wages and permanent employment. Only thus could he actually lead "the mass," which from tradition and under the new opportunities brought about by economic growth was actively interested primarily in these very material elements of existence.[15]

Other information on the attitude of the working class towards religion is only fragmentary. Wenzl Holek writes that the brick-factory workers with whom he worked in Saxony spent their evenings telling each other Bible stories—at the same time, however, also tales of ghosts and superstitions and events and stories from life—especially prevalent, of course, was the epic storytelling and mystery which characterized the romantic folk tales and fairy tales which were kept alive among "the people." For that matter, stories from the Old Testament did not exactly abound in Catholic piety. Towards the end of the nineteenth century superstition was still common "among the people"—in the countryside in particular people believed in anything mysterious and out of the ordinary, which the poor especially had no way of verifying (nor did they want to—mystery was exciting).

In the miners' association for formal education Volnost [Freedom], which was founded by socialist miners in 1897 in today's Sokolov (*Falkenau an der Eger*), religion was not talked about, even though the main content of its meetings was initially educa-

---

15. We have also covered this quite extensively in our other works, along with the self-confidence of the workers and other elements of the "modern discontent" of the working class which began to manifest itself from the end of the third quarter of the nineteenth century.

tional lectures (with a socialist leaning). At any rate, the association soon changed into a trade-union one, but primarily a social center corresponding to the interests of the well-paid miners.[16]

Neither in the socialist sources from the coalfield of Sokolov-Loket, nor from the North Bohemian brown-coalfields, nor in the relevant contemporary literature of predominantly bourgeois provenance, do we find anything about the piety of the working class and especially of the miners, except the assertion that the miners were "Roman catholics."[17]

The situation was obviously more complicated in Moravia and Silesia, for example in the Ostravsko-Karvinsko coalfield. There the influence of the socialists began to manifest itself rather late in the day, and they were probably careful not to oppose traditional religious feelings and ideas, especially those of the "new" miners coming in from villages in the Beskydy foothills and from Galicia, even less developed and more religious. The first May Day celebrations in the Ostravsko region in 1890 were supposed to be, at the request of the miners, inaugurated by a celebratory mass, which, together with the other celebration, was banned by the district office. This act provoked such outrage that an actual uprising broke out, lasting for three weeks, which the army had to be called in to suppress. During this time, mobs of rioting miners roamed through the countryside and in a rather brutal manner forced those who were still working to join them, committed other acts of violence and were on the verge of destroying property on a large scale. In the ironworks of Vítkovice the blast furnaces were even put out. The demand for the celebration of the mass obviously emanated from the religious traditions of the countryside (and Galicia), but at the same time it was (clearly) supposed to mean that the miners were declaring their support for the contemporary organization of society as its conscious part; the following celebration of May Day was (obviously) meant to show the independence of their interests and the self-confidence of this new social group. The actual events then took place in the confrontational style of resolving conflicts which was typical of that socially transient period.

The dangerous environment of the pit undoubtedly inspired misgivings in the miners, but it seems that in Bohemia they believed in "heathen" evil spirits, who had to be placated rather than provoked; in Ostravsko the Christian Saint Barbara was supposed to protect them. Even after 1900 the miners there still held lavish celebrations in honor of Saint Barbara, which were evidently characterized by popular merry-making rather like parish fetes, where the main lure was the dancing and various worldly attractions, or religious festivals, which had long since become a social event for the country people, an opportunity to meet, "pleasure trips," an escape from the mundane, composed of the church service and the opportunity to buy some small luxury. It is hard to determine to what extent religious exaltation and thoughts of "higher things" played a part in this—genuine religious feelings could accompany the choral singing

16. Matějček, "Český dělnický spolek Volnost," 95–116.

17. *Führer durch das nordwestböhmische Braunkohlenrevier.* Brüx 1908. This book even records what the North Bohemian workers ate, and yet it contains nothing about religion except the aforementioned sweeping statement.

of hymns and pilgrim songs. Is it clear, however, that at all times and in all places Christian moral principles were observed only selectively and as long as they didn't interfere with other interests. It is likely that popular "religious" celebrations, rather than transcendental thoughts, contained elements of rare and exciting mystery accompanying the church ceremonies, but also superstitious and spooky story telling, and at the same time elements of popular piety.[18]

In the conservative atmosphere of small-scale industry, the journeyman was for a long time, even in private matters, answerable to the master craftsman, who was in most cases also quite provincially conservative. This was similar to the relationship between the farm hands and the farmer, and in small towns too the situation could be different to large-scale industry, where for a long time the factory owner did not have either the interest or the opportunity to regulate the private life of his employees, apart from offering them some special help. He paid them for work and for him it was about the smooth running of the factory, which meant that workers were only to observe the working regulations, work hard and not turn up to work drunk and should not be socialists. In small-scale industry and in the small town the journeyman, on the contrary, was to a certain extent the "calling card" of the master craftsman and had some influence on his reputation and status. In the Catholic environment of the respectable small town, he thus made the journeyman display piousness by going to church like his family, if this hadn't already been inculcated in the journeyman by his family. The power of convention was always great.

The shoemaker's apprentice Václav Medek had his piousness impressed upon him by his bigoted mother, but once he became an adult he no longer mentions anything about religion in his memoirs.[19]

It is very likely that the boisterous Prague female factory workers of whom Němcová wrote in the 1840s wanted mainly to enjoy themselves in the new relaxed environment, attending the dancing rather than the church on Sundays, and data on the membership figures of moralizing girls' associations, which were led by pious bourgeois matrons, show that their attempts were not very successful. Similarly, K. Klostermann makes no mention of piety among the girls who came in droves to the Sumava timber works in 1870.[20] On the contrary, they were just as boisterous as the Prague factory workers of a generation earlier, and in the factories they were primarily looking for (with their parents' approval) a good income and (already, it seems, through the weak resistance of the traditional environment) social freedom, i.e., breaking away from the social control of village priests and rich farmers.[21] It is almost certain that the preaching from the traditional environment—including the church—turned them away from religion and piousness.

If required, we could certainly find many examples of similar, precisely described behaviour, just as we could find opposite examples, especially in moralizing literature

---

18. Of which more will be said later. Concisely, Zuber, *Osudy moravské církve*, vol. 2. Less succinctly Nešpor, *Náboženství na prahu nové doby.*

19. Machačová, "Prostředí drobného řemeslnictva," 101–14.

20. Klostermann, *V ráji šumavském.*

21. This is of course deduction, but it is almost certain and is inferred from a set of similar behaviour.

and ideological journalism and fiction of the nineteenth century, which extolled among other things the religious traditions of the "unspoilt" country folk, but we would also find lamentations over depravity and the "loosening of morals"; this was a frequent contemporary term of the last quarter of the nineteenth century—J. Š. Baar complained that the priest was no longer the "father of the parish" as before and that liberal and socialist agitation was infiltrating even the countryside.[22]

So far it seems that "indicators" point to changes in the tradition rather than its continuance. It would be somewhat miraculous if during the process of rapid social change which accompanied the transient period of abrupt "mass industrialization" of the last quarter of the nineteenth century, the "way of thinking"—patterns of behaviour and living—remained the same as in the agrarian period.

6. In the preceding text I have already indicated some elements of the ways of life and status of the industrial workforce in large-scale industry from which emanated its "mentality"—patterns of behaviour—and changes therein. I will now attempt to describe this "Czech model" more systematically and in more detail. First, however, I will return again to the period of agrarian society and the conditions of the rural working class, from which the workforce for industrial large-scale production was formed during the nineteenth century.

In the stationary economy and rigid society of the agrarian period, controlled completely by the aristocracy, there were few opportunities for material or social advancement. The main goal of the rural (and the not yet numerous urban) poor, which probably formed ninety per cent of the total population of the Czech lands around the year 1800, was survival, and the most vital characteristic had to be resourcefulness, the art of finding seasonal and irregular sources of livelihood, free goods, begging or stealing on a small scale. It seems that the elites were more convinced of the laziness of the peasants than of their diligence and effort, and in an inefficient system they tried first and foremost to prevent the emergence of mass discontent.[23] In this they were helped by, among other things, the conservative educational system established after 1805, and even more substantially by the Catholic church with the spiritual superiority of the priest over the majority of the population and with the ideology of submitting to the will of God, devised for the medieval period with its general lack of resources. Thus in the first half of the nineteenth century the numerous rural poor still lived in material destitution (non-fulfillment of even the most basic biological needs), submission and ignorance: "In poverty our fathers lived and died, in poverty we too live, do what you will."[24] The primitive, pre-logical thinking of the lower classes, in pictures instead of in concepts, also played a part in this, along with their habit-based and strongly emotional behaviour, in which "the wish was father to the thought" without regard for logic.[25] Another source of backwardness was the overall lack of resources (motivation, energy, intelligence, material

22. Baar, *Cestou křížovou*.

23. Mj. Machačová and Matějček, "'Kdo jediné zná,'" 141–52.

24. Salichová, *Ze starých časů*.

25. See especially Kutnar, *Sociálně myšlenková tvářnost obrozenského lidu*.

goods and especially knowledge of progressive patterns—know-how). In the sub-local existence of the working class, one reflected little and carried out almost exclusively routine, habit-based activities.[26] This naturally created an unaccustomedness to reflection and intellectual effort and with this also a resistance to learning, especially in school and from books. Logical thinking was a skill possessed only by the rural and urban elites, who of course at the same time took care to conform to the establishment line. Simultaneously, however, by the beginning of the nineteenth century even a section of the rural elite understood the role of ideas, social groups, organizations and institutions, the church being among them.[27]

The overall situation was also strongly influenced by the relative territorial stability of the population. Although migrations occurred, in the period of serfdom they were severely limited and for the most part there were still no incentives for long-distance work migration as there were later on.[28] By and large there was no reason to relocate. The fundamental truth was of course that the migrant in a new location—in a village or small town—arrived in the same environment that he had left behind: one controlled by aristocrats, conservative rich farmers or equally conservative rich burghers, and by the church, and was therefore under constant and relatively uniform supervision and pressure, both spiritual and secular.[29]

7. According to church historians, popular piety of the eighteenth century was characterized: a) by the cult of the Virgin Mary as intercessor for her son, b) by the cult of the saints, helping out in predicaments, c) by faith in miracles, d) by faith in the power of formal rituals (including prayer).[30] It was therefore a case of protection and help from supernatural forces (mythical and at the same time mystical) achieved through invocation and performing miracles (magic) in a generally mythical and mystical world where rational cognition had to be replaced by faith, and the miserable peasant, as in life on earth, had to win over the powers with his pleas—with magic. What lay outside the teaching of the church was "resolved" with "heathen" superstition, faith in spooks, ghosts and devils and an equally magical defense against them. Christian supernatural powers were primarily supposed to help (the country folk in particular) in the numerous

26. "Sub-local existence" implies interest only in one's own person, family and immediate surroundings. See "'Kdo jediné zná.'"

27. Kudlich, *Rückblicke und Erinnerungen.*

28. In the second quarter of the nineteenth century there was nevertheless a migrational movement from surrounding villages to local centers—small towns, and in the long term, of course, to regional and provincial metropolises.

29. The Bohemian chronicles written in the second half of the eighteenth century by prominent citizens of villages and towns show a very strong interest in religious, or rather church matters. This, however, disappears in the first half of the nineteenth century, both from the chronicles and from other sources such as memoirs. See Machačová and Matějček, *O středních vrstvách*, where we made use of Robek's edition of the Czech chronicles and also some memoirs. It is quite possible that Moravian Catholicism maintained a strong position, among other reasons, because it didn't have such strong "Hussite" opposition as in Bohemia.

30. Viz Zuber, *Osudy moravské církve*, vol. 2.

predicaments of mortal existence. In their view, it was the priest's job to secure the help of these "powers" for the weak and erring.

At the same time fatalism was often compensated for by an elemental joy, and as in Krušné hory in the third quarter of the nineteenth century they lived *"in der lustigen Not von der Hand in den Mund."*[31]

In the first half of the nineteenth century a poor countryman living a miserable existence which only slowly improved, to which he was sullenly or uncomplainingly reconciled, naturally did not think too much about God and Christian theology, he did not even have time for it during the incessant struggle for resources, but at the same time he lived in a sort of fatalistic optimism, which told him that surely he would always manage to scrape by somehow; after all, that was what the church constantly told him. He naturally appealed to God and the saints as protectors in exceptionally difficult situations, as the church, as well as custom, also suggested to him. He perhaps prayed more ardently to the "powers" in the emotional and mystical environment of the church and its divine services. Christian morality was internalized in him by life in rural society, which constantly reminded him of it, and he knew that within the framework of social regulation and his inferior status, from which, with very few exceptions, there was no escape, he couldn't take many liberties. Church and folk celebrations offered him moments of exaltation, but it seems that later he could become sceptical towards faith in miracles, in the help of the saints and in the power of prayer, presumably because he began to comprehend that it did not help him much. The situation for women was of course different, being more emotive but mainly more dogged by the adversity of existence than men, and the situation of people in an agricultural environment probably also differed from the proto-industrial or industrializing environment, where on the one hand there were more opportunities than in agricultural and remote areas and on the other hand social control was weaker. Linked with this was the aforementioned decline in interest in religious faith and church events in the first half of the nineteenth century.[32] The previous interest in these things might be further explained by a wave of emotion around the tolerance decree, and perhaps also by the fact that otherwise nothing much was happening in the countryside.

Fundamental changes to all this were introduced by industrialization and the emancipatory political struggle of the bourgeoisie. Industrialization led to the gradually accelerating economic development of the second half and third quarter of the nineteenth century while the emancipation of the bourgeoisie led to the partial undermining of the absolute power of the aristocracy, the farmstead and gradually even the church.

8. As well as altering the attitudes of the working class, industrialization also changed their models of behaviour. A constant demand for new workers in heavy industry arose; this gave industrial workers the opportunity for material advancement, which in the

31. Dormitzer and Schebek, *Die Erwerbsverhältnisse im böhmischen Erzgebirge.*

32. One of the chroniclers writes for example at the beginning of the 60s that "the parish priests are beginning to swarm again." He is most likely referring to their renewed public involvement, previously evident around the year 1848.

last quarter of the nineteenth century, during the period of "mass industrialization" (the movement of agricultural laborers to industry), became their principal goal. With the slow growth in the working class's wages in real terms came a development in consciousness mainly in the economically progressive sectors; under the influence of the acceptance of basic socialist ideas—anti-clericalism being among them—there originated the "modern discontent" of the working class which was connected to anti-authoritarian attitudes.[33] The workers gradually began to realize that the industrialists could not manage without them, and later the industrialists themselves began to recognize this.

The second factor was the mass migration of workers in the last quarter of the nineteenth century, connected to industrialization, and likewise the mass turnover of workers in industrial firms often connected with this migration. It was significant that the migrant did not move to the same environment which he left, but to a completely different one: industrial with different models. There was a general "loosening of morals" mainly due to the mass migration and turnover of labor, but partly due to the anonymity and laxity of the factory environment—there was a distinct weakening of the social controls of the original village society from which the factory workers came.[34] The new workers, therefore, were freed from the controls of the old authorities, and even though the majority of them maintained several conventions (for example religious christenings, weddings and funerals), at the same time they were dissatisfied with the surplice fee that the Church demanded. This contributed to a change in the social stereotype of the priest, who stopped being the generally approved and respected pastor of the village people (if indeed that was the popular stereotype and not the Church's idea which was implanted in "the people"—at the time of intensive re-Catholization in the eighteenth century more than a few priests were feared rather than respected) and under the influence of socialist propaganda became one of the "evil rich" and often also a gluttonous, immoral overweight person who exploited the working people and concentrated on increasing his property rather than on matters of the soul. These doctrinaire attitudes could be softened by personal contact with a priest and a sense of reality which was different from the doctrines, though in the industrial towns and the working-class housing areas personal contact between the workers—often immigrants—and the priest was very rare.

The changes in workers' attitudes were partly due to the seesawing changes in education—at the end of the 1860s control was wrested from the Church by German liberals, then in the 1880s it was partly clericalized, but then was gradually secularized once more.[35] The effect of education was dependent on the fact that many of the ideas and attitudes which the school imparted to children often had no relationship to their lives

33. The rise in the living standards of the industrial working class (which had been much higher than in agriculture in the first half of the nineteenth century) is shown in objective studies from the 1990s. Viz Machačová, "Tendence vývoje mezd dělnictva," 146–319. Matějček, "Reálné mzdy horníků," 217–324. The same for the metal workers' movement in the collection of the Národní technické muzeum [National Technical Museum], *Z dějin hutnictví*.

34. One reaction was the so-called anti-vagrant law of 1873 which attempted to halt the spiralling crime rate and collapse in morals which accompanied migration and the turnover of labor.

35. Even in the eighteenth century the composer J. J. Ryba complained that "the church is the master, the school the servant."

and interests and they did not think about them because they did not relate to their own experiences and were forgotten in time, or, on the contrary, were "fixed" in their minds as long-term untested a-priori attitudes or ideas—it would depend on whether individuals or groups identified with the person who supported the idea or attitude. The working-class cult of Jan Hus, tortured by the Church and "betrayed by the ginger fox," also had an effect on Czech children and perhaps even on the adults, and was disseminated in liberal schools by patriotic teachers.

There were other reasons for moving away from religion—the new situation of the working class meant there were various forms of entertainment and "worldly attractions" in the cities, but also in the workers' areas where there were regular visits to the pub at least on pay day, something which the village poor had no money for, but which the well-paid industrial workers, especially the young and the single, could afford. That there was no praying or debating Christian morality in pubs is obvious. Other attractions were offered with opportunities for glamorous behaviour.[36] With a certain exaggeration it is possible to say that in some areas and housing estates, during the period of the "loosen-ing of morals" the Church was replaced by mass alcoholism or very often by satisfying the hitherto pent-up needs for "pleasures of the flesh," as well as other entertainments and distractions which had earlier been provided to the villagers in relatively directed and controlled forms by the Church, its services and religious and folk festivals.

It was also important that with the relaxing of social controls the new workers, equipped with a new consciousness emerging from the increase in opportunities, also escaped from the preaching of the Church, which villagers had earlier accepted almost fatalistically, but which in the new situation began to aggravate them more. Few people enjoyed being rebuked, regimented, disciplined and force-fed information. This was at the heart of the modern anti-authority working class where previously there had only been passive resistance.

One of the most fundamental matters, if not the most fundamental, was that the workers of the last quarter of the nineteenth century, living only in relative poverty and with growing self-confidence, began to understand that redemption from sins after death was not so profitable (they began to have doubts about it due to the influence of socialist ideology), and that they could attain their (material) rewards here on Earth with the booming economy and the aid of socialist organizations. A new faith began to spread amongst the new working class in place of religious faith—from the transcendental in poverty there was a move to material values and a belief in their gratification, a move-ment "for the better," and in place of the old organizations appeared new protective pow-ers: organizations, unions and parties from which the organized workers gained a feeling of guaranteed security—in place of the old models. The state also started to become a protector with its "social" laws and intervention. At the beginning, though, the workers were even sceptical towards socialism: when midway through the 1870s the journeyman baker Wenzl Peter returned to his native Hrušková (*Birndorf*) from Vienna and began his socialist activities, the local miners considered him to be a "big head" and disorderly

36. As written by, e.g., Pitronová, *Haličské migrace na Ostravsku*.

individual. This was compounded by his "disorderly" death of being hit by a train when drunk. However, ten years later the socialist activist Franziska Brandl, the partner of the North Bohemian socialist Josef Šíp, allegedly had "wild success" with these self-same miners. The emotional speeches of a spirited woman had a much more significant effect on the men than the earlier impassioned preachers—the young chaplains—had had (on women). (However, historiography has more or less avoided research into the emotions over the last two hundred years).

From these attitudes it was only a small step to the opinion that the workers did not need a god and even less a church, ie to the irreligiousness of the "Czech model," which at the very least (we can say with more than 90 percent probability) has been made known to us through well-known sources.

The relationship the working class (especially in Bohemia) had towards the "transcendence" of religion and the Church was represented by the aforementioned mixture of ideas and attitudes and formed "nominal Catholicism" amongst the workers, which was common in the middle and upper classes where it had other causes.

9. In the last quarter of the nineteenth century "popular piety" changed to irreligiousness, where the main aim of the working class was to improve their material standard of living.[37] This was the Czech (heavy-industrial) model. However, other factors have to be taken into consideration alongside the influence of industrialization, in particular the growth of religious scepticism amongst the educated working class and liberal sections of the middle class who recognized the advances in the natural sciences, and in this sense had been enlightened by schools, the press and literature. The rise in Czech patriotism at the end of the nineteenth century, combined with anti-clericalism, was also significant and influenced sections of the working class. There were undoubtedly other factors at work, but at the moment these are only hypotheses and require thorough analytical research.

The regional differences within secularization are, of course, also important themes. To a certain extent (though also hypothetically), these differences can be explained by the process of industrialization as well as general cultural developments. At the moment it can be assumed that the following inference is valid: the more industrialized a region, the more secularized it was.[38]

10. Of course the question arises as to why with the renewed study of the working class we should start with secularization, or indeed the opposite: why should the study of secularization start with the working class, apart from the fact that it is an attractive international theme?

The general significance of such research may reside in the fact that it is possible to discover the conditions which allowed for the creation and development of opinions, ideas and ideologies, as well as the attitudes to life of certain classes and groups, i.e., the

37. For a concise view see Machačová, J.—Matějček, *Nástin sociálního vývoje.*

38. With the growth in industry a third sphere developed with the increase in better informed inhabitants (this has been shown with the help of correlational analyzes for the Czech lands.)

principles behind how they acted and behaved. This is one of the fundamental social questions pertaining to socio-cultural historiography. The second fundamental issue, which has only begun to be addressed recently, is that alongside the level of standard of living there is also development in the attitudes to life of individuals, groups, classes and whole populations. We can, therefore, ask what part religious faith (or what it was replaced by) occupied in attitudes to life, when in sections 6, 7, and 8 we tried to show how the popular piety (of the working class) in the nineteenth century gradually changed to irreligiousness (of the modern working class) and away from the state of superstition in which, to a certain extent, rural workers lived during the agrarian period. It is also quite clear, however, that even earlier there existed a latent desire among the working classes to better their position and to acquire material goods, and that even by the end of the nineteenth century there still existed primitive thinking, social naivety and a lack of reason among agrarian workers. Whilst by the last quarter of the nineteenth century the middle classes had more or less attached themselves to a "religion of progress"—a belief in the constant improvement of existence, particularly with the help of science—at this time among the working class there appeared the "religion of socialism," "the new evangelism," "the teachings of (principally material) redemption," the secular process of "enchantment with the world," the working class's move away from religion and the transition of the middle class to "nominal Catholicism" (which of course is only weakly reflected in the statistics due to the influence of tradition), which lasted nearly the whole century.

Almost all of the "Czech model" is of course basically a hypothesis which is in some places well documented and in others less so (although perhaps somewhat better than the concept of religion among today's population), because of course we can never achieve complete induction, and even the incomplete version is, because of the lack of primary sources, often rather weak and "patched up" by deductions. However, alongside the "irreligious" and "Catholic" hypotheses might be suggested another hypothesis.

3

The Secularization of the Workforce in Germany in the Nineteenth Century

JÜRGEN SCHMIDT

INTRODUCTION

CAN WE STILL TALK today in general about secularization? In the public debate in Germany Jürgen Habermas discovered in the still young twenty-first century the return to a "post-secular society." In Central Europe there has recently been much intensive discussion on the relationship between Islam and modern western ideas. In the science of history Olaf Blaschke spoke of a "second confessional era" when looking back at the nineteenth century. Pilgrimages and the cult of worship of the Virgin Mary in the nineteenth century gave rise to a powerful Catholic popular religiousness. Looking at the workforce and the workers" movement Sebastian Prüfer saw the socialism of the early German workers movement as a "new religion." In addition to this there emerged in the nineteenth century alongside the socialist workers' movement a Christian workers' movement with its own unions and independent organizational culture.[1] Obviously religion did not disappear in the modern world neither in society nor in the workforce.

The opposing tendencies were of course no less obvious. Starting in the early nineteenth century a tendency to "de-churching" appeared in all the social strata with different forms at different times and became stronger in the twentieth century. Radical elements in the Social Democratic movement called upon their members and union members to leave the churches. Many agitators saw phenomenal success in this. The Social Democrat Josef Peukert was of the opinion that thanks to the agitation by his party in the region of the *Fichtelgebirge* the churches were empty "even on feast days."[2] A scientification of thought and perception took further hold and left the transcendental

---

1. Habermas, "Glauben und Wissen"; Blaschke, "Zweites Konfessionelles Zeitalter," 38–75; Taylor, *A Secular Age*; Blackbourn, *Marpingen*; Stambolis, *Religiöse Festkultur*; Prüfer, *Sozialismus statt Religion*; Hiepel, *Arbeiterkatholizismus*.

2. Peukert, *Erinnerungen*, 6.

less room for development. The belief in science of the Social Democrats which gained expression in the propagation of the ideas of Charles Darwin brought secular ways of thinking nearer to sections of the workforce. In the end the Christian workers' movement remained a minority grouping compared to the Social Democrats—this applied especially to the Protestant workers' movement.

This brief comparison of both developments shows that the thesis of the secularization of society in general and the workforce in particular since the nineteenth century must be considered differently. It is a matter of the juxtaposition and opposition of these developments and a question of weighing-up and classification of these different tendencies. As a first step it is necessary therefore to define precisely the concept of secularization. Directly linked to this is the question of the definition of religion. In view of the diversity of the theological, philosophical and religion sociological inputs this cannot happen in a comprehensive sense, but on the other hand must be confined to a few fundamental characteristics which are linked to the thesis and formulation of the question of secularization processes in the workforce.[3]

In addition to the difficulties of definition and method there is the problem with the sources.[4] On the one hand numerous quantitative data exist for the Protestant churches with which the process of "de-churching" can be traced.[5] However, the sources are not firmly subdivided according to socio-structural points of view. Evidence on the behaviour of the workforce can only be derived indirectly if we bear in mind, for example, the voting behaviour or the social structure in the respective church or political communities. At any rate, if these sources lead to recognition of clear trends for Protestant churches and Protestant workforces,[6] the quantitative research into de-churching processes in the Catholic sphere will remain confined to individual case studies and local investigations because national quantitative data are not available.[7] On the other hand the thesis on secularization goes beyond the concrete quantifiable de-churching. The "disenchantment of the world" (Max Weber) had numerous facets. Discourses, debates and public discussions on the relationship between state, science, culture and religion can be reconstructed and analysed in this context. Yet, what role church, faith and religion exercised on individual workers, male and female, can only be examined in first steps. Autobiographical reports which often originated in a Social Democratic environment as well as some contemporary religion-sociological research carried out at the turn of the 20th century furnish important building blocks for this purpose. However, a more profound view of the secularization phenomenon as perceived and experienced by individuals from the workforce cannot be expected for the 19th century with the handed down sources.[8]

3. Hölscher, "Säkularisierungsprozesse," 238f.

4. For the source problem see Graf, "Dechristianisierung," 48; also Hölscher, "Möglichkeiten und Grenzen," 48–51.

5. Hölscher, *Atlass zur religiösen Geographie.*

6. Hölscher, *Weltgericht oder Revolution.*

7. See for example Liedhegener, *Christentum.*

8. See also Ritter and Tenfelde, *Arbeiter im Deutschen Kaiserreich,* 751f.; and Blessing, *Staat und Kirche.*

On the basis of the extensive literature on secularization and religion the following outline tries to analyse the development and the limits of the secularization process in the workforce in Germany since the 1840's until the outbreak of the First World War. However, the state of research developed very differently. As publications on the theme of religion are at present experiencing a boom and since the 1990's numerous works on the secularization and re-sacralising of modernity have been published,[9] interest in these basic themes in relation to the workforce are relatively rare. At the outset mention should be made of the monographs by Lucian Hölscher and Sebastian Prüfer. Hölscher brings together and compares Protestant and socialistic expectations for the future, clarifies the reciprocal dependence of revolutionary and religious ideas in Social Democracy and examines the secularization processes in the Social Democratic workforce. Prüfer examines the discourse on religion as it was reflected in the lower and middle leadership levels (for instance from local and regional Social Democratic newspapers) and asks about the relationship between class and religion. These works closed a gap in the German historiography of the workforce and workers' movement as this field of research—apart from the early work of Heiner Grote[10]—had been only occasionally examined. Especially in comparison with English historical writing this research deficit stood out.[11] Stimuli then came from the early works by Vernon Lidtke and later from Hugh McLeod.[12] Both Lidtke and McLeod turned to secularization processes in several essays: on the one hand forms of de-churching of the workforce were described and on the other hand they portrayed the development of a secular religion in the socialist ideology of the German workers' movement. Wilfried Spohn combined these approaches and put them in the context of the development of a working class. He ascribed to religious mentalities an important role in the development of a "Protestant working-class ethic in secular-religious ways."[13] With the decline of interest in the history of workers and the workers' movement in German historical science in the last few years the preoccupation with questions about the religiousness and/or secularization of the workers has also lost significance.[14]

Secularization applies to the relationship between religion and society. Secularization can also be understood as part of the modernization process and the result of such a process. Regarding growing processes of modernization, pluralization, rationalization and individualization of the world it appeared to the advocates of the secularization

9. Balbier offers a very good overview on the theme "Religion," in *Sag: Wie hast Du's mit der Religion?* On the discussion about secularization see Braun, Grab, and Zachhuber, *Säkularisierung*; as well as Jakabowski-Tiessen, *Religion zwischen Kunst und Politik*.

10. Grote, *Sozialdemokratie und Religions*.

11. Spohn, "Religion and Working Class Formation," 109.

12. Lidtke, "August Bebel," 245–64; Lidtke, "Social Class and Secularization," 21–40; McLeod, "Protestantism and the Working Class," 323–44.

13. Spohn, "Religion and Working Class Formation," 125. Spohn, however, overemphasises the significance of religion when he ascribes to the dualism between Catholicism and Protestantism as well as to the dualism between Catholic worker identity and secular-religious worker identity a central role "for the paralysis of the labor movements in the face of National Socialism" (126).

14. Some works were published on the Christian workers' movement and its organizations: see Heerma Van Voss, *Between Cross and Class*; Hiepel and Ruff, *Christliche Arbeiterbewegung*.

thesis that a linear process to a secular world had been predetermined. However, this teleological viewpoint, the apparent unambiguity and irreversibility which seemed to be inscribed in the thesis led to a criticism of the thesis. The ambivalences referred to at the beginning of the chapter and new forms of religiousness which unfolded in the nineteenth century disappeared from the viewpoint of the representatives of the secularization thesis. In addition, the scale of comparison could not be precisely defined: Was there ever a "more religious age" which could be compared to a secularized one? And yet, did not new religious interpretations emerge out of the modernization process itself again and again? In general, the secularization thesis always deals with the relationship between religion and modernity—and this relationship remained ambiguous.[15]

Secularization can be understood both as an analytical concept as well as the characterising and description for a real phenomenon in history. The first way asks above all about the conceptualization of secularization in the historical context: Who concerned himself when and for what reasons with the idea of secularization? What roots does the concept have and how was it interpreted and applied?[16] Under the second aspect secularization asks on the other hand about the shaping, about real-historical findings and the forms of secularization. In this article this aspect will be in the foreground. At the same time it is in no way about a quantitative access which exclusively rests on de-churching. In fact discourses about secularization, the development of new "political religions" or secular expectations for the future will be included in the analysis since this reflects the polymorphism of the phenomenon of secularization.

The question about the secularization of the workforce and workers' movement in the nineteenth century will therefore be embedded in the broad context of religion and modernity. In addition, secularization will be defined as a process which was carried out in three forms. On the level of de-churching, the institution of the church lost its formative power over the everyday lives of the people. Public, active participation in the church community played a more minor role. On the level of de-Christianization, Christian values lost their significance or were filled with new contents in a different environment. On the third level secularization in the end meant that religion lost its interpretational authority for society. The calling on the transcendental, on the higher, holy being which contributed to identity binding as well as coping with existential anxieties only appeared as one offer amongst many and became less attractive. This definition is on the one hand bound up with the general state of discussion about the relationship between religion and the modernity, on the other hand it can be used for historical research to ask to what extent these processes became apparent in the workforce and workers' movement and where they had their limits.[17]

15. See Pollack, "Religion und Moderne," 74; Graf, "Dechristianisierung," 1997, 62. For general information on the debate about the secularization thesis in the Federal German Republic see Hildebrandt, Brocker, and Behr, *Säkularisierung und Resakralisierung*.

16. See the conference "Reconfiguration of the Religious Field. "Secularization" and Related Semantics in Inter-Cultural, Historical and Political Perspective," Bochum, December 2009; Hölscher, "Secularization and Urbanization," 284.

17. Prüfer, *Sozialismus statt Religion*, 22f.; Blickle and Schlögl, "Säkularisation," 12; Jakubowski-Tiessen, "Einleitun," 9.

From this designation of the concept of secularization it also becomes obvious in the end that the definition of religion cannot rely exclusively on "churchliness." Religion is the attempt to find an answer to the questions concerning the meanings of existence. The reference to the transcendental and to a supernatural final authority is in this context a crucial part of the answer. Linked to this are value attitudes, doctrines, symbols, rites and behaviour patterns which affect the secular world and mould its social and political structures.[18] The question of the meaning of life, the uncertainty, the doubts and fears in the face of death did not stop in front of the workforce. Working men and women could thereby find orientation and a foothold, security and confidence both in Christian-religious conviction as well as in the "new religion" of socialism. This has to be considered when analysing the question of the secularization of the workforce and the workers' movement in the nineteenth century.

THE SECULARIZATION PROCESS IN GERMANY— PROPAGATION AND LIMITS

De-Churching

Two main forms of ecclesiastical relationships or ecclesiastical loosening can be first of all discerned. On the one hand there is the formal membership of the church, while on the other hand there is the public participation in parish life. These public forms subdivide again in the direct connection to the church community via attendance at services and communion as well as integration connected with private life such as confirmation, marriage and burial. With both main forms different developments are apparent. Although in the 1870's in various German states—1870 in Saxony, 1873 in Prussian—there existed the right to leave the church (before this there was only the right to change from one denomination to another) there was no mass defection from the church in Imperial Germany. Even the church tax introduced in 1881 which between 1882 and 1908 was constantly increased from 5.5% to 20% of income tax[19] did not lead to a marked decline in church membership in the German *Reich*. In 1875 in Prussia 64.6% of the 25.7 million population belonged to the established Protestant national church, 33.5% to the Catholic Church and 1.3% to the Jewish faith. In addition there were further splinter groups with the result that the number of "non-denominationals"—"dissidents" in statistical parlance—remained at most at 0.1%. Until the end of the century this proportion of the population had more or less doubled and in 1900 now stood at 0.2%, which also means that still 99.8% could not yet make the decision to leave one of the churches.[20] In the decade before 1914 the number of those leaving the church rose and annually remained at an average of around 14,000 to 16,000; however over 99% of the population were still formal members of a church. These high percentages however also make it clear that the

18. Pollack, "Religion und Moderne," 74f.; Lehmann, "Vor Erforschung der Säkularisierung," 11; Nipperdey, *Religion im Umbruch*, 7f.

19. Ribbe, "Zur Entwicklung und Funktion," 258.

20. Figures according to Prüfer, *Sozialismus statt Religion*, 120, footnote, 326; Blaschke, "Ein Zweites Konfessionelles Zeitalter," 42.

working class as the largest social grouping (including unskilled labourers, agricultural workers, artisans and highly skilled workers) still belonged formally to the church.

Three reasons for this tendency to continued formal church membership have been given. Firstly membership had no negative consequences for the individual church member from the workforce; leaving the church on the other hand could present problems for working people. As church taxes were only deducted from a high income the financial/fiscal aspect played no part for working people. As, in addition, especially in large town parishes, pastors, and priests were to such an extent overburdened with work (and official church members), workers did not have to fear home visits, "face to face" communication or any other direct confrontation with the priests about their now only formal membership of the church. One might belong to the church but active involvement in church affairs was not the norm. Besides this, formal membership was a protection against critical inquiries on the part of employers or relatives, and the children of workers did not have to fear harassment from teachers or priests.[21]

Secondly the Social Democratic Party remained chary with regard to supporting leaving the church. Already in 1881 August Bebel, the undisputed leadership personality in the Social Democratic Party had ascertained in the *Reichstag* that his party had never advocated that its members were committed to leaving the church, but should adopt a tolerance to the religious views of its members.[22] In the end the party was not really sure about the religious views of its members and for electoral tactical reasons restrained from an increased anti-religious polemic for fear of putting off groups of voters. The consequence was therefore not a "religion as the opium for the people"-rhetoric but rather that the party declared religion to be a private matter. To a large extent therefore the attempt by Johann Most in the 1870's in Berlin where the Social Democrats had already won over 39 percent of the votes to call for a withdrawal from the church was also isolated. After about 1,000 withdrawals from the church in 1878 this figure shrank to a few dozen in the following year.[23] The church-leaving movement after 1906 proved to be essentially more successful, but it was no longer linked solely to the Social Democratic Party. Amongst working people this movement proved itself to be more successful because the first argument referred to above no longer had any effect: Through the lowering of tax-free limits more and more well-earning worker families were now drawn into the church tax. For those families who had no contact with the church community, leaving the church was therefore an obvious consequence. In Prussia in 1908 23,000 members left the church. Taken in consideration with the total formal church membership this wave did not exceed the per thousand mark and remained essentially limited to urban centres. Of the approximately 115,000 cases of withdrawal from the church in the entire German empire between 1908 and 1914 almost half lived in Berlin.[24]

21. Ritter and Tenfelde, *Arbeiter im Deutschen Kaiserreich*, 776; Lidtke, "Social Class and Secularization," 29.

22. August Bebel, Speech to the Reichstag on 31 March 1881, in Prüfer, *Sozialismus statt Religion*, 191; see also Grote, *Sozialdemokratie und Religion*, 109–22.

23. Hölscher, *Weltgericht oder Revolution*, 161.

24. Kaiser, "Sozialdemokratie und 'praktisch' Religionskritik," 263–98; summing up in Ritter and Tenfelde, *Arbeiter im Deutschen Kaiserreich*, 756f. also Hering, "Säkularisierung," 120–164.

The third reason for the extensive unimportance of withdrawals from the church lay especially in the fact that leaving the church would have entailed an altercation with the faith, with the authority of the church or with the priest. The majority of church members were obviously not yet ready for this. To a certain extent there prevailed a related "lack of participation"—the step to a deliberate breach was taken only by a committed minority who ascribed to radical Social Democratic, anti-religious or free religious views. Viewed in this context the high formal church membership can paradoxically be interpreted as evidence for the secularization of broader population groups including the workforce: belonging to a church community had little relevance for the majority of the members; this indifference even went to the extent that it was considered as not necessary to give this institution its attention by withdrawing official membership.[25]

These pointed argumentations and hypotheses are strengthened if we turn to the public forms of participation in and sharing of church community life. The data for church and communion attendances for Protestant churches prove that formal church membership can be interpreted as indifference. Lucian Hölscher's analysis differentiated the development of these indicators and the general trend became clear. The taking of communion which is central to the understanding of religion in which communal membership was linked with the religious confession of one's own personal guilt, the plea for forgiveness together with the visualization of Jesus was perceived by ever-decreasing numbers of church members. This development had already emerged in the 18th century and was then conspicuous in the nineteenth century. In the case of Saxony it can be shown that for every 1,000 Protestant inhabitants the number of participants fell from 250 to 160 in the course of the eighteenth century. In 1862 this figure stood at 72 and by 1894 had fallen to 45. In the end only 35 out of 1,000 Protestant inhabitants took communion in Saxony in 1913. This long-term trend can be differentiated in diverse ways. In the country and in small towns the turning away from communion was less pronounced, while in urban and especially metropolitan spheres it was notably more evident. Moreover, women were predominant at communion services. In a Hannover parish in 1875 two thirds of those taking communion were women; the men present were on the other hand accompanying their wives.[26]

In Berlin, moreover, two differences with regard to social groups can be determined. While in the most affluent Berlin parishes attendance at communion—which was strongly fluctuating—stood at between 16.5% in 1875 and 23.1% in 1890, these participation figures in the poorest parishes varied from about 5% and 9%.[27] The clear distinctions resulted to a considerable extent from varied population growth in particular areas of the city. For example between 1860 and 1896 the population of the predominantly

---

25. This was also the observation of contemporary clergymen. At the inspection of the Göttingen II church district a pastor ascertained in 1896, "it is rather indifference than conscious opposition" which is responsible for church members staying away (Marbach, *Säkularisierung und sozialer Wandel*, 40). See also Lidtke, "Social Class and Secularization," 29.

26. Hölscher, "Möglichkeiten und Grenzen," 58; Prüfer, *Sozialismus statt Religion*, 200.

27. Hölscher, *Weltgericht oder Revolution*, 153f.; Prüfer, *Sozialismus statt Religion*, 200f.; Hölscher, "Möglichkeiten und Grenzen," 58.

working class quarter of Moabit rose from 6,500 to 120,000. In the district there was until 1896 only one single church built for Protestant Christians, under such circumstances it was neither logistically nor possible on a personal level to establish a close relationship between the clergy and parish members. The parishioners either accepted the church offers on community and identity formation, orientated on Christian values, and lived accordingly the Christian way of life, or the overwhelming majority lived in the anonymity of the metropolis remote from or indifferent to ecclesiastical offers.

At the same time it becomes clear that for the period between 1875 and 1890 secularization tendencies did not have to be linked to a continuous decline of churchliness. The ratios of increase even in the poorer quarters (from 5 to 9%) resulted above all from an increased church-oriented commitment of lower middle class groups who had retained a "relative stability of place of residence," used religion as a means of distinction with regard to the workforce and—possibly—in its partly precarious independence turned increasingly to the spiritual interpretations of the church. Above all this new churchliness of individual urban groups prompted the building of new churches and the establishment of new parishes in the rapidly expanding town areas. After 1890 this "petit-bourgeois churchliness´ peaked and attendance at the church services and communion steadily declined. The building of new churches certainly improved the pastoral care of those members who were still active, but contributed little to the enlargement of spiritual guidance for the mass of the city's inhabitants.[28]

In essence similar to the taking of communion the general trends in Sunday church attendance continued. In the villages churches were still better attended than in the towns, and yet, on the whole, ever fewer people attended Divine services and priests found themselves faced with mainly female congregations. In the church community of Göttingen this development was shown in a confined area: while in the small villages since the 1880's the share of parishioners who attended a church service fell from about 20% to 10% before the outbreak of the First World War, the share of church-goers in the village of Geismar, which was developing more and more into a suburb of Göttingen declined already in the 1890's from 10% to 8% and then further to 3%. The "core of church-goers" consisted above all of the "resident agricultural population." Seasonal workers on the other hand who still mainly had access to a small agricultural plot of land, went on Sundays to their agricultural part-time work and contributed thus to the "disruption of morality so that amongst those who were by no means in a similar embarrassment also mowed or carried out other work on a Sunday morning, even during the church service." Thereby the feminization of church attendance progressed further. While the number of women attending main church services in the more urban structured Geismar stood already in 1902 at 75%, it increased in rural areas as recently as in the two decades before the First World War from about 55% to 66% to 75%.[29]

De-churching in the form of less communion and church service attendance pervaded society as a whole and in no way affected the workforce alone. However, counter-

28. Hölscher, *Weltgericht oder Revolution*, 158–60; Sauter, "Die Sorge um den Menschen," 13.

29. All statements and source quotations are according to Marbach, *Säkularisierung und sozialer Wandel*, 48.

tendencies became apparent too, which can be portrayed under three points of view. Firstly participation in church affairs became more and more dominated by women.[30] This gender-specific aspect was also perceived and discussed in the working-class milieu. Two examples from Hamburg can illustrate this quantitative trend on an individual level. In 1893 a stonemason said in a conversation in a pub that pastors had "repeatedly" tried to induce "the women and children of Social Democrats to keep their husbands away from Social Democratic ideas. These pastors know quite well in which way they can work on women and children in this respect." In 1894 a carpenter explained to his neighbour in a Hamburg pub that he had been a Social Democrat for a long time and had declared himself opposed to the baptism of his son. As an independent and successful carpenter he had in the course of time distanced himself from Social Democracy and told his wife that he was now prepared to have his son baptized. His wife had replied, that "she had already had the child baptized against his will, when he was still involved with the Social Democrats."[31] The Social Democrat *Reichstag* member Paul Reisshaus from Erfurt on the other hand did not have any of his children baptized in the 1880's and yet the daughter attended religious instruction classes while the sons stayed away from them. Religiousness and churchliness were obviously also in the Social Democratic core milieu practiced differently according to gender-specific roles.[32]

Secondly in especially robust village regions the de-churching process in the nineteenth century proceeded less dramatically. In Baden even in 1906 in a state-wide average 23% still went to church, while in the Prussian working-class town of Bochum the figure—in spite of a high Catholic share of the population—already in 1880 the figure was only 10%. In the villages of Saxony 20% to 40% of parishioners attended church services, in the Saxon industrial parishes only 3%–8%.[33]

Thirdly, if rural structures moreover coincided with Catholic faith the de-churching process in these areas could not be stopped but it certainly proceeded in a weaker form. In the predominantly Catholic kingdom of Bavaria, church attendance fell from 77% in 1867 to 62% in 1880 and to 43% in 1913. In spite of the highly visible decline: the Protestant churches were far removed from such high quotas of church service participation. Still in 1906 in a report of a clerical visitation from Upper Swabia, a Catholic-agriculturally dominated region it was stated: "it has to be said again and again that the people are largely strict believers, are loyal to the bishops and the priesthood, especially when it counts [in *Reichstag* elections when they vote for the Catholic party, JS] and that even the men also show this loyalty and adherence." Although the report criticized the gradual "incursion of modern ideas," yet only after the First World War—and decidedly with reference to the few industrial areas in the region (for example Friedrichshafen)— swayed between resignation and hope: "the influence of anti-religious socialism on the industrial workers of the two cities and their neighbouring environs is dangerous. In

30. For general information on the feminization of faith and religion see Götz Von Olenhausen, "Die Feminisierung der Religion und Kirche."

31. Hamburg police reports from 1893 and 1894, in Evans, *Kneipengespräche*, 170f.

32. See Schmidt, *Begrenzte Spielräume*, 144.

33. Nipperdey, *Religion im Umbruch*, 119f.

the flood of faithlessness Catholic workers are also sinking, but as long as they live in a Catholic environment there is still hope that these same men will return to the faith of their childhood."[34]

If we sum up the results of de-churching as was shown in the formal membership in church and public participation in the divine service and taking of communion, there emerges the picture of a society which (apart from the exceptions described) had to a large degree loosened itself from the forms of religious churchliness without consequently taking the second step of leaving the church. One of the essential reasons lay in the fact that the "church framework" still played an important role in celebrating individual or respectively family events. Ecclesiastical Christian mores adorned the transition from adolescence to adulthood (confirmation), the transition into family life (marriage, baptism), and the departure from life (burial). Obviously the overwhelming majority of Christians did not renounce Christian church baptism, for baptism was of course the pre-requisite for the virtually ubiquitous churchliness in the form of mere membership. During the entire imperial era clearly more than 90% of all children were baptized throughout the *Reich*. Until 1875 moreover a marriage was mainly only possible within the framework of the church. Whoever wanted to get married had to be a member of a church denomination.[35] After the introduction of civil marriage in the German *Reich* in 1876 church weddings experienced a short decline—above all in the metropolitan parishes: in Berlin between 1873 and 1879 the number of church marriages fell from 11,331 to only 2,642. However, after this the number of Protestant church marriages in metropolitan Berlin quickly increased again. While the church marriage quota of all marriages in Berlin lay at 29.4% in 1876, it quickly increased again to 60% in the next six years. On this level the quota moved until 1900, after which it gradually fell to 50% in 1913. And the percentage of church funerals in Prussia even rose between 1886 and 1914 from 64% to 86%.[36] From these figures it became clear that the churches remained of relevance if they could be integrated through family events. However, even when celebrating confirmation the ecclesiastical part was only a solemn ornament. Already in 1874 the visitation report of a priest in the then largely rural Gottingen church area stated that, "also well-meaning parents are in many cases under the illusion that it is the joy over the completed *earthly* period of the child's life and that it is the hoped-for relief after many cares and sacrifices which should now find expression" in celebrating confirmation. In 1912 the result turned out to be even more sobering: "the danger of the trivialization of confirmation is great."[37]

34. Inspection reports for Oberschwaben from 1906 and 1920, quoted in: Kuhn, "Rückständig," 490.

35. Civil marriage was temporarily introduced into German territories in 1800 under The Napoleonic Code, then gradually pushed back again and was reintroduced limited to local level in the 1850's.

36 All statements are according to Lidtke, "Social Class and Secularization," 23f.; Nipperdey, *Religion im Umbruch*, 118; Hölscher, *Weltgericht oder Revolution*, 156f.; Ribbe, "Zur Entwicklung und Funktion," 258. For the rural areas see especially Marbach, *Säkularisierung und sozialer Wandel*: "nobody excluded themselves from baptism, confirmation, church marriage and Christian burial" (page 38). Statements about a special relationship with regard to church marriage in the workforce are unfortunately not obtainable from the available data.

37. Inspection reports from 1874 and 1912, quoted in: Marbach, *Säkularisierung und sozialer Wandel*, 88.

On the other hand it also becomes clear that the churches were still being used and this also applied to the workforce—and as was shown by the example of Paul Reisshaus even by Social Democrat member of the Reichstag. On the whole therefore the general trend to de-churching needs to be put into perspective. The turning away from the archaic-ritualistic Lord's Supper was in opposition to the turning to the churchly configuration of family feasts."[38] That the working class took part in this is shown for example in Erfurt where every spring in the Social Democrat newspaper "Tribüne" numerous adverts were published from the local stores in which they sought to outdo each other with reasonable offers of suits, clothing and shoes for confirmation day.[39]

De-Christianization

At the district synod for the church area Gottingen II of the Hannover national church, superintendent Hartwig explained: "it would be wrong to measure the degree of Christian parish life according to church attendance figures alone, but the demand for public propagation of the word for the lord certainly provides an accurate scale for the churchly sense of a parish."[40] The alienation of great parts of the population from the practice of the divine service had to lead in the eyes of the pastors to a de-Christianization. As representatives of the church as an institution for them de-churching was directly linked to de-Christianization. In the abstaining from the word of the lord, reinforced by the disregarding of communion, priests perceived a turning away from the Christian life with its values and standards. The Christian faith as a co-ordinating system in the everyday life of parishioners lost influence, the social and cultural shaping-power of the church and the canon of Christian values gradually declined.

Other values came to the fore or competed with the Christian values. Even country parsons complained that in the majority of their flock the "awareness of sin" was lacking and that in its place they displayed a high degree of "self-righteousness." The loss of the Sunday rest was therefore taken not only as evidence for de-churching, but as a symbol of de-Christianization itself. The cause of the desecration of Sunday lies in the "lamentable general direction of our day," complained the Göttingen district synod in 1906: "It is not so much work, but the need for relaxation from work and in relation to this the increased desire for pleasure and entertainment that are destroying Sunday." The complaint here was about new forms of structuring leisure time, which had distanced itself from the Christian rules and ideas. With the offers of mass culture and of an increased consumption after 1900 these complaints should still increase. Criticisms of civilization and modernization are therefore from this perspective indirect evidence for the secularization processes in society around and after the turn of the century. Already 50 years earlier the parish priest of the small country town of Büchen in the duchy of Lauenburg had made similar complaints. As an interchange station for two railway lines Büchen developed

---

38. See also Graf, "Dechristianisierung," page 49 ; Schlögl, "Rationalisierung," 63.

39. See for example *Tribüne*, no. 61, March 13, 1909; no. 35, February 18, 1912, no. 58, March 9, 1912.

40. Report of the superintendent to the area synod 1902, quoted in: Marbach, *Säkularisierung und sozialer Wandel*, 1978, page 42.

into a widely-used railway junction. In 1853 the angry Büchen pastor Förster wrote to the consistory in Ratzeburg: "because people from Hamburg want to enjoy themselves on a Sunday in Lübeck, or the Lübeckers in Hamburg, because people from Schwerin or from Berlin want to amuse themselves here or there, this means that here in the duchy of Lauenburg there must be no Sunday on the railways. Where in this state of affairs is the Lord's day? (. . .) The church bells call the congregation to gather together in vain. The station does not hear the bells, it listens only to the whistle of the locomotives."[41] The entry of modernity and the progress in means of transport drove the Christian tradition onto the defensive.

Since the onset of industrialization with its over-long working hours the Sunday rest crystallized into a contentious issue. For in the end work on Sunday symbolized the sacrifice of the Sabbath to a new "deity": to work, to profit and to the pursuit of profit. Capitalism and the industrial system broke with the Christian rules that had been valid until then. We quote once more the Büchen pastor Förster in his letter of 1853: "what is to become of the churchly and moral life of the parish if it is constantly faced with such an example, if a part of the village population goes to work Sunday after Sunday as if there were no God and no Eternity, and the rest now take for themselves what is not denied to those others [who go to work on Sunday], what is to become of Christian upbringing, if the children already see how the father does not respect the Sunday, if the father does not even see his children on a Sunday any longer?"[42] The working class was especially affected by this development, they were either the ones who suffered because of Sunday work or they used Sunday to rest from work. The church and with it, its Christian edification moved into the background.

And yet the change of values was not noticeable only in the sphere of economics and the working world. Earlier central fields of the propagation of Christian knowledge and Christian rules had been made increasingly disputed for the churches. The elementary school, where according to region between 70% and 90% of all school children received their knowledge at the end of the nineteenth century, was removed from the sphere of influence of the church. Religious instruction as *the* formative school subject was taken less and less into account in syllabuses. With an eye on propaganda the Erfurt *Reichstag* member Reisshaus complained that in all his schooldays in the 1860's he had learnt nothing except for 500 verses from the Bible and church songs. However, at the end of the Imperial era religious instruction had lost some of its influence and was taught only for two periods per week in final year classes. Teachers also gradually moved away from "pure catechism lessons and churchly instruction" and included secularized materials in their work.[43] Moreover, the entry of science subjects into teaching challenged the religious basic texts such as the creation story. For the pupils concerned who mainly went to school only until the age of 14 or 16 this did not play a major role, but

41. Pastor Förster to the consistory at Ratzeburg, 23 November 1853, quoted in: Jakubowski-Tiessen, "Pastor Förster," 17; Marbach, *Säkularisierung und sozialer Wandel*, 39, 141.

42. Pastor Förster to the Consistory at Ratzeburg, 23 November 1853, quoted in: Jakubowski-Tiessen, "Pastor Förster," 22.

43. For Reisshaus see Schmidt, *Begrenzte Spielräume*, 258; Nipperdey, *Arbeitswelt und Bürgergeist*, 541.

church representatives and religious-minded members of the community saw in such developments the pushing back of their canon of values. For this new knowledge was being discussed in public, disseminated through the mass-media, found its way into the workforce via Social Democracy and led to a simple, but fundamental criticism of religion: The "creation story in the Bible has been refuted in all parts through knowledge and by philosophers, therefore out with the Bible," summarized a Hamburg worker in a discussion.[44]

The same development can be seen in social policy. In place of Christian charity and churchly care of the poor there emerged a secular based social policy that was increasingly defined by the communes and the state. Bureaucratic, rationalized procedures for the material protection of those concerned in place of Christian consolation and hope of a better life after death found expression in these movements. The view was directed to this life, which could be planned, shaped and changed. The idea of the individual as part of a Divine creation plan in which he had been assigned a meaningful place was challenged and became more and more irrelevant. From this also came the accusations of the Social Democrats against the churches as stultifying institutions and attacks on the clergy found in working-class circles. In a Hamburg pub in 1900 a worker put it as follows: "The clergy are largely to blame for the social hardship which prevails amongst all the people. The enlightened worker no longer believes in the promises in the Bible and is of the opinion that the kingdom of Heaven must be had here on earth and not as salvation after death."[45] From such positions the step towards political participation and political commitment presented itself, but also the step towards the above mentioned leisure time offers with their worldly secular temptations was possible to which the sacro-Christian culture was opposed. The traditional system of church values, morals and rites from the point of view of the clergy concerned could be shaken even by the leisure time pleasures of cycling. In a 1904 report to the area synod of Göttingen it was stated that the townspeople of Göttingen "set off touring in the surrounding area, and our villagers were faced with whole swarms of cyclists every Sunday if the weather was good." The Sabbath was therefore no longer "accorded its proper respect" and such worldly attractions were endangering the community. The bicycle became a metaphor for the temptations of the world and for the menaces to which the Christian community was exposed. Moreover it is becoming clear how broken the self-confidence in the Christian canon of values even in rural communities must have already been, if this Sunday excursion traffic gave rise to such criticism instead of ignoring it as an event of no consequence. Those doubts therefore increased that a country parson had already expressed in 1882: "In spite of proper instruction in the faith," after confirmation the parishioners lacked "in the growth of grace and in the recognition of Christ."[46]

In spite of this scepticism, disillusionment and criticism of modernization from the church representatives concerned, reference must be made to the opposing tendencies

---

44. Police report from 16 April 1984, in: Evans, *Kneipengespräche*, 174.

45. Police report from 26 September 1900, in: Evans, *Kneipengespräche*, 178.

46. Quoted according to Marbach, *Säkularisierung und sozialer Wandel*, 38.

for the process of de-Christianization, too. This is most clearly seen in the Catholic workers' movement. They were most deeply influenced by Christian values. In contrast to the Protestant workers' movement which reached only a minority amongst the workers and remained influenced by state authority thinking, the Catholic workers' movement was essentially more strongly rooted in the working class. It succeeded in linking social commitment and social demands with the Christian profession of faith. The Catholic milieu, already welded together through the years of the *Kulturkampf* maintained a Christian sense of identity and a social sense of responsibility. The Catholic "red curates" imparted to the Catholic working-class a strong feeling of belonging together as many of them had come from the lower class, whereas the Protestant pastors who came from the educated classes had rather the effect of a foreign body in the Protestant workforce.[47]

The tendency to de-Christianization—seen on the whole—took on such an extensive area in society because of two central motives. On the one hand the churches moved on to the defensive as they were opposed by the state, the sciences (natural sciences and humanistic criticisms of religion) and capitalism as protagonists which restricted the church's chances of exerting influence. New values like nationalism, rationalism and profit-seeking became important. On the other hand, de-Christianization was also able to spread, because churchliness as it was lived, as was illustrated in the previous paragraph, shrank on the individual level of church members to a "feast-day-religiousness" which was limited to only a few phases of life. De-churching and de-Christianization interacted and promoted secularization. This became especially clear amongst the urban, male working class—in spite of the existing counter-tendencies already described, above all, in Catholicism.

The Loss of the Interpretational Authority of Religion and the Churches in Society

The loss of active churchliness and Christian values went along with a loss of interpretational authority of the churches and religion for society. Counter-currents and new interpretations of the world developed a power of their own. In the case of nationalism the Protestant-established churches could to a certain extent profit from this new orientation as they were included in the connection of "Throne and Altar" in this identification process. Protestantism and nationalism joined together in the case of Germany; the example of the celebrations of the anniversary of Luther's birth in 1883 showed this clearly. Yet the interpretational sovereignty now lay in national values. The religious values were secondary. Nationalism could thereby assume forms of a substitute religion as was already formulated earlier by Ernst Moritz Arndt: "To be a united nation is the religion of our time; the highest form of religion is that which favours Fatherland more than lords and princes, than fathers and mothers, than wives and children."[48] In the form of a radical nationalism, which dissociated itself from both external as well as internal "enemies of the *Reich*" the character of a political religion also found expression in

47. See Lidtke, "Social Class and Secularization," 30–33; Budde, *Man nannte sie "rote" Kapläne*; Mooser, "Volk, Arbeiter und Bürger Volk," 266f. (example of Catholics" Days).

48. Arndt, Geist der Zeit, 1813.

the late nineteenth century. Religion did not disappear, but was instrumentalised and subordinated and adapted in an altered form to the secular phenomenon of nationalism. The development was criticised even amongst Protestant pastors who warned of a "real heathen extreme nationalist hatred against the universal in Christianity," but these remained lone voices within the Protestant church. In spite of the instrumentalization of nationalism against Catholicism and Social Democracy neither the Catholic component of the population of the German Empire nor the working-class as a whole could remain immune against this new kind of mass movement. However, Catholic and Social Democratic workers distanced themselves from close association of the throne and altar, of nation and religion.[49]

In the development of nationalism the Protestant church and religion were part of a modernization process; however, in the formation of a knowledge and science-oriented society churches stood in the cross-hairs of criticism. Criticism of religion, the church and Christianity was part of the whole nineteenth century and also influenced the (Social Democratic) working class. Not only did the criticism of religion of Karl Marx have a direct influence on the workers' movement, but also the older middle-class criticism of religion. Social Democratic agitators for example referred to this traditional, philosophical, Enlightenment criticism of religion in case they would be accused of blasphemy. Indeed, Social Democracy saw itself as the heir and executor of the old middle-class criticism of religion. While the bourgeoisie had in the late eighteenth and early nineteenth centuries originally adopted a critical attitude towards state, church and religion, they had returned to the lap and protection of state and church in the second half of the century. The Social Democrats on the other hand had adopted the "atheistic opinions" of the bourgeoisie on the basis of their "scientific convictions" and committed themselves "to spread them further and bring them to the masses."[50] In the reception history of middle-class criticism of religion in the early workers' movement Ludwig Feuerbach assumed a central role. The Social Democrats perceived him as the "great spiritual campaigner who had destroyed the idea of God."[51] Feuerbach's view that God was a reflection of man and that the thinking man could therefore free himself from God brought the Social Democratic idea of the self-responsible and (politically) self-liberating man into line.

Charles Darwin's theory of evolution stood in contrast to the biblical creation story and destroyed in the eyes of critics of religion the idea that "the world, with all it contained had been created by an all-wise, all-benign God for a definite purpose." The world could be explained in causal terms, room for transcendental descriptions was no longer available. Ernst Haeckel's books popularised the teachings of Darwin and also brought them nearer to the working class. In 1872 when August Bebel was imprisoned he read the works of Darwin and Haeckel. The criticism of the creation story was easily popu-

---

49. See Nipperdey, *Religion im Umbruch*, 46–51, 92–100, quotation by the theologian Martin Kähler from the year 1872 (quoted ibid., 94); in general see Wehler, *Nationalismus*, 27f., 62f.

50. August Bebel, Reichstag speech from 16 September 1878, quoted in Prüfer, *Sozialismus statt Religion*, 160.

51. Prüfer, *Sozialismus statt Religion*, 73–76, 88 f.; Grote, *Sozialdemokratie und Religion*, 212f., 227f.

larised and found its way into the meetings in workers' pubs.[52] This development fell at least amongst Social Democratic organised workers on fertile soil as the German workers' movement became associated early on with middle-class critics of religion, while the Christian-based artisan communism of a Wilhelm Weitling played hardly any role since the revolutionary days of 1848/49. Both in the early workers' education clubs of the 1850's and 1860's and also later in the Social Democratic Party in the Empire, scientific education was to the fore.[53] The reception of the works of Darwin, Haeckel or Feuerbach was described in worker autobiographies as milestones of a learning process in which workers distanced themselves step by step from the original religious socialization. Wilhelm Blos, later a *Reichstag* member, recalled his childhood in a provincial neighbourhood: "My grandmother used to torment me with her devoutness." While some of his classmates could dodge the Sunday Christian instruction, he "was forced to attend. This perhaps contributed to my alienation from all things religious." Only later did he find his youthful feelings aptly described when reading Feuerbach. This new knowledge made the turning away from religion all the easier.

A religious interpretation of the world was no longer conceivable for this section of the working class. "I now started to think. Hitherto I had always considered it an act of Divine destiny that we were here only to suffer for which we could expect great joy in the after-life," was how Anna Altmann described her first steps on the way to the alienation from religion and Christianity. Moritz Bromme eventually justified the turning away from the Christian faith and religion with the futility of prayer: "in such a situation [in periods of distress, JS] people sometimes advised me: "turn yourself once more with all your heart to the good Lord (. . .) Earlier when I was existing in uncertainty I tried it occasionally and prayed with all my heart when lying on my wretched bed in the evening that he would no longer have me and mine suffer hardship; but it never helped me. At least I never noticed anything of it; again and again I had to help myself."[54] The adoption of the criticism of religion both in the case of Blos as well as the turning to rationality with Altmann and Bromme rendered the existence of a superior being questionable if not even superfluous.

These testimonials gained from individual, secular, partly atheist attitudes cannot be generalised for the workforce as a whole. That they were at least not a rarity for the type of Social Democratically socialised workers of the later Empire was shown in a poll taken by Adolf Levenstein between 1907 and 1911 in which more than 80 percent of the workers questioned—most of them socialist union members—replied that they no longer believed in God or had left the church.[55] If the idea of a superior being survived in the Social Democratic party milieu, then it was most likely in the

52. Grote, *Sozialdemokratie und Religion*, 213–15 (the quotation from *Volksstaat* /The People's State/, no. 43, Maxy 29, 1872; Prüfer, *Sozialismus statt Religion*, 324; Nipperdey, *Religion im Umbruch*, 125–27.

53. McLeod, "Berlin," 76f.; Hölscher, *Weltgericht oder Revolution*, 167.

54. On the learning process see Hölscher, *Weltgericht oder Revolution*, 173–79; Blos, *Denkwürdigkeiten*, 17f.; Altmann, *Wissen und Aufklärung* (1895), 126; Bromme, *Lebensgeschichte*, 361.

55. Ritter and Tenfelde, *Arbeiter im Deutschen Kaiserreich*, 773f.; a typology on the relationship between workers and religion is contained in the essay by Lidtke, "Social Class and Secularization," 34.

form of pantheistic ideas. From the "power of nature" Moritz Bromme gained hope and confidence; and the Austrian Social Democrat Florian Gröger reduced it to the formula: "The love of nature has remained firm throughout my life. I have, in fact, lost belief in God as a result of this."[56]

Socialism itself was however much more important for the Social Democratic workforce than such alternative images of God. On the one hand socialism called into question with its criticism of religion the interpretational authority of the churches and religion and on the other hand drafted an independent interpretation system of the world which showed secular-religious characteristics.[57] Many things flowed together here that have already been presented in previous paragraphs. In addition to these factors the criticism of priests played a role in forming the "clergy-bashing" that became rooted in popular culture traditions. "The priests preached things that they themselves would no longer believe," was for example the reproach of a Hamburg worker in 1898. Besides, the clergy showed little understanding of the social situation of the working class. Social Democratic critics either bemoaned the clergy's lack of interest in the workers or reproached them for concerning themselves with the workforce only out of reasons of social control. In addition there was the propagation of the "historical register of church sins" in which ecclesiastic transgressions since the Middle Ages from the burning of Giordano Bruno and the proceedings against Galilei Galileo until the present day were listed. The church and Christianity have hampered "every cultural advance" declared the reproach of the Social Democrats, who referred to the religious criticism of the Enlightenment era. In addition to this there was the adoption and dissemination of spiritual and natural science knowledge in the 19th century which has already been mentioned.

These arguments and factors in the end fell on fertile ground amongst those workers, male and female, who gradually moved away from their original Christian socialization (baptism and confirmation). "Why were people so heartless? Why did no God help me?" wondered the agricultural worker Franz Rehbein. Adelheid Popp, a worker with a religious upbringing and who led a religious life was plagued by similar doubts; to her colleagues she argued, "that there could not be an almighty God, because so many people would then not have to suffer such hard strokes of fate." Yet at home on seeing the picture of the Virgin Mary, instinctively again and again, she thought "Maybe there is," before reports about the persecution of Russian dissidents again proved to her "that there can be no God who influenced the fate of mankind."[58] The theodicy question had its source in the experience of individual or general social hardship and political persecution. Against these obvious doubts ecclesiastic-Christian expectations of salvation and redemption in the hereafter no longer could compete as a solution and explanation model. The secular discourse had gained the upper hand.

---

56. Evans, *Kneipengespräche*, 180f.; Bromme, *Lebensgeschichte*; Gröger, "Von unten auf (1926)," 157; see also Wegner, *Alltägliche Distanz*, 37: "God will either be denied in his existence or seen as one with nature."

57. A concise overview in Langewiesche, "Die neue Religion," 83–88 and 291.

58. Rehbein, *Das Leben eines Landarbeiters*, quoted in Prüfer, *Sozialismus statt Religion*, 84; Popp, *Jugend einer Arbeiterin*, 70.

Moreover socialism with its mixture of the solution of present-day problems and visionary expectations for the future presented itself as an alternative.[59] Characteristics of a "secularised religion" or of a political religion became apparent. In this interpretation framework the idea of Socialism/Marxism was portrayed as the dogma, the party was the new church and in the association meetings, celebrations and electoral campaign events community life was lived in pre-determined forms. Here could be found consolation and hope. Solidarity, justice and brotherliness formed the ethics of the movement.[60] How religious and secular elements overlay each other is also shown once more on an individual level. For Adelheid Popp the saleroom in which she regularly bought the Social Democratic newspaper was a "shrine": "My trip to buy the newspaper had always something of a holiday atmosphere for me. On that day I would put on my prettiest dress, just as I used to do earlier when I went to church." Such perceptions and behaviour patterns were made easier by the fact that the Social Democratic workers' movement even integrated Christian, sacred and spiritual elements in a new form and language into their ideas. This extended from formulas in which the party press characterised the Social Democrats as "in fact the only real Christians nowadays," to the veneration of Ferdinand Lassalle as "The Messiah of the 19th century," up to the eschatological embellished scenarios of doom for the bourgeois-capitalist world and the utopian portrayals of the state of the future as found in August Bebel's book "Die Frau und der Sozialismus" ("The Woman and Socialism") which ran into several editions.[61]

This development makes the interpretation of the secularization process difficult within the workforce which was linked to Social Democracy. Religious orientations had been unmistakably loosened from their original connections, but they had by no means disappeared. Socialism could be perceived by working men and women "as religion" and "instead of religion." However: the alienation from the Christian faith was linked to both patterns of perception. This alienation process moreover was intensified and accelerated in Protestantism because the Protestant established national churches propagated a strong antisocialism in their alliance with "Throne and Altar." How deep the rift went (in part) can be shown in the fact that even those Protestant reformers who devoted themselves to the oppressed lower classes remained full of reproach towards urban workers. Johann Hinrich Wichern, one of the fathers of the "inner mission" of evangelical church spoke in Berlin in 1871 with the industrial workers in mind of "wild heathenised masses." And the Bochum senior consistory adviser Nebe judged after the major miners' strike of 1889 that amongst "the broad strata of our people an anti-Christian world view of life on earth and an attitude of alienation from God is becoming widespread which ridicules throne and altar." Complete lack of understanding of the plight of the workers in the leadership of the Protestant church was evident in such pronunciations as well as a total lack of communication between the church and the working-class. Above all it was

---

59. Basically: Hölscher, *Weltgericht oder Revolution*.

60. See Nipperdey, *Religion im Umbruch*, 139f.

61. *Volksstaat-Erzähler*, December 12, 1878, quoted in Prüfer, *Sozialismus statt Religion*, 281; Popp, *Jugend einer Arbeiterin*, 70.

evident that both the interpretational system "religion" and the institution "church" had reached their limits.[62]

It also has to be stressed here once more: this was a trend, which only in the course of the nineteenth century became apparent and referred essentially to a clearly-defined group within the workforce. It lived in urban, mainly even in metropolitan surroundings, had close contacts with the Social Democratic milieu, consisted primarily of men and came from a Protestant home. That Christian value systems could also have a continued existence in the nineteenth century is shown in the Catholic worker milieu. Here too, religious changes and modernization achievements took place, but in contrast to the socialist workers' movement the religious-Christian interpretational framework remained primary and the secular organization was assigned a subordinated role. The Catholic workers' associations were under ecclesiastical control, but were "no longer clubs *for* workers with also middle-class members and no longer clubs for manual workers, but genuine associations of industrial and factory workers." Before the outbreak of the First World War about 500,000 members belonged to these clubs. They had their center in western Germany. There the degree of organization amongst Catholic workers was about a third. The workers' associations imparted a sense of group awareness which built on Catholic experiences and religious values. These associations of workers' clubs and organizations achieved attractiveness and charismatic strength because they did not persist in rigid rites and forms but because they "led beyond the traditional, authoritative, church culture into the modernising world whose elements were integrated into the Catholic world." In this network of Catholic associations, mass media and the Centre Party ("*Zentrum*") a communications center emerged, "in which religious communication in symbiosis with other themes could always be shared." The Catholic workers' association movement and further mass organizations (like "The People's Association for Catholic Germany" [Volksverein für das Katholische Deutschland] which had a membership of 800,000 in 1914) contributed in this way to the "modernization of Catholicism."[63] Indirectly at least the (workers') associations achieved a contribution to the secularization of Catholicism, as they "no longer practised a pastoral form of churchliness and religiousness,"[64] inte-

---

62. McLeod, "Berlin;" Johann Hinrich Wichern, 1871, quoted in: Teuteberg, "Moderne Verstädterung," 175; business report by consistory head Nebe 1888/89, quoted in: Liedhegener, *Christentum*, 542. See also the reproaches of the pastor of the Berlin Parochialkirche in 1853 about the way of life of the lower strata in the city: "We are faced here with the most bitter need and poverty in its most wretched form. Can we find open ears here? Yes we can find open hands that are ready to receive earthly gifts, but for heavenly goods there is so little meaning available that we don't even get an answer to our question. The Scriptures are unknown and the religious practice of the people is hypocrisy" (quoted in: Wintzer, "Evangelische Predigt," 321).

63. Nipperdey, *Religion im Umbruch*, 27f., 57f.; Schlögl, "Rationalisierung," 63. However, in the long term the limits of integration achievements of the Catholic church within the workforce cannot be overlooked. "In 1915 in the working-class parish of St Michael out of 279 reported deaths there were only 102 church funerals, in the "middle-class" parish of St Matthias in the same year on the other hand out of 248 deaths there were 230 church funerals" (Escher, "Pfarrgemeinde und Gemeindeorganisation," 281f.). Besides, in the 1870's 80% of all Catholic men had voted for the Centre Party, and in 1912 this figure sank to 55% (Wehler, *Deutsche Gesellschaftsgeschichte*, vol. 3, 1060.

64. Gatz, "Katholische Großstadtseelsorge," 1990, page 29 (this quotation however refers to Catholic pilgrimages).

grated the Catholic church into very secular questions (for instance, whether Christian unions should call strikes) and in this way speeded up the separation of secular and ecclesiastical fields of action. Once more it is shown that religion and modernization were not mutually exclusive and that secularization was not a linear teleological process, but that secularization must be described in the changing relationship between the dissolution and persistence of churchly religiousness.[65]

FINAL CONSIDERATIONS

The formula of the simultaneity of the non-simultaneous applies to the relationship between secularization and the workforce in nineteenth century Germany. The findings from the second part of this article have clearly verified this. On the one hand churchliness played an ever-decreasing role in the lives of the workers, on the other hand the great majority did not want to miss church rituals like baptism, confirmation and a Christian burial. And yet, religion assumed without doubt a certain superficiality and had to "subordinate" to the private framework of feast-day-religiousness. A secularization in the sense of an alienation from Christian faith, thinking, and ideas was in fact given here, but a determined renunciation of religion and church (in the form of leaving the church) was put into practice only by a very small minority of the workforce. The churches and religion experienced the strongest competition on the level of values and systems of interpretation. Liberalism and socialism, capitalism and nationalism questioned the Christian-religious interpretations or offered alternative models of explanation. These currents had moreover a direct relationship to the criticism of religion: the Christian positions were thus forced further onto the defensive.

On the other hand it also became clear that in the Catholic milieu Christian values and behaviour patterns were also fostered further in the workforce. Besides, the aforementioned modern spiritual currents did not fully detach themselves from Christian-ethical traditions. Nationalism tried especially to integrate the Protestant church. In socialist thinking central values of brotherliness and justice showed direct references to Christian values. Moreover, both nationalism and socialism developed quasi-religious characteristics. Expectations of salvation came either from faith in the nation or from the belief in the future communist society. The interpretation system of the modern world suited religious concepts in their secular perceptions, transformed them and integrated them into new contexts. Religion therefore acquired the role of a reference system but it was no longer accorded the power of explanation. This process was the expression of secularization in the nineteenth century and the workforce was—in its Social-Democratic form—substantially greatly involved in it.

65. This becomes all the more clear if we take into consideration the strong Catholic popular devoutness which was shown in the pilgrimages in the nineteenth century. The number of annual pilgrimages in Altötting in Bavaria was estimated at around 300,000 (Wehler, *Deutsche Gesellschaftsgeschichte*, vol. 3, 189f.). For an individual perspective on the experience of the pilgrimage as a collective mass phenomenon (from a critical point of view) see Popp, *Jugend einer Arbeiterin*, 62f. See also generally Prüfer, *Sozalismus statt Religion*, 210f.

The distancing from the church by the working class as well as the orientation of the workers in everyday life and in their values on new interpretation systems were not necessarily synonymous with outright complete anti-religious attitudes or godlessness. Structural elements such as gender, age and regional loyalties exercised their influence on the behaviour of the workforce. In the end on the individual level several intermediate steps and shades of grey areas became apparent. Philip Sommerlad, one of the leading members of the Social Democrats in Bochum thought: "I had a loose relationship with the Divine ruler of the world, but I always acted in the spirit of the good lesson which Christianity imparts to mankind."[66] Secularization had many faces, unambiguity cannot, in spite of the loss of influence and function of the church and religion on state, society and culture, be restored.[67] The merit of a secularization concept used in this way, thus lies in the fact that we can point to the ambivalences in the relationship between modernity and religion without having to postulate the dominance or even the victory of the one over the other.

66. Sommerlad, *Vom "Hessebub,"* 119.
67. See also Nolte, *Religion und Bürgergesellschaft*, 52–55.

4

The Slovak Worker between God and Marx

ROMAN HOLEC

Janko Kosák was a skilled electrician who earned a tidy sum of money. If now and again he would have a beer, he always made sure he kept a clear head ... He doubted everything and didn't believe in anything. He used to say: "I only believe what I see ..." You would never see him in church but whenever there was some kind of public gathering he was the first one to gossip. Because of his protests against the ruling class he had more than his fair share of porridge in Szeged prison. It happened once that for some reason Kosák had to go to church. He was passing the church when suddenly a great storm started and he didn't have an umbrella with him, so he thought to himself: "The devil won't take me during those few minutes!" and entered the church. And as soon as he shut the door there was a "bang!" and the lightning hit the tower then went down in front of the altar and rushed out to the same place where Kosák was standing. When the churchgoers awoke from the horror they saw the vicar, old auntie Sojka and Kosak lying on the ground. And the poor souls of these three people were rushing up the same way in which the lightning had gone down—they were going unbelievably fast to heaven.[1]

T HIS IS THE START of Vaclav Chlumecky's story about a socialist, Janko Kosák. Janko Kosák is a character who proves his identity in heaven by showing Marx's pamphlet instead of a prayer-book. He also introduces socialist reforms and gradually reveals the falsity of the church, the two-faced priests and false religious demagogy. In heaven there is no equality and not even the justice which had been promised. Of course, it must be said at the outset that despite this story, the title of this article about a Slovak worker between God and Marx distorts the real state of his awareness. The rural origin and traditionally strong confessionalism meant that this worker did not know Marx's name, or at best the name was the only thing he knew, while on the other hand he grew up and lived with God from the cradle to the grave. This was the result of the deficiencies in Slovak education and the poor level of education of both the Slovak worker and the lead-

1. Chlumecký, "Janko Kosák v nebi," 9. The prose was serialized in the *Robotnícke noviny* in February and March 1914 under the pseudonym Ľudoslav Enšpenger.

ing Social Democratics, not to mention the ideological problems of Social Democratic theory. The only well-known ideology for the worker was the experience of practical religion and his spiritual life.

The very first time that the Slovak worker found himself without God was in the industrial or urban environment (it was different in Upper Hungary, today's Slovakia, as large factories were built outside the cities). Either there was not a church nearby—this was the case with large companies near raw materials and outside rural/urban areas—or he was subsumed by the urban environment. And the social impact was no less significant, even though the Slovak urban environment was incomparably smaller than Czech towns, not to mention Western European ones. With the Slovak proletarian's rural roots and mentality, he must have felt uprooted, insecure and overcome by an environment which was totally alien to him, not even being able to have lunch on a Sunday with his family or being able to work in his "field" where he could turn his mind to his faith. And these feelings still persisted even when he had his family with him in the town. A group of Social Democrats started to fight for the hearts and minds of this kind of worker at the turn of the twentieth century. The Catholic Church was also interested in him thanks to so-called Christian Socialism. There were social, tactical and strategic issues at the centre of the conflicts between these two groups.

At first sight, God and religion played key roles in this fierce struggle, while the role of Marx remained marginalized. The Social Democrats considered religious beliefs to be the private matter of every individual and their goal was not to secularize or get rid of worker's faith. What is more, they used the symbolism of Christian events to mobilize the proletariat, which was a particularly strong feature in Slovakia. The working-class press, which was called the Bethlehem star, was supposed to bring human beings to "salvation and renewal."[2] No wonder that they did not want to affect religious belief too much. On the one hand they were not prepared theoretically and on the other hand they could have frightened off the majority of the first group of proletarians rather than converting them. They mainly criticized the Church for supporting the existing system.

Despite the mentioned tactical and intellectual setting, through detailed analysis it has been clearly shown that, all other issues aside, religion really became one of the key arguments in the ideological confrontation between Social Democracy and the other different ideological trends connected with the Church and religion. Sometimes there even was the illusion that an anti-religious attitude was the only ideological position of Social Democracy. Due to the confessionality of the population this was intentional as at the time the point was to act in a discreditable way.[3]

Although the Social Democrats did not want to deal directly with religious belief, the hypocrisy of priests and the Church was criticized in a number of articles. The above mentioned Václav Chlumecký gave the reasons for the first principle in one of his stories for working-class readers as follows: "Listen to me, neighbour! I have never taken away

---

2. Ľudoslav [Chlumecký, V.], "Vianočné poznámky," *Robotnícke noviny*, vol. 10, no. 52, December 25, 1913.

3. See more in Potemra, *Bibliografia článkov zo slovenských periodík*; Potemra, "Rozvoj spoločenského myslenia," 329–72.

your belief and I will never do so. Why would I do that? Is it bad for me that you believe? In what way could I possibly take away your belief? Only if I could prove you were wrong, which is impossible because of your strong convictions . . ."[4] In some published short stories, however, he attacked the priests and the Church for their warped morality and falsehoods.

The anti-religious and anti-church tendencies were brought into the Slovak Social Democratic movement from the outside. Only a few Slovak liberals who were influenced by Thomas Garrigue Masaryk and were known as Hlasists (after the periodical *Hlas* [Voice]), and some of the most educated Social Democrats, who were mainly of Czech origin (the aforementioned Václav Chlumecký or Edmund Borek), were brave enough to criticize religious dogmas, clericalism, the Church, the priests and the hierarchy of the Church, but they were not criticizing religion in itself. The Social Democrats called for a traditional Christianity with modesty and humility, but without the prelates, luxury and pride, and the priests with their connection to an oppressive state. They also criticized using religious feelings for political objectives. The real religion of Christ identified itself with the values of Social Democracy. The attacks against religion, therefore, were not directed at God; rather it was the other way round. They were starting from the traditional principles of God and from the gospel, from the socialist character of the early Christian teachings. Secularization in the true sense of the word was not the point. The point was rather to adapt religion to its traditional values. At the very first meetings between the Hlasists and Social Democrats the question of religion was raised. The first Slovak Social Democratic periodical *Nová doba* [New Age] was published on May 1st 1897, together with another periodical *Zora* [Day-break]. It was published in Budapest with Czech support. One student of the Business Academy and a future member of the Hlasists, Fedor Houdek, subscribed to this magazine. On May the 6th he wrote down in his diary: "I have 8 issues written in a naïve style with horrible spelling, so it is not clear which language is used. Poor people, no one will ever be interested in them! If I were older and had the necessary education, I would take the side of the workers' movement and would lead them in a social national direction. I have been thinking about the magazine and I have decided to write to them, particularly to the editor Fr. Tupý, and I want to tell him to lead the party properly in our situation."[5]

We hear more of what he understood by "leading the party properly" in a detailed answer by František Tupý, who was a Czech Social Democrat originally from Slaný. Tupý wrote in the letter to Houdek the following: "Regarding your directive, we would not initially be concerned with religion. There is no need to attack religion. But we will protect ourselves against the attacks and suspicions of the clerical party because we must be mindful of what is falsely written in the newspaper *Kresťan* [Christian], which is widespread among Slovak people and is supported by the priests. We must put an end to this Jesuitism."[6]

---

4. Chlumecký, "Neznaboh," 75. The prose was published in newspaper *Hlas ľudu* in the year 1920.

5. Slovenský národný archív [Slovak National Archives] in Bratislava, F. Houdek, no. 10, reg. no. 171, Houdek, F.: Záznamy k môjmu životopisu (pražský zápisník).

6. Slovenský národný archív [Slovak National Archives] in Bratislava, 462 Slovenské robotnícke hnutie, F. Tupý to F. Houdek on 28 May 1897.

When at the turn of the twentieth century Social Democracy and political Catholicism were fighting over the worker, there were many other things that brought them into confrontation: the formation of the Hungarian Catholic People's Party (the above mentioned newspaper *Kresťan* [Christian] was its Slovak edition) and the increased attention of the Catholic Church towards the social issues under the influence of the encyclical Rerum novarum, as well as the gradual formation of a basic thesis of social teaching within the Catholic Church—so-called Christian Socialism. Christian Socialism did not deny the difficult social position of the proletariat, but it saw the main reason for this condition in unrestricted political and economic liberalism. The main enemy for them was Social Democracy, whose principles, methods and goals were rejected by Christian Socialism. And here we can see some areas for cooperation in the anti-church or anti-clerical arguments between Social Democrats and some Liberals.

In Slovak society the religious issue began to acquire specific dimensions as the Church substituted for many deficits in the social structure and in political and cultural life, while it was also gradually shaping certain attributes of civil society.[7] In Slovakia religion was a determining factor in shaping identity at the turn of the twentieth century. In 1910 Catholics represented more than 69% of the population of today's Slovakia. In some districts they even exceeded 80%. There were more than 13% Lutherans. In Hungary there were approximately 50% Catholics and 8% Lutherans. This means that in both cases the number of Lutherans is lower, which demonstrates a lower confessional variety in the Slovak area. The role of priests here was much more important. The Church-political laws of the Hungarian Liberal governments established compulsory civil marriage and register offices in the first half of the 1890s, which determined the religion of children from mixed marriages and were condemned by the whole of Slovak society. Therefore, considering the socio-ideological situation it was not productive for any political movement in Slovakia to question or openly confront religion. Decisive activities in this sphere were carried out within Social Democracy, mainly as a consequence of the cooperation between some liberal representatives of the Slovak intelligentsia and the Social Democrats who provided space for similar opinions. Houdek and Vavro Šrobár, who was a doctor in Ružomberok and a liberal freethinker, belonged to the first group. Vavro Šrobár was one of a small group of individuals who not only had a positive attitude towards Social Democracy, but in their programme they also raised the question of secularization, which in Slovakia was an unwise move.

What were the reasons for Šrobar's unusual attitudes? There were many of them: above all Šrobár was an urban person and farming was not part of his political area. Also his interest in workers, social issues and Social Democracy was increasing gradually. His ideas and opinions were formed while studying in Prague (1888–1899) and this was crucial for him. For example, from autumn 1895 we know of Šrobár's attitude to the Catholic priest Martin Kollár as well as to the solicitor František Veselovský, who later became candidates and Members of Parliament for the Catholic People's Party. Šrobár formulated some quite surprising results based on his personal meetings with both of

---

7. To this Holec, "Úloha katolíckej cirkvi," 155–73.

them. Šrobár was impressed by Kollár but he criticized Veselovský, who seemed to be too radical: "Confused by the socialist theories of Marx, Lassalle and Laveley, he is expecting the salvation of the Slovak nation from the European social movement."[8] Almost two years later Šrobár's ideas had changed and he easily defeated the views of Veselovský. He became famous for the programme statement to his partner Pavol Blaho in connection with the idea of preparing the youth movement and a magazine as a vehicle for his ideas: "We must pay attention to social issues because Social Democracy organizes people behind our back and it could happen that people's opinions might be opposed to our national rights and ideals."[9]

In the organization called *Detvan* he eagerly gave lectures and discussed individual ideological movements, attempting to apply a pan-European political and ideological approach to Slovak conditions. In 1896 in connection with the foundation of a secret youth organization he presented as one of his tasks the publication of translations of socialist articles. In April 1897 while visiting students who were members of *Detvan* in Budapest Šrobár gave a lecture called *Mravné názory našej doby* [The Moral Views of our Time]. We can mention at least three of the ten points of his working structure: the children of liberalism (German socialists, French anarchists and Russian nihilists), the reaction against materialistic atheism, and in his conclusion, Šrobár spoke about the Slovak intelligentsia and their problems.[10]

After returning to Slovakia and settling down in Ružomberok, Šrobár was influenced by the dynamically developing industrial centre on the railway line of Košice—Bohumín (Kaschau—Oderberg). Certainly, if he had lived in a village or in a stagnating town area, the influence would have been different. As a doctor in Ružomberok he took care of workers from a textile factory in Rybárpole, and due to this daily experience the level of social poverty was revealed to him: he saw the diseases caused by the bad social conditions, by malnutrition, by the working conditions and he was also aware of the high death rate.

When we talk about Šrobár and his interest in Social Democracy, there existed not only these rather subjective factors, but there was also a very strong political movement. Hlasism was looking for its base as the intellectual elite in Slovakia was very small, not even mentioning those who were "progressively" oriented. The priests and individuals influenced by the rural environment dominated amongst the youth. Šrobár, as the leader of the movement, was aware of his restricted base and the only possible way out of this was to use emancipated Slovak labourers. Although we know about the efforts to distribute the magazine *Hlas* [Voice] among the workers in Bratislava, the level of the majority of articles highly exceeded the intellectual level of the normal worker. Despite

8. V. Šrobár to P. Blaho from October 1895. Cited in Jansák, *Život dr. Pavla Blahu*, 140. The Catholic priest Martin Kollár knew well the programme documents of German Social Democracy, its press and its theoretical works. Archív Spolku sv. Vojtecha [The Society of St. Adalbert's Archives] in Trnava, fasc. 101, fol. C, no. 12, Kollár, M.: *Je náboženstvo pre človeka vecou súkromnou?*

9. V. Šrobár to P. Blaho on 6 September 1897. Cited in Jansák, *Život dr. Pavla Blahu*, 150.

10. Archív Spolku sv. Vojtecha [The Society of St. Adalbert's Archives] in Trnava, fasc. 65, no. 259, V. Šrobár to F. R. Osvald on 25 April 1897.

this "illegibility," the first two annual volumes of *Hlas* in particular were evidence of the fact that the above mentioned programme words of Šrobár addressed to Blaho were not just words on paper. Pavol Blaho, who was an editor, also played a very positive role, which, considering his rural origin was quite surprising. He was guided from Prague, not only by Šrobár, but also by František Pastrnek: "The proletariat (cities, industrial) already has its own structure, which we do not need to meddle in. But there is a need to watch with sympathy the efforts of the workers to improve their living standards, their struggle with money . . . Socio-political activity is common ground for everyone and is therefore capable of establishing cooperation with other political parties in Hungary."[11] The difficulty of the listed problems is shown best by the fact that at that time Dušan Makovický wrote to Jozef Škultéty, who was an editor of *Slovenské pohľady* [Slovak Views], about the inevitability of discussing the social issues: "Jozef, it is necessary to write some social commentary in *Pohľady* [Slovak Views]. And when do you think you will write something? The years are passing. In this way you can gain the interest of the proletariat, the youth and all those who are curious about social problems."[12]

Unlike *Slovenské pohľady* (and other periodicals) *Hlas* wrote on social issues and monitored them regularly, of course not always with the same intensity. The editors Pavol Blaho and Vavro Šrobár, the contributors Milan Hodža and the Catholic priest Ján Kempný, as well as many others, were interested in these problems from different aspects. The crucial meaning of this problem was formulated by one of the co-workers of *Hlas,* Jozef Ruman, who wrote: "We must take note of the ideas which make the world go round, we must take note of the social movement . . . because its spirit is in Europe. Nowadays, when the problem of social reforms is coming to the forefront and needs to be dealt with, these thoughts can't be ignored and must be written about."[13] Šrobár succinctly formulated this statement: "He who owns the factories owns the twentieth century."

In the first issue of the magazine *Hlas* there appeared criticism from some of the new unprepared readers: "As far as the content of the magazine is concerned, I can hear criticism from all sides, even from young Czechs who were brought up in a modern way . . . the criticism being that it is a shame that you are too modern in your opinions which are not yet suitable for the Slovaks and also that you favour the Social Democrats, which you proclaim in the first issue."[14] The attitude of Jozef Dohnány, who was a graduate of the Vienna Technical University, was not an isolated one and gradually more young conservative subscribers and supporters started to leave *Hlas*: "Thanks to Tolstoy and Social Democracy you have totally "shut the door" to the Catholic priests."[15] One very talented Catholic priest, František Jehlička, who was also interested in philosophy, was willing to

11. F. Pastrnek to P. Blaho from September 1897. Cited according to Janšák, *Život dr. Pavla Blahu*, 150.

12. Archív literatúry a umenia Slovenskej národnej knižnice [The Literature and Art Archives of the Slovak National Library] in Martin, sig. 22 H 13, D. Makovický to J. Škultéty on 23 September 1897.

13. Ruman, "Reflexie," *Hlas*, vol. 2, no. 4, November 1, 1899.

14. Slovenský národný archív [Slovak National Archives] in Bratislava, P. Blaho, no. 5, reg. no. 139, J. Dohnány to P. Blaho from the summer 1898.

15. L. Schifferdecker to P. Blaho in May 1899. Cited according to Janšák, *Život dr. Pavla Blahu*, 343.

accept discussions about socialism in the magazine *Hlas* and he was even willing to give credit to Marx and Engels and historical materialism, which "pointed to the importance of national-economic factors and broadened our view of history," but on the other hand he claimed that, "for philosophical reasons we reject materialism, evolution and atheism as being a 'coat full of holes' in which Marx and Engels wanted to 'dress' their social opinions. We consider the dreams of Social Democrats about the future of our society to be impossible, against human nature and retrogressive."[16] Soon he came into conflict with *Hlas* and he resigned his subscription. Jehlička subsequently wrote about his polemic: "I have known *Hlas* very well since its beginnings and I probably know it better than those who are editing it. I have noticed its dangerous direction, so I have started studying those who have been inspiring the Hlasists . . . I have collected a lot of material and from the Christian point of view I dare to reject the whole movement by which Hlasists want to imprison the already weak Slovak people . . . I am not afraid of engaging with anyone in a polemic because none of them are educated in philosophy and I will not even worry if Masaryk himself speaks in order to protect his followers . . ."[17]

In 1903 Jehlička published a polemic text where he summed up his opinions about the philosophical discourses in relation to religion. It is interesting that his work was released separately in the town of Martin, and also as a serial in the newspaper *Národné noviny* [The National Newspaper] during April and May 1903. The aversion to liberal Hlasism, Czech Realism and Social Democracy was obviously more important than confessional conflicts. It is therefore worth summing up precisely the core of Jehlička's attacks on the liberal *Hlas*, Masaryk and Social Democracy, as he remained faithful to these opinions in the following years and all his later works basically adopted the same viewpoint. Jehlička's ideas were based in neothomism with all its signs: rejecting modern philosophy, returning to metaphysics and thomism, partially smoothing over the arguments between science and belief, and criticizing the ideological sources of liberalism.

According to Jehlička, *Hlas* survived only thanks to people from Prague who were under the influence of Masaryk and who believed that their mission was to fight "on behalf of modern philosophy" against positive religion and against the old Churches in Slovakia."[18] Masaryk believed that ". . . there are some false prophets among us who want to withdraw our gaze from the heavenly stars, who want to destroy our belief and real religion, and they want to leave us in the storms of modern philosophy, so we might die poorly."[19] Religion and science are mutually incompatible and there is a fight between them, and the Hlasists want to deprive people of their religion. According to Jehlička, when *Hlas* was being edited by Pavol Blaho it behaved with caution, but then when it was edited by Šrobár it attacked the most holy ideals of Slovakia. When under Blaho it dared to deny "the Godship of Christ" in the article *Vznik kresťanstva (The Beginning of*

16. Margin [Jehlička, F.], "Stanovisko najmladšieho dorosta k smeru Hlasu," *Hlas*, vol. 4, no. 5, from the end of year 1901.

17. Archív Spolku sv. Vojtecha [The Society of St. Adalbert's Archives] in Trnava, fasc. 65, no. 75, F. Jehlička to F. R. Osvald on 21 March 1904.

18. Margin [Jehlička, F.] "Novoveká filosofia a Slováci," 3.

19. Ibid., 5.

Christianity) it also dared to moderately promote Tolstoyism, under Šrobár it dared to start a religious revolution with the article *Mojžiš či Darwin?* [Moses or Darwin?]. In the article *Obnovenie pekla* [The Rebuilding of Hell] (both in no. 3, volume V.) many parts of the Holy Scriptures were refuted, and according to Jehlička, Masaryk's followers wanted to "destroy idols."

According to Jehlička, there is a need to return to the beginnings of modern philosophy, which suffers from the fact that it moved away from scholastic philosophy at the end of the fifteenth and the beginning of the sixteenth century, and this we can call the "Fall of Man." It meant the end of medieval thinking and people grew tired of medieval opinions of the world, and everything which mankind had achieved was destroyed in a revolutionary manner. According to Jehlička people might have turned away emotionally from the scholastic opinions but they did not consider them lacking in logic. They rejected them because scholasticism only dealt with unworldly issues. Maybe the philosophers at the time did not pay enough attention to science, but they devoted themselves to Christ's truths. Francis Bacon is still considered to be the father of empirical and positivist philosophy, which is so unfriendly to metaphysics. Bacon's empirical one-sidedness later caused the one-sided rationalism of René Descartes.

According to the writer, Masaryk is eclectically interested in every modern philosopher and although the philosophical systems are mutually connected, he primarily starts from David Hume. Jehlička claims that positions which philosophy once considered to be a disgrace are now acknowledged, and only things which are open to human reason are accepted. There is no absolute truth, religion is a private matter, there is anarchy and each new philosophical system contemplates the destruction of all its predecessors. According to Friedrich Nietzsche, nothing is true and everything is allowed. The return to Immanuel Kant is devious. He was the one who brought chaos to German philosophy. Therefore it is preferable to return to his predecessor Hume, who established academic scepticism and disturbed the general principles of knowledge. Hume's theory of knowledge was based on the sceptical view of John Locke and it denies the essential difference between sense-perception and rational-perception. This is thought to be the fateful delusion in Hume's theory. According to Jehlička, the consequence of this was that Hume lowered himself in this theory of knowledge to the level of the animal. With this began the gradual disintegration of philosophy. Jehlička asks himself how the behaviour and the good of nations can be influenced by a philosophy which deprives people of their values and lowers them to the level of an animal. How can anyone want to save a nation with this kind of philosophy?

The Hlasists and Masaryk's followers arrived loudly in Slovakia and started to spread the need for renewal and criticized everyone's immorality, but how did they want to encourage this "depressed nation," Jehlička asks. Which of the theories of modern philosophy that were growing like "mushrooms after the rain" would be suitable? They came to Slovakia with some barbaric and immoral theories, they came to spread thoughts of love, fairness, pureness, modesty and morality and after that they wondered why there was no moral confidence among the Slovaks. They even used so-called Social Darwinism, a popular tool in the struggle against science and the new scientific knowledge: "If Darwin's theory of descent, which you promote so loudly, is right; if there is a principle that stronger individuals have the right to suppress the weaker ones and to blossom at their expense, so if it is true that any nation is able to absorb us—defenceless without punishment: Oh God, what can our self-awareness and national pride be based upon? Should it be built on those bare rocks we work on, or on the literature or the industry which we don't have, or on the crowd of people who immigrate to America, or on a terrible slowness and lack of education? If we are only "nourishment for our hungry neighbours" then what can encourage us? . . . You want to spread civilization among us, a civilization which extinguishes the flame of our self-awareness and pride and which destroys our courage, which reassures the pessimism in our spirit . . . a civilization which "is digging our grave."[20]

Instead of spreading love among the people, the Hlasists were doing the exact opposite, they were taking away any impulses for love: "Or, dear Hlasists, do you think that the writer of these lines would do anything in order to help his nation if he was convinced, according to principles of realism, that all religious truths, the whole metaphysics and the belief based on it, the belief that life after death is only a fantasy, a dream or a reflection of an insane mind? Which clever person would suffer for a nation if thanks to realism he would be convinced that as there is nothing after death a man should enjoy the passion of his life until he is unable to?"[21] When we consider Jehlička's later betrayal of the national interests, these words do not sound very convincing.

"If there are a lot of people at the moment who live the life of cattle, as if nature had given them only a belly as in the case of spiders: What would life be like in Slovakia if your poor realism forced out the Christian teaching which at least partially maintains the flame of love for the unhappy Slovak people?" asks Jehlička and continues with another question: "Why does Hlasism rail against renegades and defectors?" "What is there to stop a person who is a materialist in his thinking and in his life from joining the stronger ones where he can have more materialist advantages, where he can indulge more?"[22] And it should be mentioned again that the writer of the previous words preferred the professional career of a professor to defending the national interests in the Hungarian parliament.

If religion is a private matter, as the Social Democrats claim, the Slovaks are losing the only weapon which they could use against "the conquering Magyarizators and mean renegades." Jehlička criticizes Hlasists: "You are lost! You weaken the noble Christian teaching, which exalts man to the supernatural and expresses the true, higher supernatural brotherhood of all people with the fatherhood of the spirit! What can there be without this teaching . . . which is essential for our harmony, which today, when all the gates of hell have conspired against us, is the only requirement of our existence?"[23] The Christian religion must be essential for the ideology of a national movement and people should respect it more than material wealth. Technical and social progress is not possible

20. Ibid., 14–15.
21. Ibid., 16.
22. Ibid., 17.
23. Ibid., 19.

without Christianity. The only solution for the Slovak nation is to return to metaphysics and the religion of Thomas Aquinas.

Anton Štefánek, who was a sociologist and a journalist, responded to Jehlička in the pages of *Hlas*. He refused to give as a model to the downtrodden Slovaks a philosopher who does not see an ideal in a nation state. According to him, a philosophy is considered to be suitable if it respects modern science including Copernicus, Newton, Galileo, Darwin, Helmholz and others. He said about the Hlasists that they are as religious as other people. However, they differentiate between generally accepted Christian norms on one side, and Church practice and Church dogmas on the other. He was also against the incompatibility of thomistic philosophy and the Church dogmas with the development of modern science: "The Catholic or spiritual scholar restricted by dogmas can only be involved in those sciences which have no connection with Church belief . . . he must be careful to examine all sides in order to discover any dogmas."[24]

During the final period of its existence, when Šrobár was an editor, *Hlas* published a study by the German socialist Werner Sombart called *Socializmus a sociálne hnutie v 19. storočí* [Socialism and the Social Movement in the 19th Century]. The editorial board of the failing *Hlas* was in ruins and this study by Sombart was their pride. Many years later Anton Štefánek said that they had decided to publish Sombart after "long hesitation."[25] This was also too radical for most of its liberal followers.

Hlas was not unknown among the workers. While preparing it, Houdek asked Blaho to also think about "the craftsmen and their helpers and also the helpers in the factories"[26] when sending out the first issue. *Hlas* was distributed among the workers mainly during the first year of publishing as later on interest in it gradually decreased. In Bratislava in the years 1898–1899 the subscribers were railwaymen, craftsmen and workers, some Social Democrats and the future playwright Jozef Hollý. It is also clear from the letters of Rudolf Lapár and František Tupý addressed to the editorial board of *Hlas* that they were trying to acquire subscribers from the working class. However, Lapár claimed that the style of this magazine was too sophisticated for simple, uneducated people.[27]

After the end of *Hlas*, Jehlička used the pages of *Katolícke noviny* [The Catholic News] to present his attitudes to Social Democracy and also to attack the leader of the Social Democrats, Emanuel Lehocký. Concerning Jehlička's later betrayal of the national interests, when in 1907 he preferred the financial comfort and quiet career as a professor to the difficult work of a Slovak Member of Parliament, the attitude of Eduard Sándorfi, who was a priest and editor from 1905, was predictable. He warned against underestimating the Social Democrats, especially if they continued to demand the need for educa-

24. Štefánek, "Nováveká filosofia a Slováci." *Hlas*, vol. 5, no. 7, from July 1903.

25. Slovenský národný archív [Slovak National Archives] in Bratislava, A. Štefánek, no. 23, reg. no. 811, p. 201, Štefánek, A.: *Hlasizmus a socializmus* (handwritten).

26. Slovenský národný archív [Slovak National Archives] in Bratislava, F. Houdek, no. 2, reg. no. 27, F. Houdek to P. Blaho, n. d. (probably in March 1898).

27. Slovenský národný archív [Slovak National Archives] in Bratislava, P. Blaho, no. 5, reg. no. 48 a 50, J. Hollý to P. Blaho on 28 September 1898 and on 1 March 1899; ibid., no. 5, reg. no. 48, R. Lapár to P. Blaho on 23 October 1898.

tion in the mother tongue, whilst the Catholic priests would not stand up for the Slovak language and even kept it away from the churches. In that case it would be no surprise to see the Slovaks gather under the red flags.[28] This was an opinion from the opposing side, but in many issues it was similar to Šrobár's opinions.

Jehlička became one of the main representatives of Christian Socialism, which was based on a modern social theory of the Catholic Church. The establishment of eternal God's laws and the renewal of the love to your relatives in the spirit of Christianity stood against "the pagan, atheistic and anarchistic socialism." Only Christianity could solve the problems of society. Liberalism must be non-confessional; it must "separate Christian, earthly authority and heavenly authority, the state and the Church, the Earth and heaven, a person and God." Jehlička wanted a Catholic-Lutheran union because, "If we do not take care of the people, the Social Democrats will. And people will follow them because they always follow the one who can quench their thirst and who can feed them."[29] This produced another negative response to Jehlička's text from the periodical *Hlas*. The Czech Social Democrat Josef Václav Krejčí also entered into this discussion, not directly, but with his pamphlet from 1905 called *Náboženství a moderní ideál člověka* [Religion and the Modern Ideal of Man]. It was also distributed among the Slovak Social Democrats.

Not once did Jehlička surprise by demonstrating a detailed knowledge of German Social Democratic writings. What was more surprising was the admittance of his mistakes which quickly brought Christian Socialism to an end. He saw the reasons for this position in the lack of a modern understanding of life and a backward opinion about the world. Christian Socialists saw "the kingdom of fairness and complete equality" in heaven, whereas the socialists wanted to have it on the Earth. The first one is a slogan and the second is "tireless work." Christianity is still in many ways medieval and non-democratic, it is a castration of what it really should be in order to better the socialists.[30]

This "pro domo" criticism was in contrast to the very strict, even demagogic campaign, of the Christian Socialists against the Social Democrats, which more than once led to confrontations on the streets. In Bratislava on 1 October 1905 there was a heated Christian Socialist meeting which led to physical attacks: "There was one woman who punched E. Lehocký, the editor of Slovak Socialist's newspaper, in the belly when he started insulting the priests, and then Christian-Social workers grabbed his collar and they carried him in the air and threw him out of the square."[31] Jehlička also on occasion lowered himself to vulgar criticism when he talked about free love, abolishing the state and the Church and also when he talked about an all-powerful state, which would divide people, feed them and also bring up their children etc.[32]

28. "Obava pred slovenskou sociálnou demokraciou," *Slovenské robotnícke noviny*, vol. 2, no. 8, August 1, 1905. Sándorfi translated for the Social Democrats the text of one pamphlet from the Slovaks in the USA.

29. Margin [Jehlička, F.], "Boj o život," *Národnie noviny*, vol. 35, no. 47, April 16, 1904.

30. Jehlička, "Revisia nášho života, " *Katolícke noviny*, vol. 56, no. 29, July 14, 1905.

31. Prítomný: "Búrlivé ľudové zhromaždenie v Prešporku . . . ," *Katolícke noviny*, vol. 56, no. 41, October 6, 1905.

32. Archív Spolku sv. Vojtecha [The Society of St. Adalbert's Archives] in Trnava, vol. 101, fol. C, a, Jehlička, F. R.: Katolícka cirkev a prevrat ľudskej spoločnosti.

We can find evidence of the Slovak Social Democrats' careful attitude in the words of their leader Emanuel Lehocký. Although he is describing ". . . the spiritual and material misery" of the party, he refused an article by the teacher Jozef Maliak due to its religious character. The whole matter ". . . would harm us religiously. Everything is allowed apart from offending the priests. We think that there is no need to describe the character of the Slovak people. Our motto must be: Slowly does it! . . . We really don't doubt a single word; nevertheless we must not get into any problems . . ."[33]

It must be said again that the attacks of the Social Democrats against religion were not meant to be against the God; rather it was the other way round. They started from the traditional tenets of God and from the Gospel and from the socialist character of early Christian teaching. Secularization in the true sense of the word was not the goal. The aim was rather to adapt religion to its traditional values. We can also see this careful attitude of Social Democracy to religion in the serialisation called *Kresťanstvo a socializmus* [Christianity and Socialism] by Ján Ondra. This serialisation was published at the end of 1909 in *Robotnícke noviny* [The Worker's Newspaper]. Preservation of "pure Christianity" with its progressive role in human history could have played a positive role in the workers' movement at the time. Ondra mentioned some examples when the Church was disloyal to its own values, for example, with the system of indulgences in the past, the wealth of the Church now, or how the Church supported capitalism.

The entry of the Czech Social Democrat Edmund Borek marked a significant change in Slovak Social Democratic theoretical discourse. He also believed that Jesus as a social reformer was very close to modern socialists, but he also raised the question of atheism and the materialistic world view in Slovakia. In his view the new religion was in conflict with the scientific view of the world and also with the workers' interests. So ideologically there could have been a real readiness for making compromises. However, in the practical fight against political clericalism, progress was more gradual.

Along with Borek the ex-Hlasist Vavro Šrobár was also connected with Social Democracy and its attitude towards religion. *Slovenské robotnícke noviny* [The Slovak Worker's Newspaper] supported him in his election candidacy in the year 1906 and Šrobár's anti-clerical attitudes and attacks against the bishop Sándor Párvy were deemed suitable for the editorial board of the newspaper. Some radically oriented Catholic priests also positioned themselves alongside this agenda. For example, Štefan Mišík suggested putting forward Social Democrat candidates in Spiš with the aim of reducing not only the property of the bishops but also their pensions. He also had the same attitude when it came to bringing Church schools under state control.[34] He claimed several times that the Church was only "a stepmother" for the Slovaks. Šrobár worked with the editorial board of the aforementioned *Slovenské robotnícke noviny* (later *Robotnícke noviny*) and with its

33. Archív literatúry a umenia Slovenskej národnej knižnice [The Literature and Art Archives of the Slovak National Library] in Martin, A 897, E. Lehocký to J. Maliak on 6 January 1906.

34. E.g., Archív literatúry a umenia Slovenskej národnej knižnice [The Literature and Art Archives of the Slovak National Library] in Martin, 37 H 16, Š. Mišík to A. Halaša on 5 May 1906 and 49 AE 2, Š. Mišík to J. Škultéty on 11 July 1904 and on 30 October 1908.

main editor, Emanuel Lehocký. We can find evidence for this in the notes that had been made in the Social Democracts' treasury book.[35]

It is worth noting that in 1908 when Šrobár was in prison in Szeged he studied "the teachings of the self-saviour prophet Marx," especially his *Das Kapital* in Hungarian and he also made the acquaintance of the future leader of the Hungarian Republic, Béla Kun. Šrobár argued with him and these arguments were based on Masaryk's book about Marxism. The main controversial issues were nationalism, internationalism, historical materialism, religion and philosophical determinism.[36] At the same time Jehlička was also studying Marx, albeit more indirectly through the works of Marx's critics and apologists. From his studies emerged his books on social issues, ethics, the philosophical basis of modern social ethics and its Marxist interpretation and on the sources and bases of Marxist religious philosophy.[37]

At the beginning of November 1908, after being released from prison, Šrobár was welcomed by the Social Democratic newspaper *Napred* [Forwards] with the belief that as a democrat he would continue helping the workers in their struggle. In connection with this, Šrobár renewed his cooperation with the Social Democrats from Ružomberok, Žilina and Mikuláš. He also addressed rallies, prepared lectures for workers and wrote a number of articles that were published in the Social Democratic press. Šrobár's occasional contributions to *Robotnícke noviny* cemented their good working relationship. In 1909 *Robotnícke noviny* welcomed the publication of Šrobár's *Ľudová zdravoveda* [People's Hygiene] and recommended it to the workers. In February 1912 Lehocký emphasized in a personal letter that Šrobár was the only member of the Slovak intelligentsia to whom they turned for "any type of work." He didn't want to specify the topic, but one of the possibilities was "something about the future of Slovak politics."[38]

Šrobár often spoke highly of Lehocký: "When reading your newspaper I am really glad to see the improvement in the form and content. Your criticism is healthy and truthful, and you clearly see Slovak politics."[39] Šrobár raised his anticlericalism as the basis for his identification with the interests of *Robotnícke noviny* at a time when there were bitter attacks against the *Ľudové noviny* [People's News] and Andrej Hlinka.

1912 saw the most significant cooperation between Vavro Šrobár and the Slovak Social Democratic *Robotnícke noviny*. Šrobár had been working on a large publication since the end of 1911 and this text was to be a reliable and scientifically based weapon in their fight against clericalism. His aim was to reveal the fact that a religious worldview was unscientific and also to replace God's altar with the altar of science. It was significant that when he requested some of Marx's works on religion and the clergy from

35. Slovenský národný archív [Slovak National Archives] in Bratislava, Slovenské robotnícke hnutie, 261, Pokladničná kniha slovenskej sociálnej demokracie v rokoch 1904–1906. It is part of an archival document from the former archive of the Institute of Marxism-Leninism ÚV KSS.

36. Šrobár, *Z môjho života*, 448–56.

37. E.g., Jehlička, *Társadalmi kérdés és etika*; Jehlička, *A marxista vállásbölcsélet forrása és lényege*.

38. Slovenský národný archív [Slovak National Archives] in Bratislava, V. Šrobár, no. 4, reg. no. 196, E. Lehocký to V. Šrobár on 26 February 1912.

39. Šrobár, "K svetlu!" *Robotnícke noviny*, vol. 8, no. 42, October 19, 1911.

the leader of the Slovak Social Democrats, Emanuel Lehocký, he could only send him *Původ křesťanství* [The Origin of Christianity] by Karl Kautsky, and he ordered some more Czech Social Democratic publications from Prague. Meanwhile he continued to bitterly criticize *Ľudové noviny* and Andrej Hlinka.[40]

Šrobár's work *Moderný názor na život a na svet* [A Modern View of Life and the World] was supposed to be serialized in *Robotnícke noviny* and after this was to be published separately. This was rather too much for Šrobár who was not prepared for such a demanding task. Therefore, Anton Štefánek, who was his old friend, offered to be co-author and promised to help Šrobár with the philosophical-theoretical part in particualr. Lehocký agreed to this and also began encouraging Štefánek to work. Štefánek had a suitable philosophical-sociological education and unlike Šrobár, he did not want to write "an eclectic compilation" but a completely original work.[41] However, he also did not properly judge the time at his disposal and soon the whole work was behind schedule. Šrobár wrote a letter to T. G. Masaryk concerning two of the volumes, each containing four chapters. Eventually, only the first chapter was published with the title *Veda a viera* [Science and Belief]. The *Robotnícke noviny* wrote the following about it: "It will be a scientific work without rival in Slovak literature. It deserves the attention of all our readers and those who admire progress … It is a deep scientific work which must be read by every thinking Slovak."[42] According to Šrobár, it was supposed to be a response to Slovak clericalists. The chapter was published anonymously throughout July and August in 1912. Šrobár did not want to publish it as his original work and had it published anonymously, though if it caused an upset he would have claimed his right to its authorship.

The second chapter was supposed to be called *Metafyzika* [Metaphysics] and though Štefánek was working on it he never managed to finish it. In September Šrobár was still saying to Masaryk that he was "toiling with it," but his enthusiasm was gradually diminishing because of the lack of time and because of the demanding nature of the work. In the end several chapters were left unwritten and in 1913 the first chapter *Veda a viera* [Science and Belief] was republished as a separate booklet by *Robotnícke noviny*.[43] The struggle between science and belief was understood as the struggle of science and reason against superstition and intellectual darkness, as the struggle between progress and retrogression.

40. Slovenský národný archív [Slovak National Archives] in Bratislava, V. Šrobár, no. 4, reg. no. 196, E. Lehocký to V. Šrobár on 19 March 1912.

41. Slovenský národný archív [Slovak National Archives] in Bratislava, V. Šrobár, no. 5, reg. no. 295, A. Štefánek to V. Šrobár on 25 July 1912. According to the memoirs written after WWII Štefánek read Darwin's works as well as Nietzsche and Marx and „similar more or less materialistic and revolutionary works at grammar school." (Slovenský národný archív [Slovak National Archives] in Bratislava, A. Štefánek, no. 10, reg. no. 647, Rukopis vlastného životopisu).

42. "Literatúra," *Robotnícke noviny*, vol. 9, no. 27, July 4, 1912; and "Nepoddáme sa!"Ibid.

43. About the preparations of Šrobár's document look up Slovenský národný archív [Slovak National Archives] in Bratislava, V. Šrobár, no. 4, reg. no. 196, E. Lehocký to V. Šrobár on 15 January, 26 February, 19 March, 9 June, 19 July, 24 July, 26 July 1912; Slovenský národný archív [Slovak National Archives] in Bratislava, V. Šrobár, no. 5, reg. no. 295, A. Štefánek to V. Šrobár on 23 March and 25 July 1912. The handwriting of Šrobár's work in Slovenský národný archív [Slovak National Archives] in Bratislava, V. Šrobár, no. 23, reg. no. 1000. Together with note 39.

Despite everything Šrobár claimed, his struggle against clericalism using scientific means was not consistent. Although he made condemnatory speeches, he also claimed that religion ("the Christian teaching of Christ") had not yet fulfilled its "noble task." Therefore, it was to continue influencing the life of the people as "a source of life and world view."

The other chapters of the planned document were called: *Zjavené pravdy a katolícky názor na život a na svet* [The Revelational Truths and the Catholic View of the World and Life], *Konflikt vedy s vierou* [The Conflicts of Science and Belief], *Dejiny vývoja zeme a života na zemi* [The History of Evolution and Life on Earth], *Vývoj človeka na zemi* [The Evolution of Humans on Earth], *Kultúrne dejiny XIX. stoletia* [A Cultural History of the 19th Century] *and Laická morálka* [Laical Morals].[44]

In April 1913 (before the booklet's publication) Šrobár received an invitation from the "progressive women" from the town of Martin. They invited him to an educational social evening where he again mentioned this text from *Robotnícke noviny*. If he had not mentioned it again this whole text would probably have been forgotten. According to Hana Gregorová, in his lecture he claimed that life is the struggle of the representatives of science and progress against the hypocrites and despots who profit from people's stupidity and live in prosperity without working. Despite its success ("Many people enjoyed Šrobár's lecture, including the girls"),[45] shortly after there was a reaction against his words. These heretical statements on the holy ground of Martin were understood to be stirring up a hornet's nest. Consequentially the editorial office of *Národné noviny* [The National Newspaper] and the members of Slovak National Party organized an inquisitorial investigation. The result was that all the rooms of the industrial association and the casino were closed to other events organized by the women. But the workers from Martin helped them and offered them their rooms—"so that the Slovak national policemen would get angry." They expressed their conviction that the participants of other social evenings would feel at home in these rooms and that the participants would feel better there than among the elite of Martin.[46]

Šrobár stirred up things further with the articles he wrote for Prague's *Národní listy* [National Paper] and Masaryk's *Čas* [Time]. After agreeing with Šrobár Hana Gregorová wrote for Hodža's *Slovenský denník* [The Slovak Diary] and in solidarity her husband offered to give up his position as paid secretary of the Slovak National Party. Šrobár as well as Hana Gregorová refused as they thought this would harm "progressive thinking." As can be seen, this scandal attracted great publicity and it discredited the leadership of the *Národné noviny* in particular.

Ján Lajčiak, who was a modern sociologist and philosopher and one of the most educated Lutherans in Slovakia and who had a doctorate from Sorbonne and Leipzig, attacked Šrobár. According to him, Šrobár "poisoned the life of the Slovaks" and only showed that "he didn't have a feeling for religious issues." He also said that Šrobár's con-

44. V. Šrobár to T. G. Masaryk on 6 September 1912. In Rychlík, *Korespondence T. G. Masaryk*, 100.

45. H. Gregorová to J. Gregor Tajovský, n. d. (April 1913). In *Listy*, 99.

46. Gregorová, *Spomienky*, 163; "Chýrnik," *Robotnícke noviny*, vol. 10, no. 43, October, 23, 1913 (quotations).

ceptions were all wrong and he failed to realize the fact that religion cannot be ignored.[47] Lajčiak was aware of the many deficiencies of the Church and also among the priests, but these should have been separated from religious study—theology. Even though spiritual life was characterized by stagnation, the field of theology was quite active: "If science is the knowledge of the basis of things, then theology is the knowledge of religion."[48] Theology as a science was developed at university and within its framework different theological schools were established and each of them in a certain way helped science. Not once did it come into conflict with everyday religion and its promoters. And according to Lajčiak, Šrobár was silent on this.

The editorial board of the newspaper *Prúdy* [Currents], and its editor Ivan Markovič in particular, helped Šrobár who was being attacked from many sides. Ivan Markovič requested and then published the text of one of his lectures. The members of *Prúdy*, who were called *Prúdisti*, thought of themselves as promoters of the Hlasistic spiritual message, and even though there was a generation gap between them and Šrobár they still considered him to be close to them with his radical opinions. Markovič praised Šrobár's accessible and easy style, but he also pointed out Štefánek's slightly vague style of writing and his inability to move away from the influence of the complicated styles of various philosophical works. Markovič drew attention to the need to make the book accessible not only to workers, but also to farmers and craftsmen. The *Robotnícke noviny* could have managed this: "If only the book was cheap and Štefánek had enough confidence to promote his work."[49]

During this fight between science and belief, there was also a fight for Darwin and the evolutionary principle in natural science. Ján A. Wagner, Viktor Mikuška, Ivan Houdek and others were figures who tried to explain the newest natural scientific discoveries whilst also pointing out the fallacies in religious dogmas. However, this was too complicated and revolutionary even for the Social Democrats. Therefore they preferred to remain on the amateur level of Šrobár, where emotional statements took precedence over rational arguments. But the opposing side also did not want to remain behind. So when one side cited the possessions of the Church in order to demonstrate the contrast between rhetoric and reality, as well as the various discriminatory positions of the clergy towards socially weaker believers, the opposing side used the ever-effective vulgar anti-Semitism.

Šrobár was not discouraged and continued to work with *Robotnícke noviny*. Amongst other articles, at the start of May he published a review of Edmund Borek's

47. Lajčiak, *Slovensko a kultúra*, 40 and 109.

48. Ibid., 103.

49. Slovenský národný archív [Slovak National Archives] in Bratislava, V. Šrobár, no. 5, reg. no. 397, I. Markovič to V. Šrobár on 3. May and 26 May 1913. There is evidence about Štefanek's style in the notes written to Šrobár: "I don't think that pure mechanism and materialism in the development of the world, without any metaphysical intellect is scientific. Therefore I would advise you to stick to direct naturalistic facts and in metaphysics you should take the position of agnosticism or perhaps even positivism. And this is the way how you can remain true to Masaryk and practicaly you gain a lot more than when you reject everything from historical materialism" (Slovenský národný archív [Slovak National Archives] in Bratislava, V. Šrobár, no. 5, reg. no. 295 A. Štefánek to V. Šrobár on 25 July 1912).

work *Karol Marx—jeho život a dielo* [Karl Marx—His Life and Work]. Šrobár's view was rather naive and provided evidence that he understood the issue of Marxism only superficially. He connected it with the rise of industry and the exploitation of the working class. He was familiar with the example of a textile factory in Ružomberok. "The landowner using corporal punishment" was replaced by "a pot-bellied factory owner." Šrobár acknowledged the historic importance of Marx and for that reason this book about his life and views was supposed to become the "primer for Slovak Socialists" and an impulse for further analysis of social issues. He held the remarkable view that the publication of the *Communist Party Manifesto* in its full version was inadequate "when everyone is calling for the review of the programme. However, as a historical document it is of great significance, and a complete understanding of the social programme without any knowledge of this programme is meaningless."[50] In the conclusion Štrobár stressed that Slovak socialism's future lay only through the education of Slovak workers, which was all the more important since the level of education of the so-called intelligentsia was "poorer than poor."

The conflict arising from Šrobár's lecture, however, had yet another, wider polemical context. In 1913 arguments about the significance of religion, which had been continually put forward by the Catholic priest and philosopher František Jehlička against the Social Democrats, were resurrected. Once again he loaded his weapons and spoke out against the Social Democrats, albeit under a pseudonym which was widely associated with him. He wrote a pamphlet entitled *Sociáldemokracia a náboženstvo* [Social Democracy and Religion]. Following bitter confessional arguments within the Slovak political elite, it was not published in Martin, nor was it published in *Národné noviny* either. In his pamphlet he defended the existence of God and spoke out against the Slovak Social Democrats' assertion that religion was the private matter of every individual. He argued against the calls for separating the Church from the state, claiming that religion instils virtues in citizens and is therefore crucial for the state. He called for the combining of science and religious morality.[51]

Shortly afterwards a reply was published under the same title, with the author writing under a pseudonym. The reply clearly states that "religion and science were created by man" and it returns to the essential relationship between science and religion, between science and faith. The fundamental difference consists in the fact that while religion declares incontrovertible truths (dogmas), science attributes only relative value to the truth. The relationship between the Church and science is irreconcilable and both values are incompatible. The author adopted the tolerant attitude of Social Democracy towards believers as well as non-believers, pointing out the common features as well as differences between the teachings of Christ and the religion of the early Christians and socialism. Similarly, another typical component of the Social Democratic ideological arsenal pointed to the deviation of the Church hierarchy from Christian teachings. The morality of the Church sanctified the existing unjust social order. The Social Democratic

---

50. Kacirovaný [Šrobár, V.], "Oceňme si osvetovú prácu," *Robotnícke noviny*, vol. 10, no. 18, May 1, 1913.

51. Pater Salesius [Jehlička, F.], *Sociáldemokracia a náboženstvo*.

author then concentrated on morality and its social roots, the function of public opinion within it, as well as the relationship between ethical and legal norms. His conclusion pointed to the immorality of the Church as "morality at present can only be ascribed to something that helps in the pursuit of freedom, justice and equality for mankind . . . the Church, by helping slave owners and by being a slave owner and exploiter itself, is an immoral institution."[52] Social Democracy and its teachings are moral because their goal is the happiness of a majority of people, and its efforts are rooted in the misery of the exploited. As opposed to this, social egotism involves satisfying one's needs at the expense of one's neighbour and is the primary cause of immoral behaviour. It will lose its raison d'etre with the abolition of private ownership.

The author of the work remained unknown until the end of 1914. In December 1914 the master bricklayer Jozef Fašjank was sentenced to three months in prison and fined 400 crowns for "rebelling against the clergy." He was accused of writing the above mentioned polemical pamphlet under the pseudonym Xaver Rozkošný in reaction to the treatise by František Jehlička (written under the pseudonym Páter Salesius) *Sociálna demokracia a náboženstvo* [Social Democracy and Religion]. Fašjank's barrister, the Social Democrat and lawyer Hugo Matzner, unsuccessfully argued that Jehlička's treatise was full of rebellion against Social Democracy, and, in addition, that the "clergy" as such did not exist. Fašjank allegedly only spoke out against "bad priests."[53] In actual fact, it was highly improbable for the aforementioned master bricklayer to be part of such ideological circles. Today we know that Jozef Fašjank only assumed responsibility for the authorship of the pamphlet under the same title, *Sociálna demokracia a náboženstvo* [Social Democracy and Religio], and the real author of which was the aforementioned Czech Social Democrat, Edmund Borek. In the years before the First World War he had become the best prepared and most erudite Social Democratic publicist, capable of engaging in an argument with the university-educated Jehlička.

The polemical discussion concerning the relationship between Social Democracy and religion was not limited only to Jehlička and Borek. Another participant, supported by Spolok sv. Vojtecha [The Society of St Adalbert] and representing the Christian Socialists was Štefan Kmeť. Although he was a graduate of the Pázmáneum in Vienna and a doctor of theology, he summarized Jehlička's views in a didactic manner, and from the standpoint of religious philosophy reiterated the traditional stereotypes concerning the relationship with the Social Democrats.[54]

Another important figure of Christian socialism in the period prior to the First World War was the priest and long-standing member of the Hungarian Parliament (1906–1918) Ferdiš Juriga. Despite the fact that his main basis was Austrian Christian socialism, to begin with his ideological views did not differ substantially from those of Jehlička. Unlike Jehlička, Juriga systematically aimed at the mutual dependence of

---

52. Xaver Rozkošný [Borek, E.], *Sociálna demokracia a náboženstvo*, 25. It was being published to continue from the beginning of July till the end of September 1913 in *Robotnícke noviny*.

53. "Chýrnik," *Robotnícke noviny*, vol. 11, no. 16, April 16, 1914 and no. 42, October 15, 1914; "Zo súdnej siene," *Robotnícke noviny*, vol. 11, no. 51, December 18, 1914.

54. Špaňodolinec [Kmeť, Š.], *Sociálny demokratismus a kresťanské náboženstvo*.

Catholic and national ideas, and he was capable of being critical of the Church hierarchy as well as of Magyarization within the Church. A journalistically skilful style, colloquial language, accessible style and often populist ideas made him a much clearer author compared to Jehlička's academic style. In spite of his ideas he remained a Slovak and a priest. That did not prevent him from working with the Social Democrats, especially in the political sphere (e.g., in the struggle for universal suffrage). The ambivalent attitude of the Social Democrats towards him had its roots in a specific speech and activity. For example, during his speech in Malacky at the end of May 1909, he was criticized by *Robotnícke noviny* for his joviality and primitive jokes, which could no longer attract people's attention: "You should have seen how attentively the people listened when the sentence slipped out of Juriga's mouth that religion was a private matter of conscience for each individual, and that misery did not come from God but people." [55] Obviously, it was only a matter of time before a conflict arose.

On 10 September 1911 Juriga delivered a speech at a convention in Devínska Nová Ves together with the Social Democrats Ferdinand Benda and Štefan Príkopa. It was here that he met his match as the socialists harshly criticized the politicians and MPs representing ethnic minorities, and those present (probably mostly workers) vocally expressed their dissatisfaction with Juriga's speech: "Juriga was discredited, he responded to the compelling criticism with ridiculous arguments, and if he hadn't managed to extend his speech until the arrival of a church procession, the "enthusiastic" audience might have booted good old Juriga out . . . He tried to save his reputation and remove the bad impression by using demagogy and jokes."[56] It was the interesting connection of a Social Democratic and religious event which may have saved Juriga as a priest. He chose not to take part in another Social Democratic convention one week later in Stupava, which was all the more intriguing since it was his electoral district. Or perhaps because of that . . . Equally interesting, however, in that period were the articles about Juriga published in the Social Democratic *Robotnícke noviny*: "Juriga himself was the greatest progressive imaginable, especially among priests. He described quite openly, even in front of priests, the cult of Mary as feminism in the Church . . . He said more than once that he was ashamed of having to take money from a poor stupid peasant for mass or a funeral . . . Juriga never wears a cassock because it is . . . a sign of slavery. None of us have ever had such revolutionary ideas about the bishops and the Church order as Juriga, and when we interviewed him, what a liberal and a progressive he was . . ." [57]

Juriga's inconsistency could not have found a better formulation. Every reader undoubtedly had to deal with the dilemma of how to treat and judge this figure. The Social Democrats came up with the solution to the problem in April 1912 when by means of an open letter they ended their cooperation with Juriga, accusing him of betrayal because of

---

55. "Prestaneme hrať divadlo?" *Robotnícke noviny*, vol. 6, no. 10, June 3, 1909.

56. "Dopisy." *Robotnícke noviny*, vol. 8, no. 39, September 28, 1911 and no. 41, October 12, 1911. Of course, the interpretation of *Slovenské ľudové noviny* was different ("Dopisy," *Slovenské ľudové noviny*, vol. 2, no. 37, September 15, 1911).

57. "S barvou von!" *Robotnícke noviny*, vol. 8, no. 40, October 5, 1911.

"religious and political intolerance of the worst kind."[58] Juriga found himself in a maelstrom, or better put, he himself was swirling and escalating partisan and confessional discords in which the worker's press actively participated.

Like the Catholic Church, the Evangelical Church also adopted a disapproving stance towards Social Democracy, which was evident especially in the conservatively oriented *Cirkevné listy* [Church Paper]. This claim is confirmed by a review of a work by the Evangelical priest Ladislav Záturecký (László Zathureczky) *Szocializmus és reformáció* [Socialism and Reformation] (Nitra, 1917). According to Záturecký, there is no difference between the goals of socialism and the Church. On the other hand, not everyone identified themselves with such a concept, and it was not uncommon to come across a deliberately primitive interpretation of Social Democratic ideas. One such case was Juraj Janoška's speech at a convention in March 1918 which *Robotnícke noviny* felt compelled to object to. In spite of this no conflicts arose in practice which would be comparable to the conflicts between Catholicism and Social Democracy, perhaps due to the fact that Evangelical priests did not enter the political arena and conflicts to the same extent as Catholic priests.

The aforementioned Ján Lajčiak, like Záturecký, emphasised the role of reformation and its two elements: the negative one being resistance to all the pressures and the darkness, and the positive one being "the creation of a new, better life corresponding to the principles of Christianity as well as the struggle for the just social status of mankind corresponding to the principles of the teachings of Christ."[59] Every scientific field deems progress important and this applies to theology in full measure.

The Slovak Social Democrats departed from their original standpoint of avoiding the question of religion to formulating a clear standpoint that religion, the Church and priests in particular, along with their tools (clericalism and Christian socialism), guaranteed the prevalence of intellectual backwardness and obscurantism: "A Christian is the name of the successful product of the clerical mind. Here you shall find the same wickedness and so much more, because these toll collectors of human stupidity do their best to keep the folk ignorant, to keep them in the dark, and therefore, they spread myths and bigotry among the ignorant folk . . ."[60]

To counteract this, the education of the workers could have helped, as education was one of the key requirements. Due to the large number of articles written one thesis began to sound like a chorus—education is a superpower and a weapon that can't be taken away. The state and Church schools were used for Magyarization or for spreading religion and so there was a call for the democratization of education in the mother tongue. Until then education had been mainly provided by the worker's press and journalism. The Slovak workers were also encouraged in this direction by some Czech Social Democrats (František Tomášek, František Václav Krejčí) and by some figures from Czech culture (e.g., Karel Havlíček Borovský or Josef Svatopluk Machar).

58. "Sociálni demokrati z Dev. N. Vsi F. Jurigovi . . ." *Robotnícke noviny*, vol. 9, no. 17, April 26, 1912. To this also "Vrchol bezočivosti," *Robotnícke noviny*, vol. 9, no. 12, March 21, 1912.

59. Lajčiak, *Slovensko a kultúra*, 106.

60. "Slovo k robotníckej mládeži," *Slovenské robotnícke noviny*, vol. 2, no. 9, September 1, 1905.

Social Democratic journalism gradually formed the view that a person had science at his disposal, which enabled him to rule over natural forces, but he was still not able to control production and technological progress was turning against the proletariat. One would become a real master of the world only with the help of socialism.[61]

The relationship between science and religion can be characterized by the verses written by Jaroslav Vrchlický which were published in *Robotnícke noviny* [The Worker's Newspaper] on the occasion of his death: [62]

> The poison of the wrath from the forefathers in your blood
> Try to soften by love to which Christ challenges you
> And the truth, Darwin has already read in nature,
> Never more would grow into a poisonous flower.

An open question and topic for further consideration is the fact that reinforcing national identity also brings the sacralization of the nation, which also delays secularization. Generalizing this idea for a Slovak model still remains a topic for professional discussion.

In conclusion let us return to Janko Kosák who was engaged in a final conversation with God. Kosák asked God where he had come from and God answered: "I can't tell you that as I myself don't know the answer. I can only tell you that I am nature, that is to say, matter in eternal motion. Matter has always been here, is here and will be here forever. All matter is the world. So it means that I am the world." And then Kosák says: "I can't see you any more; I can just see the world!" God: "So now you can see clearly, that is who I really am." Kosák: "And where is heaven?" God: "It was only in your imagination, poor fellow." And at that moment Kosák came out of his coma by the grace of God just in time to take part in the funeral of the priest who had also been hit by the lightning, but the priest did not receive the same grace.[63]

There is evidence that this text about Janko Kosák was seditious as can be seen by the reaction of one embittered reader: ". . . I was thunder-struck by the boundless wrath, by how terribly it was written . . . it includes so much immorality, so many faithless thoughts, so much disregard for God, it is an arrogant and destructive pamphlet . . ." According to the writer, workers in particular need God. The writer characteristically highlighted his arguments when he wrote that "a man would be pleased if he knew that after this difficult life he would be able to look forward to the after-life."[64]

61. "Jaroslav Vrchlický," *Robotnícke noviny*, vol. 9, no. 37, September 12, 1912.

62. Chlumecký, *Janko Kosák v nebi*, 32–33.

63. Ibid., 32–33.

64. Archív Spolku sv. Vojtecha [Archives Society of St. Adalbert's Archives] in Trnava, fasc. 148, no. 14, Schwarz, V.: Odpoveď A. Horváthovi a V. Chlumeckému na dielo Janko Kosák v nebi. Podbrezová 1919, pp. 1 and 4.

PART TWO

Politics and Party Line

5

The Anti-Clericalism of Social Democracy and the Secularization of the Working Class in the Czech Lands

Jiří Malíř

Extracting the Roman blood from the veins of the workers, combating clerical politicians and undermining the bastion of the Church are vital parts of the work of socialism today.

—*Hlas lidu* [Voice of the People], vol. 25, July 2, 1910

O NE FACTOR IN THE modernization process in the Czech lands over the "long" nineteenth century was the changing role of religion and the Church in society. The ongoing process of secularization affected all groups in society to different degrees and it is evident that the relationship towards religion and the Church was of particular relevance among the working class. In the Habsburg monarchy, as in the rest of Europe, the critical approach of a significant section of the working class towards religion and the Church was one of the fundamental standpoints on which the Social Democrats based their programme and their attitudes as well as their "proletarian identity." The question remains whether and to what extent the critical position of the Social Democrat working class towards the Church and religion[1] differed from the positions of other strata of society at the time. The actual process, character, level and scope of working-class secularization within the Czech lands have still to be properly researched. There is little in the way of Czech literature addressing this theme prior to 1989 and it suffers from a Marxist bias,[2] although even within the framework of Marxist historiography there was research into the workers' movement which is applicable to this theme.[3] The work of foreign writers has also been important, even though their main interest has been in the relationship

---

1. Unless otherwise stated, the text always refers to the Catholic religion and the Catholic Church, which were the most widespread throughout the Czech lands and the Cisleithania.

2. See, for example, Černý et al., *Církve v našich dějinách*; *Náboženství, církve, klerikalismus a naše dějiny*.

3. See Kořalka, "Ateismus průkopníků socialismu," 22–43; Kraváček, "Katolická církev a dělnické hnutí na Moravě před první světovou válkou," 93–115; Galandauer, "Poměr Bohumíra Šmerala k náboženské otázce," 215–20; Galandauer, "Die Relation der Bildungspolitik," 295–302.

between the nation and the Church.[4] After 1989 the renewed interest in religious history could be seen in research themes which were important for the relationship between the working class and religion, such as political Catholicism,[5] Catholic modernism,[6] changes in spirituality,[7] the secularization of society,[8] the religious position of Germans in the Czech lands[9] and other themes, including the difficult relationship between the nation and religious denominations.[10]

In order to understand the secularization of the working class in the Czech lands it is important to be aware that this process took place in a divided social, cultural, national and economic context and was therefore necessarily influenced by many factors. Among them were the specific conditions which distinguished the secularization process in the Habsburg monarchy as well as the operation of strong lines of conflict which divided society, not only in its relationship towards the role of the Church in public life, but also nationally. The differences in character, establishment and development of the working class in the Habsburg monarchy and its constituent parts were also very significant.

Therefore, in the following interpretation there will first of all be an outline of the specific conditions for the secularization process in the Czech lands and in the Habsburg monarchy as a whole and then a programmatic view of the relationship of Social Democracy to the Church and religion; this will be followed by a look at how anti-ecclesiastical and anti-religious sentiments spread in the Czech lands in the 1860s–1890s with the aim of finding the connections and differences between liberal anti-clericalism and the anti-clericalism of Social Democracy. As to the basic question concerning the extent to which the anti-clerical position of Social Democracy was original, consistent and relevant for strengthening secularizing tendencies in a working-class setting, an answer will be attempted on the basis of an analysis of the anti-clerical stances of the Czech Social Democrats in the Czech lands from 1900–1914 with an emphasis on Moravia. Apart from the findings of the rather modest literature to date on the subject, it is possible to examine not only the programmes of the Social Democrats, but in particular its press, anti-clerical pamphlets, memoirs and other materials.

4. Blaschke, "Verbandkatholizismus in Mähren-Schlesien," 250–61; Schmid-Egger, *Klerus und Politik in Böhmen um 1900*; Hrubý, "Kirche und Arbiter," 258–68; Huber, "Nation und Kirche 1848–1918," 246–57; Huber, "Die Encyklika," 241–59; Kovács, "Die katholische Kirche im Spannungsfeld," 49–62.

5. Marek, *Český katolicismus 1890-1914*; Fiala et al., *Český politický katolicismus 1848-2005*; Marek, *Teorie a praxe politického katolicismu 1870-2007*.

6. Marek, *Apologetové nebo kacíři?*; Marek, *Česká katolická moderna*.

7. Hojda and Prahl, *Bůh a bohové*; Kaiserová and Mikulec and Šebek, *Srdce Ježíšovo*; Nešpor, *Náboženství na prahu nové doby*.

8. Kudláč, *Příběh(y) Volné myšlenky*; Fasora and Hanuš and Malíř. *Sekularizace českých zemí v letech 1848-1914*; *Sekularizace venkovského prostoru*.

9. Kaiserová, *Konfesní myšlení českých Němců*; Šebek, *Mezi křížem a národem*.

10. Schulze Wessel, "Tschechische Nation und katholische Konfession," 311–27; Schulze Wessel, "Vyznání a národ v českých zemích," 126–131; Jaworski, "Konfession als Faktor nationaler Identifikationsprozesse," 131–47; Schulze Wessel and Zückert, *Handbuch der Religions- und Kirchengeschichte*.

THE SPECIFICITY OF THE SECULARIZATION PROCESS WITHIN THE MONARCHY AND THE CZECH LANDS IN THE 19TH CENTURY

The character of secularization in the nineteenth century was determined by the medieval process of the division of the spiritual and secular worlds, and in the case of the Habsburg monarchy this emancipation of state and political power from the power of the Church led to a clear submission of the Church to state authority.[11] On the other hand, the state always needed the Catholic Church and always stood by it, even during the cultural struggle ("Kulturkampf"), linked as it was by the celebrated "union of the throne and the altar." It was the interference of Emperor Joseph II in Church affairs that greatly undermined the Church and led to it becoming a servant of the state.[12] The closure of monasteries and confiscation of Church property were not designed to destroy the Church but to provide it with a new role. The priest was to become a state bureaucrat and from the fund created from the seized monasteries a general seminary was to be financed where priests would be trained. Joseph's reforms did not cast doubt on religion or the Church as such, but rather viewed them in a different manner which suited the state better. The second well-known event which stood on the threshold of the secularization process in the Habsburg monarchy in the nineteenth century was the Patent of Toleration, which was the first, albeit modest, acknowledgment of a multi-faith monarchy.[13] Even though the Patent of Toleration of 1781 did not grant equal rights to the minority religions, but only began to officially tolerate some of them, the process towards equal rights for all religions had nevertheless begun. The principle of toleration was gradually replaced by the principle of equal rights. However, the Catholic Church remained a supporter of the dynasty and the state, while its standing in society was also incomparably stronger than was the case for other religions. The spread of religious tolerance and equality for the various churches led in Europe to a movement away from monoconfessional states towards multi-faith states, or rather non-religious states, and this was true for Catholic, Protestant and Orthodox states. In the case of the Austrian empire the state remained in principle Catholic despite the considerable variety of religions.[14]

The state authorities looked to the Catholic Church for support in the struggle with liberalism and revolutionary forces. This revealed itself in the post-Josephine development of the monarchy, particularly with the rule of Francis I (1792–1835), when, as a reaction to the French Revolution and the Napoleonic Wars and the national and civic emancipation movements, internal policy was based on Metternich's absolutism and foreign policy on the Holy Alliance, which were to become the mainstays of the Habsburg's celebrated union of "throne and altar." After the revolutionary interlude from 1848–1849 the 50-year period of neo-absolutism greatly strengthened the symbiosis of the state and the Catholic Church. In order to maintain domestic harmony and control,

11. Most recently in Georgiev, "Mezi svéprávností a poručnictvím," 169–85; Marek, "Církev a česká společnost," 143–54; Malíř, "Sekularizace a politika v 'dlouhém' 19. století," 11–24.

12. Winter, *Der Josefinismus und seine Geschichte*; Kovács, *Katholische Aufklärung und Josephinismus*; Huber, "Der Josephinismus und die staats-kirchliche Reformprogramm," 223–30.

13. Molnár and Smolík, *Čeští evangelíci a toleranční patent*; Melmuková, *Patent zvaný toleranční*.

14. See Wandruszka and Urbanitsch, *Die Habsburgermonarchie 1848–1918*, vol. IV.

the state looked to the Church for support with the signing of an accord with the Vatican (Concordat of 1855) on the basis of which the Catholic Church was given a series of powers both in the public sphere and education in particular.

With the establishment of parliamentarianism and constitutionality within the monarchy and with the rise of national emancipation movements, following the acceptance of the laws on churches in 1868 and 1874 there came about the formal dissolution of the Concordat and the granting of equal rights to all religions.[15] However, in spite of this the actual standing of the Catholic Church in the western part of the monarchy remained central and a complete separation of the Church from the state never occurred. The famed union of throne and altar was to survive, albeit under different conditions and in a changed form, practically until the end of the monarchy. This was not even altered by the Austrian version of the "Kulturkampf," which was tame in comparison to the German cultural struggle and had a different dimension and character. Whereas in Germany the cultural struggle was in the main between the national state and the church, represented by two strong Christian denominations, within the monarchy and the Czech lands in particular it was mainly between the nationally structured societies and the Catholic Church, which was identified with the state. Religious differences did not play a significant role in the Czech lands; instead national interests were at the forefront and national motives also became part of the background to attitudes towards the Catholic Church, which was the dominant church here. According to Martin Schulz Wessel, the dual nationalism in the Czech lands was comparable with the dual denominationalism in Germany.[16] Religion in the Czech lands did not play the national role which it played elsewhere, for example in the Balkans, and Catholicism was not to play the national emancipatory role it did in Poland, even though the Catholic Church in the Czech lands was much better represented amongst the population than was the case in the Polish state.[17]

The relationship between the state and the Catholic Church in the Habsburg monarchy took on a new dimension in the second half of the nineteenth century as a result of the strengthening of nationalism, which also significantly modified the secularization process in local multi-ethnic societies. Unlike the majority of countries in Europe, where the state ceased to be a religious state and a national state emerged in its place, in the Habsburg monarchy the search for a "substitute religion" in nationalism, or the search for another model of collective identity in identification with the nation state, was very difficult, if not impossible. The Habsburg Empire of the 19th century was not only a multi-faith state but also a multi-national one.[18] Therefore any attempts to create a unified Austrian national state were bound to run into opposition from the non-German national movements who were unable to identify with the idea that, due to the overwhelming cultural and linguistic dominance of the German elites, the Austrian monarchy should be a German state. However, unequivocal support for an Austrian na-

15. Vocelka, *Verfassung oder Konkordat?*; Georgiev, "Mezi svéprávností a poručnictvím," 169–85.

16. Schulze Wessel, "Tschechische Nation und katholische Konfession," 311–12.

17. Jaworski, "Konfession als Faktor nationaler Identifikationsprozesse," 131–47.

18. See Wandruszka and Urbanitsch, *Die Habsburgermonarchie 1848–1918*, vol. III/1–2.

tion state was not even provided by the Austrian Germans, whose linguistic, cultural and national ties and identification with Germans outside the Austrian monarchy were to continue even after the foundation of the German Empire in 1871. Owing to the difficulties in establishing national identification among the linguistically and ethnically divided populace of the monarchy, in an era of rising nationalism the state and the Church together with the traditionally strong dynasticism could provide one of the few means for the collective identification of the inhabitants of the western part of the monarchy (Cisleithania) with the state.

In the case of the Czech lands, which were mainly Catholic but with dual nationality[19], the Catholic Church's adherence to the state had the opposite effect, with Czech society reacting ever more strongly against it. In the first half of the nineteenth century the formation of the modern Czech nation had considerable support from the Catholic clergy and no conflict was seen between service to God and to the nation.[20] Even during the era of Austrian constitutionalism the Czech political elites did not stand against the Catholic forces; rather they joined with them in the fight against the prevalence of the German liberals. Gradually, however, the close symbiosis of the Catholic Church with the state brought it into ideological conflict with the Czech national movement, which was tending towards extreme historicism. The most important epochs in Czech history were seen as the Hussite period and the Czech Reformation, which Czech nationalist ideology credited as being of exclusively national significance. Due to the predominance of the liberal-nationalist concept of history the Catholic Church and the ruling anti-Czech elites were blamed for all of the Czechs' national losses and failures in the past, and more recently for their stance in the battle against the centralist state powers. Therefore, in the late nineteenth century Czech nationalist society began to perceive the Catholic Church as an oppressor of the nation and became increasingly alienated from it.

This was not due to fundamental changes in the religious persuasion of the population or because of an increase in atheism. The resistance of Czech society to Catholicism was not a majority position and it was not consistent; it was more often demonstrative and nationally inspired. This can be seen, for example, in the conversions to the Orthodox Church in connection with the wave of Czech Russophilia after the Russo-Turkish War of 1877, which were politically motivated,[21] or some aspects of the cultivation of the Cyril and Methodius tradition,[22] including proposals for the introduction of the Slavonic liturgy from the workshops of Czech liberals in Moravia.[23] The Czech anti-clericalism which was widespread in Czech liberal circles was shown to be quite superficial and

---

19. Kořalka, *Češi v habsburské říši a v Evropě 1815–1914*, 138–96.

20. Rak, "Dělníci na vinici Páně," 67–75.

21. The Young Czech leader Karel Sladkovský, amongst others, converted to the Orthodox Church. Tobolka, *Politické dějiny československého národa*, vol. 2, 353.

22. See Kolejka, "Cyrilometodějská tradice," 97–112; Machilek, "Welehrad und die Cyril-Method-Idee," 156–83; Machilek, "Velehrad ist uns Programm," 353–95.

23. For example, a meeting of the Lidová strana [People's Party] in Moravia accepted a resolution that in the spirit of the Cyril and Methodius tradition they would request the introduction of the Slavonic liturgy. See Malíř, *Vývoj liberálního proudu české politiky*, 96–97, 205–6.

seldom developed into atheism.[24] In this respect it also differed from the anti-clericalism which was common within the Social Democratic working-class setting, where there was a systematically critical and negative approach to the Church and religion for reasons other than national ones, which gradually developed into a permanently hostile attitude towards the Church and religion on the part of the working class.

SOCIAL DEMOCRATIC PROGRAMMES AND THE RELATIONSHIP TOWARDS THE CHURCH AND RELIGION

National interests were not the only motives which lay behind the critical reactions of Czech society towards the Catholic Church. An important source for the negative relationship towards the Church and religion throughout the course of the nineteenth century was the establishment of the civic principle in society. The Catholic Church was increasingly seen as an obstacle to liberal reforms and citizens' rights, and in liberal circles in particular anti-clerical feelings grew stronger. By the end of the century the observance of ecclesiastical and religious behaviour in everyday public life and its espousal in public began to be seen as a manifestation of clericalism, which was inconsistent with civic society—religious life was thus driven into the private sphere. Increased pressure was applied especially for the removal of the influence and standing of the Church in education, the state authorities and public life. Conflicts also increased over the actions of members of the clergy in public life—in non-religious associations, savings banks, etc—and in politics in particular. Steadfastly maintaining and defending the position of the Church in society began to be perceived as being irreconcilable with the civic principle. In a certain respect, therefore, civic and religious principles became estranged from one another. These attitudes were to be found in the German liberal camp in particular, but the Young Czechs and other sections of Czech politics—the Realists, Progressives, National Socials and later also the Agrarians—did not refrain from anti-clericalism, thus furthering the tendency towards secularization in Czech society.[25]

The socialist workers' movement, which from the 1860s–1890s had great difficulty in organizing and fighting for basic social and economic demands, was against national approaches, whether they came from the Czech or German middle classes, and therefore did not participate in the anti-Church and anti-religious movements which were motivated only by national factors. They were much closer to the anti-clerical position of the liberal sections of middle-class society, which developed from the establishment of basic civic rights and freedoms, including "freedom of conscience and equal rights for all religious persuasions,"[26] from which the working class also expected social freedoms.

24. Not even the Los-von-Rom movement, disseminated within the German national camp in the Czech lands mainly by pan-Germans, gained a mass character. See Kaiserová, *Konfesní myšlení českých Němců*, 79–124.

25. Significant in this regard was a pamphlet by Father Josef Hofer, where he defends the supporters of the Church against attacks by both the progressives and the Agrarians as well as the National Socials and the Social Democrats. Hofer, *Pokrokáři, agrárníci, sociální demokraté*.

26. See the policies of the Národní strana svobodomyslné [Young Czech Party] from 1874. Cibulka, *Politické programy českých národních stran*, 214.

It is possible to observe a basic programmatic overview of the relationship towards religion and the Church in the policy documents of the Social Democratic Workers' Party in Austria which were adopted at its conferences and meetings following its establishment in 1874. It was significant that the religious question did not merit priority and the main demands concerned addressing the social standing of the working class and gaining its civic and political emancipation. The attitude towards the Church and religion derived from the demand for an expansion of civic rights and for the transformation of the Austrian state into a democratic state, which would cancel the privileges of various groups of the population and institutions, including the Church, and would sever the long-term symbiosis of state and Church.

At the meeting in April 1874 in Neudörfl an der Leitha where the Social Democratic Workers' Party of Austria was founded, item three from a total of nine programme items demanded "the separation of the Church from the state and the separation of education from the Church."[27] The principle of dividing the state and the Church and freeing schools from Church supervision became a constant demand in all of the Social Democrat programmes that followed and was often supplemented with the statement that religion was a private matter.[28] The declaration that religion was a private matter was also contained in the programme which was agreed upon following the reconciliation between the radical and moderate wings of the Austrian Social Democratic Party at their conference in Brno-Lužánky in December 1887.[29]

The Social Democrats' policies towards the Church and religion remained the same up until the First World War, with only a refinement of some of their points. In particular they elaborated on the call for the separation of schools from the Church, with the aim that schools be removed from Church control and become entirely secular. The demand for non-religious education was one of the eight main principles of the policy programme which was adopted at the unifying congress of 1888–1889 in Hainfeld: "In the interests of the future of the working class it is an unconditional requirement to have compulsory, free and non-religious education at basic and general level, as well as free entry to all higher education institutions; an essential prerequisite for this is the separation of the Church from the state and the declaration that religion be made a private matter."[30]

The Hainfeld congress not only ended the divisions between the moderates and the radicals in the Austrian Social Democratic Party but also marked the beginning of its unprecedented organizational and political growth. During the 1890s Social Democracy greatly strengthened its organization and gradually became a relevant political force: thanks to Baden's electoral reform it entered the imperial parliament in Vienna in 1897 and after the introduction of universal suffrage in 1907 it became one of the strongest

27. Prokš, *Politické programy*, 13; Marek, *Šedesát let*, 32; Berchtold, *Österreichische Parteiprogramme*, 116.

28. Prokš, *Politické programy*, 17; Marek, *Šedesát let,* 40; Berchtold, *Österreichische Parteiprogramme*, 120.

29. Jordán, *Sjezd dělnictva českoslovanského v Brně*, 65.

30. Prokš, *Politické programy*, 28; Marek, *Šedesát let*, 67; Berchtold, *Österreichische Parteiprogramme*, 139.

political parties, particularly when, having started out as a protest opposition force, it gradually became a part of the parliamentary structure through its active politics.[31]

The emphasis which had been placed on education and its secularization in the Hainfeld programme was to a significant extent motivated by the ongoing political struggle over an imperial law which had been proposed to the Viennese parliament on January 25, 1888 by the leading representative of the German Christian Social Party in Cisleithania, Prince Alois Liechtenstein. The proposal aimed to cement the Church's position in education and was met with considerable resistance by freethinking forces and by the Social Democrats. Therefore a special resolution on general schooling was adopted in Hainfeld which stated:

> ... in consideration of the fact that ... the Social Democratic Workers' Party main-
> tains in its programme that education should be free for everyone at all levels
> of education, that there should be the complete separation of education and the
> Church, and the state and the Church ... and as Liechtenstein's proposal will re-
> move the meagre remnant of useful public education and the entire future of the
> youth will be unconditionally surrendered to that obscurantist enemy of culture
> and freedom, clericalism ... therefore today's congress declares: The working class
> holds the ruling classes responsible for the disgraceful attack on education which
> this unprecedented proposal attempts, and it will be resisted with the appropriate
> energy and indignation.[32]

Irrespective of the combative tone of the resolution, its content also betrays the deeper long-term concern of the Social Democrats that the youth who underwent a compulsory primary education in the monarchy should not be under the systematic influence of the Church in general schools and would therefore be more receptive to socialist ideas. In the majority of industrial centres and in Moravia in particular the workforce was to a large extent recruited from the surrounding rural areas; therefore, when trying to gain influence among the workers, the Social Democrats had for a long time been confronted with the predominant village mentality of the working class. In trying to inculcate social-ist ideas into the ranks of the working class, the largest obstacle they came across was the village priest and his influence over the local community and in particular the working-class youth who were educated at a school under the guardianship of the local priest.

It is therefore no wonder that the Czech Social Democrats in particular, being part of the federalized Austrian Social Democrats, paid significant attention in their programme not only to the idea of non-religious schooling but also to restricting the influence of the Church in the community affairs of the village. In policy resolution 4 of the Congress of the Czechoslavonic Social Democratic Workers' Party in České Budějovice in September 1900, alongside the section "Social Democrats and Schools," in which was declared "the complete separation of education and the Church," there was also a detailed section on "Social Democrats in the Village." The subsection entitled "The Village and the Church" requested that: "The representatives refrain from any kind of subsidy or support for

---

31. Brügel, *Geschichte der österreichischen Sozialdemokratie*; Mommsen, *Die Sozialdemokratie und die Nationalitätenfrage*; Kořalka, "Československá sociálně demokratická strana dělnická," 213–39.

32. Prokš, *Politické programy*, 31; Berchtold, *Österreichische Parteiprogramme*, 143–44.

buildings or businesses which are to serve the purposes of any religion or church. Also, refrain from any administrative speeches which would place some religion or church above others. Religion is to be a private matter and so, for this reason, institutions and schools have to be administered in this way."[33]

Apart from the systematic interest of the Social Democrats in the establishment of education without religious influence, there was also a heightened interest in the demand for the separation of the Church from the state. In the first years of the twentieth century this was aimed at the specific area of Church and religious organizations and at matrimonial law. In the final pan-imperial policy programme which was adopted at the 8th congress of the Social Democratic Workers' Party in Vienna in November 1901, apart from the usual demands—the declaration that religion was a private matter, the separation of the Church from the state and the introduction of secular schools—there were new demands: "the declaration of Church and religious societies as private gatherings, administering their affairs independently; compulsory civic wedding."[34]

All of these positions towards the issue of religion and the Church remained a consistent part of the policy arsenal of Social Democracy, even at a time when the Social Democrats were much more intensively involved with the national issue and demands for the introduction of universal suffrage and when the gulf between the clerical and non-clerical political forces in the monarchy was increasingly widening.

In a cursory comparison of the official policy documents of the Social Democratic Party in the Habsburg monarchy with the quote from the introduction, it is interesting that the policy items which touch upon religious issues were not formulated as openly anti-religious or anti-Church attitudes. Their overall phrasing did not correspond with the aggressive tone of the propaganda speeches or the sharp clashes which were part of the final decades of the Habsburg monarchy on the political scene, in publications and in everyday public life, and which even encroached upon the private lives of individuals. The content and direction of the Social Democratic policy principles in relation to the Church and religion did not differ greatly from the programmes of the liberal and progressive parties. Therefore the question remains whether in public life the declared anti-clericalism of the Social Democratic working class corresponded with the anti-clericalism which was widespread throughout the non-working-class strata of society, or rather whether, to what degree and in what respect it differed.

ANTI-CLERICALISM IN MIDDLE-CLASS AND WORKING-CLASS SETTINGS UNTIL THE END OF THE NINETEENTH CENTURY

Critical attitudes towards the Church motivated by the establishment of civic rights were especially prevalent in the German liberal camp, but the struggle against clericalism as a brake on the development of a free civic society also took place in the Czech lands in the second half of the nineteenth century.[35] It was led by freethinking individuals such as the

33. Prokš, *Politické programy*, 53, 55.

34. *Protokol o jednání společného sjezdu*, 7.

35. Vocelka, "Staat und Kirche, 74–90; Vocelka, *Verfassung oder Konkordat?* For the Czech setting, compare Znoj et al. *Český liberalismus*; Kudláč, *Příběh(y) Volné myšlenky*.

journalist and writer Karel Havlíček (1821–1856), the philosopher and priest Augustin Smetana (1814–1851) and the pioneer of women's emancipation Vojta Náprstek (1826–1894), who, due to their critical attitudes towards the Church, were either persecuted or forced to emigrate after 1848.[36]

With the resumption of institutional life in the 1860s and 1870s, the critical position towards the Catholic Church became a common element in the ideological propaganda of the Young Czechs, which in 1874 transformed into the Národní strana svobodomyslná (Mladočeská strana) [Young Czech Party]. The Young Czechs turned against the leaders of the Národní strana [National Party] (the Old Czechs), which under the leadership of František Palacký and František L. Rieger, as a result of its long-term political alliance with the conservative aristocracy, moved away from its original liberal principles and maintained good relations with the Czech clergy and the Church hierarchy. The Young Czechs were against "preferential treatment for Ultramontanist and reactionary elements,"[37] and anti-Catholic rhetoric, combined with a condemnation of the role of the Catholic Church in Czech history, became a routine part of their press and public activities. The main critics of the Catholic Church and its role in society were the Young Czech politicians and journalists such as Julius Grégr and his brother Eduard, Jan Neruda, Josef Barák and Alfons Šťastný, who were grouped around the most widely read newspaper of the time, Národní listy [National News].[38]

The resistance to the Catholic Church in Young Czech circles was mainly motivated by nationalist reasons and only in a very small number of cases was the anti-clerical criticism broadened to promote atheism. This course was mainly represented by the fortnightly paper Svoboda [Freedom], which was published in Prague from 1867–1873 by J. Barák and then A. Šťastný. As a student of natural science and later a farmer and a unique thinker, in his copious journalistic and organizational activities Šťastný promoted the requirement that Church dogma should be subject to detailed independent research and analysis using simple reason. Šťastný put forward this demand for free, independent thought (from which came the name Volná myšlenka [Free Thought] for the entire atheist movement) in countless pamphlets in which he critically challenged several Church dogmas—Dekret o neomylnosti papeže římského a jeho význam praktický [The decree on the infallibility of the Pope and its practical significance]; O spasení po smrti [On salvation after death]; K otázce školní [On the issue of education] etc. Then in 1874, in the spirit of free thinking, he established the Spolek volných myslitelů [Association of Freethinkers] in Prague.[39]

---

36. After 1848 Náprstek spent 10 years in the USA, Havlíček was forced into exile in Brixen, Smetana was forbidden from teaching either at the university in Prague or in secondary schools, and when he left the Church in 1850 he was excommunicated. See Morava, C. k. disident Karel Havlíček; Šolle, Vojta Náprstek a jeho doba; Šnebergová, Augustin Smetana.

37. Viz Cibulka, Politické programy českých národních stran, 224. Overview: Garver, The Young Czech Party; Vojtěch, Mladočeši a boj o politickou moc.

38. Vošahlíková and Řepa, Bratři Grégrové a česká společnost.

39. Zubek, Tradice protináboženského a protiklerikálního boje; Kudláč, Příběh(y) Volné myšlenky, 15.

A significant section of the working class sympathized with these liberally motivated anti-clerical positions and contributed to their expansion. This was already the case at the start of the socialist workers' movement in the Czech lands when the suppression of the 1848 revolution and the installation of a neo-absolutist regime in the 1850s strengthened the conviction among many workers that the Catholic Church was a mainstay of the conservative governing system in the Habsburg monarchy and was partly to blame for its backwardness and rigidity. The conviction that the Church's position within the state was one of the reasons for the slow introduction of political and social reforms and national demands after the re-establishment of constitutionality in Austria in 1861 only deepened within the socialist workers' movement. That is why the liberal-led fight against the Concordat and for the introduction of the church laws of 1868 as well as the negative reaction of the freethinking section of the public to the declaration of papal infallibility in 1870 were met with the sympathy and support of the working class. A number of years ago the Czech historian Jiří Kořalka showed that although the anti-Church attitude of the early working-class movement in the Czech lands developed in close connection with the anti-clerical activities of the liberals, by the 1870s and 1880s it had already begun to develop different characteristics from liberal anti-clericalism.[40]

Anti-clerical demonstrations occurred amongst the working class in the 1860s and 1870s in the most economically developed areas of North Bohemia, with the centres being in Liberec and Prague, where the workers' movement was most developed. In the 1860s a particular chord was struck among the working class in Prague by anti-clerical articles in the Czech press and demonstrations at so-called "camps" which were organized as great Czech national open-air displays and whose speakers, under the influence of Czech national ideology, proclaimed themselves Hussites as a symbol of freedom and attacked the Catholic Church as the cause of the nation's bleak situation, both in history and at present.[41]

Supporters from the ranks of the working class also discovered the anti-clerical activities of the radical Young Czechs, of whom the aforementioned A. Šťastný received the most attention from the working-class press for his atheist articles and pamphlets against "Catholic obscurantism," as well as his attempts to set up a freethinkers' society.

The newspaper *Dělnické noviny* [Workers' News] published several of Šťastný's articles and enclosed his atheist pamphlets, praising their appeal to reason and conception of man as a natural being. And many of the people who joined the Association of Freethinkers founded by him in Prague in 1874 were workers.[42]

The predominantly German working class in North Bohemia also joined in anti-Church activities, which after the declaration of the dogma of papal infallibility in 1870 were bound up with the movement leaving the Catholic Church to join the newly formed Old Catholic Church. The local workers subscribed in large numbers to the newspaper *Nemesis*, which was published in neighboring Saxony and whose attacks on priests and agitation to leave the Church found fertile ground with them—at the head of the com-

---

40. Kořalka, "Ateismus průkopníků socialismu," 22–43.

41. Purš, "Tábory v českých zemích v letech," 234–66, 446–70, 661–90.

42. Zubek, *Tradice protináboženského a protiklerikálního boje*, 7–12.

mittee of freethinkers in Liberec in 1871 was the Social Democrat Anton Fledl. Therefore, from the 1870s a combative form of anti-clericalism and atheism began to be part of the socialist ideology of the North Bohemian socialist workers.[43]

Anti-clerical positions took on new dimensions both within and outwith the working class in the Czech lands and the whole of Cisleithania in the 1880s. In European free-thinking circles there was a negative reaction to the activities of the Church following the Vatican Council and the declaration of papal infallibility. This was manifested most clearly by the Kulturkampf (cultural struggle) in Germany in the 1870s and the establishment of the Free Thought federation of atheists in Brussels in 1880. In Cisleithania this tension was heightened after the existing government of German liberals was replaced by the conservative government of Eduard Taaffe (1879–1893), which opened up far greater scope for clerical aspirations. The conflict was magnified by the successful attempt by the Catholic forces to reform the existing liberal education laws in 1883 and by the politicization of the Catholic movement. Pope Leo XIII's *Rerum Novarum* encyclical of 1891 was another trigger, awakening the Christian-Social movement and the general participation of the clergy in political life.[44]

Within the socialist workers' movement, which in the 1870s had organized itself into the Social Democratic party, anti-clerical positions were an inseparable part of the propaganda machinery. Czech Social Democratic newspapers such as *Budoucnost* [The Future], *Pravda* [The Truth], *Právo* [Justice] and *Organizace* [Organization], along with their German counterparts *Sozialpolitische Rundschau* [Social-Political Observer] and *Arbeiterfreund* [Friend of the Worker], strongly opposed religion and the Church for their alleged hunger for power, vices and dereliction of their original duties, and described the conflict between faith and science. At the same time they also aimed their sights at specific Church initiatives, such as those manifested in the papal encyclicals, at their Christian socialist rivals and the battle over the increasing influence of the Church in education.[45] However, in this regard they did not differ greatly from the anti-clerical positions of the liberal German and Young Czech press.

However, there were a few differences in the anti-clericalism of the Social Democrats. The main difference was the emphasis placed on a criticism of the Church and religion based on scientific knowledge and education in general, which was linked to the expansion of atheism. In North Bohemia in particular at the end of the 1870s there was another significant move away from the Church and new attempts at organizing individual atheists.[46] For example, the Association of Atheists in Liberec was denied official approval, while atheists from the ranks of the Social Democrats, with Franz König and Ferdinand Schwarz as leaders, formed a network of contacts in North Bohemia, shared atheist publications and literature among themselves and carried out non-religious funerals. Their appeal, which was published at the end of 1881 in the *Arbeiterfreund* [Worker's Friend] newspaper in Liberec addressed "To atheists" and which was also printed by other Social

---

43. Kořalka, "Ateismus průkopníků socialismu," 27.

44. For the Christian-Social movement see Knoll, *Zur Tradition der christlichsozialen Partei*.

45. Kořalka, "Ateismus průkopníků socialismu," 35–37.

46. Kořalka, "Ateismus průkopníků socialismu," 38–39.

Democratic newspapers in Cisleithania and Transleithania, led to the establishment of many contacts in various parts of the monarchy, notably with Eduard Schwella, a participant at the 1880 International Congress of Free Thought in Brussels and founder of the Svobodná církev rozumu [Free Church of Reason] in Vienna. [47] A section of the North Bohemian Social Democrats subsequently joined this atheist organization in 1882.

The Social Democratic workers' membership of Schwella's atheist Svobodná církev rozumu [Free Church of Reason], as with Šťastný's Spolek volných myslitelů [Association of Freethinkers] in Prague, indicates the atheist movement's connection with the working-class and non-working-class strata. However, at the same time it showed the differences in the understanding of anti-clericalism between the Social Democrats and critics of religion from the liberal middle class. Whilst Schwella emphasized the inner convictions of each individual when entering his atheist organization, the Social Democrats expected that his Free Church of Reason would help in the fight against clericalism in areas concerning the overall situation of the workers.[48] In contrast to atheism among the non-working-class, which at the time was mostly a sign of individualism and a distancing from the ignorant and uneducated masses, the Social Democrats strove to link atheism and the awakening of the working class with the attempt to tackle all their other needs. They referred to the danger of separating the atheist movement from solving social issues and other goals of the workers' movement: "Religious freedom must come after national economic freedom, which brings with it a general improvement in education. Of what use is it to the worker who is hungry and lives in subservience? First give him bread and then his religious convictions will change thanks to the influence of a free society and prosperity."[49] The question of the extent to which the atheist movement was in accord with the overall aims of Social Democracy was not answered at that time. The union of the atheist movement and all anti-religious manifestations in the working class with the atheist movement in other social strata continued even in the following period of 1890–1914, as did the arguments over the prioritizing of atheism at the expense of the other aims of Social Democracy.

Social Democracy's search for a role for anti-clericalism and atheism clearly manifested itself in the engagement of Social Democrats in the Free Thought movement. This movement developed in the Czech lands from the 1890s more or less independently of the anti-clericalism of the individual political parties and, in contrast to previous decades, continuously and with a much wider organizational and social basis. While it had previously been based around groups of individuals, in the decades leading up to the First World War they were linked into organizations. After an appeal to form a free association of atheists in the Prague press in March 1903—in the Social Democratic *Právo lidu* [People´s Justice], the Realists' *Čas* [Time] and the German *Prager Tagblatt* [Prague Daily]—in the spring of 1904 the Spolek Augustin Smetana [Augustin Smetana

47. The atheist organization registered itself as a church, because Austrian law permitted the establishment of new religious societies, but not purely atheistic associations.

48. For more see Kořalka, "Ateismus průkopníků socialismu," 37–41.

49. "Národní hospodářství a osvěta: Otevřený list svobodným myslitelům," *Dělnické listy*, May 18, 1881. Cited in Kořalka, "Ateismus průkopníků socialismu," 41–42.

Association] was established, and in 1906 it was renamed the Spolek volných myslitelů Augustin Smetana [Augustin Smetana Association of Freethinkers]. It attracted the attention of, amongst others, the editors of the Social Democratic, Realist and anarchist press, e.g., Julius Myslík, Karel Pelant, František Václav Krejčí, Theodor Bartošek, Staniskav K. Neumann, and thinkers such as Tomáš G. Masaryk, František Krejčí and Emanuel Chalupný.[50] From 1905 the Association published the magazine Volná myšlenka [Free Thought] and became a regular member of the International Federation of Free Thought. In September 1904 its representatives took part in the World Congress of Free Thought in Rome. After the formation of the Czech section in the spring of 1906, Volná myšlenka [Free Thought] became the organizational core of the entire Czech atheist movement, even achieving international recognition and prestige, particularly when in 1907 it successfully organized the XIV World Congress of Free Thought in Prague.

Volná myšlenka's demands for freedom of science and thought in everyday life were mainly focused on education and schools, as well as the issue of equal rights for women and the resolution of the relationship between Church and state. As well as the full separation of the Church from the state, Volná myšlenka called for the removal of religious acts and formalities from public life (Church registers, weddings, religious oaths in court, paragraphs concerning religious libel, etc.) and their replacement with civic ceremonies and laws. These demands were disseminated through relatively widespread journalistic activities and through events which were aimed against the influence of the Catholic Church in public life. Volná myšlenka also maintained foreign links and had contacts in the Czech atheist movement in the USA, where their representatives attended a congress in Chicago in 1907.

From the beginning of the Free Thought movement Social Democrat members took an active role: the journalists Antonín P. Veselý and Julius Myslík were there from its inception and J. Myslík, Karel Pelant and other Social Democrats were significant figures in its leadership. According to Šmeral, the workers formed a majority of Free Thought's membership from 1904–1908 and its magazines Volná myšlenka and Havlíček were also very frequently distributed at Social Democratic meetings.[51] Myslík was also one of the main organizers of the 1907 International Congress of Free Thought in Prague, in which official representatives of Social Democracy also actively participated—as well as the journalist and literary critic František V. Krejčí, there were the members of parliament František Soukup and František Modráček—and there were also representatives from many of the local organizations of Českoslovanská sociálně demokratická strana [Czechoslavonic Social Democratic Party].[52] A letter of welcome was sent to the congress and its executive committee which found a common goal in the efforts of Free Thought: "For decades our party has been leading this cultural struggle through its programme and tactics, its organization and press, its entire intellect and tradition, and it will participate in this international congress of workers for freedom of science, acting in the belief

---

50. For extensive writing on Volná myšlenka: Kudláč, *Příběh(y) Volné myšlenky*.
51. Zubek, *Tradice protináboženského a protiklerikálního boje*, 13, 15.
52. Kudláč, *Příběh(y) Volné myšlenky*, 29.

that the movement it represents is and will remain one element of a historical development which, through its efforts to free the human intellect, facilitates the fundamental social efforts of all the modern organized proletariat to transform today's anarchy of private capitalism into a collectively owned means of production."[53]

However, this harmony in the approach and aims of the Social Democratic Party and Free Thought was soon shown to be problematic. With Free Thought's emphasis on the battle against clericalism as the root of all evil in society, the leaders of the party began to see in it a certain threat to Social Democracy and its influence over the workers. That is why in 1908 there was conflict between the leaders of the Social Democrats and Free Thought. The basis and ideological background came from an extensive journalistic essay by Bohumír Šmeral entitled "Our opinion of religion, the Church, clericalism and Free Thought," which was published in the newspapers *Právo lidu* [People´Justice], *Nová Doba* [New Era] and the Viennese monthly *Der Kampf* in the summer of 1908, and published as a polemic in a special edition of the magazine *Volná myšlenka* [Free Thought].[54]

So, just as in the 1880s, there was now a polemic on the question of how much of a priority the promotion of atheism was for the Social Democrats' efforts amongst the working class and whether it was a distraction from their most pressing aims. Šmeral had formulated a stance towards religion and anti-clericalism from the position of an expert on socialist theory as a standpoint for the whole party. He started from the assumption that religion is the result of the economic and social growth of society, and as it was impossible to separate the struggle against clericalism from the class struggle and the goals of the workers' movement then Social Democracy must endeavour to transform all of society and not only to suppress clericalism: "In keeping with a materialist historical view, religion cannot be considered as something independent, which originated independently and which can be independently led to its extinction, but as the result of certain economic and social conditions. In this regard the approach to the fight against the influence of the Church and clericalism is completely different than it is for middle-class anti-clerical parties. Our fight against clericalism can never be separated from our economic and political class struggles . . ."[55] He also emphasized the fundamental difference, which according to him was between the isolated, individualistic and sometimes self-serving liberal form of anti-clericalism and the anti-clericalism of the Social Democrats, which was to be part of the struggle to change all of society. He therefore criticized those members of Social Democracy who overrated anti-clericalism and who often read more anti-clerical pamphlets and prioritized activities with Free Thought at the expense of their knowledge of the socialist classics and work for the party, even attacking other Social Democrats for not leaving the Church.

---

53. Zubek, *Tradice protináboženského a protiklerikálního boje*, 32.

54. Galandauer, "Poměr Bohumíra Šmerala k náboženské otázce," 215–20; Galandauer, "Die Relation der Bildungspolitik," 295–302. See also Zubek, *Tradice protináboženského a protiklerikálního boje*, 15, 32–33; Kudláč, *Příběh(y) Volné myšlenky*, 32–35.

55. *Právo lidu*, vol. 17, May 31, 1908, 1–2. Cited from Zubek, *Tradice protináboženského a protiklerikálního boje*, 31.

The hardening attitude of Social Democracy towards Free Thought cooled their mutual relationship and finally led to the formation of a purely Social Democratic atheist organization in 1913, the Association of Socialist Monists in Austria, whose leader was the editor of *Právo lidu* [People's Justice], F. V. Krejčí. The party's influence on the Association of Monists was assured by the fact that only atheists who were members of Social Democracy could join it.[56] Šmeral's ascendancy and the development of the relationship of Social Democracy to the question of religion in the years prior to World War I signalled that the leaders of the party were attempting to clearly demarcate the anti-clericalism of Social Democracy from the atheist movement and the anti-clericalism of other political and interest groups, and to subordinate the anti-clerical campaign and the atheist movement to the overall aims of Social Democracy, as well as keep those members of the Social Democratic Party who remained believers.[57]

The extent to which Šmeral's implied principles became successfully implanted in the everyday life of the party can be judged through an analysis of the anti-clerical activities of the Social Democrats from 1900–1914. The ideological, social and political mix in the Czech lands in the 1890s formed completely new conditions for the development of the relationship between the Social Democratic workers and the Catholic Church and religion.

Czech society was now so strong and well developed that it could allow divergences in opinion and not adhere to nationally defensive positions. The new, young generation growing up after 1882 rebelled against their fathers in the new Czech university in Prague, "opened the window" to Europe and took on board modern ideas and artistic approaches which, either directly or indirectly, undermined the Church's authority and cast doubt upon the significance of religion in the life of modern man.[58] Manifest české moderny [The Czech Modernist Manifesto] of 1895 announced the right of the individual to have his own critical view of art and society; symbolism and decadence found a home in Czech art and literature; political Realism and the Progressives brought new themes and impulses to Czech politics; national and social issues, including the role of women in society, were addressed in a new manner, as was the role of the Church and religion in the modern world. Thus criticism of the Catholic Church began to be a common, everyday occurrence within the setting of modern art and new political movements. The state of the Church became not only a target for critics but also a stimulus for attempts at change from within the Church. Sections of the clergy and supporters of Catholic Modernism wanted to confront the challenge of the modern age through appropriate reforms of the Church, and signatories of Manifest Katolické moderny [The Manifesto of Catholic Modernism] (1895) through their own modern Catholic art.[59]

Another important factor in the worsening relationship with the Church and the subsequent strengthening of secularizing tendencies was the escalation of political battles

---

56. Even with this organization, however, the monists' concentration on anti-clerical propaganda led to them splitting with the Social Democrats in the spring of 1914. Kudláč, *Příběh(y) Volné myšlenky*, 35–36.

57. Galandauer, "Die Relation der Bildungspolitik," 299–300.

58. Gabriel and Svoboda, *Náboženství v českém myšlení*.

59. See note 6.

in the twenty five years leading up to World War I. Until the 1890s more profound political differentiation of Czech society was prevented by fears of the strengthened position
of the German population. Although at that time the relationship towards the Church
represented an important dividing line between Old Czechs and Young Czechs, the political division of the Czech lands was primarily along national lines. There were other
politico-ideological factors at work apart from the relationship towards the Church—the
conflict between labor and capital and between the interests of the city and the village. A
combination of these lines of conflict separated both Czech and German society in the
Czech lands into five different socio-cultural backgrounds, or rather political camps—
National Liberal, Social Democratic, Catholic, Agrarian and National Social.[60]

Within the Czech National Liberal camp all of the parties, with the possible exception of the Old Czech National Party, which had lost all of its influence, held a critical
and detached stance towards the Catholic Church. The Young Czechs, the leading Czech
political force from the 1890s, particularly condemned the misuse of religion for political
aims, while the Progressives attacked the Church not only verbally but also with radical
actions. A very intense relationship existed between the Catholic Church and Masaryk
and his Realists (Josef Svatopluk Machar, Jan Herben, František Krejčí, etc.). Masaryk
himself, despite his attacks on Catholicism and the Catholic Church, was not against
religious faith in itself and was quick to emphasize that the crisis of modern man was due
to the religious crisis of society in the modern age, which could only be surmounted by
the search for personal faith and a new non-church religion.[61] Národně sociální strana
[The National Social Party] was also distinguished by its nationally motivated fierce anti-
clericalism. Following the establishment of Agrární strana [The Agrarian Party] in 1869,
the agrarian movement, after a certain amount of deliberation, particularly in Moravia,
also came down on the side of those critical of political Catholicism, with the Agrarians
recognizing it as their greatest opponent in the struggle for influence in the countryside.[62]
The rise of political Catholicism, which after 1906 was to become the strongest political
force in Moravia, led to the political cooperation of Social Democracy with the liberal
Lidová strana [People's Party] and Agrární strana [The Agrarian Party] in a "bloc" of
progressive parties formed on an anti-clerical basis. Therefore, in the years prior to the
First World War Czech society was divided into two distinct political camps—the clerical
(Catholic) and the anti-clerical, which was termed progressive at the time. In parliamentary and social life this development manifested itself through increasing pressure to
remove the Church's existing influence in education and the state authorities (control
of registers, marriages, etc.), and in public life there were bitter arguments and conflicts
over various issues of an everyday nature, including arguments about the clergy's influence in non-religious associations, societies and savings banks, as well as scandals
of either a fabricated or true nature concerning the misdemeanours of the Catholic
clergy, and newspaper campaigns and protests against the disciplinarian intervention

60. Malíř, *Od spolků k moderním politickým stranám*; Malíř, "Die Parteien in Mähren und Schlesien,"
705–803; Pokorný, "Vereine und Parteien in Böhmen," 609–703.

61. Nový, "Masaryk volnomyšlenkář?," 46–54.

62. Malíř, "Moravské rolnictvo," 47–68.

of Church bodies against teachers in particular.[63] Even though the anti-clericalism of the political parties was mainly superficial and pragmatic and did not lead directly to atheism, but only to pressurizing of the Church at a political and public level, it did contribute to strengthening secularizing tendencies in society and corresponded with the anti-clericalism of Social Democracy.

THE ANTI-CLERICAL ACTIVITIES OF SOCIAL DEMOCRACY 1900–1914

It is possible to view the extent to which the Social Democrats' position towards the Church and religion differed from the non-working-class by examining the content, form and intensity of the everyday anti-clerical activities of its members and newspapers, which in the fifteen years before the First World War underwent a huge expansion and became a decisive area for the dissemination of secularizing tendencies amongst the working class. The best way to approach these activities is on the basis of several studies. These were based on two years (1900 and 1914) of the newspaper *Červánky* [The Dawn]—which, with the subheading Časopis pro šíření osvěty a hájení pravdy [Magazine for the dissemination of education and safeguarding of the truth] was published from 1889–1926 as a party organ in Brno and was noted for its openly anti-religious orientation—one year (1918) of the daily newspaper *Rovnost* [Equality], which was the provincial organ of the Social Democratic Party in Moravia, and two years (1910–1912) of its entertainment supplement *Besídka* [Discussion], along with one year (1910) of the paper *Hlas lidu* [Voice of the People], which was published in Prostějov as an organ of České strany sociálně demokratické [The Czech Social Democratic Party], and three years of the monthly *Akademie* [Academy], which as the *socialist review* was also an official organ of the party and was edited by prominent Social Democrats,[64] and also articles and pamphlets by Alois M. Špera, the long-standing editor of *Červánky* and after 1920 a senator in the National Parliament, as well as numerous other anti-clerical Social Democratic pamphlets from the time. The Social Democratic journalism which touched upon the Church and religion stemmed from the basic policy principles calling for the separation of the Church from the state and religious freedom. On a day-to-day basis, however, this acquired a strong anti-Church and anti-religious focus. For the Social Democrats, the principle of free religion was interpreted as a demand for non-denominational schools, non-denominational marriages and non-denominational law for each individual and, as a main demand, the removal of the influence of the Church and its clergy from the public sphere, particularly politics: "We do not fight indiscriminately against the religious activities of the clergy, but rather against their social, economic, cultural and political involvement," wrote Edmund Burian in his pamphlet *Socialistické epištoly* [Socialist Epistles], where he spelled out these aims quite clearly for the reader: "The religious question will not be solved legislatively, but only through a free battle of

---

63. E.g., against K. Juda, A. Konečný, L. Wahrmund. More on their affairs below.

64. The publisher of the 10th (1905/1906) and 11th (1906/1907) issues was František Tomášek and his editors were František Modráček and Alfred Meissner; the publisher of the 15th edition (1910/1911) was Bohumír Šmeral and the editors were František Modráček and František V. Krejčí.

intellects. And we believe that the state should not enter into this battle of intellects, but should give the people complete freedom. The state should not be involved in either supporting or attacking religion; that is why we ask for a complete separation of the Church from the state. . . . Only in this way will there be an end to the immoral coercion of the religious state."[65] In the Habsburg monarchy the influence of the Catholic Church remained particularly strong within primary-level education. For the great majority of supporters from the lower strata of society this was the only level of education available to them and Burian therefore focused his readers' attention on this area: "The fight against free schools is directed against the interests of the non-propertied class, and it is even sadder when these interests are opposed in the name of religion. In the interests of the non-propertied class the fiercest struggle must be waged against clerical obscurantism which shouts about threats to religion, which no-one wants to or can threaten using political means, against this obscurantist power which itself threatens people's physical and spiritual well-being with venom and plague."

In their publications aimed at a cross-section of the community they emphasized that although "the basic state laws provide everyone with freedom of religion, the Austrian bureaucracy interprets this freedom rather strangely, as it is not to be seen in action anywhere."[66] In their campaign they cited cases in which parents were punished for refusing to send their children to religious instruction at school. For example, an article was written concerning the case of F. Optiz from Broumov. He was convicted on the basis that every citizen was required to send their children to school lessons, of which religious instruction formed a part. The author of an article critical of this situation, Antonín M. Špera, wrote that according to the law every citizen had the right to bring up their children in the faith which they considered appropriate; however, as soon as the child started school he had to attend religious instruction, even if he was without religion or his religion was different to the one being taught at religious instruction. He pointed to the problematic nature of such lessons, since when the child reaches the age of fourteen he has the right by law to change his religion or to leave the Church.[67] Špera also cast doubt on the reasoning behind forcing children to attend Sunday school, to participate in confession and to pray, arguing that children are not able to fully comprehend these acts and do not carry them out properly and with conviction, and that they can therefore have no educational benefit for them.[68] The Social Democratic press, meanwhile, supported attempts to secularize lessons and welcomed Free Thought's proposal to supply

65. Burian, *Socialistické epištoly*, quotations on 56, 57 and 59–60.

66. A. M. Š. /= Špera, Alois M./, "Náboženská svoboda," *Červánky*, vol. 12, 1900, 227–29, quotation 227.

67. Ibid. According to the decision of the Ministry of Education from 15. 9. 1910 a non-religious child was not required to attend religious instruction, but the constitutional court repealed this law and forced parents of non-religious children to report to the school what kind of religious instruction their children should receive. *Akademie*, vol. 15, 1910/1911, 44, 84, 175, 527.

68. A. M. Š. /= Špera, Alois M./, "Děti a náboženské výkony I–III," *Červánky*, vol. 12, 1900, 141–42, 156–57, 165–67.

their own readers to schools and the idea of introducing Darwin's theory of evolution into science lessons.[69]

Anti-clerical campaigns were also organized to tackle the issue of matrimonial law. In their publications the Social Democrats called into question Church weddings and the sanctity of marriage in general. They mustered a variety of reasons in favour of legalizing divorce and the conclusion of new marriages. They railed against the fact that when it came to the indissolubility of marriage the state yielded to the dictates of the Catholic Church, and they asked whether it were possible to have marriages between partners of different religious backgrounds.[70]

During this campaign even Bohumír Šmeral, the leading Social Democratic representative, did not hesitate to produce a pamphlet for a wider audience and "speak as accessibly as possible to those who have been duped and swindled by clericalism, and explain to them in the most straightforward way what the reform of matrimonial law entails, setting the truth against clerical lying and chicanery."[71] Šmeral made it clear why it was necessary to establish "the introduction of obligatory civil marriage and the introduction of the dissolubility of Catholic marriages," and demanded that "matrimonial law be separate from one particular religious faith." In his opinion matrimonial law was an opportune area for the assertion of the Catholic Church's influence on the state and on the ordinary life of citizens, and he therefore called for fundamental opposition to it. By refusing to allow reforms in matrimonial law he saw that the Church feared losing their own power in society. In order to convince the ordinary reader of the need to abolish Church marriages, Šmeral used graphic examples from life, attacked the hypocrisy of the Church by showing examples of the celibacy rule being broken throughout its history and condemned the Church's disdainful attitude towards women. The overall aggressive tone of the pamphlet meant that several passages were censored by the authorities and the pamphlet was published in a revised edition. The otherwise reputable socialist review *Akademie* came out aggressively in favour of matrimonial reform, demanding equal rights for men and women and at the same time emphasising that "the main battle front, however, has to be against the influence of the Church."[72]

The Social Democratic press also took part in atheist campaigns. At the head of Brno's Spolek volných myslitelů [Association of Freethinkers] was Jaroslav V. Stejskal, a Social Democrat and member of the imperial parliament from 1911. In addition to posters, the association's lectures were advertised in the Social Democratic paper *Rovnost*, which also warned of improper administrative attempts against the association by the authorities.[73] The press also covered the Congress of Czech Atheists in Prague

---

69. "Přehled školský," *Akademie*, vol. 15, 1910–1911, 260–61; Kepl, "Darwin a škola," *Akademie*, vol. 15, 1910–1911, 464–68.

70. "Svazek manželský, " *Červánky*, vol. 12, 1900, 453–55, 467–68; A. M. Š. /= Špera, Alois M./. "Pro reformu manželského práva," *Červánky*, vol. 26, 1914, 241–42.

71. Šmeral, *Klerikálové a oprava manželského práva*. Other quotations on 7, 10, and 36.

72. "Reforma práva manželského," *Akademie*, vol. 10, 1905/1906, 192–96.

73. *Rovnost*, vol. 14, July 31, 1908, 4.

on 16. 5. 1914.[74] In promoting atheism the Social Democrats did not hesitate to make use of the popularity of the anti-clerical writer Josef S. Machar: "Machar and his family are non-religious and many could take them as a model of consistency."[75] The main weapon at the Social Democrats' disposal in the campaign for atheism was the pamphlet *Bezvěrci dle práva rakouského* [Atheists according to Austrian Law] by František Soukup, an important Social Democratic member of parliament and after 1918 Czechoslovak Minister for Justice.[76] Soukup not only outlined for readers the laws relating to freedom of religion, the relationship between the state and the Church, the relationship between individual religions, matrimonial law and the role of the Church in education, but also focused on the consequences of these laws for practical living. He showed how it was possible within the given legal norms for each individual to become an atheist, have a non-religious wedding, get divorced, not baptize his children, take oaths, organize a non-religious funeral, and how his children could avoid religious instruction at school, etc. Along with these arguments he even attached a sample form with requests for carrying out the aforementioned non-religious activities and set out the legal norms which the administration could use against the campaign for atheism. According to him, the goal of these urgent reforms was to be "the establishment of the entire organization of state society on a non-denominational basis as the freedom of conscience and civic equality of today demands."[77] The campaign for atheism demonstrated that, according to the Social Democrats, atheism was not the goal in itself but had to serve in the creation of a new and "better" society.

The anti-religious arguments to be found in the Social Democratic press often referred to the findings of natural science and rationalism.[78] Science and theological teachings were set in opposition, and they made use of supposedly contradictory texts from the Bible as well as contradictions between what was written in the Bible and what the Catholic Church taught.[79] By using examples of the development of several religious dogmas in the past, such as the dogma of the Holy Trinity, or religious superstitions such as belief in the existence of the Devil, the author tried to reveal their insubstantiality and dubious nature.[80]

The lack of clarity from the Bible concerning the birth and life of Jesus Christ was even used to cast doubt on belief in his divinity and on his role as the founder of the

74. "Sjezd českých bezvěrců," *Červánky*, vol. 26, 1914, 260–61.

75. "Machar," *Červánky*, vol. 26, 1914, 129.

76. Soukup, *Bezvěrci*.

77. Ibid., 56.

78. Lev, "Křesťanství ze stanoviska rozumu," *Červánky*, vol. 12, 1900, 359–61; Špera, "Nesmrtelnost v životě," *Červánky*, vol. 12, 1900, 373–74, 381–82.

79. A. M. Š. /= Špera, Alois M./, "Věda a katolický tisk," *Červánky*, vol. 12, 1900, 421–22, 433–34, 441–43; "Zjevená pravda," *Červánky*, vol. 12, 1900, 549–51.

80. "O vývoji dogmat I–VI," *Červánky*, vol. 12, 1900, 561–63, 575–76, 585–86, 598–600, 611–12, 625–26; "Kdo holdoval pověře?" *Červánky*, vol. 12, October 31, 1900, 538–39, 551–52.

Catholic Church. They described him only as someone who denounced the abuses of the Jewish church, who was seen in his time as a prophet of God.[81]

Josef Skalák's pamphlet *Ježíš-bůh a ne člověk* [Jesus-God, not man] from 1910 is a good example of the attempts of Social Democratic campaigns of the time to cast doubt on the very basis of the Christian faith.[82] The historical interpretation of Jesus's life with reference to scientific as well as theological literature was meant to persuade the reader not to interpret a "cultural-historical development shrouded" in myth and legend, but to look clearly at the sources from which it originates." The irreconcilability of Skalák's attitude towards religion, as with all of Social Democracy, stems from the fact that it did not fit in with a socialist conception of the evolution of society. According to Skalák socialism saw its goal and ideal in a situation where "people arrange temporal matters for themselves on the basis of the equal economic conditions which are necessary for the successful growth of each individual, and do not leave their care to the heavens or to their spiritual and political lieutenants, those saviours and messiahs established by religion or theocracy."

Polemics with Christian teachings were also carried out in the Social Democratic press in several secular articles and pamphlets which, by using a popular format, enabled the reader to understand the new scientific knowledge from various fields, particularly from Darwin's theory of evolution. Alois M. Špera, the publisher of the weekly paper *Červánky*, was at the forefront of disseminating Darwin's ideas, not only in a number of articles but also in two pamphlets.[83] In *Červánky* he also popularized the philosophical ideas of Friedrich Nietzsche and Ernst Haeckel.[84] Along with this he targeted religious taboos and in his journalism he paid particular attention to health education, including sex education, as well as all manner of new scientific discoveries which the nineteenth century brought.[85] Much of Špera's anti-clerical journalism consisted of contributions on the history of religion and the Catholic Church, which were supposed to cast doubt on Catholic teachings and the authority of the Church by revealing the historical changes in Catholic teachings and the various Church abuses.[86] These pamphlets were widely distributed and one of them was even published in Slovak in Chicago.[87] Testament to their popularity with readers was the fact that they were first published in magazines and then later came out in the form of separate pamphlets.

81. A. M. Š. /= Špera, Alois M./, "Narodil se Kristus pán!" *Červánky*, vol. 12, 1900, 621–623; "Jak se Kristus stal synem božím?" *Červánky*, vol. 26, 1914, 265–66, 278–80, 290-92.

82. Skalák, *Ježíš-bůh a ne člověk*. Quotations are on page 76.

83. Špera, *O vývinu tvorstva a člověka*; Špera, *Kdo stvořil člověka?*.; Špera, "Souvislost všech žijících tvorů," *Červánky*, vol. 12, 1900, 623–24.

84. Šp. /= Špera/, "Z filosofie Nietzscheovy," *Červánky*, vol. 12, 1900, 285–86; Pelant, "Světový názor přírodovědce," *Červánky*, vol. 12, 1900, 563–64, 573–75.

85. Špera, *Stručná pohlavní zdravověda*; "Něco o vědě, zvané fysiologií," *Červánky*, vol.12, 1900, 636–37; "Pohlavní zdravověda," *Červánky*, vol. 26, 1914, 160–61; A. M. Š. /=Špera/, "Užívejme světa!" *Červánky*, vol. 26, 1914, 253–54; Špera, "Devatenácté století," *Červánky*, vol. 12 ,1900, 634–36.

86. Špera, *Jak povstalo křesťanství*; Špera, *Z dějin církve*; A. M. Š. /= Špera, Alois M./, "Sicilianské nešpory," *Červánky*, vol. 12, 1900, 347–48; "'Svatá' inkvisice," *Červánky*, vol. 12, 1900, 225-26.

87. Špera, *Z dejín cirkve*.

In the Czech lands in the second half of the nineteenth century, the Social Democratic press's criticism of the Catholic Church's past widely employed the image of the Catholic Church as an oppressor of Czech ambitions in the past. A particularly frequent theme was the burning of the Czech reformer Jan Hus in 1415 and the Hussite reformation and Hussite wars in general.[88] Apart from Masaryk and other thinkers and politicians of the "long" nineteenth century, Hus also received attention from František Modráček, an important theoretician of socialism and a Social Democratic member of parliament, in an extensive pamphlet.[89] The Social Democrats obviously interpreted Hus in their own way—as a rebel who fought against authority, political injustice and economic oppression—and adopted him as their own, since in their opinion they were fighting against the same abuses as Hus did in the fifteenth century. Hus's fight against vices within the Church, which according to Modráčka was "against the priests as a class, a class which was politically, socially and economically privileged," was thus seen by the Social Democrats as a class struggle. The Social Democratic press therefore employed Hus both in the fight against clericalism and in the class struggle of the working class against middle-class society.[90] In their criticisms of the Church the Social Democrats also made use of its transgressions against other Czech notables from the past, for example the attitude of the Pope towards King Jiří of Poděbrad in the fifteenth century or the persecution of the journalist Karel Havlíček in the first half of the nineteenth century.[91]

The Social Democrats objected very strongly to the efforts of the papal curia to support the Christian-Social movement in the name of solving the working-class issue, and objected to all the activities of the Christian Socials in general. The Social Democrats logically saw them as dangerous competition in the battle for influence over the working class: "All of Christian socialism is a copy of the teachings of socialism, made necessary by the fear that the working class will adhere to true socialism, through which the power of the Church, protecting capital, could be seriously threatened."[92] Its press did not pass on the opportunity to react critically to the traditional Catholic congresses which often took place and to anti-semitic clerical speeches.[93] They also frequently provided information on other religions and the situations of various churches elsewhere in the world, including the conditions of churches and religious societies in the USA, where there was usually an emphasis on the religious freedom that existed there.[94]

88. Heumos, "Hussitische Tradition und Volkskultur," 75–91; Rak, *Bývali Čechové* . . . ; Havránek, "Příprava Husových oslav," 235–44.

89. Modráček, *Mistr Jan Hus a jeho doba*; "Dějiny husitské války," *Červánky*, vol. 12, 1900, 142–43, 157–58; see also Urban, "Bohumír Šmeral a František Modráček," 432–44.

90. "Soudcové mistra Jana Husa," *Rovnost*, vol. 14, July 6, 1908, 1; "Hus a sociální demokracie," *Rovnost*, vol. 14, July 8, 1908, 1; *Rovnost*, vol. 14, ibid., July 9, 1908, 1.

91. "Prokletí českého krále Jiřího," *Červánky*, vol. 26, 1914, 159–60; "Havlíčkovo náboženství," *Červánky*, vol. 26, 1914 (revised edition after confiscation!), 361–63.

92. "Skrytí nepřátelé socialismu," *Rovnost*, vol. 14, August 13, 1908, 3–4; Skalák, "Moderní papežství a dělnická otázka," *Akademie*, vol. 11, 1906/1907, 220–22, 237–42, 272–6, 307–9.

93. "Katolické sjezdy," *Červánky*, vol. 12, 1900, 474; "Sjezd klerikální armády v Praze," *Rovnost*, vol. 14, August 31, 1908, 2; "Klerikalismus," *Červánky*, vol. 12, 1900, 89–90.

94. "Kristus a Konfucius," *Červánky*, vol. 12, 1900, 417–418; A. M. Š. /= Špera, Antonín M./, "Vývoj

The most widespread element of the Social Democrats' anti-clerical campaigning was the everyday smearing of alleged specific manifestations of clericalism. First in line were individual Catholic priests who were criticized by the Social Democratic press for not doing what they claimed: "in the name of religion they can smash the skulls of their opponents, in the name of religion they can denounce, prosecute and destroy lives—that is, they do everything that religion forbids."[95] The press railed most of all against the misuse of religion in election campaigns and politics in general, and against the alleged misuse of chaplains in political agitation. They criticized priests for behaving like a caste which was not concerned with religion but only with strengthening its own position, and they also noted the situation abroad, particularly in France, where the clergy had a minimal role in public life.[96] The press also condemned the false morality of God's servants, who apparently enthused about celibacy and sexual abstinence while many of them failed to observe this morality.[97]

One very effective and persuasive form of anti-clerical campaigning amongst the working class was the daily flood of short items concerning various stories and cases from the lives of specific priests and believers. These were intended as examples which would demonstrate the gulf between the values to which the Catholic faith and Church claimed to adhere and the actions of its servants. Readers were supposed to be convinced of the discreditable and malignant nature of the actions of priests and the Church in society.

To further this propaganda goal there were press campaigns and protest gatherings against several priests who were publicly accused of abusing their position or directly breaking the law. The most celebrated affair at the start of the twentieth century was that of the Olomouc archbishop Theodor Kohn, who was attacked by the anti-clerical press for his autocratic leadership of his archdiocese and persecution of unsuitable priests. He himself began to be deemed unsuitable and had to leave his episcopal seat in 1904.[98] In 1902 a similar pretext for an anti-clerical campaign was the embezzlement at the St Wenceslas savings bank in Prague, which involved the papal prelate and canon Jan Drozd. There was also the alleged bad forestry management and embezzlement of the prelate Norbert Drápalík at the monastery in Nová Říše.[99]

---

náboženství," *Červánky*, vol. 26, 1914, 145–46, 157–58; "Náboženské sekty v Americe," *Červánky*, vol. 26, 1914, 117; "Co vše bůh poroučí?," *Červánky*, vol. 26, 1914, 308–9.

95. A. M. Š. /= Špera, Antonín M./, "Moudrá slova," *Červánky*, vol. 12, 1900, 395–97, 405–7; quote on p. 406.

96. Špera, A. M. "Ku slávě boží!" *Červánky*, vol. 12, 1900, 525–27, 539–41, 552–53; "K čemu je kazatelna," *Červánky*, vol. 12, 1900, 514–15; "Boj proti kleru," *Červánky*, vol. 12, 1900, 131–32; "Chovali hada na svých prsou,." *Hlas lidu*, vol. 25, August 6, 1910, 1.

97. A. M. Š. /= Špera, Antonín M./, "Falešná morálka," *Červánky*, vol. 12, 1900, 129–31, 120–22; Š. /= Špera, Antonín M./, "Dnešní morálka," *Červánky*, vol. 12, 1900, 601–2, 609–10, 624–25.

98. Marek, *Prof. ThDr. Theodor Kohn*; Marek, *Český katolicismus*, 495–510; Marek, "Josef Hofer-Rectus," 71–106.

99. Staněk, *700 let kláštera v Nové Říši*; Šlesinger, *Z bojů o pokrokovou Moravu*, 47; Marek, *Český katolicismus*, 485–94.

However, there were also relatively large campaigns against the persecution of secular individuals who, at the instigation of Church circles, had been administratively punished in their civilian jobs for alleged misdemeanours against the Church. These cases mainly involved teachers and had ramifications that went beyond Social Democracy. The most famous case was the so-called Juda affair, involving the Prostějov secondary school teacher Karel Juda, who was punished by being transferred because in 1905 he had written a strongly anti-religious introduction to a catalogue for an exhibition of paintings by František Kupka in Prostějov.[100] There was also the affair of the teacher Alois Konečný, who was transferred in 1908 because he had taken his pupils to the non-religious funeral of his colleague.[101] The case of Ludwig Wahrmund, a professor of ecclesiastical law in Innsbruck, was also widely known. He had been persecuted for his public criticism of the Church and his persecution was seen by the liberal public as an attack on freedom of research.[102] All of these affairs were part of the "cultural battle," which in the monarchy was mainly a battle for influence in education and which in the years before the war split the whole of society into two distinct camps.[103]

In these cases the Social Democrats were on the side of the other anti-clerical forces.[104] However, their press campaigned much further in these and other causes. They used less well-known cases for propaganda purposes, often employing even alleged or fabricated transgressions by members of the Church. Among these were the alleged offences against morality by the catechist Father Kokta in 1908 at the Institute for the Deaf and Dumb in Ivančice.[105] Then there was the loan that was granted by the Catholic Cyril and Methodius savings bank to the Jewish forestry owner Baron Popper in 1902 and the political support that was afforded to him by the Catholic member of parliament Josef Kadlčák over a dispute concerning the irresponsible felling of forests.

The background to these journalistic campaigns was, of course, an attempt to discredit the representatives of the Church and weaken the entire Catholic political camp. These press attacks had a very aggressive and rough tone. Nor did they stop at occasional campaigns; rather the Social Democratic press would use the slightest pretext to blacken the Church and did not refrain from employing lies and slander. In the weekly newspaper *Červánky*, which the Social Democrats used to attack clericalism in Moravia, there were mostly petty reports or letters scandalizing various lapses by priests or ridiculing their behaviour. The attacks were personal and contained names and the places where they worked. Most of these were in and around Brno, though there were also stories from

---

100. *Judův případ*; Dostál-Lutinov, *Lutinov contra Juda*; Marek, "K Judově aféře z roku 1906," 293–311.

101. "Záležitost naďučitele Konečného," *Rovnost*, vol. 14, July 4, 1908, 6; Fischer, *Pokroková Morava*, 251–54; Marek, *Český katolicismus*, 526–29.

102. Marek, "T. G. Masaryk a Wahrmundova aféra," 145–57.

103. Balík, "Kulturní boj," 79–92.

104. E.g., on 28. 3. 1908 the Moravian Provincial Assembly J. Filipinský, J. Hybeš, J. Prokeš, F. Svoboda, K. Vaněk et al. protested in the Moravian Provincial Assembly at the punishment of A. Konečný. *Landtagsblatt über die Sitzungen des mährischen Landtags. 2. Session 1907/10*, 1126–27.

105. "Proti páteru Koktovi," *Rovnost*, vol. 14, July 9, 1908, 5; Šlesinger, *Z bojů o pokrokovou Moravu*, 58–59.

the rest of the country, and similar causes throughout the monarchy and abroad were publicized as well.

There was a very wide range of disparaging reports on the behaviour of both priests and believers, and a large number of these were focused on the inappropriate behaviour of priests in the education of children and youths. Cases were presented where the priest beat children, swore at them, behaved arrogantly and vengefully towards them, set children against their parents, etc.[106] They published with great relish stories about young girls who were the objects of the priests' immoral behaviour during lessons,[107] and even more regularly there were stories of priests who either by word or deed had gone against their self-professed claims of celibacy.[108]

Just as discreditory in the anti-clerical propaganda were examples testifying to the greed of the priests, to their hunger for money and even an affection for the rich and scorn for the poor.[109] It was also reported that in some cases the Church acquired money for the building of churches from the profits made from concerts held in churches, or even by organizing lotteries or bullfights.[110] The Catholic clergy were reproached for all manner of negative qualities—the vindictiveness with which they persecuted converts, denunciation, the misuse of confession, gluttony, hedonism, and so on.[111] They were also blamed for spreading superstition from which they themselves benefited, just as they benefited from people's stupidity, etc.[112] Clerical education and the conditions in the Church were also blamed for transgressions whereby Christian attacked Christian, as well as for crimes committed by priests or simple believers.[113] These cases of priests' improper conduct were used to disparage and satirize individual members of the Church and the Church as a whole, and they were often accompanied by judgmental conclusions, instructions for the reader and appeals for change. For example, a news item de-

106. "Bestiálnost," *Červánky*, vol. 12, 1900, 222; "Horlivý poutník," *Červánky*, vol. 12, 1900, 401; "Farář Homola v Obřanech," *Červánky*, vol. 12, 1900, 438; "Starostlivé jeptišky," *Rovnost*, vol. 14, July 22, 1908, 6.

107. "Z činnosti misionářů," *Červánky*, vol. 12, 1900, 78; "Vzdělávání učitelek," *Červánky*, vol. 12, 1900, 222; "Znamenitým nemravou v kutně." *Červánky*, vol. 12, 1900, 485.

108. "Vojna o celibát," *Červánky*, vol. 12, 1900, 221; "Nepožádáš manželky bližního svého," *Červánky*, vol. 26, 1914, 261; "Kněz se oženil," *Červánky*, vol. 12, 1900, 402; "Zase dva podaření flanďáci," *Červánky*, vol. 12, 1900, 486.

109. "Vydírání," *Červánky*, vol. 12, 1900, 79; "Mnich loupežníkem," *Červánky*, vol.12, 1900, 222–23; "Lačnost černých po penězích," *Červánky*, vol. 12, 1900, 378; "Ejhle, pastýř duchovní," *Červánky*, vol. 12, 1900, 379; "Peníze světem vládnou," *Červánky*, vol. 12, 1900, 486; "Povedený sluha páně," *Červánky*, vol. 12, 1900, 461.

110. "Chytráctví." *Červánky*, vol. 12, 1900, 401; "Bestiálnost ve službě misie," *Červánky*, vol. 12, 1900, 473–4; "Komedie v kostele," *Červánky*, vol. 12, 1900, 402.

111. "Udavačský páter," *Červánky*, vol. 12, 1900, 78; "Zneužívání zpovědi," *Červánky*, vol. 12, 1900, 222; "Pomsta náleží bohu," *Červánky*, vol. 12, 1900, 401–2; "Vychovatel mládeže," *Červánky*, vol. 12, 1900, 474.

112. "Zázraky," *Červánky*, vol. 12, 1900, 376–77; "Těžili z lidské hlouposti" *Červánky*, vol. 12, 1900, 377; "Prozrazený zázrak," *Červánky*, vol. 12, 1900, 510.

113. "Květy klerikální morálky," *Červánky*, vol. 12, 1900, 438; "Další květy klerikální morálky," *Červánky*, vol. 12, 1900, 438–39; "Klerikální výchova," *Červánky*, vol. 12, 1900, 461–62; "Květy z klerikální zahrádky," *Červánky*, vol. 12, September 19, 1900, 474–75; "Ohavný čin dvou zbožných v kostele," *Červánky*, vol. 12, September 19, 1900, 473.

scribing the improper conduct of a priest during confession, which many women had complained about, concluded with the words: "Well, then, who is breaking up marriages, honorable clerics? Certainly not the Social Democrats. Such a priest should be confined to the barracks and not to the confession box."[114]

The anti-clerical attitudes of the Social Democrats were not only aired in the press, but also in meetings, demonstrations and appearances at the Provincial Assembly in Brno and in the Viennese parliament. If we take just the year 1908, there was a strong response to the Social Democrat demonstrations against the Congress of the Catholic Association of Czech Agricultural Labourers in Moravia which took place in Brno in March 1908.

Part of the congress's programme was the struggle against the de-Christianization of schools and, as the Catholic press wrote, the participants at the congress had to pass through *"a cordon of seething socialists who swore at the villagers, jeered at them and spat on them."*[115] The sequel to the demonstration was that Vlastimil Tusar, the editor of *Rovnost* and after 1918 a government minister, was sentenced to prison for four days for the illegal distribution of leaflets at this anti-clerical demonstration.[116] Another demonstration by the Social Democrats with an anti-clerical slant took place in the Workers' House in Brno on 15. 9. 1908, the day of the opening of the Moravian Provincial Assembly, and was aimed against the harmful influence of Catholic members of parliament on the country's economy and budget.[117] Another opportunity for a fierce attack against clericalism was the autumn session of the Moravský zemský sněm [Moravian Provincial Assembly], with the slogan, *"You do not have the right to govern schools in the name of religion,"* which led to clashes between Social Democratic teachers and Catholic members of parliament over disciplinary reform, with a bill finally being passed along anti-clericalist lines.[118] A similar opportunity for the Social Democrats to attack the political Catholicism of members of parliament came with the 1908 summer session of the imperial parliament in Vienna, where MPs Assembly from the Czech Catholic parties supported the government's proposal to increase the home guard contingent, thus providing the Social Democrats with a pretext to attack them for supporting the government and militarism and criticize their politicians for being hypocrites:[119] "Who lowers religion more than those people who want to be its spokesmen and use religion only as a cover to conceal their wickedness and wretchedness. The role of the Social Democrats is thus: to unmask the clerics, and if this leads to their heightened activity then we will say to them: Through greater campaigning

114. "Jak zpovídal páter Zaplichal na Sv. Hoře," *Červánky*, vol. 12, 1900, 378–79.

115. Šamalík, *Hnutí katolických zemědělců*, 15.

116. "Dozvuky protiklerikální demonstrace v Brně," *Rovnost*, vol. 14, July 31, 1908, 3.

117. "Zemské hospodářství klerikálů," *Rovnost*, vol. 14, Sepgtember 13, 1908, 1–2.

118. "Srážky klerikálů se sociálními demokraty," *Rovnost*, vol. 14, September 16, 1908, 2–3; "Vážný projev pro svobodu učitelů," *Rovnost*, vol. 14, September 17, 1908, 1; "Moravský sněm," *Rovnost*, vol. 14, September 17, 1908, 1–2.

119. "Proti militarismu, válkám a militaristickým stranám," *Rovnost*, vol. 14, July 11, 1908, 2–3.

across Moravia there will be a systematic raising of people's awareness of the mendacious and deceptive policies of the clerics in the imperial council!"[120]

THE INFLUENCE OF SOCIAL DEMOCRATIC ANTI-CLERICALISM ON THE SECULARIZATION OF THE WORKING CLASS

From the above examples of anti-clerical campaigns by the Social Democrats it is obvious that in the final years of the monarchy their activities involving the working class were very intensive and systematic and had a clear goal: to discredit the Church using all possible means. However, the actual impact of Social Democratic anti-clericalism on the widening of secularizing tendencies within the working class can only be very approximately surmised.

The statistics do show a rise in the number of atheists, but the increase before 1914 could not be said to be dramatic. In 1910 only 0.13% of inhabitants of the Czech lands claimed to be atheists. However, the small number of atheists does not mean that the secularization of society did not proceed dramatically during this period. A loss of faith or a cooling in the relationship towards the Church at this time was not accompanied by a move away from the Church, but by an increase in so-called nominal Catholics, who formally remained within the Church but did not take part in religious life. However, anti-clericalism became far more widely established in the years after the war, with 1.5 million people in the Czech lands leaving the Catholic Church in 1918, and the number of atheists in Prague, which had stood at only 0.4%, rose in 1921 to 18.3% and in Bohemia to almost 10%. To a large extent these atheists came from the working class who were recruited from the great industrial centres—Prague, Pilsen, Kladno and Most. An example of this were the Social Democratic functionaries: of 17 MPs Assembly elected to the Viennese parliament in 1907 in Bohemia, 6 had no religion; in Moravia it was one from five.[121]

The fact that the Social Democratic press was offering instructions and forms for leaving the Church, having a non-church baptism, marriage, funeral, etc., either in the form of a template or offering them for purchase, [122] is testament to the existence of a certain demand for these services among the readers, and indirectly points to growing secularization in the Social Democratic working-class milieu.

A similar indicator of the growth in the distance between the Church and religion and the working class was the huge number of advertisements for anti-clerical literature to be found in the Social Democratic press. Under the recommendation *"pamphlets with an educational and scientific content"* could almost always be found works of an anti-clerical nature. *Rovnost*, the Social Democrats' newspaper in Moravia, regularly advertised Darwin's *The Descent of Man and Selection in Relation to Sex*[123] and anti-clerical

---

120. "Otravovači studní," *Rovnost*, vol. 14, July 22, 1908, 1.

121. Havránek, "Příprava Husových oslav," 235–38.

122. See also "Formulář ku vystoupení z církve," *Rovnost*, vol. 14, July 1, 1908, 8, which was offered at 10 hal.

123. *Rovnost*, vol. 14, July 1, 1908, 8; August 13, 1908, 8; August 20, 1908, 8.

pamphlets such as: *Z dějin církve* [From Church History], *Zpověď papeže Alexandra VI.* [The Confession of Pope Alexander VI], *Řeč generála jesovitů* [The Jesuit General's Speech], *Jak povstalo křesťanské náboženství* [The Rise of Christianity], *Katolický názor světový a svobodná věda* [The Catholic World View and Free Science], etc.[124] The weekly newspaper *Červánky* also offered similar anti-clerical works, advertising them to "everyone who wants to fill their library with good, entertaining and informative reading."[125] Advertisements for anti-clerical pamphlets could also be found in otherwise specialized Social Democratic works. The advertised pamphlets sold very well, partly because a significant number of them were sold to the libraries of workers' associations and Social Democratic organizations.[126]

The appeals to workers to "subscribe, read and distribute their party's press (pamphlets, books, newspapers)" and to strengthen their local party organizations, which in the final years before the war had been set up in smaller villages as counterpoints to the parish and the town hall, were imperative for the Social Democrats: ". . . the clerics have their parishes and capitols. Every town hall and every parish is the secretariat for a local political organization of the middle class against working-class people and for their money . . . That is why it is our duty today to have a local Social Democratic political organization alongside every parish. The enlightenment and organization of the proletariat is at the heart of the programme of the Social Democratic Workers' Party."[127]

It is possible to judge the popularity of the anti-clerical Social Democratic press amongst its readers by the differences in the number of copies[128] and indirectly by the fact that many copies were confiscated by the censors due to their disparaging and defamatory style of writing about the Church and religion. For example, in 1900 six of the 52 editions of *Č ervánky* were confiscated on the basis of press law for offences against public peace and order committed by the magazine against the Church or for inciting hatred against the Catholic clergy or defaming the foundation of the Catholic Church.[129] However, even this did not prevent the editorial boards from publishing other similar articles or readers from subscribing to these publications. This was also the case with the newspaper *Rovnost*, which had 27 editions confiscated between 1885 and 1905 for

124. *Rovnost*, vol. 14, August 17, 1908, 8; August 19, 1908, 8; August 20, 1908, 8.

125. "Všem," *Červánky*, vol. 26, 1914, 324.

126. The advertisements occasionally offered pamphlets compiled into one book with the appeal: "Library associations and organizations, do not miss out on this chance to acquire good books for little money—buy now while stocks last. We can also offer these books to organizations, groups and associations with monthly payments." See Vaněk, *Co dělat?*, 2. That the majority of the anti-clerical pamphlets were sold out can be seen in *Protokol VI. sjezdu českoslovanské sociálně demokratické strany dělnické dne 30., 31. října a 1. listopadu 1904 v Prostějově*. Prague 1904, 74.

127. Vaněk, *Co dělat*, 7–8, 19.

128. In 1900 *Červánky* sold 11,000 copies, *Akademie* only 1,600 and *Rovnost* 3,000. In 1911 the number of copies of the anti-clerical paper *Plameny* was 50,000 and the *Akademie* only 2,800. *Protokol čtvrtého řádného sjezdu Českoslovanské strany sociálnědemokratické konaného ve dnech 8., 9., a 10. září 1900 v Českých Budějovicích*, 23; *Protokol X. sjezdu českoslovanské sociálně demokratické strany dělnické ve dnech 23. až 27. prosince 1911*, 43–44.

129. "Jménem Jeho Veličenstva císaře," *Červánky*, vol. 12, 1900, 81, 129, 225, 285, 369, 417. For an overall view of the persecution of the workers' press, see also Malý, *Policejní a soudní perzekuce*, 166–89.

crime paragraph 122 and offence paragraph 303 of disturbing religion and defaming the Church.[130]

Naturally it is difficult to ascertain the extent to which the anti-clerical press expanded, how much it was read and what its real impact was on the spread of secularizing tendencies. We can only infer these facts on the basis of a few fragmentary notes in the sources. From people's memoirs it is clear that, permanent subscribers aside, the distribution of the press was mainly dependent on the work of colporteurs, at first attached to the editorial board, who sold *Rovnost* and other publications in Brno's factories and railway stations. Later a significant section of the press was distributed through local political organizations of the party.[131] In the case of smaller, more remote areas, the publications would be sent to one customer, who would then distribute them to other subscribers.[132] A significant role was played by individual Social Democrat activists in attracting new subscribers, offering the party paper when attending local meetings in various areas of Moravia and Bohemia.[133]

Initially calendars published by the Social Democrats were widely subscribed to and read amongst the working class.[134] For example the Workers' Club in Náměšt ordered 50 copies of the *Kalendář českoslovanského dělnictva v Rakousku* [Calendar of the Czechoslavonic Working Class in Austria] in 1888 and after all the copies had been sold the editor J. Hybeš had to set about printing more almanacs.[135]

Amongst the working class the attachment to almanac literature contributed significantly to the formation of a world view, as we can see that the number of almanacs at the start of the 1880s was twice the number of other party publications, and there was also a great interest in them among Czech workers in the USA, where 2,000 copies were sent at the end of the 1870s.[136] In 1913, 100,000 workers' almanacs were published and 10,000 anti-clerical readers were distributed in a week.[137]

This almanac literature also contributed to a clear anti-clerical feeling amongst the workers. Alongside the amusing anti-clerical stories in the Social Democratic almanacs it was also possible to find caricatures ridiculing members of the clergy.[138] In this anti-

---

130. From 1885–1894 an average of 40% of all editions were confiscated annually; from 1895–1905 it was only 6%. Musilová, "Konfiskace Rovnosti," 278–99.

131. Hybeš, *Práce a vzpomínky*, vol. 1, 146.

132. E.g., 10 copies of *Červánky* were sent to one customer in Lipnice u Humpolce, with a population of 1,300, who then distributed them to the other 9 subscribers in the town. "Chikanování," *Červánky* 12, 1900, 126–27.

133. Filipinský, "Vzpomínky," 127–28.

134. Svobodová, "Nástin dějin," 239–43.

135. Hybeš, *Práce a vzpomínky*, vol. 1, 146; The calendars which were published from 1887–1893 by the editor of *Rovnost*, Josef Hybeš, were anti-religious in character. See Svobodová, "Nástin dějin," 240.

136. Svobodová, "Nástin dějin," 241–42. Here there are many references to the distribution and spread of calendar literature.

137. *Protokol XI. řádného sjezdu českoslovanské sociálně demokratické strany dělnické konaného ve dnech 7., 8. a 9. prosince 1913 na Žofíně v Praze*. Prague 1913, 45.

138. See Krejč, *Dělnický kalendář*. The satirical magazine *Rašple* in Brno was filled with anti-clerical caricatures (1890–1924).

clerical crusade the Social Democrats also made use of literature and as well as the almanacs there was scarcely a copy of *Červánky* which did not contain a short story or a
serialized feuilleton where the stories featured something which pointed to the negative
influence of the Church.[139]

To make their anti-clerical campaigns effective and simple the Social Democrats
often used linguistic and literary forms from religious literature which were then supplemented by their own anti-ecclesiastical content. One of the first socialists, Josef B.
Pecka, often used biblical expressions when spreading socialist ideas, as did the Czech
Social Democratic theorist B. Šmeral.[140] For the speedy education of their readers Social
Democratic authors often referred to the epistles,[141] and for their propaganda aims they
also used biblical figures.[142] *Rovnost* drew up a series of principles to which the working
class should conform in the form of a kind of Ten Working-Class Commandments.[143] The
Social Democrats' trips to the country also did not differ greatly in form from Catholic
pilgrimages.[144]

Indirect evidence of the spread of secularization within the working class can be
gathered from the court cases for the crime according to paragraph 122 and the offence
according to paragraph 303 of disturbing religion which were heard at the Regional
Criminal Court in Brno.[145] 40 percent of these offences were committed in Brno and
its environs and the large majority of the offenders were manual laborers. Even though
there were various motives and they did not always indicate a well-thought-out position, they nevertheless testify to the fact that there was a decline in respect towards the
Church and religion in the mentality of the working class.

CONCLUSION

From the outlined explanation it is apparent that the negative position of Social
Democracy towards the Church and religion played a key role in its campaigns and in its
overall political and public behaviour, as well as helping to spread secularizing tendencies throughout the working class. The anti-clericalism of the Social Democrats grew
from the same ideological background as liberal anti-clericalism, which aimed to push
religion and the Church into the private sphere, and for a long time the atheist movement
was able to coexist with liberal anti-clericalism. Despite similarities in character and mu-

139. Often the authors were the editors themselves; see Špera, "Byli spaseni," *Červánky*, vol. 12, 1900,
231–33; "Inserát," *Červánky*, vol. 12, 1900, 308.

140. Kořalka, "Ateismus průkopníků socialismu," 26; Galandauer, "Poměr Bohumíra Smetala
k náboženské otázce," 219.

141. Burian, *Socialistické epištoly*; Havíř, *Epištoly k rolnictvu a k pracovníkům*.

142. "Kašpar, Melichar a Baltazar, na cestách po Moravě," *Besídka.* Humorous supplement to no. 140 of
Rovnost, vol. 18, October 20, 1912.

143. "Desatero přikázání dělnických," *Rovnost*, vol. 14, September 22, 1908, 3.

144. "Veliký všedělnický výlet brněnských organisací sociálně-demokratických," *Rovnost*, vol. 14, July
26, 1908, 4.

145. Řepa, "'Rušení náboženství' na Jižní Moravě," 125–34.

tual cooperation in society, Social Democratic anti-clericalism had its own unique traits which separated it from non-socialist anti-clericalism.

1. At the heart of Social Democracy was the concept of changing society, which meant not only removing the working class from the influence of religion and the Church, but preparing it for a completely new social order.

2. Therefore, the anti-clericalism of Social Democracy did not only concentrate on a few selected demands but functioned as a totality, its criticism touching upon all aspects of Church life in the past and present and also upon religious faith, where the critics used the findings of science and linked it to human enlightenment.

3. Unlike other non-Catholic parties, which were often pragmatically anti-clerical and whose anti-clerical activities were often a matter for individuals or targeted campaigns, in the case of Social Democracy the critics of the Church and religion were single-minded, systematic and had the complete support of the party at all levels.

4. The anti-clerical activity of the Social Democrats was also much more intensive, bitter and ruthless. In order to discredit the Church and religion they used various means, they did not restrict themselves to one-off campaigns and their anti-clericalism was a permanent part of their public activities.

5. The concern expressed by B. Šmeral in 1908 that too great an emphasis on anti-clericalism might lead Social Democracy to undervalue its other everyday tasks was to a certain extent justified. On the one hand the anti-clerical campaign was much more understandable and easier to put into practice for the working class than the principles of socialist teaching, and on the other hand anti-clericalism could easily become an instrument for achieving specific political goals and could therefore be elevated to a priority for the advancement of Social Democracy. This occurred principally in Moravia, where anti-clericalism was the link for a political bloc of progressive parties with the aim of forcing the Catholic parties from leadership in provincial politics.

6. As had happened earlier in Germany, the religious discourse of the Social Democrats in the Czech lands turned to the historical delegitimation of the Catholic Church, offering significant competition to the religious discourse led from positions of Catholicism and liberalism and significantly contributing to the hastening of secularizing tendencies.[146]

7. Even if it is difficult to state the extent to which the anti-clerical activities of Social Democracy helped in the propagation of secularizing tendencies amongst the working class before the First World War, their effect was without doubt substantial. This was not even a case of workers leaving the Church en masse, but rather a deepening of their alienation from a traditionally religious view of the world, and their negative attitude towards the Church became an integral part of their socio-

---

146. Prüfer, *Sozialismus statt Religion*.

cultural environment. The fruits of this process were obviously harvested in the subsequent decades when the Czech nation—also thanks to Social Democratic anti-clericalism—became one of the most atheistic nations in Europe.

6

Catholics and the Issue of Working-Class Secularization

PAVEL MAREK

T HE AIM OF THIS study is to show the response of the Catholic elite in society in the second half of the nineteenth century to the process of secularization occurring within the working class. The paper is divided into three parts. Following the introductory passages, which look at the general situation within the Catholic Church, the example of a leading Czech Catholic philosopher, sociologist and politician of the time, Antonín Lenz, is used to analyse the relationship of the Catholic Church towards socialist teachings and towards visions of a modern secular society which, with their offer of addressing social problems, led to a large section of the working class moving away from Catholicism. The third part then considers whether Catholicism had the ideas necessary to solve the problem of secularization in society, with emphasis on the working class. This paper follows up on our research into the development of Czech Catholicism during the period mentioned which has been published in previous works: primary sources are also cited, as well as a broader list of national and international literature. This contribution does not intend to set out in a detailed, exhaustive manner how to approach the issue, rather it explores the material that requires more detailed study in the future.

I.

From the outset it is necessary to state that the Catholic Church responded to the rise of industrial society and the new phenomena and realities accompanying this process in a very negative and disapproving manner.[1] We need only recall some of the initiatives which were connected in the 1860s and 1870s with Pope Pius IX[2] or the trends following the establishment of the first Vatican Council. However, alongside this rather destructive

---

1. See e.g., Kryštůfek, *Dějiny církve katolické*, vol. 2, 509 f; Putna, *Česká katolická literatura*, 39–159; Wandruszka and Urbanitsch. *Die Habsburgermonarchie 1848–1918*, vol. 4, 155–62; Weitlauff, *Kirche zwischen Aufbruch und Verweigerung*, 281–315.

2. Benz, "Die Stellung der Modernismus," 93; Marek, "Církve a česká společnost," 143–54; Marek, "K problematice církevního rozkolu," 87–88; Weis, "Proměny vztahů mezi církví a habsbursko-lotrinskou dynastií," 15–16.

approach there also existed a constructive response which could be labelled as creative and which did not reject the model of modern society. The Catholic elites did not hide the fact that they held serious reservations about it, but they looked for a way to come to terms with it, to render it tolerable and acceptable to Catholics to such a degree that they could live with it. In this context we might mention the encyclical series and speeches of Pius's successor Leo XIII[3] or the approaches of the Catholic modernists as representatives of the unofficial Church structures.[4] The proposals were aimed at changes in the law, for example in the legislative relationship between the state and the Church. Globally they sought the construction of an alternative model of society to that of the liberals and the socialists in particular. However, at the same time, in response to the inability to transform these visions into reality in political life, we will reflect on the efforts to build a Catholic camp as one of the main "pillars" of society. This concerns an "alternative society" which is a self-contained whole where Catholics might live "from the cradle to the grave," if possible far from their enemies. The steps taken by the Catholics in this area were not particularly original, rather they were a response to the trends existing in the political and social scene at the time, adapting to the efforts of their competitors, rivals and opponents.

The Catholic analysis of industrial society looked unfavourably at the attempts to secularize life, which removed religion and the Church from the center of people's attention. It recognized this both in rural and urban life and set about trying to find a way to address the problem—i.e., to stop it. If we were to carry out an analysis of the aforementioned Catholic documents concerning the issue of the urban, working-class environment, then we could come to these conclusions:

1. The Catholic Church maintained that the loss of religious faith and trust in its institutions was a result of the proletariat losing their way. They had been entrapped by the socialists and were in their ideological and organizational grip. For them, the secularization of the working class was evidence of the penetration of socialist theories into society and the adoption of a socialist, atheist model of society by some individuals.

2. The Catholic-orientated elite realized that a section of the working class had turned to socialism mainly because the leaders of the proletariat had offered them the hope, possibility and ideas to find a way out from their hard lives: for the working people they offered a vision of how to solve social issues.

3. Catholic thinkers then came quite logically to the conclusion that if the Church wanted to get these workers back on their side then they would have to offer at least the same, if not more, through a realistic Catholic vision of society and, along with it, ideas for dealing with social issues.

3. Lenz, *Socialismus v dějinách lidstva*, 263; Gelmi, *Papežové*, 247–51; Schmidlin, *Papstgeschichte der Neuesten Zeit*, 138–69; Schwaiger, *Papstum und Päpste*, 105–60.

4. On Catholic modernism see Marek, *Apologetové nebo kacíři?*, 9–70.—More literature there. See also Veverková, "K problematice studia osvícenství u nás," 25–47; Weitlauff, "'Modernismus' als Forschungsproblem," 312–44.

4. If they were able to get the working class on their side then they believed the process of secularization would stop. It was their one recourse and the one real way to solve the problem. The question of the secularization of the working class and their re-Christianization formed in the minds of Catholic thinkers an inseparable part of the effort to encourage a Christian-Social model of society, the fundamental character of which was contained in the famous and often quoted encyclical of Leo XIII—*Rerum novarum* from 1891.

It is understandable that ushering in this constructive Catholic concept of social change was not a simple matter, not only because of the organization and strength of the opposition, but also due to complications because of the lateness of their offensive and disputes within their own ranks. That is why in the second half of the nineteenth century we can not only see a predominantly intellectual struggle over the introduction of an optimal model of society, where Catholics offered a Catholic-theistic idea of society as opposed to the liberal and socialist concepts, but at the same time we can follow the struggle to introduce their own vision of how to deal with social issues. We are witnesses to efforts to win over the working class. At the same time this struggle touches on attitudes towards trends in the secularization of the proletariat and the whole of society at the time. If we are talking about a collision of ideas and those who held them, it is necessary to remember that this was about a confrontation of viewpoints, attitudes and arguments of irreconcilable opponents. They were irreconcilable largely because in the case of the socialists and Catholics they held diametrically opposed concepts of the world and the meaning of human existence. For Catholic believers the highest virtue is God, redemption and eternal life, and life on earth is a preparation and test for fulfilling this goal, whilst socialists concentrate on man and his earthly existence, and the idea of eternal life is only a mirage, a fairy tale, a product of restricted and limited thinking and knowledge.[5] If we look at the axioms of the socialist political parties concerning religion which were contained within their political programmes, starting with Eisenach in 1869 up until the fifth congress of the Czechoslovak Social Democrats in Prague in 1902, we discover that there are several leitmotifs running throughout: demands for separation of the Church from the state, the removal of religion from schools and the belief that questions pertaining to faith belong in the private sphere of life and not in the public sector. With the Heinfeld programme of 1888 the Social Democrats literally mobilized themselves in a war against obscurantism and the power of the clergy which allegedly violated man's freedom.[6] The views of the nationally oriented Czech socialists towards religion are at first sight more tolerant. The Klofáč programme of 1898 spoke of the need for complete religious freedom, which was expanded upon two years later with the proposition that the party should respect "real and sincere religious feeling," and then two years later was crowned by the thesis that the National Socials were good Christians who would not work against religion because that

5. August Bebel, cited in Lenz, *Socialismus v dějinách lidstva*, 242.

6. Prokš, *Politické programy Československé a Československé sociálně demokratické strany dělnické*, 13–61.

would prevent their programme from being realized.[7] On the other hand, they called for the removal of religion from schools and a separation of the interests of the Church and the state in which the Church would be liable to state laws, and they also drew up the battle lines for the fight against "pernicious clericalism," which is not always understood as being merely a stand against political Catholicism.[8]

II.

Czech Catholicism cannot boast of the existence of a wide range of original thinkers who wrote about the need for changing modern society and were able to formulate this transformation through the ideas of the Church into a concept of Christian-Social teaching. Rather it was more about authors developing and popularizing foreign concepts, or even epigons following in the footsteps of religious and Catholic scientific authorities. If we were to attempt to list them we would have to mention such names as Bernard Bolzano,[9] Augustin Smetana, František Matouš Klácel, as well as Matěj Procházka, Placid Jan Mathon, Václav Štulc, Václav Žižka, Rudolf Vrba, Antonín Skočdopole and Robert Neuschl, and from the group of practitioners and journalists Tomáš Jiroušek, Rudolf Horský, Prokop Šup, Emil Dlouhý-Pokorný, Václav Myslivec, Jan Šrámek, etc.

For our interpretation we chose another representative figure, the Canon of Vyšehrad,[10] later provost and municipal politician Antonín Lenz, who was a conservative Catholic author. The choice of this man led to the theme of the secularization of the working class moving somewhat into the background of our interpretation, as we concentrate more on his attitude towards socialism and concepts for dealing with social issues. However, this also allows us to view Canon Lenz as one of the leading Czech Catholic sociologists of the time, who subjected the growth of modern society to a wider analysis with all its positives and negatives. It was Antonín Lenz who, twenty years prior to his central work, which focused on our theme—*Socialismus v dějinách lidstva, jeho povaha a církev katolická jedině schopná k řešení sociální otázky* [Socialism in the history of humanity, its character and the Catholic Church's unique ability to deal with social issues] (1893) entered into extensive polemics[11] and critiques of the ideas of one of the first modern atheists in the Czech lands, Alfons Šťastný.[12] In his later years, and on the basis of the ideas contained within the *Rerum novarum* encyclical, Lenz supplemented and expanded upon his ideas on secularization in society and the various classes.

Before we enter into an analysis of Lenz's ideas, it is perhaps worth looking briefly at his life, as the name of this thinker is known today only in reference books or amongst a small circle of specialists. The priest, theologian, philosopher and historian Antonín

7. Harna, *Politické programy českého národního socialismu*, 61–62.

8. Ibid, 37–65.

9. Kořalka, "František Palacký a čeští bolzanisté," 23–47.

10. Cabalka, *Vyšehrad, svědek české minulosti*.

11. See Lenz's work: *Jan Brázda, farmer from Zlámaná Lhota, arguing with the farmer Alfons Šťastný* (1873); *The philosophy of Jan Brázda; The learned debate of Jan Brázda; The disastrous moral principles of Padařov; The syllabus of his holiness Pius IX.*

12. See e.g., Marek, "K náboženskému profilu Alfonse Šťastného," 129–54.

Lenz (February 20th 1829, Bartlov u Netolic—October 2nd 1901, Prague)[13] came from an agricultural background and his father was in the service of the Schwarzenberg family. This gifted boy graduated from a German gymnasium and a school of divinity (1850–1854) in České Budějovice and in 1854 he was ordained as a priest by Jan Valerián Jirsík (1798–1883).[14] He worked as a chaplain for five years in South Bohemia (Jilovice u Třeboně, Budislav, Deštná) and studied for another two semesters at the Faculty of Arts in Prague (theology, philosophy, natural science) and took his viva voce examinations at the theological faculty (ThDr., 1866). From 1861–1881 he was professor of dogmatics and later of fundamental theology at České Budějovice's seminary for bishops and priests. In 1881 he was elected Canon of Vyšehrad and then in 1887 as the provost of the capital.[15] However, his main area of interest was science and he belongs among the first Czech neo-Thomists. He was an ardent, uncompromising apologist for the Roman Catholic Church and wrote more than fifty theological, religious and polemical works (*Antropologie katolická* [A Catholic Anthropology], 1882). He is also known as a historian of Jan Hus (*Učení Jana Husi* [The Teachings of Jan Hus], 1875)[16] and for his interest in the history of the Reformation (works on J. Wycliffe,[17] P. Chelčický,[18] J. A. Comenius, etc).[19] His contemporaries bestowed several Church awards and posts upon him. However, he also became a member of the Imperial Czech Society of Teaching and he worked on the committee of the publishers Matice česká and the Czech Museum. Alongside his books he also wrote widely (prolifically in Bohemia) for magazines, for example the *Časopis katolického duchovenstva* [Magazine of the Catholic Clergy], *Vlast* [Homeland] and *Pastýř duchovní* (The Spiritual Shepherd), etc. As a theorist he was interested in social issues (*Socialismus v dějinách lidstva, jeho povaha a církev katolická jedině schopná k řešení sociální otázky* [Socialism in the history of humanity, its character and the Catholic Church's unique ability to deal with social issues], 1893) and in politics. This was during the initial phase of forming a Czech political Catholicism when he was a member of Katolicko-politická jednota pro Království české [The Catholic-Political Union for a Czech Kingdom][20] and was part of the circle around *Vlast* [Homeland].

13. See *Komenského slovník naučný* (vol. 7), *Masarykův slovník naučný* (vol. 4) and *Ottův slovník naučný* (vol. 15). Also obituaries in: *Český časopis historický* 7 (1901) 499; also *Časopis katolického duchovenstva* (1901), 583–84; Tumpach and Podlaha, *Bibliografie české katolické literatury náboženské*, vol. 1, 525; *Österreichisches biographisches Lexikon 1815–1950*, vol. 5, 139; Čáňová, *Slovník představitelů katolické církevní správy v Čechách*, 51; Marek, "Antonín Lenz," 154.

14. Veber, "J. V. Jirsík a jeho kruh," 98–108.

15. Kotous, *Portréty vyšehradské kapituly.*

16. *Učení Mistra Jana Husi*; further works—*Pan dr. Eduard Grégr; Hus a svoboda; Slušno-li zváti M. Jana Husa; Je pravdou nepochybnou?*

17. See Lenz's work *Apologie sněmu kostnického; Soustava učení M. Jana Viklifa; Byly články.*

18. See Lenz's work *Učení Petra Chelčického o Eucharistii; P. Chelčického učení o sedmeře svátostí; Vzájemný poměr učení.*

19. See Kutnar, *Přehledné dějiny českého a slovenského dějepisectví*, 226–7; Kutna and Marek, *Přehledné dějiny českého a slovenského dějepisectví*, 323–24. The authors reproach Lenz because in his essays he triumphs over the historian of theology; he judges and evaluates the problems of the time from a contemporary position.

20. Marek, *Český katolicismus*, 19.

Although he was not directly involved in the process leading to the establishment of Catholic political parties, he did support Catholic interests from a conservative position as a representative in the Czech municipal assembly (from 1888) of an entailed estate, and from 1889–1901 as a member of the House of Lords in Vienna.

Now we shall examine in more detail Lenz's ideas and his position towards socialism and the socialists. Lenz argued that the various socialist theoreticians basically agreed that there was no place in modern society for religion and the Church. They only differed in how radical they were in their position. If we leave aside Karl Marx and his assertion that religion is the "opium of the masses" and look elsewhere, we discover that while Mikhail Bakunin might proclaim, "Away with God. God is the main enemy of the nation, away with faith in its supernatural order, away with God's authority . . . ,"[21] Karel Liebknecht promised somewhat less radically in a speech to the Berlin parliament in January 1883 that "once the Social Democrats are in power the Catholic Church will be a fairy tale from the past,"[22] and in Nuremburg he said that." . . . first of all we will get rid of the Catholic priests. We will sharpen our knives on them the African way and skin them without soap and without water."[23] However, like August Bebel he recommended that it was better to fight against religion using non-violent methods, as insults and force overcame nothing. "No man has the right to impinge upon religion with brutish hands."[24] Radical phrases apparently did not damage the Church; no idea could be eliminated through violence or decree, no matter how truthful or untruthful it may have been. The best way to get rid of religion was through schools and science. That is why Liebknecht recommended: "We will encourage science, we will set up good schools . . . the teacher and science will act against religion."[25] In his programme he argues for freedom of religion and that it should be a private matter.

Lenz's rejection of socialism can be simply summarized into two sets of arguments:

1. From the outset the socialists' attempts to deal with social issues are mistaken because they only look at the issue from the position of the proletariat, whilst social issues do not affect only one class in society, but society as a whole. If social issues are to be addressed successfully then they must be dealt with in the interests of all groups and individuals in society.[26]

2. The concept of social change set out by the socialists is one without God and is atheistic. Its creators, from Saint-Simon through to contemporary thinkers including Marx, Lassalle, Liebknecht and their followers, are people who have lost their

---

21. Lenz, *Socialismus v dějinách lidstva*, 243.

22. Ibid., 247.

23. Ibid.

24. Ibid., 242.

25. Ibid.

26. According to the Catholics the injustice of the socialist concept of society resulted in violence towards the propertied classes and threats against the non-working classes, as well as jeopardizing the "traditional state."

faith in God. They consciously and openly distance themselves from religion and form a vision of society in which there is no room for faith and religion, because there is not even room for them in the life of man. A common denominator in their positions is a hatred of the Church and the Christian community which lies at the heart of their principles. The radicals want to destroy the Church, monastic orders, religious congregations, associations and institutions; the more liberal believe that under the guise of asserting that religion is a private matter they will allow them to go off somewhere into a corner to pray until such a time as science and teachers quietly rid the world of them.[27]

Lenz expands upon this thesis and says:

a) The socialist model of society denies human dignity and respect, since at its base is lacking love of one's fellow man.[28]

b) The socialist model of society has man ruling over man. No person has this right as power over this world comes from the authority of God and not from the authority of the masses. "And because those who rule by the authority of God are Christians and dependent on the Lord's laws, they are required to uphold them: if they live in faith, they can never be despots . . ."[29]

c) The socialist model of society is materialist, it rejects the Catholic interpretation of the world and its formation, and replaces it with the theory of evolution. It repudiates faith in the inherited sins of man and the holy sacrifice of Christ for the sins of humanity. It rejects the physical unity of mankind and divides countries into the mature and the bestial. It is reluctant to concede that man is naturally good. It rejects the articles of faith concerning God's mercy.[30]

d) The socialist model of society rejects moral law. Socialists do not want to recognize the authority of God and his ten commandments. They reject the inviolability of marriage, the Christian family and religious schooling. They give priority to the absolute freedom of human action where man himself is the law. It is impossible to build an orderly society on such a basis.[31]

---

27. One of the organisers, a prominent member of the society Vlast, which witnessed the birth of the Christian-Social movement in the Czech lands, was Tomáš Škrdle, who wrote: "Free thinkers, Social Democrats, Young Czechs and some of the Liberal Agrarians, if they were to be part of the Imperial Parliament they wouldn't hesitate to vote for similar laws [facilitating divorce, free schools, the limited functioning of priests in public life] and take the Church to where it is in France." Škrdle, "Katolíci, do voleb!," *Naše listy*, vol. 16, no. 33, April 13, 1907, 22.

28. Lenz, Socialismus v dějinách lidstva, 243.

29. Ibid., 244.

30. Ibid., 246.

31. Ibid., 247.

Antonín Lenz's negative view of socialist teachings leads to the belief that the Social Democrats want to destroy the social, political and religious order and that if they were to achieve power the result would be "immeasurable chaos."[32]

At the same time he arrives at the conclusion that the only institution capable of addressing social issues is the Catholic Church. Social issues and society's problems, the basis of which is the discrepancy between the standing and quality of life of various groups in society, are nothing new. They are not the product of industrial society, which only brought the issue closer to the surface. If the Catholic Church was able to govern successfully during the agricultural era, then there is no doubting its ability to do so in a modern industrial society. Lenz's faith here came from the conviction that the Catholic Church would use everything at its disposal in order to be successful.

How was Lenz going to convince the public of the truth of his convictions?

Again it is possible to summarize into two areas the means which Lenz believed the Catholic Church had at its disposal:

1. The Catholic Church offered direction, programmes, teachings and theories. The theoretical section is a comprehensive analysis of the problem, and the direction is applied to its solution. The humanization of industrial society is at the basis of Christian beliefs, the attempt to transform society into one where belief in God would be the alpha and omega of people's activities. Theoretical and practical Christianity would once again find their place in families, communities and nations.

2. At the same time the Catholic Church had at its disposal the means with which to help eliminate specific cases of destitution, poverty, material deprivation and lack of security, which were a breeding ground for social problems and for the socialists' ideas. In 1893 he saw an example of this in the missionary activities of the monastic orders, at the forefront of which were the Salesians and the work of the Vincentians, as well as other voluntary associations and institutions of the Church and Catholic laymen.[33]

By examining the means which the Catholic Church has to deal with social issues, Lenz ranks amongst the Catholic authors and thinkers who see the situation primarily as being the remit of Catholic charity. However, he is unable to solve the basic problem of how to put the established Catholic social teachings into practice and into the life of society, transforming modern society and harmonizing it through the Church's example.

Although Lenz's work came out during the period following the publication of Leo's social encyclical, it represents a current of thought in the Church which was superceded by the *Rerum novarum* encyclical.[34] Without wanting to unnecessarily glorify the publication of the *Rerum novarum* encyclical, its reception in the Czech lands alone shows that new elements in the approach towards dealing with social issues had begun to appear

32. Ibid., 10.

33. Ibid., 362–64.

34. Knoll, *Zur Tradition der Christlich-soziale Partei*, 150–66.

in Church circles by the second half of the 1880s. The future would not only be about charity and voluntary work, even though these would continue to form a fundamental, perhaps even decisive part of the Church's activities in the social sphere, but efforts were moved to the political sphere, to the struggle to establish a concept of social change on the principles of solidarity. Here the most significant role was to be played by political Catholicism. The Catholic political parties, in the spirit of their religious-apologist efforts, began to concentrate on placing Catholics within the structures of civic society, within representative organizations and committees which influenced the character of society. At the same time they (in particular their Christian-Social branch) became essential to the Catholic camp, where they saw the chance to immediately implement their ideas for a Catholic life.

III.

According to the vision set out in the *Rerum novarum* encyclical it was assumed that the process of secularization of the working class would stop when the Catholic vision for addressing the proletariat's basic problems had been achieved. In other words the Catholics would have to put into practice their concept of society and substitute the model of secularization and civic society which the state stood for, whilst winning over the working class. If we overlook the problem of whether this vision was viable, it is necessary to ask the question whether it had sufficient strength, means and potential to achieve this. The analysis of the situation in the Habsburg monarchy contained within Jiří Malíř's study *Sekularizace a politika v „dlouhém" 19. století* [Secularization and Politics in the "Long" 19th Century][35] convincingly summarizes the reasons why it could not be successful in its efforts. Alongside this, it is necessary to reflect on the fact that Leo XIII's proclamations brought new and fresh impetus to the life of the Catholic Church, though on the whole the papal policy was evidence of a restoration which influenced the mentality and behaviour of the heirarchies in individual countries and subdued those elements struggling for change and dialogue. The Church set out a programme, but it failed to find adequate resources for its implementation, as though there was a lack of will, interest and resolve to support its vision and attract laymen and allies to it. Undoubtedly some steps were taken towards initiating the programme of change, but they were relatively hesitant.

In the policy and position of the Catholics there was a preference for a defensive, apologetic programme of isolation, closing inwards and self-sufficiency, which quite concisely characterizes the ideas for building the Catholic camp. If we accept that this was more important than moving towards dialogue, presenting their virtues and claiming to be at the heart of society, then it is necessary to realize that a Catholic camp was never established as a functioning model for linking the threads of society and protecting all, or at least the basic, human needs from "the cradle to the grave." Perhaps it stopped halfway, maybe it did not have enough room to develop, more likely it was unfeasible

---

35. Malíř, "Sekularizace a politika v 'dlouhém' 19. století," 11–24; See also Weis, "Osvícenští panovníci," 5–21; Georgiev, "Mezi svéprávností a poručnictvím," 169–85.

and was more about a symbolic and theoretical concept than a formula for an alternative functioning of interest groups in society. Perhaps more apposite than the term "camp" for an image of reality is Catholic "milieu,"[36] indicating the awareness of belonging to a specific environment with specific features which differed from the conditions in society at the time.

A detailed analysis of the character of the Czech Catholic camp at the turn of the twentieth century is lacking.[37] The authors engaged in this topic mention the establishment of association structures and talk about the building of Catholic houses as a focal point for local businesses and events, economic activities, cultural gatherings, etc.

The Catholic camp can be seen as the connection between the clergy and believers. Its basic building blocks are the Church structures, which according to the custom of the time also had a leading role in the operation of the camp.[38] For the main part they did not reveal themselves obviously, but indirectly. The overwhelming majority of the Church elites in the Czech lands at the turn of the twentieth century accepted the restoration policy from Rome; they were conservative, politically neutral and distant from the national movement, which to a large extent was due to their national ancestry.[39] They opposed many of the public activities of the lower clergy, which were halted and restricted. Their ideal was the priest in the sacristy, and that is why for the most part they prevented the public and political activity of the chaplains from becoming a driving force of the Catholic camp, as they wanted to keep it under complete control. In 1910 there was a decree from the Consistorial Congregation which advised the clergy against becoming involved in the established authorities, savings banks, banks and lending institutions.[40] On the other hand, the Catholic camp benefited from the existence of organized Church structures which developed regular activities, had a stable character and managed finances, the distribution of which focused more inwards to the Church than outwards—that is if we discount charity and focus more on political and public life.

The second pillar of the Catholic camp were undoubtedly political parties[41] which developed more slowly in comparison to other contemporary interest groups because they originated mainly due to apologist reasons and came to the defense of the Church and believers; their goal was to gain political power, to influence the laws being introduced, to prevent legislation that would move the Church away from public life and to use power in conjunction with their aims and programmes. The main weakness of Czech political Catholicism was its lack of unity due to a territorial split which brought about separate developments in Bohemia and Moravia, and this mental (social) division resulted in the existence in parallel of two party currents, with Bohemia in particular

36. Klöker, "Das katholische Milieu," 241–47.

37. See Malíř, *Od spolků k moderním politickým stranám*, 254–59.

38. See e.g., Hanuš, "Kněz a politik," 48–49.

39. See e.g., Marek, "Biskup Eduard J. N. Brynych," 248–60.

40. Hanuš, "Kněz a politik," 48.

41. See Malíř, *Od spolků k moderním poitickým stranám*, 161–73; Trapl, *Politický katolicismus*, 49–58; Marek, *Český katolicismus*, 13–166; Marek, "Český politický katolicismus a politické strany," 255–311; Marek, "Počátky českého politického katolicismu," 8–170.

facing complicated organizational regrouping which weakened the political work. The overall fragility of the political structures came to the fore in the elections at a Cislethian and municipal level as the crucial factors for establishing Catholics in such areas and positions where they could protect Catholic interests. The Catholics came into conflict with the Social Democrats and the liberal-oriented parties, but they even had to oppose party bloc politics which completely undermined their gains. The tension within the Christian-Social Party in the Bohemian organization was so disruptive that they abandoned their original priority of the working class and became representatives of the rural, Catholic-oriented population. In contrast to the disarray in which political Catholicism found itself in Bohemia, the growth of the Catholic political party in Moravia led to it becoming the flagship party. Due to the accommodating and tolerant position of Mořic Hruban and the inventiveness of Jan Šrámek, the Catholic "dual party" was established in a system of branch satellite organizations on the principle that the proposed "Catholic column" would not remain fictitious, but would start functioning, underpinned by the "hands of the workers" as an essential component of the system; here the formation of a bulkhead against the secularization of the working class began at least to approach reality. The expanding association structures formed the backbone of the Catholic camp[42]— we have already mentioned one of its branches in the form of organizations affiliated with political parties. The personal relationships and informal environment in evidence were perhaps more effective in countering the process of secularization. The effectiveness of the influence of these factors was strengthened by other interest groups of a social, cultural[43] or leisure character. Here we also see the largest growth being in publication activities which reflected the heterogenous composition of the Catholic camp as well as playing an important role in unifying the ideas of its supporters.[44]

However, there were only a few short-lived manufacturing concerns which applied some of the teachings and principles of Catholic solidarity as mentioned in the *Rerum novarum* encyclical and which could transform the position of the primary producer. Only very seldom was there news of groups attempting to build Catholic businesses on associative principles, and even these did not last very long.

The above outline of the situation in the Catholic camp shows that not even the tendency towards building an enclosed and impervious social environment was an effective remedy against the process of secularization of society—it could only slow these trends at best. At the same time it has to be noted that the complete secularization of society has not occurred even one hundred years later. Although the pressure on religion and the Church intensified throughout the twentieth century and totalitarian communist regimes attempted not only to confine them to the private sphere but to destroy them completely, the new wave in Christianity demonstrates that faith in a transcendental human civilization is a timeless value.

42. Marek, P.: *Český katolicismus 1890–1914*, 221–39.

43. On Catholic literature see Putna, *Česká katolická literatura*, 801.

44. Marek, "Tisk českého katolického tábora," 53–88.

7

Secularization and the Working Class's Response to Marxism

LUKÁŠ FASORA

ANSWERING THE QUESTION TO what extent the working-class movement in the Czech lands was Marxist is one of the most important and at the same time most difficult historical issues of the nineteenth century. Even if we look at this question in a narrower sense, that is by examining the working class's relationship towards the Church and religion, we are still faced with an exceptionally difficult task. Socialism in general, rather than just the variety based on Karl Marx's works, has often been characterized in research into secularization as the second wave of the "religion of humanity." This "new religion" began exerting an influence on Western Europe from the end of the eighteenth century and among the most important manifestations of its initial phase can be counted positivism. However, its influence was restricted to the upper and middle classes, only reaching the lower classes when it had transformed into socialism.[1] Although comparing Marxist socialism to religion is still somewhat intellectually controversial, I support the idea that Marxist socialists were not merely a political lobby or pressure group, but rather people working with teleological and utopian ideas, while the whole of the socialist movement was increasingly built on a belief in the truth of Marxism rather than on a comprehensive understanding of it. There are also elements of a "new religion" in the socialist cult of the hero, the characteristic mass, the May Day marches and so on. The search for similarities between religion and (Marxist) socialism is not merely a superficially constructed debate.[2] Marx's analysis of the economic aspects of capitalism was certainly an exceptional scientific and intellectual achievement, although at the same time we find many (deliberately) vague and uncertain aspects in his interpretation of the world. In particular his interpretations of parliamentary democracy, revolutions, the dictatorship of the proletariat and the future "classless society" are ideas with an obvious utopian basis, and this is not altered by the fact that in his works Marx always firmly

---

1. McLeod, *Náboženství a lidé*, 66.
2. See Hölscher, *Weltgericht oder Revolution*.

set himself apart from the old views of the pioneers of socialism and used the label of utopian socialists with pejorative overtones. Strengthened by the teleological elements of Marxist theory and implemented by the luminaries of German Social Democracy, Karl Kautsky and August Bebel, it became clear that socialists were not to prepare for revolution, but to expect the *"großer Kladderradatsch"* of capitalist society.[3] This, therefore, was not active politics, but rather patiently awaiting the inevitable.

MARXISM WITHIN THE SOCIALIST MOVEMENT

Marx's theory gradually began to displace all other socialist teachings within the movement, particularly so-called Lassallism. According to the American historian Gary Steenson, Austrian Social Democracy, compared to its German, French and Italian counterparts, was one of the most rigid in its relationship towards Marxism, though the author did not always distinguish the separate interpretations of Marx's works (Kautskyanism, Bernsteinism and Austro-Marxism) and did not observe thoroughly the understanding of Marx's works at a grassroots level.[4] It is no wonder that in Germany and Austria the success of Marxism was basicaly due to the repression linked to Bismark's law against socialism in 1878 and the state of emergency in and around Vienna from 1884–1890. It appeared that Marx's remarks concerning the class-enemy character of the state were fully justified. The important Social Democratic publisher Heinrich Dietz wrote on this matter in 1886 to Kautsky: "For us now only exists either—or! Here, the proletariat with their emancipatory struggle in the Marxist sense of the word; there, a moribund form of society which wants to prolong its existence using socialist trinkets."[5]

At the same time, very few politicians amongst the active comrades were able to read Marx's works because they were "too hard to digest." Even that icon of German Social Democracy, August Bebel, admitted in his memoirs that he struggled in vain over the years to read Marx's economic works.[6] In her microanalysis of the workers' movements in Leipzig and Pilsen Adina Lieske reaches similar conclusions and speaks of their education as being at best "primary school" Marxism, even if the situation in Saxony was fundamentally better than in the towns of Western Bohemia.[7]

To what extent, therefore, were the members and sympathizers of Austrian Social Democracy true experts on Marx's works?

THE STATE OF RESEARCH

Older Czech research into the working class and working-class movements understandably tiptoed around this issue. From the viewpoint of the main representatives of Czech Marxist-Leninist history, the wholehearted acceptance and practical application of Marxist revolutionary theory by the working class was a sign of their progressiveness

---

3. Berger, "Marxismusrezeption," 193–209, here 201.

4. Steenson, *After Marx, Before Lenin.*

5. Berger, "Marxismusrezeption," 199.

6. Ibid., 198–99.

7. Lieske, *Arbeiterkultur und bürgerliche Kultur*, 159–62.

and readiness for revolution. The words of the chief ideologues of the movement, beginning with Marx and Engels, then progressing via Lenin to Stalin, who was of course expelled from this pantheon in the 1950s, were sources of unassailable wisdom and milestones along the proper path. The theoretical knowledge of the works of Marx and Engels among Austrian Social Democrats was traditionally judged to be relatively poor.[8] Every digression from the tactics established by them was thought to be due to a lack of ideological education on the part of the leadership, whilst the unerring proletariat moved relentlessly forwards towards fulfilling its historical role. Pressure from the grassroots was therefore directed either towards the rehabilitation of the "lost sheep" or to their expulsion from the working-class camp.[9] After the theme was rehabilitated in 1989, apart from a few exceptions,[10] there was a general "flight" from research into the workers' movement and only a few provocative voices were to be heard in the resultant dearth of debate. Jana Machačová and Jiří Matějček formulated an uncompromising stance towards the issue whereby "the majority of the working class were not interested in social emancipation, voting rights, parliamentary representation and politicians but above all wanted 'a cheap organization' with low contributions . . . which would fight for higher wages and permanent employment."[11] Both authors connect the mentality of the working class with the notion of "primitive thinking," of being easily susceptible to "simple slogans and demagogues when they conformed to the mood of the crowd." According to them, the socialist movement was marked by aggressive behaviour, petty arguments, shouting, coarseness, intolerance, violence, jealousy and hatred, slander, constant schisms and informing for the police.[12] The authors viewed the contribution of the workers' associations as being chiefly the cultivation of workers' entertainment after the model of the bourgeoisie, and as an area of emancipation for working-class women.

MICROHISTORICAL INVESTIGATION

To substantiate Jana Machačová and Jiří Matějček's thesis, I examined sources from the Moravian cities of Brno, Prostějov and Nový Jičín in order to investigate the influence of Marxism on the ordinary members of the Social Democratic Party and those sympathetic towards it. The sources come from the societies' activities, especially educational societies in the broadest sense of the word, as well as from the local, regional and trade press,[13] and police notes from public gatherings organized by socialists are also examined. I take into account Jürgen Habermas's thesis on the evaluation of sources, which emphasises the press as being the main element in the formation of a primary independent and

8. Šolle, *Dělnické hnutí v českých zemích*, 103 ff.

9. Šindelář, "Přehled dějin dělnického hnutí na Moravě," 3–57; for a concise formulation of the approach see Šolle, *Dělnické hnutí v českých zemích*, 9 ff.; for an example of the ideological thesis see 105, 142.

10. Machačová, *Mzdové a stávkové hnutí dělnictva*; Machačová, "Výzkum stávek z 19. a 20. století," 139–51.

11. Machačová and Matějček, *Nástin sociálního vývoje*, 270.

12. Ibid., 270–71.

13. Excerpts from the magazines *Rovnost, Volksfreund, Křik lidu, Arbeiterstimme* (Brno), *Hlas lidu* (Prostějov), *Volksrecht* (Nový Jičín); the satirical magazine *Rašple* (Brno); specialist magazines *Kovodělník, Zájmy textilníka/Textilník, Dělník v tabákové továrně, Der Tabakarbeiter*.

potentially critical area. In this regard he did not consider independent public gatherings or organized movements as the most important elements, only independent journalism.[14] The three selected cities represent three levels of development in socialist organizations within the Czech lands. Brno was undoubtedly a center for movements of a Central European significance with a developed working-class subculture, although not reaching the importance of Vienna (in this category it is more comparable with Pilsen, Liberec, or Ostrava in Moravia). Prostějov was more a center of regional significance, where the politically conscious center of the working-class subculture was relatively small but the larger surrounding area of supporters represented in provincial terms an immeasurable strength and alternative to the dominating city culture (into this category could also be placed Třebíč, Šternberk, and Ústí nad Labem). Nový Jičín represents one of the cities where the workers' movement was "dormant" and posed no real threat to the dominant bourgeois culture.[15] There were many similar towns across the Czech lands and Nový Jičín was by no means the most "dormant," as not long before the First World War the local socialists enjoyed significant success and were able to print their own magazine. Into this category we could place cities where the workers' movements were less successful (e.g., Znojmo, Uherské Hradiště and Benešov).

The milieu theory is useful when analysing reactions to Marxism, in this case the socialist milieu and the observation of the so-called column organization of the whole socialist camp. We must first focus our attention on the leaders of the socialist movements of these towns and establish their theoretical education and level of understanding of Marxism. The leaders represent the core of the movement as the most ambitious and active elements. We can count several dozen figures in the towns under research, the great majority of those being active in Brno, where they held political office, were members of the regional party leadership or editors of the party newspapers. It is assumed that trade union secretaries, the chairmen of the health insurance unions, the insurance unions and the large consumer unions all had looser relationships to the party and its ideology, although generally these people can be characterized as being functionaries of the movement.

Another grouping was made up of the grassroots, the ordinary party members, whose numbers rose, though with many fluctuations. Even though it is difficult to quantify exactly, we estimate that for Brno and the surrounding area the number for this group was approximately one thousand people, in Prostějov barely over one hundred, and in Nový Jičín a few dozen. The third grouping of supporters was made up of members of satellite organizations controlled by the socialists, with some of them being very large, numbering tens of thousands of members.

THE MARXISM OF THE FUNCTIONARIES

According to German historians, amongst the leadership of the movement it is possible to differentiate between the members of the first generation (the so-called Bebel

14. Habermas, *Strukturální přeměna veřejnosti*, 125.
15. See Saldern, *Vom Einwohner zum Bürger*.

generation) and the following, so-called Ebert generation. Even if the whole concept of generations is methodologically debatable, the fact remains that a different view of the world amongst working-class leaders was formed by their experiences of the period of victimization—i.e., from around 1890.[16] J. Machačová and J. Matějček described those people who had experienced victimization as "Marxist idealists." They felt that with their successors there came to the fore an inclination towards bureaucratization and a concept of politics as being a clear battle for power.[17] However, amongst the Marxist idealists in the towns under research, we do not find many people who could be regarded as theoretical thinkers with the ability to properly apply a Marxist interpretation of the world. One exceptional figure in this regard was the editor of the magazine Rovnost, Pankrác Krkoška (1861–1888), who during his brief life made exceptional progress in his independent reflections on Darwin's theory of descent and attempted to translate the works of Marx, devising a Czech Marxist terminology in the process. However, Krkoška was not a worker and he could rely on the support of the teaching institute for his intellectual endeavours, which for most of the people classified as working-class functionaries was a very distant dream. Krkoška's work as the editor-in-chief (1885–1886) was therefore characterized by a gulf between the editorial board of the paper and its potential readers. The paper suffered from a lack of subscribers, for whom Krkoška's prescriptive educational style was too hard to swallow, and Krkoška soon realized that the comrades simply did not read his often original and valuable theoretical arguments.[18]

After his departure as the head of the editorial board, Alois Sobotka (1886–1890) took over the running of the paper and gave it a far more popular character with a simplistic style and a complete absence of theoretical ambition.[19] The third of the editors-in-chief, Josef Hybeš, then began to direct this, the most important Czech socialist newspaper in Moravia, firmly behind the task of agitation work. In 1897 Hybeš set out the following aims of the newspaper: "We have to choose the tactic which will provide us with the most widespread agitation, because agitation, spirited agitation, can only swell our ranks, and for the moment what we need the most is to swell our ranks. When we are numerous, we will be strong and powerful, and only then will we be able to realize our principles."[20] Even Hybeš's Marxist hagiographer Otakar Franěk admits that Hybeš was primarily a practical politician; theoretical issues were relatively insignificant in his works, although his theoretical knowledge was still far superior to that of ordinary socialist functionaries.[21]

One of the most educated socialist leaders, the poet Josef Krapka-Náchodský, explained in 1893 that the difference between Marx and Lassalle was that Lassalle was a promoter of Marx's work. According to Krapka, despite having devoted 36 years to socialism, Marx was not particularly well known among the ivory-tower scholars or the

16. Welskopp, "Die 'Generation Bebel,'" 51–68; Braun, "Die 'Generation Ebert,'" 69–86, here 70.

17. Machačová and Matějček, *Problémy obecné kultury*, 270.

18. Franěk, *Pankrác Krkoška*, 57–8.

19. Ibid., 58.

20. *100 let literatury v Rovnosti*, 16.

21. Franěk, "Josef Hybeš," 9–53, here 30–31.

working class. On the other hand, Lassalle's life was "scintillating," as his death in a duel demonstrated. Krapka, who was otherwise well read, translated Marx's works and travelled widely, was not aware of theoretical differences between the teachings of the two great socialists.[22]

Explaining the basic postulates of Marxism was carried out in a very didactic form, mainly through literary texts and minor political and local news sources—simpler means which would awaken the "class ethos." This was how Pierre Bourdieu defined one of the three means by which a political opinion was formed, in this case an opinion with a strong connection to immediate (non-political) moral experience. However, these were based solely on everyday practical problems, not on a deeper understanding of reality.[23] Brno's police director reported to the governor that the ability for theoretical thinking amongst the local socialists was more inherent to the leaders of the German working class,[24] which might have been due to their understanding of Marx's works in the original language, as well as closer links to the movement's Viennese center and intellectual leaders. Even though in the most important German Social Democratic newspaper, Volksfreund, there are attempts by the Brno leaders to write articles with more theoretical ambitions than might be seen in Rovnost (e.g., on the relationship between the party and the unions, or on the polemic between K. Kautsky and R. Luxemburg), even here the theoretical aspects of the paper were not particularly striking. According to H. Mommsen, this was partly due to the fact that Viktor Adler personally disliked the ideological Marxists, in particular personalities such as R. Luxemburg, and much preferred pragmatism to idealism, which he judged to be a completely unsuitable, fragile position, and one in which Austrian Social Democracy found itself.[25] Even Brno's police director in the mid-1880s noticed that the success of Marxism had been to the detriment of the established, open, albeit relatively shallow theoretical discussions on the works of F. Lassalle or H. Schulze-Delitzsche, though of course he did not link this change with the persecution of the movement and the escalation of social tensions.[26]

Adina Lieske also noted the definite triumph of agitation over education in the activities of Pilsen's workers' educational association. At the same time she discovered the existence of a "working circle" of functionaries, whose activities had the elitist character of preparing the leading cardres of the party.[27] However, even here we do not come across the study of Marxist theory; instead it involves a (speedy) education in law, politics and rhetoric, graduating towards a specific form of applied Marxism.[28] We can also observe a similar process in Prostějov's Český politický klub dělnický [Czech Political

22. Franěk, *Rebel a básník*, 71.

23. Bourdieu, *Distinction*, 419.

24. Moravský zemský archiv [Moravian Provincial Archives] in Brno, B13 Místodržitelství presidium, bk. 357, no. 2782.

25. Mommsen, "Arbeiterbewegung in Deutschland und Österreich," 424–49, here 435.

26. Moravský zemský archiv [Moravian Provincial Archives] in Brno, B26p Policejní ředitelství Brno, bk. 218, no. 1230/1873.

27. Lieske, Adina: *Arbeiterkultur und bürgerliche Kultur*, 159–61.

28. Ibid.

Workers' Club],[29] although in the activities of Brno's Volksfreund association (with a large membership outside Brno) even these educational aspects are absent, with political agitation again being at the forefront. A slightly different direction was taken by the most important workers' association in Nový Jičín, the Arbeiter-Bildungs-Verein [Worker's Education Association] (est. 1869), which developed from a non-Marxist educational association with a significant representation of impoverished craftsmen into an association with a more working-class, "class-defined" character in the 1880s, although most of its activities were centered around entertainment.[30]

This was similar to the Dělnická beseda [Workers' Community Center] Barák in Jihlava and the workers' centers in Brno.[31]

The need for the movement to focus on generating agitators to address the masses seemed to be incompatible with acquiring a broad-based education. When comparing Pilsen and Leipzig, A. Lieske notes that the workers educated in Saxony had a much better knowledge of modern science and were more oriented towards mastering modern techniques, which increased the opportunities for skilled workers in the labor market. However, Leipzig, within a German framework, was a town whose workers' movement was unusually oriented towards the politics of the educated, which A. Lieske explains was due to the significant representation of skilled craftsmen and small-scale production workers amongst the supporters of the local socialists.[32] In Pilsen, on the other hand, the core of the socialist movement was made up of workers from heavy industry, for whom, in view of the technology used, it was very difficult to secure further education, and they lacked the motivation for social advancement which was present in small-scale industry. In Prostějov from 1878–1880 there functioned an association which belonged to the wider circle of socialist organizations, but its educational activities were not linked to agitation and it had as its central aim the improvement of education predominantly for young journeymen. At a lower level there was a revision of reading, writing and stylistics, while at a higher level there were courses in technical drawing and physics (magnetism, electricity). The courses were based on readings and discussions of articles from scientific periodicals or of the works of Jules Verne. This was a unique association, as in the other towns we do not come across any similarly oriented workers' educational associations, and even the Prostějov association was of little significance to the overall direction of the workers' movement as their school operated for no more than two years.[33]

Agitation and entertainment were at the center of the Czech socialists' interests, or more precisely, agitation in the form of entertainment.[34] The most valued characteristic

---

29. "Rozmach sociálně demokratické strany v Prostějově," *Ječmínek*, vol. 1, no. 1, October 3, 1908, 2; *Ječmínek*, vol. 1, no. 3, October 17, 1908, 1; *Ječmínek*, vol. 1, no. 5, October 31, 1908, 1.

30. Czuczka, "Geschichte der Arbeiterbewegung," *Volkspresse*, May 19, 1931, 4; Schuster, "Die Geschichte der Arbeiterbewegung in Neu-Titschein," *Das Kuhländchen*, vol. 12, 1931, 19–11, 24–29, 42–45, here from 42–45.

31. Krupička, "Hrst vzpomínek," 1. *Stráž Vysočiny*, vol. 2, no. 5, January 31, 1947, 1.

32. Lieske, *Arbeiterkultur und bürgerliche Kultur*, 139–42.

33. "Vývoj sociálně demokratické strany v Prostějově," *Ječmínek*, vol. 1, no. 2, October 10, 1908, 2.

34. Lieske, *Arbeiterkultur und bürgerliche Kultur*, 139–42.

of a workers' leader was his ability to captivate a crowd—the delivery of a fiery speech was more highly prized than an article in the newspapers.[35] In the better cases these people had the command of an applied version of Marxism, which consisted of a few basic theorems drawn from the difficult works, which they were then able to "graft on" to the daily experiences of the public. And they enjoyed undoubted success with this tactic, as was shown by the growth in supporters and influence. After 1900 there was widespread political and ideological opportunism, particularly among the functionaries of the socialist satellite organizations. One of the most influential of the Brno socialists, Karel Vaněk, entirely dismissed a political interpretation of activities in his main power base, namely health insurance;[36] Rudolf Bechyně[37] similarly ruled out a politico-ideological interpretation of the work of the socialists in Prostějov's general committee; Antonín Školák, the secretary of the textile workers' union, was often sharply criticized by the textile workers for "non-Marxist negotiations," and so on.[38]

Marxism amongst the Grassroots

If there were no experts in Marxism amongst the socialist functionaries, we can hardly expect to find them amongst the grassroots. Understandably, we come up against a lack of sources here, and we can only partialy reconstruct the situation on the basis of scattered references and notes of varying provenance.

When A. von Saldern examined the same issue, he used Edward P. Thompson's thesis that the lower classes' response to Marxism depended on two fixed approaches, or rather feelings:

a) workers whose experiences were from small-scale industry connected Marxism with a sentiment linked to the demise of a considerably idealized old world of craft industries, where the owner of the firm was at the same time its (sole) employee.

b) workers who had no experience of small-scale industry harboured a sense of injustice which had its roots in the notion of the "moral economy" and therefore a critical view of the allegedly immoral attitudes of the representatives of capital towards the value of human labor.

From the pleiad of Marxist opinions to emerge from all of his theories, the most popular dictum amongst the workers was: "Class oppression leads to class struggle." From a discursive angle, one typical statement to be heard from the camp of orators was: "The capitalists suck the blood of the workers," which, along with others, attacked in a com-

---

35. Moravský zemský archiv [Moravian Provincial Archives] in Brno, B13 Místodržitelství presidium, bk.290, no. 3239/75, fol. 455.

36. "Sjezd českých nemocenských pokladen z Moravy a Slezska v Brně," *Svépomoc*, vol. 19, no. 24, November 15, 1912, 284.

37. Státní okresní archiv [State District Archives] in Prostějov, Archiv města Prostějova, bk. 605, no. 936, Zasedání obecního výboru 1912–1913, fol. 263–67.

38. Halas, *Kemka*, 100–101.

prehensible form the exploitative nature of the capitalist system, dependence on labor relations and the division of the world of work and capital.[39]

Also available are two useful memoirs of workers connected through their activities in Brno and several observations of the position of the socialists from the point of view of their opponents (mainly from the Catholic camp). In both these rare cases where the workers left behind their memoirs there is an immediate wariness—the records only date from the beginning of the 1950s, and as a result of poor memories and a certain degree of manipulation, there are many gaps and question marks.

The first one is concerned with the life of František Halas Sr, a party member and local trade union leader, based mainly in Brno from the 1890s. Halas's memoirs have already been thoroughly analyzed by J. Machačová and form one of the main points of the authors' thesis (along with J. Matějček) concerning the clear signs of ignorance amongst this group of people.[40] Halas had been exposed to the influence of socialist agitation even before his arrival in Brno, a role being played here by paternal connections with socialists from Březová nad Svitavou. Halas was led to the socialist movement through reading the satirical magazine Rašple,[41] distinguished by uncomplicated, visually rich depictions of the dark side of the "world of capital" and the hypocrisy of the representatives of the non-socialist parties, and in particular of the Catholic Church. The cartoonists in Rašple worked on pictures of rotund, repellently slimy priests, the lazy, obese factory owner was pictured beside the downtrodden, rickets-afflicted workers, and there were also sketches of representatives of the army, Jews, landlords etc. In Halas's mind, all rich people were a priori evil and corrupt, and he considered Jews to be extortioners and spiritual hypocrites.[42] There are no indications in his writings of a deeper understanding of Marx, with Halas only applying extracts from Marx's teaching onto his very basic picture of a mean and unfriendly world.

The second of the workers, Antonín Kittnar, a weaver from Lysice, came to Brno with a progressive interpretation of the world, untouched by socialism. The seventeen-year-old boy joined in a street demonstration in 1910, and later wrote in his typically simple language that the demonstrations for wage demands were "fun, but I only understood the depth of this demonstration much later on, when talking to the older workers during breaks at the factory."[43] Kittnar later became a party member, though he never had aspirations towards high office, nor did he achieve it.

There is even greater scepticism in the case of the truly mass satellite organizations of the Social Democratic Party. In connection with this it was written in Rovnost: "We admit, though it is not our mistake, that over the past few years the workers' movement has grown to such an extent that we social democrats are unable to keep it in check, to make sure it remains on the tracks as we would like . . ."[44] Amongst the thousands or

39. Saldern, "Latent Reformism and Socialist Utopia," 195–221, here 200.

40. Machačová, "Prostředí továrního dělnictva," 63–100.

41. Halas, *Kemka*, 29.

42. Machačová, "Prostředí továrního dělnictva," 75.

43. Moravské zemské muzeum [Moravian Museum] in Brno, Muzeum dělnického hnutí Brněnska, no. S 11837.

44. Quoted from: Těhle, *Přehled dějin československého odborového hnutí*, 47.

even tens of thousands of members there was evidently a "grey zone" of individuals who joined the movement purely for material reasons, the so-called "stomach" or even "sandwich" socialists. Rudolf Tayerle, the secretary of the Metal Workers' Union explained the "lack of fighting spirit" in the unions by quoting from Kautsky: "Yes, I say to those who doubt the unions, it might all be true—the trade union member pays a certain contribution for which he receives services in return, in some cases support when unemployed etc, and if he goes on strike then he acts thus in the hope of some material benefit, to shorten his working hours or gain higher wages. Fine! This is undoubtedly one of the most important things that unions struggle for. But these struggles cannot be said to be the mark of the class struggle. Very often it is about recovering and maintaining the worker's dignity."[45]

A list of the periodicals subscribed to by the enormous socialist-controlled association Vzájemnost (Solidarity) with its six thousand members (1913) shows that the socialist agitation press represented an insignificant element here, with even the calendars printed by the association having a very traditional character in their depiction and emphasis on the Catholic name days.[46] According to numerous accounts in the sources, the small libraries of the "socialist" associations in the countryside around Brno had a similar appearance.[47] However, this moderate, peaceful form of agitation was in its own way also very effective: "The cultivation of an economic politics gained widespread support, whereas an emphasis on a higher politics brought about stagnation in growth and expansion."[48] The Prostějov Catholic magazine Ječmínek did not perceive the association of socialist sympathizers in satellite organizations as the basis of revolutionary activity, but rather as a threatening gate that would lead to doubts about the traditional (that is religious-medieval) interpretation of the world and its authorities: "The organized masses want some kind of material benefit from the organization. We can see that Catholic organizations do not stand on a sound basis economically speaking. That is why people who are otherwise good Catholics rush to the socialist society shops where some purchases allure them, and then over time, without even knowing how, through contact and by reading, they become Social Democrats . . ."[49]

As can be observed from Eduard Bernstein's own experiences, it is possible to assume that for many workers the association meeting was a truly free and sociable oasis, a healthy distraction from the cycle of monotonous work, the dictates of industrial time and the employee's feeling of complete inferiority.[50] It was also clear, however, that there was not even the most basic ideological schooling, rather only some fragments of an alternative picture of the world that paid lip service to Marxist theory and was more

45. "Odborové hnutí a idealism," *Kovodělník*, vol. 21, no. 42, October 19, 1911, 1.

46. *Vzájemnost. IX. Zpráva účetní za rok 1906*, no page number; *XVI. Ročenka Dělnického potravního spolku Vzájemnost 1913*, no page number.

47. Compare e.g., Fasora, "Sekularizace a 'klerikální bašty'," 253–66, here 257.

48. "Rozmach sociálně demokratické strany v Prostějově," *Ječmínek*, vol. 1, no. 1, October 3, 1908, 2; *Ječmínek*, vol. 1, no. 3, October 17, 1908, 1; *Ječmínek*, vol. 1, no. 5, October 31, 1908, 1.

49. "Katolický konsum v Prostějově?," *Ječmínek*, vol. 3, no. 28, January 11, 1911, 3.

50. Bernstein, *Sozialdemokratische Lehrjahre*, 15, 66–67.

about the communication of everyday experiences and the emotional urge to speak out against (alleged) suffering and injustice. In contrast to J. Machačová and J. Matějček, I do not think that just because the working class expected material gains and entertainment from their socialist societies, this somehow points to the movement's "lower" character. Even if the association was not being particularly ideological in providing cheaper food or organizing dances, in Prostějov the editor of the Catholic Ječmínek noted that this brought mutual support, from which grew self-confidence, the ability to defend your own position publicly as a civic virtue. German historians work with the inspiring category known as *Konfliktfähigkeit*, that is defending one's own position with courage, preparing and using arguments etc.[51] In this context it is necessary to appreciate, for example, how in a relatively small town like Prostějov the entry into a consumer association concealed within it a huge potential for conflict: after all, the business and trade lobby, whose economic interests were obviously greatly limited by this association, exercised a considerable power over the town and its inhabitants—it owned property, it was a significant employer and certainly also the creditor of a number of individuals. When the project of establishing a Catholic consumer association, an action originating from within the party which was supported by a considerable number of traders, later came up, it brought great unrest to the town.[52]

SOCIALISTS, FAITH, RELIGION AND THE CHURCH

If we go along with the assertion that the intellectual activities of the socialist associations were reduced to fragmentary agitation activities, albeit connected to fulfilling material and cultural-entertainment requirements, there is the question of what place the church, religion and faith occupied within this agitation. According to K. Kaiserová, the agitation of the North-Bohemian German socialist press offered two basic interpretations in this sphere which are also connected to the socialist press in Moravia.

1. Faith is a private matter, the merging of the Church with state powers is a deviation from the original true meaning of Christianity, Jesus Christ is portrayed as a worker

2. The Church has completely forgotten its egalitarian traditions and has turned to forces that maintain modern extreme social relationships. The central concept of religious thought is a god who "arranges" matters, whilst socialists believe in the possibility of taking your destiny into your own hands.[53]

In comparison with other socialist interpretations of the world which do not directly touch upon religion, with the above-mentioned statements we come across five basic and, for agitation to be a success, very advantageous aspects.

a) People emerging from the countryside formed a very important element of the working class and this agitation touched on very familiar territory and prob-

51. Lieske, *Arbeiterkultur und bürgerliche Kultur*, 162.

52. "Katolický konsum v Prostějově?," *Ječmínek*, vol. 3, no. 28, January 11, 1911, 3.

53. Kaiserová, "Katolická církev, politika a sociální otázka," 217–24, here 221–22; See Prüfer, *Sozialismus statt Religion*, here 101–77.

lems of a very close, personal nature. It was not for nothing that Brno's *Rovnost* printed anti-clerical articles by the atheist teacher František Holub (pseudonym Šimanovský, who alongside Josef Svatopluk was the main author of anti-clerical attacks in the newspaper) with close ties to life in the Moravian region of Slovácko.[54] The countryside becomes the stage for injustices committed by or tolerated by the church and the "men of the cloth"[55]; on the other hand, the city is a place for portraying scenes critical of social injustice committed by or tolerated by employers and representatives of the state.

b) As analyzed by, among others, M. Řepa, the agitation here is connected with a level of popular culture which is given to obscenities, ridiculing authority figures and being vulgar towards religion.[56] The Church offered itself up as a target through its use of highly formalized rituals, the cult of the Immaculate Conception etc. The "Quasi-Marxist" explanation of the functions of the Church, religion etc., was suitable for the mental and educational level of those being addressed by the agitators, certainly far more suitable than the difficult economic category, a central pillar of Marx's interpretation of the world.

c) Venting frustration and dissatisfaction via attacks on the Church was relatively simple and was only seldom accompanied by any appreciable form of retaliation, particularly in the towns. Although religion and the Church were protected by the Austrian criminal code,[57] in comparison to retaliation by employers, the second source of frustration for the workers, the punishments were as a rule lenient. The employers, however, could retaliate by using the feared black list or marks in the work books. These were very effective measures; for example, due to his involvement in strikes František Halas was forced to find work outside of Brno, as far afield as Saxony.[58]

d) The polemic with the Church and its interpretation of the world was not only limited to socialist agitation, but also led to a merging of the positions of the socialists and the so-called progressive blocs of the bourgeois parties. The socialists' anti-clerical position was one of the issues which brought them closer to the educated sections of the bourgeoisie.[59] It is also important to remember that sections of the working class also read the bourgeois press (albeit with some delay due to the high price of the new editions) as its more regular publishing times gave its readers the

---

54. *100 let literatury v Rovnosti*, 28.

55. For typical extracts see "Svatá hloupost," *Rovnost*, vol. 22, no. 204, September 7, 1906, supplement; "Z nejtemnější Moravy," *Rovnost*, vol. 22, no. 257, November 10, 1906, supplement.

56. Řepa, "'Rušení náboženství na Jižní Moravě," 125–34, here 133.

57. §§ 122–24 and 303 of the Austrian Penal Code of 1852.

58. Halas, *Kemka*, 58–59.

59. Compare e.g., Moravský zemský archiv [Moravian Provincial Archives] in Brno, B26p Policejní ředitelství Brno, bk. 2203, no. 1995, collection Hieronymus Schloßnikel, Nový Jičín, the affair connected to the article "Jesus aus Nazareth auf dem Anklagebank," where the important leader of the Moravian socialists was defended in court by the top Brno lawyer Kornelius Hože, who waived his fees.

opportunity to follow daily events—something which even the management of Rovnost came to see as an urgent problem faced by the socialist press.[60]

e) According to K. Tenfelde there was also a significant section of the working class who, as a result of their schooling, harboured doubts as to the veracity of the religious-medieval interpretation of the world. Tenfelde naturally makes an important distinction between the level of education in village schools, where the Church had much greater social control over the teacher, and in town schools, where the teacher had more freedom to use a scientific approach to understanding the world.[61] The proportion of workers who had at least some degree of elementary education of the "town" variety began to gradually grow, perhaps more rapidly after the structural crisis in Austrian industry from 1900–1902, which was connected to the rise in industrial branches with higher demands on the qualifications of the labor force—and therefore forcing a "nomadic" working-class lifestyle, as noted by J. Machačová and J. Matějček.[62]

Why was it then, when there existed such co-ordinated anti-clerical agitation pressure, that only an insignificant number of workers actually left the Church and spoke out about their relationship towards religion? Even amongst the socialist functionaries, many remained so-called registered Catholics, and the few cases of people actually leaving the Church are to be found among the editors of the socialist political press, those who were in the front line in the battle against the "clerics." Alongside the previously mentioned teacher František Holuba-Šimanovský and the working-class poet and visionary Josef Krapka-Náchodský, we can also name the editor-in-chief of the German Social Democratic magazine Volksfreund, the famous hothead Wilhelm Nießner. On the other hand, particularly among trade unionists, leaving the Church was a very unusual phenomenon, and with members of other mass organizations controlled by the party it was unheard of. That is why the funeral of a local worker and aetheist in the outskirts of Brno caused such a scandal.[63]

The Austrian working class lived in an environment where the working-class socialist subculture had only partialy taken root, where the politically aware section of the working class was in a significant minority or was only a marginal section of employees, which seemed to be in stark contrast to the enormous Social Democratic Party in Germany. Apart from Brno, Liberec and Pilsen, there were few places which enjoyed a strong enough working-class subculture to be able to sufficiently shield and protect an apostate from the (particularly social) consequences of leaving the Church. The label "pagan" was still a threat which in the eyes of the family, the wife or the employer disenabled the person. When there are no crowds of dissenters to be registered even amongst

60. Franěk, *Pankrác Krkoška,* 54. In addition, especialy in the early days of *Rovnost,* a copy of the magazine was a kreutzer dearer than the competing bourgeois periodical.

61. Tenfelde and Ritter, *Arbeiter im Deutschen Kaiserreich,* 771–72.

62. Machačová and Matějček, *Nástin sociálního vývoje,* 184–8; Also *Problémy obecné kultury,* here 89, 286.

63. Archiv města Brna [Brno City Archives], S 18 Římskokatolická fara Sv. Jiljí v Líšni, no. 242.

the self-confident socialists in Brno, then there should be no illusions as to the situation in Znojmo, Nový Jičín or Jihlava.

The issue was very gender specific. Women in particular, socio-culturally "imprisoned" within their three roles as worker-mother-housewife, had not been influenced by socialist agitation to the extent that they would properly support their husband-dissenter.[64] That is why there is more of an emphasis on the exceptional role of women-comrades who supported the political activities of their husbands, such as Františka Skaunicová, Mína Hybešová and Běta Krapková, a mother of six children.[65] The attitudes of the wife's parents, therefore a generation older and much more closely linked to the village way of life, were not open to question. Even the rebellious Halas apologized to his life-long partner, not for his anti-religious or anti-church views, but apparently because he "didn't have any money to give the priest" for the wedding ceremony, which for a qualified spinner with a good salary was a poor excuse. The immunity of women to socialist agitation and their indifference were sources of great frustration to Brno socialists as in the local textile industry women made up 70 percent of all workers.[66]

CONCLUSION

Even though Marx's theories and interpretation of the world were only superficially understood by the working class, some of these ideas, in simplified and fragmentary form, focused the latent frustrations of sections of the lower classes on a common denominator and opened the door to their political exploitation. In this sense the theme of the Church, faith and religion was relatively simple to exploit to create a picture of the (joint) culprits for the state of poverty and injustice, and that of culprits whose ability to defend themselves had already been weakened and increasingly restricted.

The discrepancy among Church representatives of the evangelical defense of the religious-medieval view of the world and a modern understanding of science and the reality of society was very marked, and in the towns the Church lost social control of the masses from the lower levels. However, this trend did not affect all levels of the working class with the same intensity and was often less significant in those areas with a high concentration of female labor or workers with a strong connection to the countryside.

Despite the widespread changes which affected three generations of members of the lower social classes, and in particular the urban section in the second half of the nineteenth century, these did not entail a departure from traditional religion and the (Catholic) Church; faith remained a sacrosanct value in the socialist movement in the 19th century, an attribute of human freedom, and its application to certain theological aspects of Marxist teaching became a very important keystone for the whole movement. It is precisely this position which justifies the classification of the socialist movement,

---

64. Canning, *Female Factory Work in Germany*, 328ff.

65. Franěk, *Rebel a básník*, 203–4; http://encyklopedie.brna.cz/home-mmb/?acc=profil_osobnosti&load=345 (15. 9. 2009).

66. "Levné síly pracovní," *Odborný list dělnictva textilního v Rakousku*, vol. 2, no. 11, Apríl 16, 1891, 81.

especially in questions of freedom of thought, as the "second wave of the religion of humanity"[67] or even the "bridgehead between bourgeois values and liberalism."[68]

Social Democracy in the period when it was a mass movement after 1890 no longer had the ethos of intellectual Marxism and the class struggle of the previous ten years, and especially on the theme of the struggle against clericalism the socialists often found themselves agreeing with the representatives of the so-called progress or free-thinking bourgeois camps. Therefore, it was undoubtedly a theme which was a significant milestone in the transformation of Social Democracy into a standard parliamentary party, and also a theme which helped the (re-) integration of the working class into society.

67. McLeod, *Náboženství a lidé*, 66.
68. Kocka, "Arbeiterbewegung in der Bürgergesellschaft," 487–96, here 491.

8

The Influence of Secularization on German Workers' Parties in Northwest and North Bohemia within the Intellectual Milieu of Imperial Germany[1]

Kristina Kaiserová

THE UNINTERRUPTED DEVELOPMENT OF the workers' movement brought about constitutional changes which were to arrive in Austria-Hungary after 1867. Northwest Bohemia, and in particular the Ústecko and Liberecko regions, were the areas with the strongest political commitment among workers.[2] To this period is linked the era of the organized elites in the 1870s and 1880s. Germany had the greatest influence on the organisation of workers through travelling journeymen, as well as the reading of foreign publications, whilst at the same time the domestic Social Democratic press systematically reflected developments in German society.

The activities of German Social Democrats in North Bohemia were also important. For example, in Eisenach, August Bebel, founder of the German Social Democratic Party in 1869, organized a channel through which banned socialist literature could be brought into Germany via North Bohemia. As a co-founder of the 2nd International he was an advocate of the solidarity of workers of all nations. He was in close contact with the Austrian Social Democratic movement, he visited the Liberec Social Democrats frequently in the years 1879–1883, and from 1881–1885 in Teplice he was in regular contact not only with German Social Democrats, but also with representatives of the Czechoslovak section of the Austrian Social Democrats.[3] He was one of the most popular Social Democratic politicians in Europe prior to World War I. Alongside Karl Marx's portrait, his picture became a modern political icon in the homes of social democrats

---

1. This paper was funded by the grant GA ČR č. 404/08/0029 "Intellectual and Popular Religion in the Czech Lands in the 19th Century between Nationalism and New Confessionalism".

2. See Houfek, "Nacionalizace společnosti a dělnictvo na Ústecku do roku 1918," 279–315; Strauss, *Die Entstehung der deutschböhmischen Arbeiterbewegung*; Kořalka, *Vznik socialistického dělnického hnutí na Liberecku*; Gawrecki and Machačová, *Dělnické hnutí v severozápadních Čechách*.

3. Englová, "August Bebel a severní Čechy," 109–16.

before the First World War. Karl Kautsky also had an important relationship with the Czech lands.[4]

Nonetheless, the first impulse which partialy influenced ideas in the Czech-German areas was the emergence of the free-thinking religious community (Freireligiöse Gemeinden) through the activities of Johannes Ronge and Robert Blum, who after his execution "from an apostle became a martyr."[5] The original reforming German-Catholic movement gradually established a system of a scholarly obsolete faith, although it is sometimes difficult to find the border between an official faith and another form.

Within the Habsburg monarchy the German-Catholic movement was represented mainly in the areas around the borders of Saxony and Silesia, whilst Ronge's ideas reverberated even more widely, for example amongst the representatives of the socialist movement. One example is the journeyman carpenter from Srní in the Šumava Mountains, Franz Eggert (1815–1884), who during his stay in Innsbruck, along with other journeymen, read the works of utopian socialists as well as Ronge.[6]

Then in 1859 an association of these communities was formed—Bund Freirelingiöser Gemeinden, which went on to be active along the Czech-German borders.[7] The magazine *Menschentum* [Manhood], the organ of the German Freidenkertum, was also published, which often reacted to articles in the *Nordböhmischer Volksbote* [North Bohemian People's Messenger].[8]

From varying permutations of these early groups, Deutscher Monistenbund [the German Monistic Association] was founded by Ernst Häckel.[9] Ernst Häckel was known by the educated German workers in the Czech lands due to his anti-clerical ideas.[10] The works of the German-Catholic preacher Heribert Rauh were also read in this spirit of religious freedom—*Evangelium der Natur* [Nature's Gospel] (1853); *Feuerflocken der Wahrheit* [Sparks of Truth] (1854); *Katechismus der Kirche der Zukunft* [Catechism of the Church of the Future] (1855) and *Neue Stunden der Andacht* [New Hours of Devotion] (18763) etc.[11]

---

4. See Šolle, *Karel Kautsky a Československo*.

5. Randák, "From an apostle he became a martyr," 34–51.

6. Strauss, *Die Entstehung der deutschböhmischen Arbeiterbewegung*, s. 32–37. Franz Eggert was arrested in February 1846 and after his release in May was kept under police watch and barred from completing his master craftsman's qualifications. He decided to move to America, where he left his revolutionary activities behind him.

7. Sächsisches Hauptstaatsarchiv [The Saxon Central State Archives] in Dresden, 12520, no. 134, Acta Landeskirchenvorstandes der deutschkatholischen Gemeinden Sachsens, Zittau betreffend; See also Kaiser, *Arbeiterbewegung und organisierte Religionskritik*.

8. Sächsisches Hauptstaatsarchiv [The Saxon Central State Archives] in Dresden, 12530, no 31, Druckschriften. E.g., Menschentum. Organ für deutsches Freidenkentum. Gotha, vol. 30, no 128, August 8, 1909.

9. Weber and Di Bartolo, *Monismus um 1900*.

10. Holek, *Unterwegs. Eine Selbstbiographie*.

11. Compare Artikel "Rau, Heribert" in *Allgemeine Deutsche Biographie*, edited by the Historical Commission of the Bavarian Academy of Science, Vol. 27 (1888) from page 376, full text in digital form Wikisource, Online: http://de.wikisource.org/w/index.php?title=ADB:Rau,_Heribert&oldid=681972 (19.7.2009). An overview of similar publications in: Daum, *Wissenschaftspopularisierung im 19. Jahrhundert*.

In the 1860s Ferdinand Lassalle was to have a widespread influence on the socialist movement within the monarchy. Lassalle was by no means a Marxist materialist, he was by persuasion a Helgelian, which sections of the working class used to sharply attack him as did the aforementioned religious free-thinking (freireligiöser) preachers. Thus Leberecht Uhlich from Magdeburg, who apart from this was also chairman of the local workers' education association, attacked Lassalle for serving the church, which was followed by a sharp rebuttal from Lassalle's followers.[12] Even though Lassalle was still venerated in the monarchy at the start of the 1870s, these intellectual discussions did not have any great influence on the religious ideas of the local workers.[13]

From the end of the 1870s, however, Karl Marx, August Bebel and Wilhelm Liebknecht were to dominate, promoting Bebel's slogan, *that socialism and Christianity stand opposed to one another like fire and water.*[14] Bebel spoke clearly on this question in his addresses to the German Reichstag. On June 17th 1872 he proposed a law which would restrict the residency of Jesuits in Germany. Bebel viewed this law as part of the complex problem of the church, whereby he considered the Catholic Church to be a relic of the Middle Ages, whilst Protestantism was a powerful tool of the modern state. After applying certain preconditions, he thought it would be possible to deprive all the churches (he also named the Old Catholic Church) of any type of influence. First of all there would have to be separation from the state, the result of which would be the church's loss of influence in schooling. One of the main tasks would then be to invest in education at the widest levels. He proposed that the money for the development of schooling, teachers and education in general would come from a reduction in armaments. He was convinced that if society was open to the most modern scientific knowledge then the churches would be empty within a decade, no matter what church representatives tried to do.[15]

However, for the majority of factory workers the old village models of behaviour still dominated, emphasizing emotion and tradition. From this came a resoluteness and bluntness of expression, a tendency towards both verbal and physical violence, and also towards sharp reversals of fortune among the movement's protagonists as well as damage to the fortunes of the movement as a whole. Nor can it be said that someone joining the Social Democrats automatically became an atheist. The level of participation in church life varied widely (and at times an individual's religion altered in a very complex manner[16]), and very often faith was presented as a private matter.[17] Therefore, when arguing against the Catholic Church, this position had to be taken into account. It was for this

---

12. Prüfer, *Sozialismus statt Religion*, 245–50; Also Grote, *Sozialdemokratie und Religion*, 93–96.

13. Keplinger, "Lassaleanismus," 147–46; compare also Sewering-Wollanek, *Brot oder Nationalität?*, 7–17.

14. *Nordböhmische Volksstimme*. Organ für arbeitende Bevölkerung der politischen Bezirke Rumburg, Schluckenau und Umgebung. Publisher August Hecker, vol.7, no. 30, July 26, 1903, 1–2.

15. *Stenographische Berichte über die Verhandlungen des Deutschen Reichstages*, 1079–82. Online: http://www.payer.de/religionskritik/bebel01.htm.

16. An example is the famous workers' leader Josef Schiller, who lost his faith in life after death, compare. Strauss, *Die Entstehung der deutschböhmischen Arbeiterbewegung*, 205.

17. "Darf ein Christ und guter Patriot Sozialdemokrat sein?" *Nordböhmische Volksstimme*, vol. 2, no. 2, January 8, 1898, 11.

reason that it was repeatedly stated either that Jesus and the early church were basically socialist, or they would use church ideas in the spirit of socialist terminology.[18] Such themes as infringing the principles of poverty laid down in the Scriptures or payment for church services (christenings, wedding, funerals, etc) would therefore be analyzed with great relish.[19] Within the environment of an industrial city the links to a specific priest were also, of course, far weaker, which often made a worker's decision to leave the church easier to make than solely due to economic reasons. On the other hand, in smaller localities, preaching against specific individuals could become a significant test for the active socialist.

For the educated workers, and activists within the socialist movement in particular, the setting up of a library within workers' associations played a significant role.[20] Their hunger for knowledge was insatiable and they read practically everything which came to hand—gradually they moved from the pamphlets of the above-cited free-religious thinkers (Haeckel, Rauh) to the works of German philosophers, Darwin and the leading works from all fields.[21]

Secularisation within social democracy in Germany had several general traits, which were taken on board by the socialists in Northwest Bohemia, and in some cases, were generally applicable:

- the difference between the regions, the city and the village, the role played by historical traditions;

- a lack of time—work on Sunday, free time taken up by reading, alcoholism etc.;

- impossible to say that trends in secularisation were straightforward, a similar situation here as with reconfessionalisation.[22]

When assessing the church both in Germany (the Evangelical Church) and in the Habsburg monarchy (the Catholic Church), it is important to note their connections to the powers of state—the famous alliance of "altar and throne." August Bebel logically concluded that if the authority of the church was shaken, the state authorities would subsequently be undermined. In the Reichstag in 1872 he said that, "the consequences will be republicanism in politics, socialism in economics and atheism in religion."[23]

The workers' movement was specifically represented by the German National Workers' Association and later Deutsche Arbeiterpartei [The German Workers' Party]. Various associations were formed in the second half of the 1880s and 1890s, particularly

---

18. *Nordböhmische Volksstimme*, vol. 2, no. 2, January 8, 1898, 11. Here Jesus appears as a worker. Further *Nordböhmische Volksstimme*, vol. 2, no. 15, May 28, 1898, 115–16, in the text Whitsun becomes an analogy for revolution (Volkspfingsten).

19. See also Měchýř, *Bouřlivý kraj*, 109–10.

20. Tippelt et al., *Handbuch Erwachsenenbildung*, 33–34

21. Strauss, *Die Entstehung der deutschböhmischen Arbeiterbewegung*, 179–80.

22. Hölscher, "Weltgericht oder Revolution," 144–56.

23. Ibid., 174: "daß auf dem politischen Gebiete der Republikanismus, auf ökonomischen Gebiete der Sozialismus und auf dem Gebiete, was wir jetzt das religiöse nennen, der Atheismus seine volle Wirksamkeit ausübt."

in Northwest Bohemia, prinicipally with the aim of protecting the German workforce against the tide of Czechs coming from the central agrarian areas (as well as other nationalities—Galician, Balkan).

In Cheb in 1893 Franz Stein founded the German National Union of Workers. Stein supported Schönerer's Pan-German movement and published the magazine *Der Hammer* [The Hammer], whose editorial board he transferred from Vienna to Cheb in 1898. In 1898 Verband der deutschen Gehilfen und Arbeitervereinigungen [The Union of German Auxiliary and Workers' Associations] was founded in Moravská Třebová, which was to protect the interests of German workers. Then in Cheb in 1899 the first congress of the German National Workers was held. A programme was presented which was later known as the Cheb programme, which set out the intentions of Schönerer's party. Subsequently in October 1899 Steiner founded Bund deutscher Arbeiter "Germania" [The Union of German Workers "Germania"].

The break-up of the "Alldeutsche Vereinigung" [Pan-German Association] parliamentary club (Schönerer versus Wolf) paved the way for the establishment of professional as well as workers' parties. The initiative came mainly from the Czech lands and the first negotiations took place in Žatec on April 24th 1902. The participants at the meeting had not entirely dispensed with the notion of forming a "large Pan-German party." However, as early as December of the same year at the imperial conference in Liberec, the idea that the German National Workers should follow their own path already held sway. At a conference in Ústí nad Labem in 1903 the decision was taken to establish a party and this was formalized a year later on the 14th and 15th of August in Trutnov. At the party's founding congress, Hans Kirsch referred to the dedicated work that had led to this day. To a resounding ovation, Alois Cihula's (Ciller's) manifesto for Deutsche Arbeiterpartei (DAP) [The German Workers' Party] was announced.[24]

How did the Trutnov programme deal with the issue of the church? The basic thesis was a complete separation of the church from the state, educational reform and its separation from the church.[25] The Trutnov programme was basically a modification of the so-called Cheb programme, which in turn had only been a modification of the programme set out in 1882, with the addition of some workers' demands. However, some points had not previously featured, the most important from our perspective being the support of the movement Out of Rome.[26] However, the leaders of the party were not sympathetic to their ideas. When Josef W. Titta founded the Deutscher Volksrat für Böhmen [The German People's Council for Bohemia] in 1903, he gained the support of Hans Knirsch in activities directed towards the support of the Evangelical Church.[27]

---

24. We can discover more about the origin of the DAP from the texts of the "founding fathers": Ciller, *Sozialismus in den Sudetenländern*; Burschofsky, *Beiträge zur Geschichte*; Fuchs, *Geistige Strömungen in Österreich*; Also compare: Gawrecki, "Německá dělnická strana," 29–41, 81–90; Gawrecki, "Německá dělnická strana a její trutnovský program," 123–37; Malíř and Marek et al., *Politické strany*, 476–80; Wladika, *Hitlers Vätergeneration*.

25. Ciller, *Sozialismus in den Sudetenländern*, 183.

26. Gawrecki, "Německá dělnická strana," 33.

27. Wladika, *Hitlers Vätergeneration*, 537.

Walter Riehl was an unconventional DAP politician. This Viennese lawyer studied law in Vienna and economics in Berlin, Leipzig and Munich. At the start of his career he worked alongside Pernerstorffer, but after working in Liberec from 1906–1908 he moved away from the Social Democrats and began to work energetically for the DAP.[28] However, in 1908 he was one of the last politicians to convert to Protestantism.[29]

Support for the Evangelical Church therefore did not mean direct support of Schönerer, as in this period many German politicians and other subjects in the Czech lands searched for a path to the Pan-German Union in Wilhelm's Germany individualy, often through lobbying matters of a different kind.[30] On the other hand, Schönerer refused to associate with the Volksrath as he did not want to be under one roof with the social Christians, which with their increasing nationalism and antisemitism led them closer to the DAP, but the basic tenet of the Trutnov programme that was against the clericalisation of society remained in place.

Overall it is possible to say that the party became increasingly nationalist and supported antisemitism—the influences from Germany are apparent here (the ideas of Dühringo, the influence of the Pan-German Union, etc),[31] and religious questions remained separate.

28. See http://www.landtag-noe.at/service/politik/landtag/Abgeordnete/ZAbgR/Riehl_W.pdf.

29. Wladika, *Hitlers Vätergeneration*, 552.

30. Werner, *Der Alledeutsche Verband*, 124–27.

31. Nachrichten deutsch-katholischen Gemeinden. Organ für deutsches Freidenkentum, Gotha, vol. 30, August 8, 1909—often comments in the Nordböhmischer Volksbote, e.g., 128.

PART THREE

Case Studies

9

The Crisis of Identity in the Priesthood
at the Turn of the Twentieth Century

Jiří Hanuš

WHEN EXAMINING THE THEME of secularization at the turn of the twentieth century, one may touch upon issues concerning the priesthood during this period. Here we shall limit ourselves to the Roman Catholic Church, the religion of the majority of Czech society. What can we discover about the problems facing the priesthood, and in particular parish priests and curates, i.e., the lower clergy; what were their worries and impressions; what were their opinions regarding "church and nation," social and working-class issues; how were they influenced by foreign and domestic trends; what angered them or inspired them; did they encounter any problems due to their identity as priests; what things tarnished this identity and how was it possible to trace church groups or rather the early beginnings of movements? The Catholic Modernists (the Czech modernist movement) have been fairly well documented, as have some of the leading figures who were involved in building a new national church. However, the above questions—not all of which can be answered in this paper—point to a wider field of interest than is represented by Catholic Modernism, whether we conceive of this term in its literary or religious reformist element. There is an attempt here to outline various connections, contexts and concrete examples, principally in the relationship to political and social issues.

> In the course of my fight with the clergy I had a public debate at Hradec Králové with Father Reyl and Father Jemelka. It was a sign of progress that such a discussion was possible. I had a large following of young students and priests, anxious for me to advise them whether or not to leave the Church, since they had some sort of doubts. As a rule I advised against such a step, for I saw that their doubts were not strong enough to lead them to another positive faith. One young curate admitted to me that the only thing which interested him in the exercise of his office was hearing the confession of women and girls. I did not advocate leaving the Church so long as the cause was only indifference, or a political impetus like the "Los von Rom"

movement, or the desire to marry; I wanted people to be honest in their religious feelings.[1]

What is interesting in this excerpt from the conversations between Karel Čapek and the future president of the Czechoslovak Republic, Tomáš G. Masaryk, is the following: it concerned a relatively well-known argument between several Catholic priest-theologians and representatives of the organization Volná myšlenka [Free Thought] which took place in Hradec Králové in 1906. These types of debates were a feature of the period when clerical and liberal circles attempted to address the wider public as well as minorities within the cities. Evidently many of the aforementioned young priests were either preparing for service in the priesthood or were curates working within a diocese in a village or small-town parish. It is interesting that they were not on the side of Reyl, Šulec and Jemelka, but on the side of the political writers Bartošek and Masaryk. Their doubts were "not so strong" that they were inclined towards a coherent doctrine; rather they were vague "feelings." However, at times these doubts were so strong that they would resign from the service of the Church and on occasion leave the Church completely. The journalist Ladislav Kunte, who will be mentioned again later, also took part in this learned debate, although by this time he was not known as a supporter of the Catholic side as he had left the Church and was fully involved in the Czech atheist movement.

The first context for our extensive theme could be what is termed *the religion of humanity,* which influenced all aspects of religion across Western Europe from the end of the 18th century. In historical literature the central manifestation of this new religion is seen as positivism, which had not reached all social classes but was influential mainly among the elites of society—particularly in the French Third Republic and among the liberals in Spain and in Latin America. The wider masses, however, were more attracted to the second wave of this *religion of humanity,* which was socialism. Of course, it is difficult to label socialism as being a religion, though it is possible to do so from the viewpoint that socialism and its supporters are not mere political pressure groups acting on behalf of the working class. They are the new "missionaries" who offer "a formula allowing for the general renewal of society,"[2] who have the key to man's emancipation, from which everything else will proceed. This affected not only Western Europe, but also influenced the Czech lands at the turn of the century. A pattern was established by political events in France and political organizations—whether socialist or non-socialist—in Germany. As Paul Göhre, a pastor in Kamenice and later a Social Democrat, remarked, "the working-class issue was not just an issue of the stomach—it was a demand for respect and recognition, for greater equality in society."[3] Liberal values—science and education—were added to socialism and together formed a combination which was very much indicative of the age. Socialism was not the only element of the "religion of humanity" at the turn of the twentieth century—there was also the atheist movement, represented principally by "Volná myšlenka." It is worth drawing attention to the fact that the Czech section of this

1. Čapek, *Hovory s T. G. Masarykem*, 144.

2. McLeod, *Náboženství a lidé západní Evropy (1789–1989)*, 66.

3. Ibid., 67.

organization was very active, as was seen in 1907 at the World Congress of Free Thought in Prague, which enjoyed a relatively large degree of success. It is also worth remembering that there were areas of conflict within this religion of humanity—in his book on Volná myšlenka, Antonín K. Kudláč mentions arguments with the Social Democrats, who were represented by the Social Democrat Bohumír Šmeral and his articles in *Právo lidu* [People's Justice] and in the Viennese paper *Der Kampf*.[4]

The promoters of this new "religion of humanity" in the Czech lands were the conservative and liberal writers and historians who represented the Czech nation in the 1840s and who were active in the revolution of 1848–1849, albeit at a more moderate and less radical level. The historian and "father of the nation" František Palacký[5] became the symbolic figure in this area, along with his companion, the journalist Karel Havlíček (Borovský), who was more radical in religious matters. These two men determined the main form of the "religion of humanity" in the Czech lands, a lineage which leads to the thinking of T.G. Masaryk and to Václav Havel today. The basic features of their approach are a distancing from theology, an emphasis on the national interest which is free of superficial "banner-waving nationalism," a tolerance of other religions and opinions, and sometimes an effort to democratize the Church and have it become more involved in social issues (Karel Havlíček). It was concerned with a distinct "philosophy of history" which became one of the dominant themes in Czech society following the break-up of Austria-Hungary and the establishment of the Czechoslovak Republic after 1918. Catholic priests were confronted by this approach in their seminaries or later as curates in their first placements, and, willingly or unwillingly, they had to develop a definite stance towards it. The constituent elements of this theory were officially criticized by the Church; however, it also had an undoubted magic which exerted a growing influence on the younger priests.

The second context could be the notion of "anti-clericalism." This is a very interesting term that requires further study and accurate definition.[6] There is no doubt that even the lower clergy in the Czech lands were affected by this multilayered trend, which included a number of aspects: intellectual protests against the papacy and its relationship to the modern era, the ongoing dispute between religious indifference of the "Austrian type" and the requirements of the gospel, the modern Czech ideology founded on historical interpretations, the use of historical religious themes for the promotion of new political theories (Jan Hus, Jan Ámos Komenský, Augustin Smetana), protest against the excessive politicization of the gospel, the continuing conflict between "science and faith" involving on the one hand "scientific dogmatism" and on the other the Church's defense of the old ways and fear of the new, which could threaten apostolic faith. Political parties

---

4. See Kudláč, *Příběh(y) Volné myšlenky*, 32–34.

5. The latest book on Palacký in Czech is: Štaif's *František Palacký: Život, dílo, mýtus*, which concentrates on an analysis of the "second life" of Palacký in Czech society, on the formation of the picture of "father of the nation" and "father of Czech historiography".

6. The term anti-clericalism was first used in 1864 in the Saturday Revue in the headline "Lively protest against anti-clericalism." The author attacked the clergy for their inability to understand modern thinking and to learn from the case of Galileo. The anti-clerical movement has been excellently researched in Great Britain: see the collection *Anticlericalism in Britain c. 1500–1914* by Aston and Cragoe.

in both Western and Central Europe used anti-clericalism in order to attract supporters. There was also another side to anti-clericalism consisting of ultramontanist and conservative groups—it is typical that Czechs found this model later in Western Europe, in France. For the purposes of this theme it is important that the term "clericalism" was even used by the clergy, whose identity was in flux for several reasons. Within this context the term is most often understood as "the contradiction between the theory and practice of Christian principles," not exclusively the unsuitable application of Christian principles to political life. It is also interesting that one component of anti-clerical thought was a criticism of the fact that the Church represented a pillar in the order of society. (This was accepted by both revolutionaries and conservatives, with one group establishing it as grounds for revolt while the other saw it as a bulwark of political stability!) Within a Czech context, explicit anti-clericalism is connected to political differentiation. In the 1860s, the Národní strana [National Party], which had started off as a united group, began to splinter, with the first party disagreements having distinctly religious overtones. Anti-clerical speeches were common in the new "Young Czechs Party," with more radical currents appearing in this party alongside liberalism, atheism and free-thinking (Josef Barák, Alfons Šťastný). It is necessary to add to this that the anti-clericalism which was to be found in Bohemia and parts of Moravia was very vigorous, whilst pronounced anti-religious views (even amongst the working class) were less frequent. As has already been noted, a significant role in this type of anti-clericalism was played by historical hindsight regarding the real or alleged "guilt" of the Catholic Church in the history of the nation (the burning of Jan Hus in Kostnice, the counter-reformation of the seventeenth century), which was employed not only by the Young Czechs, but by other political parties after the 1890s, in particular the Social Democrats.

It is necessary to add that at the seminaries the majority of the diocesan clergy had been supplied with defenses against anti-clerical arguments (apologetic courses within the study of theology), but these were often inadequate against the specific new ideas coming both from historical and scientific areas. One priest who responded in an interesting manner to this anti-clericalism was Ladislav Kunte—to whom we shall return later—who wrote that from the 1880s a type of "compromised priest" was widely evident in Bohemia, whom he characterized thus: "They act as priests in church, but it is always easy to recognize that this priestliness is only a mask; a compromise in which they prefer to operate, which also spreads to the wider populace that deteremines the character of the Czech public. They tend to be quite liberal in their opinions and in their lives—in accordance with their surroundings; liberal again in the sense of compromise. Certainly not intransigent, intolerant—at least not unless it involves their most personal interests. The most widespread type, more or less corresponding to the state of today's Catholic Church, a state of religious superficiality and compromise . . . That is also why there tend to be relatively few disrupters and apostates among them. Naturally, if they encounter strong anti-clerical pressure then against their will they are driven to make their office to be taken more seriously: they become combative, they stand at the vanguard of the clerical organizations, selling Renewal and the Sword and not suffering the liberal magazines

Čas or Osvěta lidu in the inns that they visit daily."[7] Even though Kunte wrote these lines when he was no longer working as a priest, he still managed to describe the distinct lack of certainty in the priesthood that was shared by many curates and parish priests.

A third connection which should not be overlooked is the question of religious identity and religious consciousness, which at the turn of the twentieth century was under pressure from various influences. These issues have been covered relatively thoroughly in Western Europe, but less so in Central Europe. What is apparent though is the diversity in how they operate in various European countries and the interesting "combinatorial analysis" of these influences and the responses to them. There are not only the issues of loyalty to one's own camp and mutual stereotyping between groups.[8] The late 19th century was a time when religious consciousness was sharply defined. This development took on an extreme character in the Netherlands, but it was also clearly visible in other countries—in France and in Germany. By far the most interesting area is the relationship between religion and nationalism, which also played a significant role in the multi-state Habsburg Empire. Towards the close of the century in Western Europe there was a merging of religious, national, racial (imperial) and class ideas, with nationalism influencing members of both religious and non-religious parties and denominations. It is interesting that each of these large groups espoused a different version of nationalism (in Germany there were at least three major varieties of national narrative—Protestant, Catholic and Jewish).

In Austria several factors contributed to the specificity of this area: the previously mentioned religious heterogeneity and multi-state nature of the territory and, in the Czech case in particular, growing Czech-German friction gradually alienated society from the Catholic Church from the second half of the nineteenth century and by the end of the century manifested itself in politics and through a preference for the aforementioned "non-Catholic national narrative," strengthened by anti-Austrian rhetoric after the First World War.[9] Of great value to researchers are the actions of priests who found the courage within themselves to criticize their own church, and in some cases to eventually leave it. As we have already noted, the activities of the organization Volná myšlenka

---

7. Kunte, *Cesty,* 177.

8. A good example for Western Europe is given by Hugh McLeod in his book *Secularization in Western Europe 1848–1914,* in the chapter on identities: "In Baden, where Protestants were on average more economically successful than Catholics, they made fun of the numerous Catholic saints' days, claiming that Catholics were lazy, as well as being 'primitive beings'. Catholic farmers complained of unfair competition from Protestants who worked non-stop, including Sundays, and accused them of being pagans. In Preston Protestants claimed that the local custom whereby Catholics concentrated in particular places of work applied even to the town's brothels, the prostitutes being of course Catholics, which could be told from the fact that they turned out to kneel on the pavement when religious processions passed down the Manchester road." In McLeod, *Secularization in Western Europe,* 222–23.

9. According to Jiří Malíř, Czech "secularization was not consistent throughout the 19th century, Czech resistance to Catholicism was often more demonstrative, nationally motivated and instrumentalized. For example, this can be seen in the conversion to the Orthodox Church which became popular in connection with the wave of Russophilia after the Russo-Turkish war of 1877, especially among Czech liberals, and even certain characteristics from the Cyril-Methodius tradition including proposals to establish a Slavonic liturgy from the workshop of Czech liberals in Moravia." See Malíř, "Sekularizace a politika,"19.

are very interesting in this context, in particular the publications to which several former priests contributed. Alongside publishing, it is also possible to come across several other activities such as propaganda lectures and disputes between the "clericalists" and "anti-clericalists" at the start of the twentieth century. In connection with this the pamphlets by Theodor Bartošek are inspirational. He was a well-known free-thinking activist who not only analyzed the harmful effects of the Roman Catholic Church but in his texts also referred to cases and examples of priests who attacked "Masaryk's doubts." In the publication *Moderní společnost a církev* [Modern Society and the Church][10] he analyzes the orientation of modern society towards more profound social feeling which will be facilitated by liberation from the obscurantism of the Church; he criticizes state support of the Church and the Church's emphasis on simple, rural believers. The national view is also brought to bear when he criticizes the foreign Church organism (an objection which continued to be raised throughout the twentieth century), which asserts itself primarily in education: "What applies to national life applies especially to the national school. 'The Czech child belongs in a Czech school' is something which can be read today even on a box of matches. However, the struggle for a Czech school cannot be restricted only to opposition to Germanization, it is not only about language in schools, but rather about spiritual life, and therefore even a Roman school is not a Czech one. Our struggle for a national school must oppose both Germanization and Romanization."[11] The issue of the "sincerity" which must be set against the Church's hypocritical morality runs like a leitmotif through the free-thinkers' publications, with a particular emphasis on "modern knowledge" which in the future will supersede the old religious thinking based on miracles (in today's terminology, old religious paradigms): "The conflict between the medieval Church and modern knowledge (less accurately: between religion and society) is that modern man recognizes the rules governing all of nature and therefore the impossibility of so-called miracles, and this has furthered our understanding of precision and truth: we are no longer content with only possibilities, fantasies and likelihoods, which were sufficient for people during the Middle Ages, rather we strive to attain a truth which is genuine and precise."[12] It is also significant that the ideas of Volná myšlenka reached the smaller regions and villages, particularly through the magazine "Havlíček," which was distributed in the villages in an attempt to "educate the people" and which often caused difficulties for the Catholic clergy as it made its way into schools, affecting religious education.

For a specific example of a priest involved in political and social activities we can turn to the figure of Ladislav Kunte (1874–1945). He is a very interesting and provocative character who found his way into the lexicon of Czech philosophy thanks to his concept of "new religion."[13] His life was very interesting. He was born on March 22nd 1874 in

10. Bartošek, *Moderní společnost a církev.*

11. Ibid., 36.

12. Ibid., 20.

13. "Religion is the response to the definite needs of individuals and of society. These needs change, they are subject to development, however they can never be extinguished. Religion develops and changes alongside them, but not even it can disappear. Only transient religious forms and specific historical systems

Čestína na Kutnohorsku, his father was a smallholder and all of his siblings learned a trade. However, the talented Ladislav studied at the gymnasium in Hradec Králové and then, after some hesitation, entered the seminary. In 1896 he was ordained as a priest and in the autumn of the same year he became curate of the deanery of Dobruška. In 1900 he was transferred to Třebechovice and in 1906 he left the service of the priesthood and became the editor of liberal and then later anti-Catholic magazines. During the First World War he was involved in the home resistance and he was imprisoned from 1916–1917. After the war he worked again as an editor (*Čas* [Time], *Národní osvobození* [The National Revival]) and wrote his most important works on religious, social and national themes. From 1924 he was a clerk at the embassy in Vienna. At the start of the Nazi occupation he collaborated on the illegal magazine *V boj* [The Struggle]. He was arrested in 1940 and spent 1941–1945 imprisoned in Ebrach. He died on March 19th 1945 during an evacuation of prisoners from Straubing.[14] For the purposes of this paper it is particularly significant that Ladislav Kunte was a Catholic priest who left us an important eyewitness account of his journey to the "new religion" in his book entitled *Cesty, kterými jsem šel* [The paths which I have taken].[15] It is a publication worth examining in more detail as it explains his motivations for leaving the Church in a form which is not unlike a confession, delving into the most intimate corners of the soul of L. Kunte. Amid the stylization and subjective opinions there are several areas where he describes the activities of the Roman Catholic clergy and their manifold problems in ecclesiastical administration, especially in smaller towns and villages—in the celebration of the liturgy, religious teaching, club activities, etc. The book is of interest to the historian in five respects:

a)   As a record of an extreme position which was arrived at as the result of a profound crisis of faith and a crisis of trust in the Church's institutions (after several years of inner struggle, Kunte sees the Church as being simply untrustworthy, and in his view its teachings lead to hypocrisy and a deformation of character). Kunte underwent a relatively long journey during which he must have encountered a whole series of doubts—for example, that as a priest he was a figure of authority for many ordinary people (he mentions, for example, the tanners) whose own identity he helped to form. That was why he kept his real opinions secret for years. It is also interesting, though, that at the time of his greatest doubts the Hradec Králové episcopal seat was occupied by Eduard Brynych (1852–1902), a very active bishop, who was recognized even outwith the Catholic sphere for his national and pastoral work. Paradoxically, however, his activities were to cause Kunte the greatest difficulties because they were aimed against the modern age, with this rallying cry: "We must oppose a book or letter with a book or letter, oppose an

---

die out. Religion fulfils a function which science (since it does not satisfy our emotional needs) and art cannot." In Gabriel et al. *Slovník českých filozofů*, 322; for Kunte the religion which is disappearing is evidently dogmatic Roman Catholic Christianity.

14. For details of L. Kunte's life, see Smutný, "Srovnání činnosti."

15. Kunte, *Cesty*.

association by setting up an association, oppose action with action, money with money, oppose hatred and fanaticism with love and determination." This bishop became a promoter of the Catholic press (Politické družstvo tiskové [Political Press Society], Obnova [Renewal], Časové úvahy [Reflections on the Time]) and as a result of his activity there was an increase in the number of Christian social clubs, journeymen's clubs and other associations in the whole diocese.[16] Kunte was left outraged by the intransigent position of Catholicism towards everything modern, including socialism (there was an internal contradiction associated with "religious socialism" or "Christian socialism": according to the Church of the time, no-one could be a Catholic and a real socialist at the same time.[17])

b) As a record of a specific situation in a particular setting (Kunte describes in detail the situation in the Hradec Králové seminary and his work in Dobruška, Třebechovice and other areas in the foothills of the Orlické mountains), in which is described the standing of parish priests and their curates, the activities of Catholic associations and their disputes with "progressive" associations. (For example, Kunte describes a time when—during his period of zealous religious activity—he denounced a teacher for eating a sausage on a Friday, or when he protested that through schoolchildren parents were being supplied with magazines such as *Školský obzor* [The Scholastic Horizon], *Osvěta lidu* [People's Enlightenment], *Čas* [Time] etc.). He notes a significant political matter during his time in Třebechovice—the publication of the priests' magazines *Rozvoj* [Progress] and *Bílý Prapor* [The White Flag], which attempted to formulate a political programme which was relevant to Catholicism in a modern setting. Kunte describes meeting the priest Emil Dlouhý-Pokorný, a well-known activist and politician who was a Christian-Social candidate for the Imperial Council (in November 1900). However, even this "progressive current" proved to be insufficient for Kunte—it was not radical enough and was still "clerical."

c) As an interesting eyewitness account of the activities of Tomáš G. Masaryk, whom Kunte met at the time of his spiritual crisis and at the time when he left the Church, and also of an ambivalent relationship between a younger clergyman and a professor of philosophy who was engaged in anti-clerical politics. After meeting him in person, Kunte reappraised this ambivalent relationship and began to admire Masaryk for his belief in a personal god, for his emphasis on ethics and for his philosophical and religious insights. This influence began to make itself apparent in his own work, where he started to follow TGM's example in devoting himself to "contemporary issues," sociology and the relationship between politics, religion and science. He tried to become a writer and after leaving the Church he began to contribute to liberal and then the aforementioned anti-clerical magazines. Masaryk remembers the young curate in his book of discussions with Karel Čapek—they

16. See Kadlec, *Přehled církevních českých dějin 2*, 222–23.

17. This view was part of so-called Christian (Catholic) sociology until the 1940s, especially in the works of the sociologist Bedřich Vašek, translator of the pope's social encyclicals.

even continued to co-operate during the First World War and afterwards. At this time Kunte became something of a "moderate" socialist, producing works with socialist themes[18] and trying to interpret Marxism using Masaryk's model.

d) As a record of the social feeling of sections of the Catholic clergy, which relates to the previous observation. Catholic priests only had the opportunity to be activists within the framework of Catholic "standards" and within the framework of social religious teaching, which attempted to stand up against extreme solutions to social problems—both liberalism and communism were considered to be forms of extremism. For many people, however, this was much too restrictive, as was demonstrated by Ladislav Kunte's decision to leave the Church. He became involved in plans to reform society and issues concerning industrial and agricultural workers, which came to the fore following the creation of the new republic in 1918. Several of his ideas from that time are excellent analyses of the contemporary situation (weaknesses in the Marxist approach, warnings against ill-thought-out nationalization),[19] whilst some of his ideas are an expression of a somewhat utopian notion of economic life (proposals to involve workers in the management of factories, etc).

e) As a record of the dual life which was experienced by some priests, for whom the principles and activities of so-called Catholic modernism were not a sufficiently persuasive alternative to the feeling that the Church was in a wretched state. Kunte described the division of his life into the "priestly," in which he fulfilled the most essential tasks and obligations, and the "human," in which he read Masaryk, frequented Prague's cafes and strengthened his conviction that Roman Catholicism was a pre-modern and therefore antiquated institutional form, which led him to what he later described as his "liberation"—although along the way Kunte encountered several obstacles which he analyzed quite convincingly. The most important of these were probably the emotional ties to his family, who may have been disappointed with their son's development, as well as questions of subsistence, which for a priest leaving the priesthood were (and still are) very burdensome issues.

In conclusion, it is possible to consider the Catholic clergy at the turn of the twentieth century within the framework of certain typological characterizations, without confining oneself to the persuasive account of one of them (L. Kunte). To a certain extent this is more of an outline, but perhaps it has a certain significance. It describes the differences in the diocesan clergy (not the rank and file, as that would be a whole other chapter) more than one hundred years ago and the birth of the modern differentiation which I believe continues to this day, albeit with certain variations. Into the first group we could place priests who vehemently joined in the arguments which modernity brought,

18. See Kunte, *Socializace*.

19. "The transfer of ownership of industrial captial from private hands to the state—which is all that nationalization is—only changes the situation of ownership, not the legal position. Capital, which following nationalization belongs to the state, remains the master and work the servant. And the state-master in this case means bureaucracy-master." See Kunte, *Socializace*, 41.

on the side of the so-called clerical camp. One example of such a priest was František Alois Ermis from Bludov na Moravě, whose work in and around that area was referred to by my colleague, Stanislav Balík.[20] The activities of this type of priest were directed mainly in the struggle against the "progressive side," represented by the majority of the local elites—the mayor, doctor, teacher and some of the richer tradesmen. The clergymen belonging to this group found their identity precisely in this struggle, and through it they were strengthened in their conviction. This stemmed from the belief that many of the modern trends threatened the "legacy of the fathers" and it was therefore necessary to increase their efforts to confront this unfortunate development. This was more or less the position of the Vatican and the Pope at the time, albeit with distinct differences which were due to specific developments in Austria-Hungary. The second group of priests, whose center was in Moravia, consisted of clergymen who tried to reconcile Catholicism with the modern age and aimed to increase the cultural prestige of the Catholic elite. These were priests connected to the Catholic Modernist movement, who were particularly active from 1895 to 1907—that is, until the publishing of the Pope's anti-modernist documents, which had a profound effect even in the Czech lands. This group included the Catholic writer-priests, who left behind a literary testimony to the identity of priests and the upheavals they faced at the time. An excellent example from this group is the writer Jindřich Šimon Baar (1869–1925), who developed a picture of the life of a priest in shorter works and larger novels. With Baar we find not only a critique of the capitalist cult of property, which was normal amongst so-called Christian-Socials, but also a critique of the contemporary situation in the Church.[21] The third type of clergymen are the extreme cases, such as Ladislav Kunte. Although it is possible to label this type as extreme, they were not as rare as might appear at first sight. (This is shown by the attention which conservative priest-writers devoted to such cases in the 1930s.[22]) In the 1910s a position started to be formulated which was then developed during and after the First World War by several priests who had left the Roman Catholic Church to become involved in the new national church (the Czechoslovak Church and later the Czechoslovak Hussites). These were clergymen whose Catholic identity had been eroded in the two decades before 1920 and for whom the challenges of the modern age became so pressing and at the same time so contradictory to Roman Catholicism that they gradually decided to risk the struggle for existence and leave the Church, despite the fact that it provided them with a living. For this group the issue of celibacy was not the most fundamental matter, even if it did play a significant role. What was more important was the ongoing conflict between the ideas of the modern era and the state of religious teaching and practice, with the impossibility of finding a reconcilable position. A significant role was played here by the fact that it was impossible to become involved in any association or political activity other than a strictly Catholic one.

20. See Balík, "Politika vedená z bludovské fary," 104–21.

21. *See Putna, Česká katolická literatura, 304–12.*

22. For example, Doležal, *Český kněz.*

10

The Move away from the Catholic Church by Journeyman Cloth Makers in Liberec (*Reichenberg*) around the Middle of the Nineteenth Century

JIŘÍ KOŘALKA

THE JOURNEYMEN'S INSTITUTION TUCHKNAPPENBRUDERSCHAFT [The Brotherhood of Journeyman Cloth Makers] of Liberec (*Reichenberg*) dates back to 1619, when it regulated the relationship between journeymen and master cloth makers and their guild, and established codes of behaviour and the access of journeymen to workshops, hostels and mutual contact with other journeymen.[1] The Brotherhood originated as part of the guild and was under its supervision. Normally at the head of the Brotherhood you would find the sons of master cloth makers, and they were guaranteed to become masters themselves with the full rights conferred on guild members. The leadership of the Brotherhood influenced all aspects of a journeyman's life—according to one expert's evaluation of the journeymen's institution this involved "regulations, wage contracts and a criminal and moral code all at the same time."[2]

The Catholic Counter-Reformation from the second half of the seventeenth century also reached the Liberec cloth-making guild and its brotherhood of journeymen, where only a short time before the Lutheran influence from Saxony and Lower Saxony had been relatively strong. The journeymen, along with the master's family, had to take part in the Sunday Catholic worship, whilst one of the duties of the younger journeymen was to serve the priest at the altar. The masters' and journeymen's clothing for services and funerals were all regulated and the journeymen had to carry the deceased master to the cemetery. Another of the journeyman's duties, which continued until 1859, was to sing every Sunday in the church choir—failure to do so resulted in an investigation and

---

1. Hallwich, *Reichenberg und Umgebung*. More recently—Scholz, "Die Reichenberger Tuchknappen-bruderschaft," 145–61.

2. "Statut, Lohnvertrag, Strafgesetzbuch und Sittenkodex zur gleichen Zeit." Grunzel, *Die Reichenberger Tuchindustrie*, 47.

punishment.[3] The strict regulations and the lack of money in the Brotherhood's funds fuelled disagreements and opposition in the first half of the nineteenth century amongst the journeymen, which reached its height in 1848 with the demand for an independent organization which was not under the guild's leadership. The dissatisfaction also turned against the overdependence on the Catholic Church.

A group of young journeyman cloth makers associated with Anton Fledl, who arrived in Liberec from Jihlava on March 1st 1858,[4] became involved with the opposition activity of the German liberal movement in North Bohemia. They were supported most of all by the Ketzerklub [Heretics' Club], founded in Liberec in 1846 from a society of master cloth makers, shop owners and inn-keepers who were dissatisfied with the social and political situation prior to March 1848.[5] They read books and newspapers in the club, especially the Augsburg daily *Allgemeine Zeitung* [General News], lectures were held on aspects of cultural life and there was even an amateur theater, though a club charter was never officially adopted. The anti-clerical nature of the association was reflected in criticisms of the Catholic Church and individual priests. Following a practical stand-still in the association's activities in the decade following the revolution, there was a large upswing after 1859. The Heretics' Club took part in a large celebration for the 100th anniversary of the birth of Friedrich Schiller, it published a humorous magazine, and organized balls as well as plays, recitals and musical evenings.

The young journeyman cloth makers who joined the Liberec Heretics' Club at the end of 1860 enthusiastically took part in the association's activities.[6] It expanded their horizons and they participated primarily in the cultural events. However, after a few months they began to be dissatisfied with the standard of the association, especially when in 1862—at a time when German liberals had a majority in the Viennese government—the Club lost its original oppositional character and changed its name to the *Geselligkeitsklub* [Social Club].[7] The local liberal daily *Reichenberger Zeitung* [The Reichenberger News] praised the former club of heretics for now being "one of the best registered clubs."[8] In the first half of 1863, Anton Fledl and his supporters left the former Heretics' Club, now the Social Club, and attempted to set up their own association in cooperation with prominent local liberals. In August 1863 a 12-member preliminary committee was established, which was represented not only by the prominent journeyman cloth makers Anton Fledl, Wenzel Gross and Franz Kasper, but also by several master cloth makers, the engineering works owner Ferdinand Gerhardt, the printworks owner Heinrich Stiepel and the liberal town clerk, lawyer Anton Jahnel. The central figure in establishing the association was the doctor and co-owner of a cotton mill Wilhelm Herzig, a leading liberal

---

3. Hübner, *Geschichte der Reichenberger Tuchmacherzunft*, 145–46.

4. Státní okresní archiv [State District Archives] in Liberec, Soukenický cech Liberec IIA-2b/4, kniha cechovních tovaryšů, fol. 261, no. 1043.

5. Soyka, *Der Fortbildungs- und Geselligkeitsklub*, 6–8.

6. Hannich, *Ein Beitrag zur Geschichte*, 1.

7. Soyka, *Der Fortbildungs- und Geselligkeitsklub*, 10.

8. "Reichenberger Leben," *Reichenberger Zeitung*, vol. 11, no. 37, February 14, 1869.

who represented Liberec (*Reichenberg*) and Jablonec nad Nisou (*Gablonz*) from June 1848 until February 1849 in the German Parliament in Frankfurt.

In accordance with the North Bohemian liberals' idea that a "worker" was anyone who was involved in industrial production, not only the paid employees but also the employers,[9] in September 1863 the journeyman cloth makers together with Liberec factory owners established the Arbeiterbildungsverein [The Workers' Educational Association], whose charter was ratified on the third attempt in July 1865 with the proviso that the name of the association be changed to Industrieller Bildungsverein [Industrial Education Association]. Disregarding the number of association members, it was stipulated in the ratified charter that the employers and salaried workers were to have the same number of members on the association's committee. From 1863–1865 the journeyman cloth makers around Anton Fledl always acted as library representatives on the committee and contributed to the growth of the library with several hundred volumes and association reading rooms where there were numerous political and non-political newspapers and magazines.[10] The future leaders of the socialist movement were also close to the German liberals in Bohemia in their activities against the excessive influence of the Catholic Church.[11] These efforts reached their height in the Chamber of Deputies of the Austrian Empire Council with the acceptance of Church laws which Emperor Franz Josef sanctioned on May 25th 1868, and the enforcement of the education law from May 14th 1869.[12]

When the leaders of the journeyman cloth makers in Liberec identified themselves with the principles of international socialism, they became staunch atheists and launched stinging attacks against clericalism and the strong influence of the Catholic Church in society. The working-class poet Josef Schiller, who, like many of his kind, had started out as a journeyman cloth maker, in 1870 wrote an extensive poem *Der Konfessionslose* [Without Religion], in which he wrote about the need for human thoughts and feelings to oppose blind faith:

> . . . I did not find the deity
> There, where in gilded missal garments
> A priest preaches about the commandments and duties;
> Or that what he teaches means: to suffer, to endure, to bear!
> My inner voice, however, teaches me: to create, to struggle, to risk!
> . . .
> Never limit your own powers,
> Otherwise you will make a wretched slave of yourself:
> Blind faith cannot take away your powers,
> Always discover for yourself what is true or false.

9. "Alle sind wir Arbeiter, auch die, so ihnen Arbeit geben. Die Arbeit ist eben die gemeinsame Nährquelle beider. Arbeitgeber und Arbeitnehmer lassen sich nicht getrennt denken; es muss daher auch das Interesse des Arbeitgebers und des Arbeitnehmers, weil auf derselben Quelle beruhend, ein gemeinsames, eng verknüpftes sein." *Reichenberger Zeitung,* vol. 11, no. 178, August 1, 1869. Compare Kořalka, *Vznik socialistického dělnického hnutí,* 113–15.

10. *Rückblick auf die Verwaltung und Tätigkeit,* 5–6.

11. In detail in Vocelka, *Verfassung oder Konkordat?*

12. Leisching, "Die römisch-katholische Kirche," 42–51.

> If you use human feeling and human thought
> Then you will recognize what is right and wrong.
> And this thought is what I call prayer, Brothers,
> So pray in this way—do not kneel before idols!
>
> . . .
>
> If you know yourself, then spring will come,
> Free the spirit—heaven is on Earth.[13]

One observer who witnessed the start of the workers' movement in Liberec wrote that: "A good comrade, naturaly, had to be without religion . . . The principle applied that each comrade had to elicit from his convictions the principles for his personal life, and if they differed from the Church then he could no longer belong to the Church."[14] In April 1871 the district office in Liberec confirmed that almost all the leaders of the Liberec Social Democrats had left the Catholic Church.[15] According to registry notes and the newly established birth certificates submitted during a court trial of North Bohemian socialists in Prague in December 1882, Franz König had been without religion since January 1871, Josef Schiller since May 1872, Ferdinand Schwarz since September 1872, Josef Ulbrich since November 1873 and Antonín Behr since June 1878.[16]

The feeling of opposition to the Catholic Church was strengthened in Vienna and other parts of the Habsburg monarchy after the Vatican Council of 1869–1870, especially following the acceptance of the dogma of papal infallibility.[17] The German liberals in North Bohemia attempted to use this situation to strengthen their own political influ-

---

13. „. . . Ich fand die Gottheit nicht
Dort, wo im goldgestickten Messgesande
Ein Priester predigt von Gebot und Pflicht;
Denn was er lehrt, heißt: Dulden, leiden, tragen!
Mein Inn'res lehrt mich: Schaffen, ringen, wagen:

. . .

Ihr sollt die eig'nen Kräfte nicht beschränken,
Sonst stempelt ihr euch selbst zum nied'ren Knecht;
Nicht blinder Glaube soll die Kräfte lenken,
Prüft immer selbst, was falsch ist oder echt.

Ihr mögt nur menschlich fühlen, menschlich denken,
Dann wisst ihr ja, was gut ist oder schlecht:
Und dieses Denken, nenn' ich—beten, Brüder,
Drum betet so—kniet nicht vor Götzen nieder!

. . .

Erkennt euch selber, soll es Frühling werden,
Lasst frei den Geist—der Himmel ist auf Erden."

The poem was first published in the magazine *Nemesis* in May 1871. Reprinted in the collected works Schiller, *Gesammelte Werke*, 115.

14. Rieger, "Nordböhmische Reminiszenzen," 159.

15. Brügel, *Geschichte der österreichischen Sozialdemokratie*, 325.

16. Státní oblastní archiv [State Regional Archives] in Prague, Zemský soud trestní 1850–1897, C 1882/754, part XX.

17. See Hoyer, "Die altkatholische Kirche," 618–20.

ence. Albert Springer, the Liberec district officer, attempted to describe the mood at the time amongst the opponents and representatives of the Roman Catholic Church in and around Liberec: "For the first time the issue of the dogma has appeared publicly here, to which almost all of the educated population is bitterly opposed, but which also has many opponents among the lower orders, so that judging by the current mood, we could say without exaggeration that the announcement of infallibility has served Catholicism very badly. On the other hand, however, it has to be admitted that a large part of the bourgeois and village population is still strongly Catholic, whilst the working class leans more towards atheism."[18]

On the 27th of March 1871, the liberal Politischer Verein [Political Association] in Liberec called a public meeting which was intended to express its support for the "Old Catholic" movement and send a message of confidence to the Munich professor Johann Ignaz Döllinger. The meeting was very well attended and of the two and a half thousand participants a significant section consisted of supporters of the Social Democratic movement. After the opening speeches by the member of parliament Hermann Hallwich and other liberals, the working-class leader Josef Schiller took the floor. He supported a submitted proposal for a resolution against the dogma on papal infallibility, and attacked the Catholic Church and papal policies even more strongly than the liberal speakers. He received thunderous applause from the crowd when he described cases of "historical oppression for which the popes were responsible."[19] However, at the same time he said that workers could not solely be involved in anti-clerical activities and had to continue in the struggle for equal political rights.[20] The district officer in Liberec commented that Josef Schiller's radical speech caused political problems for the local liberals. "It appears that the Political Association did not count on such numerous and active participation by the Social Democratic Party, so the generally embarrassing impression emerged that the association was seen to be in alliance with this party." The leader of the Catholic political movement in Liberec, Professor Theodor Böhme of the School of Economics, had announced that he would give a defending speech, but he did not appear at the meeting, while the Liberec Catholic Deacon Simm, who was present, did not address the meeting.[21]

18. "... und so tritt die Dogmafrage hier das erstemal öffentlich zutage, von der sich beinahe die ganze intelligente Bevölkerung mit Entrüstung wendet, die aber selbst in den untersten Schichten viele Gegner hat, so dass schon bei der gegenwärtigen Stimmung wahrgenommen werden muss, dass dem Katholizismus mit der Unfehlbarkeitserklärung, mindestens gesagt, schlecht gedient sein dürfte. Hingegen muss aber auch zugegeben werden, dass ein großer Teil des Bürgerstandes und der Landbevölkerung noch streng katholisch ist, während sich die Arbeiterklasse der Konfessionslosigkeit hinneigt." Liberec district office to the presidium of the Czech governorship 25. 4. 1871. Národní archiv [National Archives] in Prague, Presidium místodrž[hacek over z]itelství 1871–1880, 8/5/22/2, no. 1159/1871.

19. Josef Schiller "ergriff das Wort für den Antrag, indem er mit scharfen Ausdrücken die historischen Bedrückungen, welche sich Päpste zu Schulden kommen ließen, unter vielen Ausbrüchen des Beifalls der Versammlung schilderte." Liberec town council to the presidium of the Czech governorship 28. 4. 1871, Národní archiv [National Archives] in Prague, Presidium místodržitelství 1871–1880, 8/5/22/2, no. 1189/1871.

20. Hannich, *Erinnerungen*, 26–27.

21. Liberec district office to the presidium of the Czech governorship 16. 5. 1871. Národní archiv [National Archives] in Prague, no. 1390/1871.

At this time the anti-clerical mood amongst the workers in Liberec was heightened by the free-thinking magazine *Nemesis,* which was published in Saxony by the former teacher Franz Josef Dittrich, originally from the area of Šluknov (*Schluckenau*) in North Bohemia.[22] At the time of its widest circulation 1,100 copies were printed, of which around 700 were for subscriptions in North Bohemia. The main propagator of the Social Democratic and other opposition press, Wilhelm Schiller from Liberec,[23] received as many as 500 copies of *Nemesis* every fortnight. The paper was aimed at "democrats, free thinkers, internationalists or whatever all you pioneers of freedom call yourselves." It was a public voice critical of the activities of priests in various parishes and of the Catholic Church as a whole, but it also provided space for the activities of workers' associations and encouraged the support of strikes. As well as the magazine *Nemesis,* Dittrich also published several independent anti-clerical pamphlets, the most famous being *Epistel an die Dummen* [Epistle to the Stupid].[24] However, his activities were interrupted because he was not allowed to distribute his magazine and pamphlets in Austria.

In the Saxon town of Pirna thirty-year-old Franz Josef Dittrich was accused of slandering the Christian church, attacking the state offices and insulting His Majesty, for which he was sentenced to ten months in prison and expelled from Saxony.[25] Dittrich's short time as a free-thinking activist ended ingloriously. His imprisonment and ban from public activities ruined Dittrich. His new attempt at publishing an anti-clerical magazine in Podmokly (*Bodenbach*) foundered, despite being supported by several of Děčín's businessmen. Under their influence he decided to abandon his "anti-state" activities, promised to co-operate with the authorities and disclosed the whereabouts of the secret meetings of the North Bohemian Social Democrats in Svojkov (*Schwoika*).[26] Just before the end of 1874 the Liberec Social Democrats accused Dittrich of taking advantage of his fellow workers and of financial fraud.

Before Franz Josef Dittrich arrived with his radical newspaper *Nemesis,* the working-class opponents of Catholicism in Liberec had attempted to organize public meetings with an anti-clerical bias in and around the town. The city council in Liberec, under the German liberals, banned two meetings announced in Liberec on the grounds that according to the planned programme "it intends to proselytize (turn to a new faith) the public, which would threaten public security and the public good." Similarly in December 1870 the district officer in Liberec banned an announced public lecture in Františkov

22. A more detailed account was sent by the Viennese Ministry of the Interior to the presidium of the Czech governorship 27. 12. 1871. Národní archiv [National Archives] in Prague, Presidium místodržitelství 1871–1880, 8/4/15/7, no. 4796/1871.

23. Wilhelm Schiller moved to Lawrence, USA in September 1877 and died there in June 1880.

24. Liberec district office to the presidium of the Czech governorship 23. 11. 1871; Národní archiv [National Archives] in Prague, Presidium místodržitelství 1871–1880, 8/4/15/7, no. 3955/1871.

25. Pirna public prosecutor's office 21.1.1872 to the presidium of the Czech governorship. Národní archiv [National Archives] in Prague, Presidium místodržitelství 1871–1880, 8/4/13/2, no. 553/1872; also 8/4/15/7, no. 1847/1872.

26. Děčín district office to the presidium of the Czech governorship 1.2. and 8.2.1874, telegraph agreement from the Ministry of the Interior 12.2.1874. Národní archiv [National Archives] in Prague, Presidium místodržitelství 1871–1880, 8/1/15/1, no. 604/1874, 756/1874, 804/1874.

(*Franzenthal*) as the fundamental points of the lecture were "evidently aimed against the central teachings of the Catholic religion, that is the Church as legally recognized by the Austrian state, and any public discussions would only cause animosity and outrage amongst the mainly Catholic residents."

In May and June of 1871 there were two subsequent failed attempts in Liberec to set up firstly a free-thinking society and then a free religious association. In the first case the experienced journeyman cloth maker Anton Fledl was chosen as interim chairman. However, in both cases the Liberec authorities refused the application to set up a free-thinking society or association. The initiators then appealed unsuccessfully to the Czech governorship in Prague.[27]

Unlike the beginning of the 1870s, when the anti-clerical propaganda of the liberal socialists came in many different guises and attacked individual priests and chaplains, whilst lacking a coherent programme, at the end of the 1870s a new situation emerged. The Social Democratic magazines edited in and around Liberec, but printed under the editor-in-charge Ladislav Zápotocký at the J. R. Vilímek publishers in Prague, marked the arrival of the international Christian-Socialist movement. The monthly *Sozialpolitische Rundschau* [Social-Politikal Observer], which from 1878 expressed the opinions of the Social Democratic leadership in Liberec,[28] commented midway through 1878 on the rise of Christian-Socialist agitation in Germany and Austria. According to the Liberec social-ists, although neither the Catholic nor Protestant priest was concerned with "delivering the people from destitution," in politics they were "at least a horse's length" in front of the liberals because they managed to comprehend the significance of social issues and attempted to take socialist ideas "on a different course." It was, of course, unrealistic to expect social issues to be solved by "prayer and song," nor could there be a rebuilding of the "disrupted harmony" between labour and capital through religion. Ferdinand Schwarz, one of the leading figures of the Liberec Social Democrat leadership, provided in an article several examples from the Catholic Church's history where the pope had deemed slavery and serfdom to be justified. "Where humanity has achieved progress it has been in spite of the Church, and often in fierce struggles against it," wrote Schwarz in summation of his argument.[29]

Six months later the position of the Liberec magazines *Arbeiterfreund* [Worker's Friend] and *Sozialpolitische Rundschau* [Social-Political Observer] became worse due to the new social encyclical of Pope Leo XIII, *Aeterni Patris*.[30] The encyclical was aimed at "godless" socialism, which the pope termed a "deathly plague," and accused it of trying

27. Liberec district office to the presidium of the Czech governorship 25.4.1871 and 20.5.1871. Národní archiv [National Archives] in Prague, Presidium místodržitelství 1871–1880, 8/1/1/1, no. 1422/1871, 1580/1871. On the termination of both attempts see Presidium místodržitelství 1871–1880, 8/5/22/2 (as-signed call number 5/1/6), no. 1580/1871.

28. Subscription to this monthly publication was considered part of the membership fee of the semi-legal Social Democratic Party. See more in Kořalka, *Severočeští socialisté*, 212–18.

29. "Wenn die Menschheit Fortschritte gemacht hat, so geschah es trotz der Kirche, ja vielfach unter harten Kämpfen gegen sie. " [Schwarz], "Pfaffensozialismus in Österreich," *Sozialpolitische Rundschau*, vol. 1, no. 6, June 1, 1878.

30. Kaiserová, *Konfesní myšlení českých Němců*, 60.

to "fill society with revolt, theft and murder," of contributing to "the division of property, the break-up of marriages and the disruption of the foundations of every civic society." The editor of the magazine *Arbeiterfreund* [Worker's Friend], Josef Hannich, a skilled journeyman cloth maker, wrote in a critical article that in this case it was not a great spirit who had spoken, only a pious man, and he referred to the well-known phrase by Gotthold Ephraim Lessing that "what is good in this work isn't new, and what is new isn't good."[31] This good perhaps alluded to the many references to the Old and New Testaments and the writings of the church fathers. If the pope made claims for the Catholic Church's good work against the fury of war, Hannich brought forward numerous examples of wars and murders which had the blessing of the Church: "If society can really be led by the Church towards more moderate behaviour, then it must have had the opportunity long ago to influence morality, as for centuries the Church has been the greatest power in Europe; however, if the Church believes it has only just acquired this power, then its efforts to turn things around must be carried out principally where wars are planned and decided upon." A critical commentary in the Liberec paper *Arbeiterfreund* [Worker's Friend] targeted the attempt of the papal encyclical to turn back the wheel of history. "The leader's idea is to restore to the Church its old powers, with which it will lead nations once more to the submission of previous centuries, through the comfort and joy of the hereafter."[32]

According to Ferdinand Schwarz, Pope Leo XIII's encyclical was an expression of the contrast between science and faith, between recognition of the new and entrenched prejudices. "The clergy advocate faith as the opposite to science: humanity's joy has to wait for an invisible, supernatural world. They disguise and excuse the hardships and injustice in this earthly vale of tears with the consolation of a better life in the 'hereafter.'" In several places in the papal encyclical there is an attempt to blame the scientific knowledge of the past two centuries for causing the "poisonous teachings" of socialism. With this presentation of the "red terror" the Pope tried to incite government circles to repress freedom of belief and conscience as well as independent inquiry.[33]

An important demand of the socialist workers in Liberec remained the separation of the Church from the state, and of schools from the Church. Ferdinand Schwarz

31. Lessing's idea was popularized around the end of the 18th century by Johann Heinrich Voss. See Büchmann, *Geflügelte Worte*, 220.

32. "Wenn die Gesellschaft durch die Religion zu milderen Sitten gebracht werden könnte, so müsste sie dieser Sitten ja schon längst teilhaftig sein, da ja die Kirche durch Jahrhunderte die höchste Gewalt über die Völker Europas besessen hat; wenn sie aber diese Kraft erst heute zu besitzen glaubt, so müssten die Bekehrungsversuche vor allem dort gemacht werden, wo die Kriege geplant und beschlossen werden. [...] Der leitende Gedanke ist der: man setze die Kirche wieder in ihre alten Vor-Rechte ein, und sie wird den Völkern wieder den Gehorsam vergangener Jahrhunderte beibringen, und das zwar durch den Trost auf die Freuden im Jenseits." [Hannich], "Papst Leo XIII.," *Arbeiterfreund,* vol. 6, no. 2, January 23,1879, 2–3.

33. "Das Pfaffentum lehrt den Glauben als Gegensatz zum Wissen; es verlegt das Heil der Menschheit in eine unsichtbare, übernatürliche Welt. Mit dem Troste auf ein besseres Leben im ‚Jenseits' lassen sich die Leiden und Ungerechtigkeiten im irdischen Jammertale beschönigen und entschuldigen. [...] Es handelt sich nur darum, die leitenden Kreise durch Vorführung des ‚roten Gespenstes' für Maßregeln zur Unterdrückung der Glaubens- und Gewissensfreiheit und des freien Forschens empfänglich zu machen." [Schwarz], "Pfaffentum und Socialismus," *Sozialpolitische Rundschau*, vol. 2, no. 2, February 1, 1879.

clarified this demand in a policy article with the words that Social Democracy, ". . . does not want atheism at all costs, rather it wants religion to be a private matter. Everyone can find bliss according to their needs, but they also have to contribute to the costs of their salvation."[34] Josef Hannich expressed himself similarly in July 1879 in the magazine *Arbeiterfreund*: "We are also demanding the complete separation of schools from the Church and the Church from the state, which in other words means: we want religion to become a private matter. To declare religion to be a private matter does not mean atheism in itself. Everyone can and should find bliss in their own way. Everyone can have their god if they need him to satisfy an intellect which longs for god, but everyone has to meet the costs for this gratification of the intellect, for their salvation. . . . Honesty, morality, integrity and decency are purely earthly matters, which are closely linked to our circumstances, and in conjunction with them we rise and fall. Transgressions against them will be punished according to purely earthly laws or according to purely earthly human traditions of censure. These are, therefore, not dogmatic issues, their existence is not bound to divine revelation, but to human experience, and that belongs to the realm of knowledge . . .[35]

The leading group of Liberec socialists used this approach to try to influence religiously sensitive workers so that they might be sympathetic to the other demands of the workers' movement. However, Liberec City Council complained that from 1879 there was a new wave of workers leaving the Catholic Church, which was reminiscent of the increase in free-thinking at the start of the 1870s. The city council saw this as evidence that the Social Democrats "want as little order in the Church as in the state."[36]

From February 1879 the working-class poet Josef Schiller took over the editorship of the monthly *Sozialpolitische Rundschau* [Social-Political Observer], disseminating his atheistic position not only in his verses but also in his deliberations concerning the incompatibility of faith with the wisdom found in science. The relatively fast development in the sciences over the previous 100 years was accompanied by a rise in atheism and conflict with the traditional Catholic Church, which, of course, did not always mean the strengthening of a scientific interpretation of the world, but also allowed for the widespread growth of religious sects. According to Josef Schiller it was possible to compare religious views with the prehistoric age when generation after generation lived from hand

34. [Schwarz], "Was wir wollen," *Sozialpolitische Rundschau*, vol. 2, no. 2, January 1, 1879.

35. "Auch fordern wir vollkommene Trennung der Schule von der Kirche und der Kirche vom Staate, das heißt also mit anderen Worten: wir wollen die Religion zur Privatsache machen. Die Religion zur Privatangelegenheit erklären heißt aber nicht Religionslosigkeit an und für sich. Jeder mag und soll auf seine Art und Weise selig werden, Jedem mag sein Gott belassen werden, soweit er ihn benötigt, um sein gottbedürftiges Gemüt zu befriedigen, aber Jeder mag auch für die Kosten dieser seiner Gemütsbefriedigung, seiner Seligwerdung aufkommen. [. . .] Ehrenhaftigkeit, Sittlichkeit, Redlichkeit und Anstand sind rein irdische Dinge; sie sind mit unseren Zuständen eng verwachsen, sie steigen und fallen mit ihnen. Ein Verstoß gegen sie wird auch nach rein irdischen Gesetzen bestraft, oder nach rein irdisch menschlichem Herkommen getadelt. Es sind dies also keine Glaubenssachen, sie verdanken ihr Dasein nicht der göttlichen Offenbarung, sondern der menschlichen Erfahrung, mithin gehören sie in das Bereich des Wissens." [Hannich], "Was wir wollen," *Arbeiterfreund*, vol. 6, no. 13, July 10, 1879, 2–3.

36. Státní okresní archiv [State District Archives] in Liberec, Magistrát města Liberce, pres. I/2, no. 42/1881, report from z 18. 6. 1881.

to mouth. "There is a significant difference between religion and science in that religion is founded on emotion whilst science calls on reason. Where it is possible to influence people individually with reason, thousands of people are controlled by emotion with its accompanying passions. This explains why religion moves forward so quickly, whereas science, hindered by so many prejudices, creeps forward so slowly that its progress can only be observed from one generation to the next." This fact was not intended to cause consternation, rather it was to be encouraging so that people might raise their awareness at least slightly.[37]

Verein der Konfessionslosen [The Association of Non-Believers] was established in Liberec in October 1880 on a much wider basis than nine years previously. The former journeyman cloth-worker Franz König was chosen as its chairman. After returning from working in Hannover and Saxony from 1873–1875, he set up a workshop in Liberec as an independent master cloth maker, also employing several other leading Social Democrats.[38] The newly established association set forward its goals thus:

1. to unite non-believers in a common association

2. to spread amongst its members the fundamental principles of a non-believer's morality

3. to contribute to the development of the intellect in the sense of a naturalistic or unified world view through lectures and debates at meetings.[39]

Once again it proved impossible to legalize the association because the governorship in Prague rejected the proposed charter on the grounds that a non-believers' association "would be in contradiction to the religious-moral basis of the state."[40] A new appeal was also turned down by the Austrian Ministry of Culture and Education on the grounds that the proposed association was illegal and a danger to the state as the spread of atheism "is in conflict with the highest principles of Austrian education and culture."[41]

37. "Zwischen der Religion und der Weisheit herrscht der bedeutende Unterschied, dass sich die erstere auf das Gefühl, die zweite aber auf den Verstand beruft. Wo sich ein ein einziger Mensch durch den Verstand beherrschen lässt, werden Tausende Menschen durch ihr Gefühl und durch in demselben gipfelnde Leidenschaften beherrscht. Dadurch ist es erklärlich, warum die Religion so schnell vorwärts schreitet, wogegen die Wissenschaft, befreit von allen Vorurteilen, so langsam vorwärts geht, dass man erst von einem Geschlechte zum andern ihren Fortschritt bemerkt." [Schiller], "Die Wissenschaft verdrängt den Glauber," *Sozialpolitische Rundschau*, vol. 2, no. 7, July 1, 1879.

38. Behr, "Erinnerung an Franz König," *Vorwärts*, vol. 41, no. 41, February 17, 1929. The workers' leaders returned to the workshop after being set free from prison during the first half of 1883.

39. "[. . .] 1. um die Konfessionslosen ein gemeinsames Band zu schlingen; 2. die Sittlichkeit nach den Grundsätzen der von aller Religion losgelösten Moral unter seinen Mitgliedern zu fördern; 3. durch wissenschaftliche Vorträge und auch durch Besprechungen in seinen Versammlungen der Entwicklung der Vernunft im Sinne der naturalistischen oder einheitlichen Weltanschauung Vorschub zu leisten." *Arbeiterfreund*, vol. 8, no. 23, December 8, 1881, 4, Lokales.

40. The handwritten copy of the association's charter and its rejection in the confiscated material of Franz König in the trial of the North Bohemian socialists in December 1882. Státní oblastní archiv [State Regional Archives] in Prague, Zemský soud trestní 1850–1897, C 1882/754, part XIII.

41. ". . . im Widerspruche mit den obersten Gesetzen des österreichischen Unterrichts- und Bildungswesens." *Arbeiterfreund*, vol. 8, no. 23, December 8, 1881, 4, Lokales.

Disregarding the refusal to ratify the association's charter, the socialist non-believers in Liberec went on to form a strong organization which met regularly. One or two activists operated in each region whose task it was to link up with other non-believers in the area.[42]

In Liberec this work fell to Franz König and Josef Ulbrich, the long-serving chairman of the workers' sickness fund; in the Liberec environs this work was mainly carried out by Ferdinand Schwarz from Stráž nad Nisou (*Althabendorf*), a baker and leading figure in the pan-Austrian Social Democrats from 1877; and around Tanvald (*Tannwald*) principally by the glass worker Anton Schwödler from Desná (*Dessendorf*). House searches conducted before the trials of the North Bohemian socialists uncovered lists of citizens without religion along with the places and regions where they were invited to non-religious funerals and other events. In the home of Ferdinand Schwarz in Stráž nad Nisou (*Althabendorf*) a store of freethinking literature was discovered which Schwarz had bought and often distributed to others.[43]

In June 1880 the Prague police headquarters acquired a copy of Schwarz's funeral speech for the final farewell to an atheist worker. "It has been mentioned that he to whom we now say farewell preached the gospel of love towards humanity, and that he carried in his heart the welfare of his fellow man; he did not search for heaven 'somewhere above,' but here amongst his fellow brothers, and he adhered to his code of love towards humanity right up to his final breath."[44]

In November 1880 the Liberec *Arbeiterfreund* [Worker's Friend] refused to accept the state administration's ruling that the South Bohemian farmer Alfons Šťastný have his right to be a juror rescinded due to his non-religious beliefs.[45] "If atheism brings with it a prejudice in the law, then all citizens are not equal before the law as is guaranteed by the constitution."[46]

In the lists of financial collections for the families of imprisoned socialists featured in the Prague and later the Viennese *Dělnické Listy* [Workers' News], the contributors did not want to sign their full names for fear of persecution, and from the Liberec region the signature "Non-believer" appeared alongside socialist and other slogans.[47] It was indicative of the attitude of the state authorities towards atheism that the district offices in Děčín (*Tetschen*) allowed several socialist-oriented poems by Josef Schiller to be read in public

42. As remembered by Beranek, "Aus dem Leben," *Vorwärts*, vol. 38, no. 102, May 1, 1926.

43. An extensive list of works confiscated from Ferdinand Schwarz in: Státní oblastní archiv [State Regional Archives] in Prague, Zemský soud trestní 1850–1897, C 1882/754, part XVI.

44. Prague police headquarters to the presidium of the Czech governorship 21. 6. 1880. Národní archiv [National Archives] in Prague, Presidium místodržitelství 1871–1880, 8/4/15/7, no. 4686/1880.

45. Zita, *Alfons Šťastný*, 14–17.

46. "Da die Konfessionslosigkeit aber eine Rechtsverkürzung mit sich zieht, so sind die Staatsbürger nicht mehr vor dem Gesetze alle gleich, wie es durch die Verfassung gewährleistet wird. " *Arbeiterfreund*, vol. 7, no. 22, November 25, 1880, 3.

47. *Dělnické Listy*, no. 40, September 20, 1882, 4.

at a workers' association festival in Františkov nad Ploučnicí (Franzenthal), while the reading of his popular poem *Der Konfessionslose* [Without Religion] was forbidden.[48]

At the end of 1881 a small event in Liberec was the spur for the further integration of Social Democratic non-believers. The tradesman Franz Peuker, who was without religion, had been repeatedly challenging the authorities—the latest incident had been his refusal to have his child christened in a Catholic Church as demanded by the Czech governorship. The authorities argued that prior to announcing their non-religious status both parents had belonged to the Catholic Church and therefore their children had to be brought up in the Catholic faith. To declare your children to be without religion was allegedly in contradiction with the highest principles of Austrian schooling and upbringing.[49] However, Peuker refused and turned to the leaders of Liberec's Social Democrats for advice. As this was not an isolated case Ferdinand Schwarz, Josef Ulbrich and the Czech locksmith František Nechvíle issued a public appeal "To Non-Believers," in which, with an eye to the political situation in Austria, they suggested establishing associations of citizens without religion. In the proclamation published in the Liberec magazine *Arbeiterfreund*[50] [Worker's Friend] they invited all non-believers to send their addresses to Liberec. The appeal was printed in several other papers including the Viennese socialist magazine *Die Zukunft* [Thew Future], the Budapest *Arbeiter-Wochen-Kronik* [The Worker's Weekly Chronicle], and without the knowledge of the authors in several newspapers such as *Deutsche Zeitung* [German News] in Vienna.

The letters which Josef Ulbrich received from 52 people in answer to this appeal were very disparate in nature.[51] As a resolute non-believer the socialist activist Hermann Wanke sent two letters in the name of the socialists from Rýmařov (Römerstadt), as did several Social Democrats from Vienna. Two young workers who had just reached the age of majority asked how they should go about leaving the Church. Josef Ingruber from Graz informed the Liberec Social Democrats of the state of the non-believers' movement in Steiermark where, following a large upswing at the start of the 1870s, the freethinking community had collapsed. Some supporters of Social Democracy questioned the usefulness of a non-believers' campaign at a time when workers were going hungry. Letters also arrived in Liberec from the fanatical founders of a "new religion" and from a greater number of freethinkers outwith the sphere of the workers' movement.[52]

In connection with this Eduard Schwella from Vienna wrote in solidarity to the Liberec Social Democrat non-believers. He was the founder of the local "free church of reason," which represented Austria at the World Congress of Freethinkers in Brussels in 1880.[53] As the authorities did not allow associations of non-believing citizens, Schwella

---

48. Děčín district office to the presidium of the Czech governorship 5. 7. 1880. Národní archiv [National Archives] in Prague, Presidium místodržitelství 1871–1880, 8/5/1/1, no. 5137/1880.

49. *Arbeiterfreund*, vol. 8, no. 21, November 19, 1881, 4, Lokales.

50. With the appeal in *Arbeiterfreund* printed in: *Wahrheit*, vol. 2, no. 2, January 20, 1882.

51. Státní oblastní archiv [State Regional Archives] in Prague, Zemský soud trestní 1850–1897, C 1882/754, part X, interrogation of Josef Ulbrich 3. 8. 1882.

52. Ibid., part XI.

53. Among the fundamental works was the book Schwella, *Geschichte der Glaubens-Mythen*.

recommended to the Liberec socialists that they set up a religious society in accordance with the liberal Austrian constitution of 1867, perhaps even establishing a branch of the Viennese "free church of reason," whose charter, magazines and textbooks for children he sent to Liberec. The Liberec non-believers called a meeting and set up a special committee to investigate the charter and direction of Schwella's church. After lengthy discussions a section of the non-believers decided to maintain links with it and some of the others, notably Ferdinand Schwarz, personally signed up for the "free church of reason."[54] During these discussions significant differences between the socialist workers and the middle-class freethinkers in their understanding of atheism came to light. The Liberec socialists wanted to work with the "free church of reason" on the practical everyday issues faced by non-believing families, particularly the refusal to christen children and the non-religious education of school children, but other than that they advocated the principles that were common to workers' organizations. In one of his letters to Ferdinand Schwarz, Eduard Schwella disagreed with mass discussions on the principles of the church because each man had to deal with his relationship to the church individually according to his convictions. In a letter dated March 20th 1882 Schwella had to answer a question from the Liberec socialists about his relationship to the issue of the working class, and his evasive explanation of the arguments he had had with the socialists from the Alpine territories failed to convince. Ferdinand Schwarz had grave doubts about the usefulness of Schwella's "free church of reason," but over time practical issues concerning the possibility of legal atheist lectures on the basis of an authorized charter were to prevail.[55]

Josef Beranek, one of the most active Social Democrat non-believers in the Liberec area following Ferdinand Schwarz's retreat into seclusion,[56] was the co-organizer of regular Sunday meetings of non-believing citizens and sympathizers in Liberec's Vereinshalle [Public Hall]. Part of the programme for these well-attended meetings consisted of regular lectures on various scientific issues. After several unsuccessful attempts, permission for a non-believers' association was finally granted in 1892.[57]

54. Ferdinand Schwarz joined Schwella's church in June 1882 and took from Schwella 10 copies of his *Geschichte der Glaubens-Mythen* and a further 10 editions of *Religionslehrer*. Státní oblastní archiv [State Regional Archives] in Prague, Zemský soud trestní 1850–1897, C 1882/754, part XVI, interrogation of Ferdinand Schwarz 18. 8. 1882.

55. Ibid., part XXVI.

56. Ferdinand Schwarz was twice convicted by the federal criminal court in Prague, in January 1879 to two months and in December 1882 to four months imprisonment. After acquiring significant debts he was forced to give up the bakery business and he had also become disgusted by the fights with the radicals and anarchists in the Austrian workers' movement. His life was described by Ferdinand Schwarz in three letters to Karl Kautsky in Stuttgart from 12. 6., 4. 9. and 12. 12. 1883. Kautsky, *Briefwechsel mit der Tschechoslowakei*, 82–89.

57. Beranek, "Aus dem Leben," *Vorwärts*, vol. 38, no. 102, May 1, 1926.

11

The Social Democratic Atheist Movement in Interwar Ostravsko

MARTIN JEMELKA

INTRODUCTION

O NE OF THE MOST important, if not the most important, apolitical, non-physi-
cal education organizations in interwar Ostravsko was the Sdružení českých
bezvěrců [Association of Czech Atheists] (1919) which quickly became the Sdružení
sociálnědemokratických bezvěrců [Association of Social Democratic Atheists] (1919),
and from 1933 the Unie socialistických svobodných myslitelů [Union of Free Socialist
Thinkers]. It was easily the largest atheist organization in the region and, together with
Volná myšlenka [Free Thought] and the Communist atheist movement, was the main
ideological rival to the Catholic Church and to religion in general. The development
of an organized atheist movement in Ostravsko, capitalizing on ineffective Christian
social teachings and the anti-Catholic position of the majority of the socialist-oriented
workers, was facilitated by the establishment of the Czechoslovak state and the postwar
liberalization of association life, regulated by an amendment to the law on the rights of
associations from Nov 15, 1867. Before World War One, when Moravian Ostrava and
Vítkovice served as bastions of Austrian militarism and where most of the local industrial factories were under military supervision, organized atheism in Ostravsko lacked a
fertile breeding ground: the middle-class oriented Volná myšlenka tended to avoid social
issues and featured only in short news items in the socialist daily *Duch času* [The Spirit
of the Time]. People without faith in Moravian Ostrava and the outlying areas were very
much in the minority in comparison with the situation after 1918.[1] However, the tradi-

1. Jemelka, "K náboženskému životu," 41. In 1900, out of the 30,115 inhabitants of Moravian Ostrava
there were only 16 people without religion (0.05 %), ten years later for every 1000 inhabitants of Moravian
Ostrava 1,4 people were without religion (the city then had 36,754 inhabitants), in 1921 41,765 people lived
in Moravian Ostrava and 2,214 people were without religion (5.3 %) and in 1930 among 45,885 inhabitants
4,236 were without religion (9.23 %).

tionally strong religious sentiment of the local coalminers and industrial workers was not to have a significant influence on the postwar standing of the atheist movement.[2]

The immediate postwar development of the atheist organizations in Ostravsko was therefore not determined by the prewar traditions of Free Thought, as it ceased to exist during the First World War and developed only slowly after the war, but by urbanization with its generally civilizing value changes, the anti-clerical propaganda of the socialist press (*Duch času*), the experience of war, the anti-Catholic ideology of the infant Czechoslovak state and by generations' experiences of a religion which only partially reflected, or failed completely to reflect, the social reality of life in industrial Ostravsko. The more active and important interwar atheist movements in Ostravsko and Czechoslovakia (SSDB in Moravian Ostrava, the Socialističtí bezvěrci [Socialist Atheists] in Most, Obroda [Renewal] in Prague, the SDB Union in Roudnice, the Federation of Communist Cultural Units, Bund der proletarischen Freidenker, etc) were affiliated to the socialist parties, with Volná myšlenka being allied to the Atheists' International from 1924, and there were some 35,000 paying members in just four socialist-atheist organizations in the Republic by the middle of the 1920s.[3]

THE UNION OF SOCIAL DEMOCRATIC ATHEISTS IN MORAVIAN OSTRAVA

The fact that interwar Ostravsko, an industrial center of the Czechoslovak state on the borders of a geopolitical and ethnographical region, was at the center of the Czechoslovak atheist movement is illustrated by the rapid establishment of the Sdružení českých bezvěrců on 6. 5. 1919 at the Slavia Hotel in Moravian Ostrava at a meeting of the nineteen founding members led by the editor Bedřich Čurda-Lipovský (1893–1962).[4]

An initial step towards the founding of the first Czechoslovak atheist organization was the establishment of the *Volné slovo* [Free Word] magazine, which from 1919–1939,

---

2. Skalníková, "Problém Ostravska," 362.

3. *Volné slovo*, vol. 7, no. 34, September 11, 1925, 1: the SDB in Moravian Ostrava, Bund der proletarischen Freidenker, Federation of Communist Cultural Units and the Union of Socialist Atheists in Most had 35,000 paying members altogether.

4. Jiřík, "Čurda-Lipovský," 31: Bedřich Čurda-Lipovský (20. 11. 1893 Smolkov, local part Háje u Opavy—21. 10. 1962 Ostrava), journalist, writer, astronomer and founder of the atheist movement in Ostravsko, he was born into a shoemaker's family and after studying at a German business school in Opava in 1912 he became a shipping clerk for the František coking plant in Přívoze. After that he was the manager of the crematorium in Moravian Ostrava (1924–1928), a correspondent for the Moravian Ostrava electricity company (1929–1940) and librarian at the Národní odborová ústředna (National Trade Union Centre) in Moravian Ostrava (1943–1944). 28. 8. 1944 he was arrested by the Gestapo and interned in Terezín until May 1945. 1945–1949 he was the secretary and chairman of the Regional Trade Union Committee in Ostrava. From 1950 he worked on the development of Ostrava's observatory, of which he was director until his death. In 1919 he set up the SSDB (after 1933 the USSM), as well as being editor of the atheist Volné slovo (The Free Word) he regularly attended atheist conferences both at home and abroad. From 1924 he was a Social Democrat representative on the town council and a member of Moravian Ostrava City Council (1935–1939). He actively participated with the Moravian Ostrava regional amateur actors, undertook study trips to several European countries and was interested in astronomy from his youth onward. He was the author of hundreds of newspaper articles and several books.

according to the subheading of the first edition that came out in Přívoz on 1. 3. 1919 "defended and promoted the interests of Czech atheists" and used Machar's slogan that "a Czech man cannot be a man of Rome."[5] At first *Volné slovo* came out fortnightly, then weekly, and by the end of the 1930s monthly, whilst in 1927 and 1930–1931 it was published as a weekly supplement to the newspaper *Náš kraj* [Our Country], otherwise it came out independently despite constant economic difficulties.[6] The first issue of *Volné slovo* mainly supplied practical information on how to leave the Roman Catholic Church on the basis of existing legislation, including the State Fundamental Law on the General Rights of State Citizens from 21. 12. 1867, no. 142 of the Imperial Law, and the Interconfessional Law from 25. 5. 1868, no. 49 of the Imperial Law, according to which those wishing to leave the Church at the age of 15 had to send a form to the local political authorities which would inform the relevant parish council of their removal from the Church (the priest's only role in the whole process of leaving the church was as a state clerk in charge of the registry, any other intervention could be punished by a month in prison for defamation). Immediately in the first edition of *Volné slovo*, edited by B. Čurda-Lipovský, alongside the normal features (various news items, editorials, public notices, the atheists' chronicle: "From the Roman sheep pen they left and remained without faith," letters page, printing fund) it also opened up themes which over the following years were honed and reduced to ideological slogans (the separation of the Church from the state, free schools), but also to stereotypes aimed at Czech clericalism, the Roman Catholic Church and religion in general (e.g., the article Pravda o svatém Janu Nepomuckém [The Truth about St Jan Nepomucký] from 1. 4. 1919, reacting to the street protests in Prague's Old Town Square, Týn Church and Charles Bridge in March 1919 and discussing Jan Nepomucký as a kind of Catholic *"replacement for Hus"*).[7]

Whilst the first postwar meeting of Volná myšlenka to take place with the participation of Ostravsko delegates was on 8. 6. 1919 (among other things at the meeting Čurda-Lipovský described the difficult beginnings of the Ostravsko anti-clerical struggle, which had been supported by the workers but practically ignored by the local intelligentsia),[8] one month before the Prague meeting of Volná myšlenka on Tuesday 6. 5. 1919 at 7.30pm at the Slavia Hotel in Moravian Ostrava there was the first confidential meeting of Ostravsko atheists called by the publishers of *Volné slovo*. Over 100 participants of both sexes from Velká Ostrava, as well as from Orlová, Polská and Německá Lutyně, Příbor, Rychvald and Sedlice u Opavy proceeded to establish an apolitical atheist organization, which was to "proceed independently in local matters and in nationwide matters in co-operation with the central atheists' organizations in Prague (Volná myšlenka, Svaz monistů [Union of

---

5. *Volné slovo*, vol. 1, no. 1, March 1, 1919, 1.

6. *Volné slovo*: a magazine defending and promoting the interests of Czech atheists (1919–1920), a magazine defending and promoting the interests of Social Democratic atheists (from 15. 5. 1920), a magazine defending the interests of Social Democratic atheists (1921), a cultural paper for Social Democratic atheists (1922–1930), a cultural paper for proletarian atheists (1931–1933), an organ of USSM (1934–1938), a cultural paper defending the interests of atheists (1939).

7. *Volné slovo*, vol. 1, no. 3, April 1, 1919, 2.

8. *Volné slovo*, vol. 1, no. 8, June 15, 1919, 3.

Monists], Svaz československých bezvěrců [Union of Czechoslovak Atheists])." At the inaugural meeting, for which there had been little in the way of preparation and only a few newspaper announcements in the pages of *Duch času* and *Volné slovo*, a twenty-one member preparatory committee was chosen which discussed the current state of the anti-clerical struggle and the hegemony of the Social Democrats in the struggle against clericalism in Ostravsko.[9] It is interesting to note the reaction of the conservative press to the first meeting of the Ostravsko atheists, for example the Ostravský kraj [Ostravsko Region] had the following report on the meeting: "The meeting of the heathens took place on May 6th at the Slavia Hotel in Moravian Ostrava. According to reports around 100 heathens gathered there. A presidium and committee were elected. This sparked a debate. The first to speak was the editor-in-chief of the Ostravsko daily, citizen Knotek, who warmly greeted the new organization. He pointed out that it was necessary to de-Catholicize those millions who were still in the Church and wished them much success in their work. Otherwise nothing happened. It drizzled a little and draught beer was available."[10]

The Sunday members' meeting on Aug 17, 1919 in the Moravian Ostrava's Lidový dům [People's House] can be considered to be the founding act of the first atheist organization in Ostravsko, the Sdružení českých bezvěrců, during which, apart from drawing up telegrams to send to atheist organizations in Brno and Prague (Volná myšlenka, Svaz socialistických bezvěrců), it established the first local atheist divisions in Ostravsko (Heřmanice, Hrabová, Hrabůvka, Hulváky, Mariánské Hory, Michálkovice, Moravian Ostrava, Přívoz, Přívoz Odra pit, Radvanice, Rychvald, Slezská Ostrava, Šenov, Vítkovice, Zábřeh, Zárubek) and agreed on the union's charter proposed at the previous meeting of 6. 8. 1919 in the Slavia Hotel in Moravian Ostrava, according to which the Sdružení českých bezvěrců would be developed by lectures, debating evenings, the promotion of educational literature, discussions and speech-making courses "working towards the Czech nation divesting itself of the disastrous influence of the various churches, the Roman Catholic especialy, which has always been the worst enemy of the Czechs."[11]

Immediately in its first year of existence the Sdružení českých bezvěrců and its press organ *Volné slovo* diversified into a range of activities: they reflected on the Prague preparations for the establishment of the Socialistický svaz bezvěrců [Socialist Union of Atheists] (21. 6.), there was great interest shown by Ostravsko atheists in the dignified demonstration for the first postwar celebration of the anniversary of Hus's death (6. 7.), the development and arguments within Volná myšlenka were viewed with alarm, the reforms within Czech Catholicism leading to the establishment of the Czechoslovak Church were judged critically (*"new firm, same old swindle"*), there were ironic comments about the marriage of priests, the ceremonies performed by the Radvanice priest P. Ferdinand Stibor (1869–1956), a future bishop of the Czechoslovak Church, who in

9. *Volné slovo*, vol. 1, no. 6, May 15, 1919, 1.

10. Cited from *Volné slovo*, vol. 6, no. 10. May 16, 1924, 6.

11. Archiv města Ostravy [Ostrava City Archives]. Spolky na území města Ostravy: Župní výbor Unie socialistických svobodných myslitelů, Pamětní zápis schůze Sdružení českých bezvěrců, August 6, 1919, 216, no. 1, reg. no. 1.

1919 alone consecrated 105 weddings of Catholic clerics, but a survey was also written for *Volné slovo* entitled Why did I leave the Church?[12] and the regional committee of the Volné sdružení sociálnědemokratických bezvěrců [The Free Union of Social Democratic Atheists] was elected. From the very first year *Volné slovo* started what were to be several years of verbal attacks on Andrej Hlinka and the age-old struggle with alcoholism and prostitution, incompatible with the ideals of a secular morality.

The year 1920 saw much activity among the local atheists in Ostravsko: whilst at the time of the conference of the Sdružení sociálnědemokratických bezvěrců (SSDB) [Union of Social Democratic Atheists] in the first half of February 1920 the association had only 13 local divisions with 825 members, at the district conference in the Lidový dům on October 10th of the same year it was noted in the presence of 45 guests and 37 delegates from 28 local divisions that there were 2,500 regular paying members organized in the district. In the programme for the district conference there was mention of holding 120 lectures and two mass meetings to discuss increasing membership contributions, the financial support of *Volné slovo*, the translation of a French-language pamphlet of Belgian origin into Czech and establishing co-operation with Belgian atheists. There were also presented newly prepared slide lectures.[13] In 1920, with the active Čurda-Lipovský as leader, the Ostravsko atheists took part in the 1st meeting of the SSDB in Prague (Mar 21, 1920), which focused mainly on the arguments concerning the increase in membership contributions and the central print organ (Čurda-Lipovský had to support the primacy of *Volné slovo* in Ostravsko), and the XVIII world congress of Volná myšlenka in Prague (Sept 5–9, 1920). Through *Volné slovo* there were several commentaries concerning the law from Apr 15, 1920 which altered some of the statutes of the Interconfessional law of May 25, 1868, no. 49 of the Imperial law, and according to which children between the ages of eight and fifteen could change their beliefs. A great deal of attention was also focused on the struggle over Czech schools, the blossoming of the activities of the SSDB's theater division, repeated complaints about the tardiness of the district political authorities when dealing with applications to leave the Church, and also cremation and crematoria, the building of which had led to an architectural competition in Velká Ostrava in the autumn of 1920. However, in *Volné slovo* there continually cropped up in the undercurrent of regional socialism and atheism a socially determined antisemitism that was outraged by the combination of "Catholic landowners and Jewish capital."[14] Finaly, there had to be some mention of the death (4. 11.) and funeral of Petr

12. *Volné slovo*, vol. 1, no. 15, October 1, 1919, 3: "Why did I leave the Church? We have extracts from the survey 'Why I left the Church.' We ask all our friends to take part in the survey. Describe in brief your life history by answering these questons: 1. What was your school education like? 2. How were you brought up by your family? 3. Through which resolution did you enter into public life? 4. Which books and works led you to your path today? 5. For what reasons did you leave the Church? 6. What wrongs did you suffer as a result, both from the authorities and society? 7. Do you feel happy now that you are without the Church? 8. How does this disengagement affect you? 9. Do you believe you are now on the road to a better life? 10. What do you think of the issues regarding smoking and abstinence? If everyone can write even roughly about their experiences, the editor will tidy it up. We intend to publish the most interesting cases in the newspaper in this new section. Now, to work, friends!" The survey either did not attract enough readers or the results were never published.

13. *Volné slovo*, vol. 2, no. 16, October 15, 1920, 4–6.

14. "Beat the Jews," *Volné slovo*, vol. 2, no. 11, August 1, 1920, 3.

Cingr (Nov 13, 1920), which was attended by a crowd of around 100,000, and the 300th anniversary of the tragedy of the Battle of White Mountain (Nov 8, 1920).

In 1921 the Ostravsko atheists demonstrated their readiness for the anti-clerical struggle with the 300th anniversary of the executions on Old Town Square, the Jan Hus celebrations and the celebration of the birth of Karel Havlíček Borovský (Oct 31, 1921). The SSDB's district conference in the Lidový dům on June 12, 1921 demonstrated not only the increasing influence of the local atheists (around 4,000 paying members were organized in 40 divisions and *Volné slovo* now had a print run of 6,000), but principally it articulated the most pressing problems of the movement—the separation of the Church from the state, land reform, and the conflict and subsequent break with the Communist atheists. The November meeting of the SSDB in Prague (Nov 6, 1921), where from the 47 delegates present J. Nehyba was voted as Ostravsko's representative to the presidium, though it did not agree on a new charter, clearly showed that Ostravsko was one of the regions with the best organized atheist movement, which was confirmed in the same year at the end of 1921 with the establishment of Svépomoc [Self-Help], a section of the SSDB in Moravian Ostrava whose aim was to provide dying members of local divisions with a dignified non-religious funeral, coffin, floral decoration, a decorated room for the service, a funeral cortege and orator, which initially cost 12 crowns a year for every paying member.[15]

The first half of the 1920s was a particularly busy part of the interwar period for the Ostravsko atheists: in the period between Jan 1 and Dec 1 1921 alone the district organization of the SSDB brought together 40 divisions with 4,175 members (958 women and 2,585 men), and the majority of the organized atheists were members of the Dělnická tělovýchovná jednota (DTJ) [The Workers' Physical Education Unit] and the Social Democrats (only 636 members were non-party members or members of different socialist parties). Apart from the so-called heretics' parties, theater performances and countless slide lectures, during this period there were also held 305 member meetings, 353 committee meetings and 209 public meetings, 28 mass meetings and 50 non-religious funerals.[16] As the notes from the annual and work conferences show, the number of local divisions in the 1920s fluctuated: whilst at the time of the annual conference on Mar 26, 1922 the district organization had 49 local divisions, four months later during the work conference the SSDB only had 41 local divisions. The main themes of 1922 were establishing contact with the Dělnická akademie [Workers' Academy] and the issue of the secularization of Czech education, which the SSDB brought to people's attention at mass meetings in Přívoz (June 14) and Místek (Aug 20, 1922).

In 1924 the Ostravsko atheists entered into their fifth year as a local atheist organizaton: on Sunday Mar 23 there was a fifth-anniversary celebration of the SSDB at the Národní divadlo moravskoslezské (NDMS) [The Moravian-Silesian National Theater]. Instead of the originally planned premiere of the play *Přijde den!* [The Day is Coming!] by B. Čurda-Lipovský, which due to its disparaging of the teachings of the Roman Catholic

---

15. *Volné slovo*, vol. 3, no. 21, November 15, 1921, 3.

16. *Volné slovo*, vol. 4, no. 6, March 15, 1922, 7.

Church had been banned by the regional political authorities in Brno, despite urgent reminders by the SSDB, only 24 hours before the premiere,[17] there was only a celebratory meeting for the 800 participants, with a number of anniversary as well as protest speeches. After the celebratory meeting was over, a protest procession left the NDMS building, filed past the Catholic House and after speeches of indignation and an assurance from the police commissioner that he would convey the anger of the Ostravsko atheists to the regional political authorities in Brno, the crowd dispersed in front of the police headquarters in Moravian Ostrava.[18] The meeting of the central office of the SSDB also took place in this spirit of protest in Moravian Ostrava on Sunday Apr 13, attended by 186 delegates from 61 divisions and guests from several associated organizations (at the meeting the cultural and educational activities of the SSDB were recognized for the first time by the official bodies of the Social Democrats),[19] as did the SSDB divisions' autumn work conference in the Lidový dům on Friday Oct 24, when, among other matters, letters of protest were drawn up against the continued confiscation of Czech socialist magazines. Another theme of the autumn work conference was the participation of six delegates from the SSDB, the daily Duch času and the Dělnická akademie at the Whitsun World Congress of Atheists in Vienna and at the autumn meeting of the Atheists' International in Vienna (Oct 4–8, 1924), at which the Ostravsko delegates were worthily and actively represented by B. Čurda-Lipovský, František Čepek and Bohuslav Šída (topics for discussion included the constitution of the Atheists' International, the relationship of European socialist parties towards atheism, subsidies for atheist institutions and press, the separation of the Church from the state and the role of the Volná myšlenka Brussels International).[20]

Powerful examples of the size and influence of the membership base of the Ostravsko atheists were the celebrations at the opening of the Ostrava crematorium, for which the atheists had been campaigning since 1919, and an enormous demonstration for freedom of conscience which took place in 1925. Even before the First World War, the local politicians of Moravian Ostravsko had been considering the idea of building a crematorium in a city with a rising population and an unsatisfactory city cemetery with unsuitable clay subsoil. The architectural competition, which was won by Prague architects Vladimír Hofman and František Mencel, was announced on June 1, 1920, but actual construction of the crematorium did not begin until Apr 10, 1923. The construction was carried out by the building contractor Rudolf Slezáček, the central entrance to the cemetery was designed by the builders Kolář and Rubý, with the decoration of the archway being assigned to the sculptor Augustin Handzel, a native of the nearby Šalomoun settlement. It was only after the opening of the Moravian Ostrava crematorium, the first crematorium

---

17. On Feb 29, 1924 the play was submitted to the censors at the The Regional Political Administration in Brno, on 17. 3. a reminder was sent to the administration, and only on Mar 22, 1924 did the police office in Moravian Ostrava issue its refusal.

18. *Volné slovo*, vol. 6, no. 7, April 1, 1924, 2f.

19. *Volné slovo*, vol. 6, no. 8, April 15, 1924, 6.

20. Ibid., 1f.

in Moravia, [21] that crematoria began to be built in Brno and Olomouc. Due to the large degree of public interest, the crematorium was given a ceremonial opening on Sunday Feb 1, 1925, with cremations beginning the following day, and by Feb 14 there had been fifteen cremations including members of the atheist division of Svépomoc. [22]

Alongside the regular meeting of the SSDB at the start of July 1925 in the Lidový dům in Moravian Ostrava [23] and the propaganda activities of *Volné slovo*, which centred particularly on the new Interconfessional law (March) and the Marmaggi affair (July), the attention of the atheists was captured by the large demonstration for freedom of conscience which took place on Sept 6, 1925. The demonstration, which was initiated by the German Bund der proletarischen Freidenker (BPF) [Union of Proletarian Freethinkers] as a protest against German Katholikentag [Catholic Day], was organized by the BPF and SSDB as well as members of Volná myšlenka and the Federace komunistických osvětových jednot (FKOJ) [The Federation of Communist Educational Units]. The demonstration, whose themes were the struggle against clerical reactionism, the separation of the Church from the state, the abolition of the "unnecessary" embassy in the Vatican, and freedom of conscience, included the organization of four huge marches in Vítkovice, Přívoz, Mariánské Hory and Silesian Ostrava, which from Boleslav Pecka Street in Moravian Ostrava joined with local atheists and continued along Nádražní Street and October 28th Street to Masaryk Square, where Czech and German speakers addressed a crowd of over 10,000 people, asking them to end the gathering with a rendition of the International. *"If you are a real socialist, you cannot be a member of any church,"* read the accepted resolution, which went on to demand the removal of the Church's influence from the army (abolishing the institution of the chaplain) and the completion of land reforms. [24]

What was to be a large demonstration for freedom of conscience in September 1925 became the high point for the Ostravsko atheists in the 1920s. In the following years, alongside a definite slowing down of activities, and even doubts over the operation of the SSDB, there were attacks from the FKOJ, whose aim was to take over or at least split the SSDB. Whilst in 1927 the local atheists commemorated the first anniversary of the death of the socially engaged writer František Sokol-Tůma († Dec 31, 1925) and during the

21. The crematorium building with adjacent columbarium cost 770,000 Kč, and the portal, in which there was a dissecting room and morgue, caretaker's flat and other rooms, cost 730,000 Kč.

22. *Volné slovo*, vol. 7, no. 3, 1925, 6 and no. 4, 1925, 3 f.

23. *Volné slovo*, vol. 7, no. 24, July 3, 1925, 1: On Sunday June 28, 1925 there was a meeting of the SSDB at the Lidový dům in Moravian Ostrava which was chaired by B. Čurda-Lipovský and was attended by delegates from 85 divisions with 7,516 members. 12 new divisions had been added since the last meeting and there had been 849 committee, division, member and educational meetings, 10 public meetings, 59 Jan Hus celebrations, 290 public lectures with slides, 59 theatre performances and 28 funerals. Since its last meeting 859 members had joined the SSDB and it had established a close working relationship with the Dělnická academie and the Atheist Congress in Vienna and was involved in extensive discussions over the removal of children from religion, the restitution of the independent publication of *Volné slovo*, the election of a new central committee and comments on the implementation of the Malý školský zákon [The Lesser Educational Law] (so that parents could have their children exempted from religious education at the start of the school year).

24. *Volné slovo*, vol. 7, no. 32, August 28, 1925, 1 and no. 34, September 11, 1925, 1.

autumn election campaign called for the restriction of the SSDB's activities to the bare minimum,[25] the following two years were marked by celebrations, firstly the tenth anniversary of the formation of Czechoslovakia and then the tenth anniversary of the SSDB. The main celebrations reached their peak on June 2, 1929 in the NDMS, where members of Ostrava's theaters and amateur performers from the theater divisions of the SSDB from Vítkovice, the Šalomoun settlement, Mariánské Hory, Přívoz and Moravian Ostrava put on the anti-clerical play *Hvězda* [The Star] by Hanuš Müller, the main character of which was Galileo Galilei. The June celebration was preceded by a district conference on Sunday May 22, 1929, which was attended by 112 delegates from fifty divisions, who were told that in the period 1927–1928 alone there had been 1,423 meetings and lectures and 105 children's parties, which were attended by 85,600 people (in 1928 activities were put on hold due to the 10th anniversary of the Czechoslovak state and attacks by Communist atheists).[26] Nor did the beginning of the 1930s see any abatement in the anti-clerical struggle of the Ostravsko atheists, when, following the stabilization of Czechoslovak-Vatican relations after 1929 and reconciliation between the state and the Church, there arose in Ostravsko a new "ideological enemy" in the form of the Czechoslovak Church, whose clerics lured atheists to their ranks: "The Czechoslovak Church remained silent while its roots were not imbedded in the state, but as soon as it achieved what it wanted, albeit through state support, it has shown that it has not relinquished the spiritual method of the Roman Catholics."[27] However, the main opponent of the local atheist movement remained the Roman Catholic Church, against whose eucharistic conference in Moravian Ostrava was advertised a "meeting of non-religious and progressive citizens against the eucharist meeting" at the Lidový dům on June 22, 1920, under the slogan "down with the church and religion in schools," which was attended by representatives of the SSDB, VM and BPF.[28] In the autumn of 1930 there were preparations for the annual conference in Vítkovice's Odborový dům [Union House] (Oct 12, 1930),[29] at which was discussed the forthcoming census of the people of the Czechoslovak Republic, Dec 1, 1930 ("Czech Brother, are you still in the church?" wrote *Volné slovo*) and the transformation of *Volné slovo* into the joint press organ of the SSDB, the BPF in Podmokly (a regular subscrip-

25. *Volné slovo*, vol. 9, March 13, 1927, 2f.: Not counting guests, the annual conference of the SSDB in the Lidový dům in Moravian Ostrava included 116 representatives from 74 divisions, who were presented with slide lectures on topics such as Papal Rome, Travels across Africa, the White Mountain, Albania, the Crematorium, Jan of Pomuk, Hus and his Time, the Inquisition, Journey to the North Pole, Kutná Hora, Prehistoric Life and Phrenology.

26. *Volné slovo*, vol. 11, no. 11, May 23, 1929, 1.

27. *Volné slovo*, vol. 12, no. 3, February 6, 1930, 1.

28. *Volné slovo*, vol. 12, no. 13, June 26, 1930, 1.

29. *Volné slovo*, vol. 12, no. 21, October 16, 1930, 1f.: On Sunday Oct 12, 1930 the annual conference was held in Vítkovice's Odborový dům, at which every division was represented by its chairman, secretary, treasurer and educator with sworn mandates. The room, which was decorated with palms, pansies, red flags, and busts of Masaryk and Marx (a red flag flew from the building), welcomed 159 delegates from 45 divisions as well as representatives from the Central SSDB, the CSSDS and the Sdružení proletářských bezvěrců [Union of Proletarian Atheists] from Brno. Included in the discussions were plans for the population census of Dec 1, 1930, with special posters to provide information on how to fill out the sections on religious belief.

tion of 300 copies) and the SPB in Brno (950 copies),[30] which represented another step towards the unification of the domestic atheist movement.

However, the key period for the unification process of the Czechoslovakian atheist movement was 1932: first of all, on Apr 24 in Česká Třebova there was a working meeting of representatives of the socialist atheist organizations (SSDB in Moravian Ostrava, SPB in Brno, the Provincial Committee of the Prague SPB), the main purpose of which was to agree on guidelines for a joint approach to the unification of the organizations. Among the Ostravsko Social Democrat atheist delegates at the Dělnický dům [Workers' House] were B. Čurda-Lipovský and František Ladislav Koudelka, who decided that the joint central atheist organization would be sited in Prague, with the provincial secretariats in Brno and Moravian Ostrava, and the joint press organ would be *Volné slovo*, which was again to be published independently as either a fortnightly or monthly edition and which was to be subscribed to by every atheist family. They also did not forget Svépomoc, a division of the SSDB which had grown over the years into a large organization and which was to continue helping with the funeral arrangements of members of the united socialist atheist organization.[31] Another meeting aimed at the further integration of the above-mentioned organizations was held in the Odborový dům in Prague II Perštýn (Nov 19–20, 1932) and was attended by 116 delegates (27 from Ostravsko, 67 from Bohemia and 22 from Brněnsko), who were welcomed by Dr. František Soukup. On Jan 1, 1933 the Unie socialistických svobodných myslitelů (USSM) [Union of Socialist Free Thinkers] was established, the heir to the fifteen-year operation of the leftist atheist organizations in the Czechoslovak Republic.

The preparations and process of the merger inevitably had an influence on the operation of the Ostravsko SSDB, which, with a parallel district meeting with the DTJ on June 26, 1932 in the Lidový dům in Moravian Ostrava, met to discuss the ongoing financial crisis, the unification process, "the general rise of the movement" and the increasing costs of the once again independently published *Volné slovo* (from Oct 1, 1932).[32] Soon afterwards there was the sacred remembrance of Jan Hus, which was jointly organized by the SSDB, the Dělnická akademie and the Svaz národního osvobození [The Union for National Liberation] and which led participants through the city from Boleslav Pecka Street to the Výstaviště [Exhibition Ground] where a stake was burned and speeches were given. However, the Ostrava atheists also understood the significance of everyday educational work, especially among the youth, and so in 1932 they proceeded to introduce talks on natural morality (in the specified year alone in the Moravian Ostravsko area 1,690 non-religious children studied at primary and civic schools, a further 300 children at secondary schools; the greatest number of children without religion came from the boys', girls' and civic schools in the areas of the mining settlements in Hlubina and Šalomoun), and to print textbooks for teachers on natural morality for children

30. *Volné slovo*, vol. 12, no. 23, November 13, 1930, 1.

31. *Volné slovo*, vol. 14, no. 9, May 5, 1932, 1.

32. *Volné slovo*, vol. 14, no. 13, July 16, 1932, 2.

without religion,[33] the authors of which were, with only a few exceptions, non-religious teachers.[34]

Reports of the organization's activities in 1933 are only fragmentary and so it was only possible to find out that on Nov 14, 1933 there was a committee meeting of the USSM in Moravian Ostrava, the main task of which was to alter the charters of the individual local divisions of the former SSDB in the presence of 29 delegated members, to bring them into accord with the charter of the USSM and the district committee for the Moravian-Silesian district based in Moravian Ostrava, agreed on Sept 23, 1933, issued by the Provincial Committee in Brno number 35.589/V-13. At the next convened meeting there were also established 68 local branches of the USSM in the district of Moravia-Silesia, which apart from the area of Moravian Ostrava (Přívoz, Šalomoun, Hlubina, U Dubu, Vítkovice, Zábřeh, Mariánské Hory, Hrabůvka, Nová Ves, Hulváky, Hrabová, Krmelín, Stará Bělá) also had divisions in the areas of Frýdek (Hrušov, Heřmanice, Michálkovice, Zárubek, Řepiště, Kunčičky, Kunčice nad Ostravicí, Vratimov, Frýdek, Dobrá, Bartovice), Místek (Brušperk, Frýdlant, Čeladná, Místek, Palkovice, Frenštát, Paskov, Kunčice pod Ondřejníkem, Lichnov), Valašské Meziříčí (Valašské Meziříčí, Krhová, Hutisko), Nový Jičín (Nový Jičín, Kopřivnice, Trnávka, Kateřinice, Příbor, Štramberk, Košatka, Petřvaldík), Bílovec (Bílovec, Bítov, Tísek, Studénka, Slatina, Svinov, Poruba, Pustkovec, Vřesina, Krásné Pole, Čavisov, Polanka, Klimkovice, Horní Lhota, Dolní Lhota), Fryštát (Nový Bohumín, Dětmarovice, Prostřední Suchá, Petřvald, Petřvald-Březiny), Opava (Háj u Opavy) and in areas around Hranice, Přerov and Vsetín.[35]

Although the annual conference of 1932 gave the impression of an expanding atheist movement in Ostravsko, the opposite was true, and neither the demonstration for democracy and the Republic on May 27, 1934, with 8,000 marching in honor of the newly elected President Masaryk and 18,000 people gathering at Masaryk Square, made up from the ranks of Social and National Democrats, the USSM, VM, DTJ and Legionnaires, nor the conclusion of the International Congress of the Union of Free Thinkers in Moravian Ostrava and Vítkovice (Apr 14, 1936) could prevent the weakening influence of the atheist movement, whose high point had already been reached. Despite this, the second event in particular was connected with the unveiling of a monument to Francesc Ferrer i Guàrdia (Jan 10, 1859—Oct 13, 1909), "the martyr of the Spanish free school," which was the highlight of the demonstration by the Ostravsko USSM. The

33. The Sunday Talks on Natural Morality for Non-religious Children, printed from 1932–1934 by the Ostravsko SSDB, then the USSM, included the following exercise books: The White Mountain, War and Peace, Gustav Habrman—What it Means to be Non-religious, Nature—the Generous Provider, The Legend of Nicholas, About our Families, Christmas and the Solstice, New Year—New Life, The Work of Prayer, The Black Watch, A Happy Mind—Halfway to Being Healthy, About our President, The Resurrection, Religions of Different Countries, and Alcohol the Enslaver.

34. The authors of the Sunday Talks on Natural Morality for Non-religious Children were Drahomíra Šelongová and Milada Vojtoňová, teachers in Moravian Ostrava, Evžena Gavlasová, a teacher in Mariánské Hory, František Haněl, a teacher in Prostřední Suché, as well as Bedřich Čurda-Lipovský, František Ladislav Koudelka and Jiří Přívozský.

35. Archiv města Ostravy [Ostrava City Archives]. Spolky na území města Ostravy: Župní výbor Unie socialistických svobodných myslitelů, Stanovy Unie socialistických svobodných myslitelů, 216, no. 1, reg. no. 1.

International Conference of Unie svobodných myslitelů [The Union of Free Thinkers] met in Prague's Obecní dům [Municipal House] before Easter 1936 (Apr 10–13) with the participation of 75 foreign delegates, of whom 37 arrived at Přívoz station at 3pm on Tuesday Apr 14 so that after visiting the New Town Hall and resting in the town hall restaurant they could arrive in the evening at the Masaryk gardens beside Vítkovice's Odborový dům, where 5,000 people had gathered, and after speeches by F. L. Koudelka (in Czech), Čurda-Lipovský and the chairman of the Atheists' International Dr. Modeste Terwagne (in French), a bust of Francesc Ferrer by Augustin Handzel was unveiled. After the unveiling by Dr Terwagne, the bust of Ferrer was taken by the senator and mayor of Velká Ostrava, Josef Chalupník, to the municipal authorities, after which came the celebrations of the International Academy and an anti-clerical exhibition in the Lesser Hall of the Odborový dům in tribute to Francesc Ferrer.[36] From that time, every year until 1939 on the eve of the anniversary of Ferrer's execution wreaths were laid at his memorial.

The Ferrer celebrations in the middle of May 1936 were, together with the demonstrations for freedom of conscience (Sept 6, 1925) and free schools (July 5, 1935), the most important events of the interwar atheist movement in Ostravsko, which attracted the attention of thousands of participants and observers. However, at the same time the following years were to usher in a difficult period, the weakening of the influence of the atheist organizations on the polarizing society and political life, and finally the complete cessation of activities. At the district conference on Oct 16–17, 1937, those present (80 on the Saturday and 114 delegates on the Sunday) were informed that the lessons on secular morality in the form of talks had started at the same time as religious instruction in thirteen Ostrava city schools (March 1937) based on the curriculum of Karel Kapička, and went on to mention the death of President Masaryk on Sept 14, 1937, for which a meeting of mourning by the district committee of the USSM was held with an introductory speech by F.L. Koudelka, who described Masaryk as a fighter against clericalism, a modern-day Hus and a man who came from a poor background.[37] The actual October conference in the DTJ room in the Lidový dům in Moravian Ostrava was attended by delegates from 88 branches with 3,500 paying members, for whom 1,137 meetings and lectures were held between 1934 and 1936 with the participation of 162,000 people (apart from Čurda-Lipovský and Koudelka, the most active lecturers were Antonín and Jan Janta from the Šalomoun settlement in Moravian Ostrava). The last significant event of 1937 was a memorial service for all the deceased from the Ostrava crematorium, which was also broadcast by Ostrava radio on the morning of Nov 1, 1937.

The clouds which began to gather over Czechoslovakia in 1938 and 1939 cast a shadow over the activities of the USSM in Czechoslovakia and the same was true in Moravia-Silesia. Despite this, the first edition of *Volné slovo* in 1938 was dedicated to the 20th anniversary of the publication of the Union's press organ (along with many reminis-

---

36. *Volné slovo*, vol. 18, no. 3, March 1, 1936, 1, no. 4, April 1, 1936, 1, no. 5, May 1, 1936, 1–3.

37. *Volné slovo*, vol. 19, no. 16, October 1, 1937, 2.

cences and congratulations, it covered Baťa's attitude towards the Catholic Church)[38] and in June the Czechoslovak atheist movement came back to life through its participation in the 60th anniversary celebrations of Social Democracy (June 4–6, 1938), with the atheists joining in a march on June 5 with banners and an allegorical float with portraits of Gustav Habrman and Francesc Ferrer. In autumn 1938, the preparations to unite the USSM with Volná myšlenka (the Communist atheists and, for national political reasons, the members of the BPF would remain excluded) and finally the disbanding of the USSM in Czechoslovakia[39] brought about the rapid extinction of the atheist organizations in Moravia and Silesia. On Nov 20, 1938 a special meeting of the Moravian-Silesian USSM was held in Moravian Ostrava, at which, with a restricted number of delegates due to the banning of meetings and speeches, it was decided to change the charter and name: Osvětový svaz [Educational Union].[40] B. Čurda-Lipovský was unable to attend the special meeting as he had been at his mother's grave in Háj u Opavy on All Soul's Day and when he was crossing the border at Svinov the Gestapo arrested him, held him first of all in the local library and then moved him to a prison in Opava from which he was released at the beginning of December.[41] The country's occupation cost the USSM in Ostravsko 39 branches with 860 members and 1,900 subscribers to Volné slovo, the final edition of which was apolitical in character (astronomy, the medieval inquisition, the history of the swastika) and came out on Oct 1, 1939. Shortly after the establishment of the Protectorate of Bohemia and Moravia, Osvětový svaz transformed into a non-political association which was "to guide the behaviour and education of members of the working-class in modern views of life, deriving from the results of scientific research and the teachings of scientific socialism."[42] The activities of Osvětový svaz were brought to an end in 1940, definitively so after the events of May 1942, and the postwar attempts to revitalize the atheist organizations in Ostravsko never recaptured the significance of the interwar atheist movement.

THE ŠALOMOUN PIT LOCAL DIVISION OF THE SSDB AS AN EXAMPLE OF THE ACTIVITIES OF THE OSTRAVSKO ATHEISTS

It was not only through the example set by the neighboring mining settlement at the Hlubina pit (Juen 6, 1920) that the local group of the SSDB was established "at the Šalomoun pit". According to Volné slovo, the SSDB division of the Jáma Šalomouna [Šalomoun Pit] in Moravian Ostrava came into being after the lecture "Why are we leaving the Church?" by the editor Čurda-Lipovský on Aug 27, 1920, during which Ferdinand Gvožď (also Gvoždž, Gvozdž) was elected as chairman of the local group, B.

38. "Baťa and morality," Volné slovo, vol. 20, no. 1, January 1, 1938, 10.

39. Because the USSM in Moravia-Silesia had its own charter, the USSM was only disbanded in Czechoslovakia (Prague).

40. Volné slovo, vol. 20, no. 12, December 1, 1938, 1.

41. Volné slovo, vol. 21, no. 1., January 1, 1939, 2.

42. Archiv města Ostravy [Ostrava City Archives]. Spolky na území města Ostravy: Župní výbor Unie socialistických svobodných myslitelů, Stanovy Unie socialistických svobodných myslitelů, 216, no. 1, reg. no. 1.

Talpa as secretary, K. Piontek as treasurer, Josef Cebula as vice-treasurer, F. Gvoždž and
A. Skotnica as account auditors and M. Skotnicová and H. Czemburová as members of
the committee.[43] By the end of 1920 the Šalomoun atheists had taken part in several
events (e.g., a lecture on Sept 30 entitled "School and the Church"), though detailing
their activities over the subsequent years has proved difficult due to a lack of archive
or newspaper material. The charter for the association of Šalomoun atheists, who at a
general meeting in January 1924 elected František Novák as the new chairman, whose
successors were again the Karolin coking-plant worker Ferdinand Gvožď (1926–1936),
Božena Pospíšilová (1936), Petr Kalina (1936–1937) and, for the atheist movement, the
unusually enterprising Antonín Janta (1937–1940), was approved by a ruling from the
Provincial Political Authority in Brno on Aug 19, 1922.[44]

However, the local Šalomoun pit division of the SSDB had already embarked
on intensive activity before then, as can be seen by the public protest meeting which
was held in the works' canteen of the Šalomoun living quarters (Jan 6, 1924), where
the Vítkovice orator Karel Langer gave an inflammatory speech in front of 70 people
about the strengthening of clerical reactionism and the results of the last parliamentary
elections. Just as with the Ostravsko atheist movement as a whole, the pinnacle of the
Šalomoun atheists' activities fall into the period at the end of the 1920s and the beginning of the 1930s, as is testified by the number of articles in *Volné slovo*: on Nov 8, 1929
F. L. Koudelka gave a slide lecture on The White Mountain, two days later there was a
children's talk in the canteen of the Šalomoun living quarters and the amateur dramatics
association Probuzení [Awakening] gave a performance of Legionář Lanc in the Czech
Joint Stock Brewery, on Jan 19, 1930 the 11th general meeting of the local division of the
SSDB was held in the living quarters' canteen with 70 members in attendance, and the
activities of the division culminated in November when they put on film parties for children, "Tears and Laughter" and "Monty Banks amongst the Cannibals" (Nov 12, 1930 in
the works' canteen), a lecture by Čurda-Lipovský entitled "The French Revolution" (Nov
13, 1930 in the pub U Kopolda), the celebratory children's academy and children's talk
with Jindřich Janta (Nov 23 and 26, 1930 in the canteen) and a celebratory meeting to
mark the tenth anniversary of the local division of the SSDB (Nov 29, 1930). A great loss
for both the Šalomoun and Ostrava atheists was the sudden death of František Novák (†
Oct 22, 1932), an atheist pioneer and member of the Central Committee of the SSDB and
the Šalomoun division, which was also reported by *Volné slovo*.[45]

In 1932 the association held its regular January general meeting in the canteen of
the Šalomoun living quarters to discuss the change of name and charter; for all other
activities they used rooms in Adolf Haas' pub or a deconsecrated wooden chapel at the
army barracks on the outskirts of the Šalomoun settlement. As well as educational lec-

43. *Volné slovo*, vol. 2, no. 15, October 1, 1920, 6.

44. Zemský archiv Opava [Opava provincial archives]. Policejní ředitelství Moravská Ostrava, Spolkové
oddělení: Místní odbočka Unie socialistických svobodných myslitelů v Moravské Ostravě (Šalomouna),
1071/2, no. 1082.

45. *Volné slovo*, vol. 14, no. 22–23, November 1, 1932, 7.

tures on anti-clerical and current political themes,[46] the local SSDB group organized regular July mass meetings on the grounds of the former brickworks of a local resident, Vítek, at which the 2,000 Šalomoun participants would remember Jan Hus.

The attention of the police authority was particularly aroused by a slide lecture called "The Idolaters." The association had distributed leaflets on the morning of Oct 20, 1933 advertising the lecture for that evening in the works' canteen. One of the leaflets fell into the hands of P. Tomáš, who was so irked by its contents that he complained to the police headquarters in Moravian Ostrava: "From hundreds of thousands of voices came the pilgrimage song of that hot August day. Enormous processions of barefoot, pitifuly dressed women with children bundled onto their backs made their way to the Virgin Mary of Częstochowa to beg her for blessings in future life, boiled potatoes and tea having been their only sustenance for several days, and so that they might have something to lay down before the Mother of Częstochowa and the monks of Pavlán (Minims of Saint Francis of Paola), one of them, Damazy Mazoch, in the name of the Lord under a picture of the Holy Virgin, murdered and stole. And amongst those pilgrims wandered our own ubiquitous editor BEDŘICH ČURDA-LIPOVSKÝ, who enjoys collecting impressions of the Catholic world, and who will be among us once again on Friday October 20, 1933, when he will be in the canteen at 7pm with 100 slides to accompany his talk on his pilgrimage to Čenstochová, to Loretta in Italy and to other places of pilgrimage. The name of the lecure is "The Idolaters" and you are most cordially invited. Bring with you some well-known zealous Catholic women so that they might see for themselves what a holy pilgrimage is. SDB Association of Šalomoun."[47]

The transformation of the association to a Local Branch of the USSM in Šalomoun (28. 1., change in charter Apr 19, 1934) was celebrated by the members with the February lecture "The French Revolution" in the pub U Haase. The lecture was given by F. L. Koudelka, chairman of the USSM for Moravian Ostrava, who also called for a memorial ceremony for fallen comrades in Austria. On St Wenceslas' day the following year the Šalomoun atheists celebrated with a jubilee members' meeting commemorating fifteen years of activity: the society which was established at the start of the 1920s with 45 members had in the decade and a half of its existence organized 145 public lectures and several hundred meetings (in 1925 it had 335 members, in 1935, as a result of the economic crisis, unemployment and the closure of the Šalomoun pit, this had fallen to just 167 members, of whom 85 were pensioners and three unemployed).

From 1935–1938 the activities of the USSM in Šalomoun gradually slowed, the local organization was temporarily dominated by younger, extreme leftist members, and to the tried and tested anti-clerical lectures[48] were added more frequently the themes of

---

46. "Increasing reactionism" (Apr 9, 1924), "15 Years in a Monastery" (28. 2. 1924, Dr. Schacherle), "The Separation of the Church from the State" (June 27, 1925), etc.

47. Zemský archiv Opava [Opava provincial archives]. Policejní ředitelství Moravská Ostrava, Spolkové oddělení: Místní odbočka Unie socialistických svobodných myslitelů v Moravské Ostravě (Šalomouna), 1071/2, no. 1082.

48. "History of the Cross" (Nov 10, 1933, B. Čurda-Lipovský), "Witches" (Jan 19, 1935, lecture of B. Čurda-Lipovského).

current politics: "The Dogs of War" (Apr 4, 1936, F.L. Koudelka), "Spain, land of eternal revolution" (Sept 21, 1936, B. Čurda-Lipovský), "How do they live in Russia?" (Dec 12, 1936, Jaroslav Kocián), "Race Theories" (Apr 20, 1937, B. Čurda-Lipovský). Even though attendances at these political lectures grew slightly and seldom fell below 100, the lectures with the highest attendance were Professor Oldřich Stránský's "Spiritualism—and what comes after Death?" (Mar 9, 1937) and a popular reading by the favorite Čurda-Lipovský on the theme "Is there Life on the Stars?" 480 people attended this lecture in the Blaník Catholic House, where in the 1930s the Šalomoun division of the USSM met with increasing frequency.[49] The Šalomoun section of the USSM was also involved with children, and not only through the long-term promotion of education in secular morality in primary schools, but also by sending children of local atheists to Sunday talks on natural morality for non-religious children, which were held in the neighboring Hlubina settlement by the teachers Drahuše Šelongová, Evžena Gavlasová and Milada Vojtoňová.[50] The sharp increase in the association's activities was halted by the post-Munich events—at the beginning of June 1940 the atheist branch in the Hlubina settlement voluntarily disbanded and 14 days later (June 21, 1940) the activities of the Šalomoun Educational Union came to an end (officially due to insufficient membership).[51]

Probuzení [The Awakening], the drama circle of Social Democratic atheists, was linked to the atheist organization in the Šalomoun settlement both in terms of personnel and world view.[52] Although the name of the association would lead one to the conclusion that it was merely the theater division of the Šalomoun SSDB, it developed its own independent activities within the SSDB. The SDB's dramatic circle Probuzení was founded before August 1925, when at its first general meeting its members elected as chairman F. Gvoždě, who remained in the post from 1925–1926, 1934–1935, 1936–1937, and for the last time from 1941 until its premature closure following the assassination of Heydrich. Gvoždě twice changed posts with Augustin Gaj (1929–1931, 1935–1936).[53] The dramatic circle, which could be joined by all men over seventeen and girls over fifteen, promoted the reading of appropriate books and magazines, lectures, trips, and principally dramatic and musical exercises for the "cultivation of dramatic art, singing and music, inspiring

49. Zemský archiv Opava [Opava provincial archives]. Policejní ředitelství Moravská Ostrava, Spolkové oddělení: Místní odbočka Unie socialistických svobodných myslitelů v Moravské Ostravě (Šalomouna), Policejní hlášení z přednášek, 1071/2, no. 1082.

50. Archiv města Ostravy [Ostrava City Archives]. Spolky na území města Ostravy: Místní odbočka Unie socialistických svobodných myslitelů v Moravské Ostravě—Hlubině, Nedělní besídky přirozené mravouky pro děti bez vyznání, 216, no. 2

51. Zemský archiv Opava [Opava provincial archives]. Policejní ředitelství Moravská Ostrava, Spolkové oddělení: Místní odbočka Unie socialistických svobodných myslitelů v Moravské Ostravě (Šalomouna), Úřední list zemského úřadu v Brně of July 1940, 1071/2, no. 1082.

52. Zemský archiv Opava [Opava provincial archives]. Policejní ředitelství Moravská Ostrava, Spolkové oddělení: Dramatický kroužek Sociálnědemokratických bezvěrců „Probuzení", no. 2155 (no. of the association register 1977).

53. Chairmen of Dramatický kroužek SSDB „Probuzení": Ferdinand Gvožď (1925–1926, 1934–1935, 1936–1938, 1941), Vítězslav Simurda (1926), František Novák (1926–1927), Jan Klimčík (1927–1928), František Vavříček (1928–1929), Augustin Gaj (1929–1931, 1935–1936), Ladislav Magiera (1931–1934), Eduard Abrahamčik (1938–1941), Filip Kurečka (1946–1948), Stanislav Indrák (1948).

and cultivating intellectual and social life, supporting beneficial public, charitable and educational establishments and other cultural establishments."[54]

The association, whose first activity was the general meeting of 40 members on Aug 23, 1925, had regular annual sessions in the works' canteen of the Šalomoun living quarters, which they shared with the "Šalomoun Pit" SSDB. Their first public productions were staged in the canteen and then in Haas's pub, and then from the 1930s the amateur players regularly put on performances at the Blaník Association House. At the close of the interwar period Probuzení was affected first of all by a generational changeover (1938–1941), in February 1941 they reappeared but only as the Dramatic Circle Probuzení, but the events of 1942 simply decimated them. In 1945–1947, the Šalomoun amateurs returned to the Blaník stage without their costumes, which had been stolen during the war, and in February 1948 they had their final general meeting where Stanislav Indrák was elected chairman. However, they were unable to resuscitate the interwar tradition and at the beginning of 1958 Probuzení broke up once and for all due to a lack of interest.

THE ATHEIST MOVEMENT AS REMEMBERED
BY OSTRAVSKO EYEWITNESSES

"The people in the settlement had strong religious convictions, but when the men returned from the front they became atheists," Marie Filipská (*1907), who lived in the Silesian Ostrava working-class district of Zárubek during the First Republic, recalled in 1977.[55] In her seemingly elliptical statement she not only captures the experience of the generation who lived through the First World War, but also points to the ideological viewpoint of the postwar atheist movement in Ostravsko and beyond, where the association of the throne and the altar or the blessing of weapons were some of the most effective tools at the disposal of the atheists in their intellectual struggle against the Roman Catholic Church.

The links in personnel and ideology between the atheist movement and Social Democracy, and their common struggle for a secular education and against a depersonalized and institutionalized religiosity in the coalminers' environment are shown by the following account of the Hrušov miner Matouš Salomon (1897–1988): "I was a member of the general council, a member of the school board for the Social Democratic Party. I was also a member and on the committee of the Unie svobodných myslitelů [Union of Free Thinkers], a member of the Social Democratic party and on the committee as well. I was a member and instructor of the DTJ workers' physical education unit in Muglinov because in 1919 a workers' physical education unit hadn't yet been set up in Hrušov. After the First World War lots of people left the Roman Catholic Church, so there were eighty children in the school who didn't go to religious education. Religious education was a compulsory subject and non-religious children had to leave this class. In 1926 a

54. Zemský archiv Opava [Opava provincial archives]. Policejní ředitelství Moravská Ostrava, Spolkové oddělení: Dramatický kroužek Sociálnědemokratických bezvěrců „Probuzení", Stanovy Dramatického kroužku SDB „Probuzení" z 25. 9. 1925, no. 2155 (no. of the association no. 1977).

55. Bilová, "Dělnické bydlení v Ostravě," 132.

law was passed on education—secular morality. The "Unie svobodných myslitelů" took responsibility for this type of education. It was difficult to find a teacher for this subject. Two teachers put themselves forward—Sýrovatka and Kudělková. Instruction was given on how to teach the lessons. I was in charge of this training, I provided teaching aids and if a teacher didn't turn up, I also taught.

In Austrian times there was a room called the "cechovna" at the works where you would punch in your shifts. In it there was a raised statue of Barbora surrounded by kneeling angels. The miners would pray in front of the statue of Barbora before going underground. It was compulsory at that time and the Catholic Church was careful to ensure that the religious ceremony was upheld. During the First World War soldiers saw to it that everyone went to the "cechovna" to pray. Miners who were under military command had a black and yellow braid on their shoulder."[56]

As the next account from Jaroslava Houžová (*1925), who grew up in the Šalomoun settlement in Moravian Ostrava, shows, atheism was not only an institutionalized world view, but also reached into all the intimate spheres of Ostrava working-class families and in many cases also divided their members (it was usually a case of atheist men living with their religiously inclined wives) who usually came from a traditional, agricultural, religious background: "Grandpa was the strictest atheist. One of the family once told me that when he was a boy in the village (he came from Trnávka near Nový Jičín) he had to work at the rectory and that he had to run barefoot in the snow. I guess he saw something at the rectory. He must have seen something at the rectory, otherwise he wouldn't have been such a strict atheist. He must have seen something that didn't go along with the Christian faith. Maybe there was a paedophile priest at that time. Grandpa forbade us from going to church or even being religious. The schools under Masaryk were such that if you didn't take religious education you could go out or take a walk around the school. I remember taking advantage of this, and because I wanted to be an actress or a director or an editor I got all the girls to play at theater with me. I was in charge and I told them we were going to play Snow White and the Seven Dwarfs. Of course I was Snow White and the girls were the seven dwarfs. We rehearsed using a book that I had found somewhere. And I remember that there were swing doors in the school and I got the girls to hold the doors open for me so that I could walk along like a queen (laughter).

The only book in our home was called Francisco Ferrer, who was a Spanish free thinker whose statue was in the park behind the Record cinema in Vítkovice. Grandpa was a big free thinker: I remember that when he was dying in hospital they called the priest to his bed and he shouted at him to go away. In his childhood Grandpa must have seen something at that village rectory, because otherwise he wouldn't have been so against religion.

I didn't go to the Salesians because by then we had left Šalamoun. But I'll always remember how they played football with the boys, running about in their cassocks. But I couldn't go to the Salesians because Grandpa was an atheist. So Gran would pray in secret, though only when Grandpa wasn't at home. He didn't behave very nicely towards

---

56. Brtvová, "Kolonie Ida šachta do 1918," 1–12.

her and was coarse, as miners often were. I think Gran was religious because she would pray at night when Grandpa was away. Once when Grandpa wasn't home I came back from school and passed two or three women in the hall. Gran sent me away and never explained who those women were. When I returned from my aunt's, or from wherever I'd been, Gran was in tears, she had terribly tear-stained eyes. Apparently they were spiritualists who went about the settlement calling up the spirits of the dead. They were in the bedroom and called up my mother who spoke to Gran. Apparently Mum said that she knew I was studying hard and that she was in purgatory and that we had to pray for her so that she would go to heaven. For some time I believed this because Gran had been crying so much. However, not long ago I read a book by a Hungarian writer and he explained all the practices of these spiritualists."[57]

In order to retain some sort of parity and bring attention to the reality that atheism did not always have to mean a lifelong conviction and that there were also cases of the return or conversion of atheists to Roman Catholicism, I offer the following account by Mons. Erich Pepřík (*1922), who grew up in the Zárubek Silesian-Ostrava mining settlement, and who from childhood was confronted by active, sometimes even aggressive, atheist propaganda. There are further accounts from the Ostravsko atheist movement to be found in the collection *Lidé z kolonií vyprávějí své dějiny* [The People from the Settlement Tell their Story] which is to be published at the end of 2009 in Ostrava. "I began going to confession more regularly, usually on a Saturday afternoon. You went to the church past the miners' settlement along the 'old path.' In a courtyard by a fence there often stood a girl who was a year or two older, and almost every time she mockingly said: 'The holy boy's coming!' I had already counted on this happening and so I kept a dignified silence. When the girl left school I think she started to train to be a shop assistant, later, however, she entered a convent and became a nurse, and during some epidemic she volunteered for the infectious ward. There she became ill herself, and as a sacrifice of love for those around her—and for Christ the Lord—she died . . . She who—obviously under the influence of the spirit of the time—laughed at me childishly, has certainly reached the kingdom of heaven before me."[58]

57. Houžvová, "V naší havířské rodině," 234–35, 239.

58. Pepřík, *Neboj se a pojď!*, 19.

12

The Question of Piety in State Tobacco Factories

Marie Macková

T HE WORKFORCE OF THE state tobacco factories in the Habsburg monarchy was a very distinctive group, differing from other state industrial workforces in the monarchy in many respects. It began to take shape at the end of the eighteenth century, when the state had taken over control of all tobacco production in the monarchy on the basis of Emperor Joseph II's edict of 8th May 1784. At that time the hitherto piecemeal processing of tobacco also began to be concentrated into state workshops in such a way that there was roughly one such producer located in each of the lands of the Habsburg monarchy. This process, in which the workshops were transformed into modern factories, had several phases and continued until virtually the end of the nineteenth century. By the time it had finished Bohemia and Moravia were in this respect among the most thoroughly utilized of all the lands of Cisleithania. Because the Hungarians had their own administration for tobacco production after 1850,[1] as did the subsequently annexed area of Bosnia-Herzegovina,[2] in this sense the area of Cisleithania formed an independent whole earlier than it did in the political sense. From the end of the 1830s to the end of the 1850s factories arose there at such a rate that the continually growing demand for tobacco products in the individual lands was satisfied. Between 1869 and 1874 more factories came into being, primarily in Bohemia, Moravia and Galicia. The setting up of these factories is usually termed "social" or "emergency." This is the term used in the case when a state factory helps to resolve a complicated economic situation, especially in the old industrial regions, which ran into problems and where there was a threat of social instability. The last burst of development took place in the 1890s, when tobacco factories sprang up in Písek, Tachov and Vienna-Ottakring.[3] In the course of the nineteenth century the operation of the state tobacco factories was standardized not only from the

1. For more detail, see e.g., Wandruszka and Urbanitsch, *Die Habsburgermonarchie 1848–1918*, 348ff.

2. *Tabellen zur Statistik des österreichischen Tabak-Monopoles.*

3. Hitz and Huber, *Geschichte der Österreichischen Tabakregie*, 53, 56, 174–75; Ventura, *Dějiny c. k. továrny na tabák v Sedleci*; Sommer, *Československý tabákový průmysl*, 32; Macková, *Tabáková továrna*, 69–73.

point of view of production and technology, but also in terms of the way it was managed and the position and the security of the workforce. On the other hand, it is clear that each of these factories was distinct in the sense that it introduced this increasingly uniform way of existence and prosperity into often quite diverse regions. It was because of this that the perception of each of these factories was somewhat different: it corresponded to the changing realities of places and regions and the people who lived there.

The actual workforce of the tobacco factories was also quite special, just as the production was. For a very long time this was manual work demanding a great quantity of manpower; naturally the workers did not have to be very qualified and for the most part did not have to have great physical strength, on the contrary they had to be dexterous and able to carry out precise operations very quickly and yet with reasonable care. The result of these requirements was that, for the majority of posts, female manpower was ideal for tobacco factories. One exception was the handling of materials, which throughout virtually the whole of the period in question were packaged in units exceeding 15 kg, a quantity which a single woman was not allowed to handle alone, and in these cases it was economically more advantageous to employ one man than two women. Furthermore, women were not involved in the handling of fire (drying chambers and lighting or heating), not even in the factories' fire brigades, or in the craftsmen's workshops, taking care of maintenance and producing packaging. Of course, all this only ever represented a small part of the work. The vast majority of the factory workforce in the state tobacco factories was composed of women, or more precisely usually of very young girls. Because the only qualification required was the ability to read and write, girls could enter the workforce immediately after they finished their compulsory schooling. In the course of the nineteenth century this age changed, varying between 13 and 15 years old. Girls did not always go to work in the factory straight away but it was frequently the case. At first they were temporary workers, but if they stayed the course and were skillful enough, after a year they could receive a permanent post. According to the internal guidelines of the state tobacco monopoly's board of management, women over thirty years old were not to be newly employed as workers. In practice this rule was continuously breached, but never systematicaly, only on a case-to-case basis.[4]

There were several ways in which a female worker might leave her job: she could leave at any time through her own decision, she could be dismissed as a punishment, she could be retired or she could die. The last possibility was difficult for any of those concerned to influence, but death hardly ever occurred as a result of workplace injuries. Unlike other factories of the time, the tobacco factories were not life-threatening: the most common workplace injury was sliced fingertips and the most common reason for sick leave was childbirth. Voluntary departure depended entirely on the will of the employee, though of course her reasons had to be serious because as a result of this she lost any claim to a pension. The number of workers who were dismissed as a punishment was extremely small. It was a final punishment, which could be preceded by a wide range of considerably milder punishments, and in the whole period in question it concerned

4. Macková, *Tabáková továrna*, 98–114.

individuals, almost never larger groups of people. Retirement was not dependent on the worker herself. It could be granted or imposed only by the factory doctor, because the sole justification for it was this: incapable of further work in the factory.[5] Of course, in many cases this did not mean she was incapable of other work.[6] The outcome of these conditions was that the majority of the workers were young or very young women, often below the legal age of majority, either single or married. Men practically never featured in production (women even occupied the posts of foremen) and in other factory operations they made up just a fraction of the number. On the other hand, there was almost always a large number of women concentrated in one place. In the last quarter of the nineteenth century, the biggest of the tobacco factories employed around two thousand female workers at a time.[7]

A factory workforce composed in this way was certainly not the usual model of the Habsburg monarchy. In addition, the state in its role as employer also had quite specific requirements, even if in this case it contented itself, for example, with minimal qualifications. On the other hand there is no indication in the working regulations that they embodied principles which can also be found in guidelines such as those for public officials.[8] And this was not just because a female worker with a permanent post in a state tobacco factory also had, under specific, strictly laid out conditions, the right to a pension, just like an official in public service. The female worker was also, not just during working hours but in private too, supposed to behave in such a way that she would not damage the good name of her employer. In practice this meant that she should not only display at least a reasonable degree of loyalty, or rather at least passive neutrality, but she should keep within the bounds of the law, observe the rules of good behaviour and not cause a public nuisance. On the other hand, the state as employer did not feel the need to regulate some other aspects in any specific way: for example, the relationship or designation of the worker to her nationality was never regulated in any way. It was not only that nobody inquired into an employee's nationality when she joined the workforce, but it was not even verified indirectly in the form of languages spoken. Although for a very long time, until the issuing of the first language decrees, the tobacco monopoly as a state office used German in its official communications, it did not demand the same of its own workforce. Even all the decrees which were binding for the workforce had to be both in German as well as in the languages "usual in that country," as the official wording put it.[9] And the state treated the religious or denominational affiliation of its workforce in the tobacco factories in a very similar way.

As previously mentioned, the department began its administration in 1784, that is after the issuing of the tolerance edict. It was therefore no longer necessary for the

---

5. For more detail see Macková, "Lékaři v rakouské státní tabákové režii," 131–49.

6. Macková, "Penzisté a penzistky," 170–78.

7. Macková, *Tabáková továrna*, 99–102.

8. *Organische Bestimmungen und Verhaltungsregeln für die Arbeiter der k. k. Tabakfabriken*; *Arbeitsordnung für die Tabakfabriken*; *Arbeitsordnung für die k. k. Tabakverschleißmagazine und die k. k. Tabakeinlösungsämter sammt deren Expozituren*.

9. Macková, "Projevy nacionalizace společnosti," 200–28.

religion of individual male and female workers to be uniform. In the course of the nineteenth century this position gained firmer legal footing until it culminated in a full granting of equal status to all churches recognized by the state. In spite of that, no passage ever appeared in the internal directives which ordered that the religion of a job applicant be established. Nor was it determined through any indirect, related information. This approach was followed even in the course of employment: books known as workers' registers, which listed temporary as well as permanent workers and recorded the course of their employment as well as its termination (changes in job and pay grade, changes in qualifications, marriage, widowhood, punishments and appraisals, even the date of departure or death or the amount of pension), made no reference whatsoever to religious or denominational affiliation.[10] And all this at a time when, for example, every school catalogue contained compulsory data on the religion of each pupil. As long as the female worker did not violate the general laws which applied to the whole population of the monarchy, then her state employer left religion to her as a private matter.

Since, especially in the second half of the nineteenth century, the state naturally had to look after the workforce in its own way, a few provisions appeared in the working regulations concerning precisely this part of the private life of male and female workers. These primarily related to the obligation to work on Sundays and religious holidays, which as a minimum made attendance of church services impossible. However, regular working hours in the tobacco factories did not include work on Sundays and the usual holidays. Moreover, the imperial exchequer was not particularly keen on overtime work, so it was ordered only in quite exceptional circumstances. Nevertheless, in a few cases the technology of processing tobacco demanded uninterrupted operation. In particular the drying chambers for the raw material and the maturation of some products had to run either without interruption or at very precise intervals of time, regardless of whether it was a Sunday or a holiday. First and foremost it was established that these workers must have not only time to rest, but also the chance to attend a religious service in accordance with their own religion at least once a fortnight. Therefore they had to be free when it was taking place. On top of this, it was within the authority of the managers of individual factories to extend the whole workforce's time off to include local holidays, or even parts of the days immediately preceding them. From the practical application of this decree it is clear that it exclusively concerned religious holidays. Generally no work was carried out in any of the factories the afternoon before Ash Wednesday, before Easter Sunday and Whit Sunday and before Christmas Day. In some places the whole day was a holiday. A further extension of time off could apply to locally celebrated holidays.

For a long time no other decree relating to the religious life of the workforce of the tobacco factories appeared in the official communications. Only in the time of the long-reigning Emperor Franz Joseph I, with the rise of his cult, did a request appear, directed towards the management of individual factories, that it be made possible for the workforce to take part in religious services on the emperor's birthday on the eighteenth

10. Preserved in their entirety are, for example, workers' registers for the state tobacco factory in Lanškroun. Státní oblastní archiv [State Regional Archives] in Prague Rakouská tabáková režie, továrna Lanškroun, bk. 5/I-V.

of August.[11] Nowhere was it laid down that they should participate collectively, as was the case for example with the state administration. On the other hand, it is almost impossible to determine whether it actually happened in this way. Sources of information, both internal and from other areas than that of the tobacco monopoly, make no mention of such matters.

The relationship of the church in general, and even individual representatives of the church-administered structures in particular, to the workforce of the state tobacco factories can only be found sporadically expressed and recorded. It almost always involved representatives of the Roman Catholic church, which of course is not surprising given its majority in Bohemia as well as Habsburg Cisleithania. One well-known account was the resistance of priests in Linz and subsequently in Šternberk in Moravia to girls from the region becoming factory workers, which even manifested itself in their refusal to issue them with the birth certificate needed to get a job in a factory. Their justification was the same: protecting them from the life of a factory worker.[12] That is, from the almost certain ruin of body and soul which the factory environment brought about. This was of course the view not only of the clergy but also of a considerable section of the middle classes of society in the middle of the nineteenth century. Nowhere in Bohemia was a similar stance recorded.[13]

The early existence of the state tobacco monopoly in the Habsburg monarchy belonged to a period which, with respect to the Josephinist suppression of the monasteries, presented an unusual cross-section, time-specific but subsequently living on in its own legend, of the state's approach towards the church and the tobacco monopoly. There is an anecdote, still repeated from time to time, in which Joseph II turned the abolished monasteries into either a barracks or a tobacco factory. This is accepted by the general consciousness, even if it corresponds only partialy to reality. While there was no great technological problem in converting a monastery building into a barracks, adapting the same building for factory use was always more difficult. The state tobacco monopoly abandoned this idea very early on and began to construct modern, purpose-built premises, which in the final reckoning were considerably cheaper and entailed fewer problems and especially expenses for the future. Nevertheless in some exceptional cases tobacco factories did operate in the premises of the abolished monasteries: in Bohemia there was (and still is) the former Cistercian monastery in Sedlec u Kutné Hory,[14] while in Moravia the oldest one was established in Hodonín through the reconstruction of the local castle. However, these examples are certainly not indicative of the relationship of the tobacco monopoly to the Roman Catholic church, but rather time-specific views on the welfare of the state and public benefit, brought about by the Enlightenment and developed in the

11. *Arbeitsordnung für die Tabakfabriken.*

12. Hitz and Huber, *Geschichte der Österreichischen Tabakregie,* 175–76.

13. On the contrary, the majority of places in which a state tobacco factory was eventually sited sought its location there, the town taking some pains to ensure it. One exception at that time was Jáchymov, where there were protests against the factory on the grounds that it would draw necessary manpower away from agriculture. But even there the reasoning was entirely economic and the church played no part in it. Hitz and Huber, *Geschichte der Österreichischen Tabakregie,* 176. See also Národní archiv [National Archives] in Prague, Presidium pražského místodržitelství, card 647, call 12/6/1.

14. Ventura, *Dějiny c. k. továrny na tabák v Sedleci,* 12.

context of the Josephinist administration and its successors in the monarchy. From these attitudes, current in the early phases of the existence of the state tobacco monopoly, it is certainly not possible to derive any later opinions or practical consequences.

On the other hand, it is possible to detect a certain distance which the administration of the tobacco monopoly, of course not until the second half of the nineteenth century, maintained from the usual social models of the time in terms of the participation of church representatives in life, or more precisely in various public events. For example, in the otherwise staunchly Catholic town of Lanškroun, where in the second half of the nineteenth century the local Roman Catholic dean, or at least some of his chaplains, were actively present at almost all public celebrations, with the mass or ordination playing a significant part, the celebrations connected with the newly constructed and already operational state tobacco factory took place without the presence of church representatives. That is to say, those celebrations which came under the authority of the officials of the tobacco monopoly. One example of this is the laying of the foundation stones for a new factory building, which was indeed a large public celebration, proceeding entirely in keeping with the tastes of those days, with honourable guests, celebratory speeches, music, flags and popular merry-making. The only thing missing was a celebratory church service or at least consecration of the foundation stones. Similarly, among the speakers there was nobody from the local deanery or from the higher church authorities. In the context of the time and place it was so conspicuous that it was even remarked upon by the local chronicler (in his personal politics a German liberal), but he did not feel the need to comment further nor to offer any explanation.[15]

What is missing from all of these discussions are reflections from the other side: the personal expression of at least some of the female workers of the state tobacco factories of Habsburg Cisleithania. However, so far we have not turned up a suitable source of a personal nature authored by such a woman or girl, or even a man. In the period before the First World War, when it was very common (even fashionable) to write a diary or explain one's opinions and attitudes in long letters, the female factory workers did not have much opportunity or even desire to do this. The majority of them were not employed in the factory for reasons of self-fulfilment, but from the necessity of earning a living. What is more, many of them regularly walked long distances to the factory. So, even if their working hours were shorter than in many other industries of the time and all of them had to be able to write (it was a condition for employment), they most likely did not have the strength left for such activity and in many cases they probably did not even feel the need to do such a thing. The few memoirs of female workers from the tobacco factories which were published at the beginning of the second half of the twentieth century mainly cover the interwar period in Czechoslovakia and reflect the older situation only very sporadicaly. However, it is interesting that they make no mention of any attitude (either positive or negative) of any of the factory bosses towards the church or religious

15. Státní okresní archiv [State Distrikt Archives] in Ústí nad Orlicí, Mezifondová sbírka kronik, bk. 152, 507–11. It is unfortunate that it is not possible to compare this record with an evaluation, for example, from the press, but in Lanškroun at that time newspapers were not yet being published, and none of those from the wider region, as far as we know, remarked on this situation.

issues, even though this kind of recollection would certainly have suited the more or less biased opinion of the time when the memoirs were written and there would have been no problems with the publication of a negative one in particular.[16]

If the state employer demanded that the behaviour of its workforce, both during and outside working hours, support its good reputation, then through its implied approach to the church authorities it unambiguously assigned both religious affiliation and dogmatic attitudes to the private sphere. Even the workforce in public service was required to obey only the generally applicable laws in this matter; there was no other specific decree which would further tie them or on the contrary untie them from the sphere of the church. This can be explained partly by a large dose of liberalism, primarily dominant among the decision-making bodies of the state tobacco monopoly, which was responsible for establishing this type of set-up, and partly by the utilitarianism of the same masters, for whom the crucial issue was the prosperity of the area entrusted to them and who did not consider a firmer attachment to the church to be an appropriate means for its consolidation and growth. And finally it is not possible to ignore, even in the society of the time, a generally perceptible formalism, which became more and more apparent in relations with the church. Roman Catholicism in particular was so commonplace and accessible that it was not necessary to pay special attention to it or to display some form of exceptional activity. Not even at that time, at least in the case of the state workforce, for whom the state to a certain extent constantly tried to be the one who "guides their steps": at least in such a way as to derive some benefit from them. The Habsburg monarchy, particularly in the last quarter of the nineteenth century and the very beginning of the twentieth century, was definitely not a great supporter of the church, as is sometimes depicted, in its actual activities. Perhaps this was because, like a large section of its population, it considered it to be self-evident, requiring no help or support.

16. See e.g., *Sto let jihlavské tabákovky*; *175 let tabákového průmyslu v Hodoníně 1783–1958*; By implication also Kopecký, *Sto let tabákového průmyslu ve Svitavách*.

13

The Workers' Song

An Element of Secularization in Nineteenth-Century Czech Civic Society?

JOSEF ŠEBESTA

"Will governments help the worker?
Will he be helped by prayer?
Or will his pleas be heard
By the saints in heaven?
. . .
Will he be helped by miracles?
Will he be helped by God's church?
None of these will help him,
He must help himself."

(Rašple, July 1st 1904)[1]

IN THE INTRODUCTION TO this historical outline allow me to cast a shadow of doubt on the relevance of the theme "The Secularization of the Working-class in the nineteenth Century," as Czech civic society had already been gravitating towards secularization in everyday life since the sixteenth century, most markedly following the storming of the Bastille. The start of the nineteenth century presented opportunities for even more grandiose secularization and it is evident that this concerned intellectuals rather than the working class. The effects were to become apparent in the second half of the nineteenth century, as can be seen by many specific examples, such as in the travel article Velehradská pouť [The Velehrad Pilgrimage] written by Svatopluk Čech in 1881. In the introduction he warns against religious themes and at the same time calms his readers with the words: "Do not worry, we will not be singing or carrying crosses, there will not be a priest or rector and we can merely walk around the church as we tour the city. I shall take you to Velehrad with the profane purpose of showing you a significant and interesting part of the Moravian lands and the Moravian people." There then follows an enthusiastic and detailed description of village events, although only as far as the church doors. Svatopluk Čech and his readers refuse to participate in the local rituals and cer-

1. See Petrmichl, *Bičem a Rašplí,* 203.

emonies in the church.[2] To single out from this whole process the working class and its social development, in which secularization only played a supporting role—as opposed to the conscious and deliberate self-secularization of the educated citizenry, for whom village piety appeared as something exotic and actual participation in urban worship as a social misdemeanour—means to impose on this section of the Czech population a role which I feel to be debatable.

The workers' song belongs to a cultural category which came about suddenly, almost without any developmental process, and which reflected in a fascinating manner the political situation in Europe around the middle of the nineteenth century. In 1819, on the initiative of the enlightenment society Gesellschaft der Musikfreude des österreichischen Kaiserstaates zu Wien [The Society of Music Friends of the Austrian Imperial States in Vienna],[3] the minister of the interior and supreme chancellor Count František Saurau ordered the gubernatorial collection campaign, which brought together a large number of Czech national songs.[4] It was from these that the director of the Prague Conservatory, Bedřich Dionys Weber (1766–1842), compiled the so-called barrel-organ manuscript, which in 1825 formed the basis of a printed version by Jan the Knight of Rittersberk (1780–1841).[5] Within a short period of time this ethnographic publication was entirely sold out and it was subsequently widely copied. It contains a total of 300 Czech songs, fifty German songs and fifty instrumental dance tunes.[6] For the contemporary historian, the Rittersberk edition with its 300 Czech national songs is an important gateway into the social and communal mindset of Czech citizens at the beginning of the nineteenth century. Alongside drinking, spiritual, recruitment, shopkeepers' and love songs, a large section of the collection is made up of songs of up to twenty or thirty verses which reflect minor social conflicts.[7] For our topic it is important to realize that none of those participating in the gubernatorial collection campaign had any notion of the song category which the social and political developments of the next fifty years would, under the title of *worker's song,* raise to the level of a historico-cultural phenomenon.

A distinct community of people expresses its spirit in the form of a song. The songs, which originate from shared ideas and experiences, from the shared causes and effects of these experiences, and which through melody, rhythm and lyrics identify a common goal and the means to attain it, are an important source for studying the politico-cultural contexts of the period. What is more, a song category is capable of capturing in a broad spectrum a contemporary social "sign," which over time becomes lost in other sources, for example, of a bureaucratic, legal, religious or statistical nature. Therefore, if the histo-

2. See Rak, "Exotismus doma aneb Venkov versus město," 221–27.

3. This musical society was established in 1812 and is active to this day. It holds concerts and works with the best contemporary musicians.

4. On the 14th of May 1819 Chrudim was one of the first district offices to announce its collection, which consisted of 151 songs and 8 dances.

5. *České národní písně (Rittersberkův tisk),* 1825. Library of the Institute of Musical Science, Faculty of Arts, Charles University in Prague, H 7. Only a few examples remain.

6. Markl, Jaroslav looks at this issue in detail: *Nejstarší sbírky českých lidových písní.*

7. See Šebesta, "Pivo jako inspirační zdroj," 199–215.

rian wants to step back into the past and hold a dialogue in the language of the symbols of that time—so that upon his return to the present he can translate these into contemporary linguistic symbols for other interested parties—then the songs of communities and societies are an ideal means for achieving this. As far as the origin and development of workers' songs is concerned, I will not go into great detail here. This has already been admirably carried out by Vladimír Karbusický and other experts.[8] In the following text I will concentrate on the symbolism of secularization in workers' songs of the second half of the nineteenth century.

When Karl Marx came to Vienna at the end of 1848, he characterized the working class as still being "unorganized, distrustful, barely extricating themselves from the emotional ties to the old regime."[9] As the lyrics of the first workers' songs demonstrate, the hatred of the working classes was primarily aimed at the Jews, their wealth, factories and businesses. They blamed them for high prices and unemployment. There were workers' uprisings against Jewish factory owners in Prague and Liberec in June 1844. The clashes between soldiers and workers in front of Poříčská brana in Prague even resulted in deaths. From these arose the first attributed workers' songs.[10] The themes of these songs were poverty, the spilling of blood and, above all, hopelessness.[11] In *Nová píseň* [New Song] from 1848 there began to clearly emerge four basic directions that would define the struggle of the workers' movement. The emerging workers' organizations were opposed to the nobility, the Church, the bureaucracy and the Germans.[12] However, *Nová píseň* was not an original work. The first attempts at a distinctive category of expression were focused mainly on changing the lyrics of well-known tunes, mostly broadside ballads or cabaret songs, set within the framework of the Singspiel.[13] In the case of *Nová píseň* it was based on Josef Vorel's *Že peníze světem vládnou* [Money Rules the World].[14]

8. See Karbusický, "Idea vlasti v nejstarších dělnických písních," 5–9; Karbusický and Pletka, "Soupis českých a slovenských dělnických písní"; Karbusický and Pletka, *Dělnické balady*; Karbusický and Vanický, *Český revoluční zpěvník*. See also. Kotek, "Městská lidová zpěvnost a dělnická píseň," 117–32.

9. See Marx, *Die wirtschaftlichen Ursachen der Revolution von 1848 in Österreich,* 254. Quoted according to: Sked, *Úpadek a pád habsburské říše,* 98.

10. See Karbusický and Pletka, *Dělnické balady.*

11. Friedrich Engels wrote that "the active proletarian movement begins with the rebellions of the Czech and Silesian workers in 1844" See. Engels, *O rozkladu feudalismu a rozvoji buržoazie,* 72–73.

12. As far as the anti-German mood is concerned, there are no surprises here: the whole of Czech society, across all levels, was forming this antipathy towards the Germans. Antal Stašek best characterized this trend in 1868 with his reaction to the laying of the foundation stone of the National Theatre: "Everyone who was once subjugated is now calling out for freedom and self-determination. Such is our call and that of the politicians. It is not enough. We also have to emancipate ourselves from the influence of culture, which has always been our enemy.... One of our tasks is to free ourselves from German culture.... If we build our own culture and on that basis our own life; if we have our own world view, our own independent character; if we refuse to adhere to foreign models and stop looking back wistfully at them, then we will have our own great drama." See Stašek, "Hrst úvah, chumáč vzpomínek," 61–76.

13. From the plays of Josef Kajetán Tyl (1808–1858) *Strakonický dudák* comes the well-known tune *Peníze jsou pány světa*, with music by Josef Balanda (1825–?).

14. The tune by Josef Vorel (1801–1804) *Že peníze světem vládnou* accompanied the one-act play by Jan Nepomuk Štěpánek (co-director of the Estates Theatre) *Hastroš*, which played in the theater Na Žebráce from 1837.

New Song

If, dear brothers, a nobleman comes up to you,
Do not bow down to him, as oft times before;
We are all equal in the eyes of the Lord,
So why is it not the same on Earth,
Noblemen, robbers, we want you no more:
Fear nothing and string him up at once!

And those priests who preach to you, it's all a lie,
For the priests ever have been a deceitful bunch;
They live by the sweat of the people, and from the Lord's Prayer drink wine,
Thus turn them all out,
The whole Papal tribe,
Fear nothing and string him up at once!

And those bureaucratic lads, the offspring of hell,
You will not find bigger scoundrels in the whole world,
He comes as a penpusher, they make a crook of him,
The poor work themselves to the bone,
They have to learn:
Fear nothing and string him up at once!

And those Germans, foreigners, a land of leeches,
Stick a pitchfork ten inches into their backs,
They got their property by stealing and through the toil of the people
Where a greedy grabber comes,
It must be one of those Huns:
Fear nothing and string him up at once![15]

Here it is clear that, among others, the Church is portrayed as one of the main enemies of the workers' movement. However, in the course of defining its own path and the obstacles upon it, there is no trace of animosity towards individual devoutness. This animosity is directed at the application of piety and obedience through church ideology and propaganda.

In his conversations with Karel Čapek, Masaryk said: "It goes without saying that every organization, especially one as huge as the Church, is ipso facto political."[16] It was also for this reason that the Austrian chancellor Metternich had Pope Pius VII[17] construct in the Papal state a centralized, efficient and well-organized administration run by industrious and capable bureaucrats. Along with this went a stable legal system, a taxation system and a strong police force with a full range of repressive powers.[18] It is certain that the politics of the Church were not the politics of the workers' movement at that time. I speak of a movement because the principles of mass movements—as opposed to

15. Karbusický and Vanický, *Český revoluční zpěvník,* 51–52.
16. Čapek, *Hovory s T. G. Masarykem,* 122.
17. He reigned in 1800–1823.
18. See Sked, *Úpadek a pád habsburské říše,* 31.

totalitarian systems—do not repress the spirituality of an individual to such an extent that he cannot maintain his individual devoutness.[19]

Jiří Wolker described this aspect well in the poem *Svatý Kopeček* [The Holy Hill]:[20]

"... and I am a procession eager for the Lord's word,
I come from faraway Prague and my native Prostějov,
a mature lad, student and socialist,
believing in myself, iron inventions and Jesus Christ ..."

It is evident that on its journey towards a secularized political ideology, the Czech workers' movement was inspired by foreign political centers which formed around 1848 in Paris, Bonn and London, predominantly as a response to the ideas of Karl Marx. In Erich Fromm's *Marx's Concept of Man*, which was published in the United States, he demonstrated that: "Marx fought against religion exactly because it is alienated and does not satisfy the true needs of man. Marx's fight against God is, in reality, a fight against the idol that is called God. ... Marx's atheism is the most advanced form of rational mysticism, closer to Meister Eckhart or to Zen Buddhism than are most of those fighters for God and religion who accuse him of godlessness."[21] Karl Marx (1818–1883) himself wrote in 1841 as the motto for his dissertation: "Not those are godless who have contempt for the gods of the masses but those who attribute the opinions of the masses to the gods."[22] It was from these views that after 1848 he fashioned a whip which the workers' movement used to beat their enemies. In order to understand the "weapons" of the early struggle of the workers' movement—and secularization was one of them—we have to remind ourselves of their political context: in 1847 the Communist League was formed in Germany, for which Karl Marx and Friedrich Engels wrote the Communist Manifesto, which was published in February 1848.

On September 28th 1864 the International Workingmen's Association First International was founded in London, in whose charter Karl Marx wrote: "The International was founded in order to replace the socialist or semi-socialist sects by a real fighting organization of the working class," in 1867 the first volume of *Das Kapital* was published, in 1871 the Paris Commune was declared and in 1878 the Social Democratic Party was legalized in Prague.

In the same year a leading representative of the Social Democrats, Josef Boleslav Pecka (1849–1897)[23] published his own lyrics to the tune of the song *Hej, Slované* [Hey, Slavs] which reflected the new strategy for struggle as well as naming the new enemies of society. The church was not absent![24]

---

19. See Grunberger, *A Social History of the Third Reich*. See also Arendtová, *Původ totalitarismu I–III*.

20. Wolker, "Svatý Kopeček," 55.

21. See Fromm, *Obraz člověka u Marxe*, 47.

22. Quoted from Fromm, *Obraz člověka u Marxe*, 47.

23. Josef Boleslav Pecka, František Josef Hlaváček (1853–1937, pseudonym Podleský), Leopold Kochmann (1845–1919, pseudonym V. L. L. = Vive la Liberté) and Norbert Zoula (1854–1886) worked from the 1880s for the compatriots' workers' movement in the USA, where they continued with editions of workers' songs.

24. See *Zpěvník českých dělnických písní*.

Rise, brothers, the time has come when we are needed!
From every corner of the wide world the important news:
The new movement claims its right to justice.
From the ruins of tyranny, rule by the people will rise!

Long has ruled terrible injustice sanctified by the Church,
long has the impoverished class been crushed under tyranny!
But now there's a thundering in the ears of the murderers: thus far and no more!
Otherwise you'll be stricken by a fate as cruel as King Ludwig's!

Hunger imposes itself among our ranks, it rouses the movement,
your boundless avarice forces us to take revenge.
Look out, sir, poverty beckons, judgment day approaches
We are not going to drink our own bloody sweat!

(J. B. Pecka, Chicago 1887)

In the supranational organizational process the workers' organizations functioned as units with a strong fighting spirit: this influenced the melody and rhythm of the songs, especially during public performances. In his feuilleton Byl prvni máj 1890 [It was the First of May 1890] Jan Neruda wrote: "With calm, iron steps, battalions of workers gathered on May 1st 1890, innumerable, as far as the eye could see, formed into a human battle line, so that forever they advanced with the rest of us towards the noble goals of the people, equally righteous, equally burdened and equally jubilant ... How extraordinary—those colors: black on a dark red field which fluttered above the heads of the Hussites, fighters for religious freedom. Today these colors flutter above the heads of the fighters for complete equality for all citizens! ... The Lord always has both hands full of work for them, and so cannot bless them. Well then, God bless you!"[25]

The 1st of May 1890 was also depicted in song form as an important source of inspiration for the expression of emotions through lyrics set to a well-known melody. The most important was a song by Josef Krapka-Náchodský (1869–1909), *Dělnická hymna k 1. máji 1890* [Workers' Hymn to the First of May], to the melody of the broadside ballad *Na hranicích města německého* [On the Outskirts of a German Town]. Also important was the song *Pokrokářská* [Progressive], which was set to the melody of *Když jsem já šel tou putimskou branou* [When I Went Through the Putim Gate] by Jindřich of Štemberk (1867–1926). In the second verse can be found the notion of the downfall of Austria, which around 1890 was still far from being a bon mot.

When the nation stopped fearing its government,
The old orders began to collapse,
In one fell swoop the progressives
United in a strong formation.

They united hand in hand,
The vanguard of the revolutionary spirit,
And joyfully tore down
The rotten empire of Austria.

(Jindřich Štemberka, Polička 1890)

25. Neruda, *Nechť nový cíl dá nový den*, 408–11.

At that time, however, the workers' song as a socio-cultural category already contained hundreds of original songs with lyrics. By 1918 this number had risen to over 5,000 songs, as is shown by Vladimír Karbusický and Václav Pletka's *Register of Czech and Slovak Workers' Songs*.[26] From a total of 5,325 songs, only five have lyrics which are based on anti-clerical themes,[27] with a further fourteen satirizing the priesthood.[28]

An overwhelmingly large number of the songs could be described as workers' spiritual songs, or even workers' songs based on liturgical texts.[29] Over the course of time, all the secularizing undertones of the workers' songs practically disappeared. They were no longer necessary. The battle had been won on that front. Around 1880 the struggle for freedom and equality became the principal theme. Songs such as *Proč jsem sociál* [Why I am a Socialist]—1879, *Vězeňská* [Prison Song]—1886, *Píseň práce* [Song of Work]—1887, *My dělníci* [We the Workers]—end of the 1880s, *My jsme proletáři* [We are the Proletariat]—beginning of the 1890s, *Pryč s tyrany a zrádci všemi* [Down with Tyranny and all Traitors]—1891, *Milion paží* [A Million Arms]—1905, and hundreds of others pointed to, in a significant range of lyrics, only one enemy, who came to be symbolized as the "exploiter." Apart from the eternal struggle with this enemy, one of the most significant sources of inspiration in workers' songs from the nineteenth century was the idea of the homeland and nation. I am reminded at this point of the conference Národ místo boha v 19. století [Nation in Place of God in the nineteenth Century] which was held in Ústí nad Labem in April 2005.[30] There Jiří Rak quoted Alexis de Tocqueville that, "religion has abandoned the human soul but has not left it empty and weakened."[31] Into the empty space entered values which the revolution and faith in progress considered to be more important from the point of view of enlightened reason, from the point of view of a new way of looking at the world and its social ills, as well as from the point of view of the new hierarchies of values which the various mass movements created and adapted. All the movements—not just the workers' movement—thus proclaimed a new era in which man would be freed from his old prejudices. However, they did not realize that the new spiritual conditions would also bring about new prejudices, leading to a new "dogmatism." The organized workers' movement simply—on the basis of its social standing and set goals—adopted a form of "religion" that, to all extents and purposes, replaced the one it had rejected.

26. Karbusický and Pletka, *Soupis českých a slovenských dělnických písní*.

27. Lidé, co jste katolíci (Karbusický—Pletka 2050); Nevolte klerikálů (K-P 2843); Od Příbrami k Svaté hoře (K-P 2992); Pan farář se rozstonal (K-P 3068; Rozmarná píseň o nešťastných ptácích (K-P 3307).

28. e.g., Pan farář také rád (K-P 3069; Šla Bětuška k zpovídání (K-P 4068); Ten zdejší pan farář (K-P 4256).

29. Blíž tobě, Bože můj; Otčenáš; Te Deum laudamus; Svatý Václave; Pane Bože náš; Již jsem dost pracoval; a další.

30. See Kaiserová, *Národ místo boha v 19. a první polovině 20. století*.

31. Tocqueville, *Starý režim a revoluce,*187.

Caricature, Rašple, 27th August 1896: "This is what the liberal and clerical bigwigs think of the workers' movement, when they are being nice."[32]

CONCLUSION

The worker's song is a cultural category which was created suddenly, almost without any developmental process, and which reflected the political situation in Europe around the second half of the nineteenth century. 1819 saw the gubernatorial collection campaign in the Czech lands, which brought together a large number of Czech national songs. None of the participants had any notion of the song category which the social and political developments of the next fifty years would, under the title of "Workers' Song," raise to the level of a historico-cultural phenomenon. As the lyrics of the first workers' songs demonstrate, the workers' hatred was primarily aimed at the Jews, their wealth, factories and businesses. They blamed them for high prices and unemployment. In *Nová píseň* [New Song] from 1848 there began to clearly emerge four basic directions that would define the struggle of the workers' movement. The emerging workers' organizations were opposed to the nobility, the Church, the bureaucracy and the Germans. The Church was clearly seen to be one of the main enemies of the workers' movement. However, in the

32. *Rašple. Humoristický list dělného lidu.* Came out every third Wednesday of the month. Publisher and editor responsible František Komprda, Brno 1890–1921. The magazine *Rašple* printed 545 workers' songs, which was by far the largest number in the area of today's Czech Republic. The first printed collection *Písně dělnické* [Workers' Songs] came out in New York in 1877.

course of defining its own path and the obstacles upon it, there is no trace of animosity towards individual devoutness. In 1878 a leading representative of the Social Democrats, Josef Boleslav Pecka, published his own lyrics to the tune of the song *Hej, Slované* [Hey, Slavs] which reflected the new strategy for struggle as well as naming the new enemies of society. The church was not absent! During this period the workers' song as a socio-cultural category contained hundreds of original songs with lyrics. By 1918 this number had risen to over 5,325 songs. Only five have lyrics which are based on anti-clerical themes, with a further 14 satirizing the priesthood. An overwhelmingly large number of the songs could be described as workers' spiritual songs. Over the course of time, all the secularizing undertones of the workers' songs practically disappeared. Around 1880 there is present in a significant range of lyrics only one enemy, who came to be symbolized as the "exploiter." Apart from the struggle with this enemy, one of the most significant sources of inspiration in workers' songs from the nineteenth century was the idea of the homeland and nation.

Bibliography

100 let literatury v Rovnosti. Brno: Rovnost, 1985.

175 let tabákového průmyslu v Hodoníně 1783-1958. Hodonín: Československý tabákový průmysl, 1958.

Arbeitsordnung für die k. k. Tabakverschleißmagazine und die k. k. Tabakeinlösungsämter sammt deren Expozituren. Vienna, 1899.

Arbeitsordnung für die Tabakfabriken. Vienna, 1899.

Arendtová, Hannah. *Původ totalitarismu.* Vol. 1-3. Prague: Oikoymenh, 1996.

Arndt, Ernst Moritz. *Geist der Zeit.* Part 2. Berlin: Hammerich/Reimer, 1813.

Aron, Raymond. *Opium intelektuálů.* Prague: Mladá fronta, 1998.

Aston, Nigel, and Matthew Cragoe. *Anticlericalism in Britain, c. 1500-1914.* Cloucestershire: Sutton, 2000.

Baar, Jindřich Šimon. *Cestou křížovou.* Praha: Vyšehrad, 1956.

Balbier, Uta Andrea, "*Sag: Wie hast Du's mit der Religion?: Das Verhältnis von Religion und Politik als Gretchenfrage der Zeitgeschichte.* " *H-Soz-u-Kult* (10.11.2009). No pages. Online: http://hsozkult .geschichte.hu-berlin.de/forum/2009-11-001.

Balík, Stanislav. "Kulturní boj v českých zemích a politický katolicismus." In *Teorie a praxe politického katolicismu 1870-2007,* edited by Pavel Marek, 79-92. Brno: CDK, 2008.

———. "Politika vedená z bludovské fary—P. František Alois Ermis." In *Osobnost v církvi a politice: Čeští a slovenští křesťané ve 20. století,* edited by Pavel Marek and Jiří Hanuš, 104-21. Brno 2006.

Bartošek, Theodor. *Moderní společnost a církev.* Prague, 1907.

Bauer, Franz J. *Das "lange" Jahrhundert: Profil einer Epoche.* Stuttgart: Ph. Reclam jun., 2004.

Beck, Ulrich. *Der eigene Gott, Friedensfähigkeit und gewaltpotential der Religionen.* Leipzig: Insel, 2008.

Bell, Daniel. *Kulturní rozpory kapitalismu.* Prague: SLON, 2001.

Benz, Ernst. "Die Stellung des Modernismus zur päpstlichen Autorität." In *Die päpstliche Autorität im katholischen Selbstverständnis des 19. und 20. Jahrhunderts,* edited by Erika Weinzierl. Salzburg: Pustet, 1970.

Berchtold, Klaus. *Österreichische Parteiprogramme 1868-1966.* Vienna: Verlag für Geschichte und Politik, 1967.

Berdiajew, Nikolai. *Der Sinn und Schicksal des russischen Komunismus.* Berlin: Junker, 1929.

Berger, Peter L. *The Rumor of Angels.* New York: Doudleday, 1970.

———. *Vzdálená sláva: Hledání víry ve věku lehkověrnosti.* Brno: CDK, 1998.

Berger, Peter L., and Thomas Luckmann. *Sociální konstrukce reality: Pojednání o sociologii vědění.* Brno: CDK, 1999.

———. "Sociology of Religion and Sociology of Knowledge." *Sociology and Social Research* 47 (1966).

Berger, Stefan. "Marxismusrezeption als Generationserfahrung." In *Generationen in der Arbeiterbewegung,* edited by Klaus Schönhoven and Bernd Braun, 193-209. Munich: Oldenbourg, 2005.

Bernstein, Eduard. *Sozialdemokratische Lehrjahre: Autobiographien.* 2nd ed. Berlin: Dietz, 1991.

Bilová, Marcela. "Dělnické bydlení v Ostravě do roku 1918." Master's thesis, College of Education Ostrava, 1977.

Blackbourn, David. *Marpingen: Apparitions of the Virgin Mary in Nineteenth-Century Germany.* New York: Knopf, 1994.

Blaschke, Franz. "Verbandkatholizismus in Mähren-Schlesien." In *Kirche, Recht und Land:Festschrift Weihbischof Prof. Dr. Adolf Kindermann dargeboten zum 70. Lebensjahre,* edited by K. Rei and D. H. Schütz, 250-61. Munich: Sudetendeutsches Priesterwerke e. V., 1969.

Blaschke, Olaf. "Das 19. Jahrhundert: Ein Zweites Konfessionelles Zeitalter." *Geschichte und Gesellschaft* 26 (2000) 38-75.

Blessing, Werner K. *Staat und Kirche in der Gesellschaft: Institutionelle Autorität und mentaler Wandel in Bayern während des 19. Jahrhunderts.* Göttingen: Vandenhoeck and Ruprecht, 1982.

Bibliography

Blickle, Peter, and Rudolf Schlögl. *Die Säkularisation im Prozess der Säkularisierung Europas*. Epfendorf: Bibliotheca Academica, 2005.

———. "Die Säkularisation im Prozess der Säkularisierung Europas: Einleitung." In *Die Säkularisation im Prozess der Säkularisierung Europas*, 11–17. Epfendorf: bibliotheca academica, 2005.

Blos, Wilhelm. *Denkwürdigkeiten eines Sozialdemokraten*. Vol. 1. Munich: G. Birk, 1914.

Bourdieu, Pierre: *Distinction: A Social Critique of the Judgment of Taste*. Cambridge, MA: Harvard University Press, 1984.

Braun, Bernd. "Die 'Generation Ebert'". In *Generationen in der Arbeiterbewegung*, edited by Klaus Schönhoven and Bernd Braun, 69–86. Munich: Oldenbourg Wissenschaftsverlag, 2005.

Braun, Christina von, Wilhelm Grab, and Johannes Zachhuber. *Säkularisierung: Bilanz und Perspektiven einer umstrittenen These*. Berlin: Lit 2007.

Bromme, Moritz Th. W. *Lebensgeschichte eines modernen Fabrikarbeiters: With an Epilogue by Bernd Neumann*. Jena: Diederichs, 1905. Reprint, Frankfurt: Athenäum, 1971.

Brtvová, Eva. "Kolonie Ida šachta do 1918." Master's thesis, College of Education Ostrava, 1965.

Bruce, Steve. *Religion and Modernisation: Sociologists and Historians Debate the Secularization Thesis*. Oxford: Clarendon, 1992.

Brügel, Ludwig. *Geschichte der österreichischen Sozialdemokratie*. Vol. 1–5. Vienna: Wiener, 1922–1925.

Büchmann, Georg. *Geflügelte Worte: Der Zitatenschatz des deutschen Volkes*. 31st edition. Berlin: Haude & Spenersche, 1967.

Budde, Heiner. *Man nannte sie „rote" Kapläne: Priester an der Seite der Arbeiter*. Kevelaer: Butzon and Bercker, 1989.

Burian, Edmund. *Socialistické epištoly*. Brno: Nákladem Rovnosti, 1907.

Burschofsky, Ferdinand. *Beiträge zur Geschichte der deutschnationalen Arbeiterbewegung in Österreich*. Hohenstadt, 1915.

Cabalka, Josef Václav. *Vyšehrad, svědek české minulosti*. Prague: Družstvo Vlast, 1941.

Canning, Kathleen. *Female Factory Work in Germany: 1850–1914*. Ann Arbor, Michigan: Cornell University Press, 1996.

Čáňová, Eliška. *Slovník představitelů katolické církevní správy v Čechách v letech 1848–1918*. Prague: Státní ústřední archiv, 1995.

Čapek, Karel. *Hovory s T. G. Masarykem*. Prague: Fr. Borový, Čin, 1937. Prague: Československý spisovatel, 1990.

Cassirer, Ernst. *Die Philosophie der Aufklärung*. Hamburg: Meiner, 1998.

———. *Substanzbegriff und Funktionsbegriff. Untersuchungen über die Grundfragen der Erkenntniskritik*. Darmstadt: Deutsche Buchgemeinschaft, 1994.

Černý, Bohumil, et al. *Církve v našich dějinách*. Prague: Československá společnost pro šíření politických a vědeckých znalostí, 1960.

České národní písně. Prague: Jan Ritter z Rittersberku, 1825.

Chlumecký, V. "Janko Kosák v nebi." In *Janko Kosák v nebi a iné prózy*, edited by Štefan Drug. Bratislava: Tatran, 1978.

———. "Neznaboh." In *Janko Kosák v nebi a iné prózy*, edited by Štefan Drug. Bratislava: Tatran 1978.

Cibulka, Pavel. *Politické programy českých národních stran (1860–1890)*. Prague: Historický ústav AV ČR 2000.

Ciller, Alois. *Sozialismus in den Sudetenländern und der Ostmark*. Hamburg:Hanseat, 1939.

Comte, Auguste. *Système de politique positive ou Traité de sociologie*. Paris, 1851–1854.

Daum, Andreas. *Wissenschaftspopularisierung im 19. Jahrhundert. Bürgerliche Kultur, naturwissenschaftliche Bildung und die deutsche Öffentlichkeit 1848–1914*. 2 nd ed. Oldebourg: Oldebourg Wissenschaftsverlag, 2002.

Dělnictvo a náboženství. Hlas lidu 30.9. 1908, year 23, no. 78.

Doležal, Josef. *Český kněz*. Prague, 1931.

Dormitzer, Michal, and Emanuel Schebek. *Die Erwerbsverhältnisse im böhmischen Erzgebirge*. Prague: Handels- und Gewerkekammer, 1862.

Dostál-Lutinov, Karel. *Lutinov contra Juda*. Prostějov 1906.

Elm, Kaspar, and Hans-Dietrich Loock. *Seelsorge und Diakonie in Berlin: Beiträge zum Verhältnis von Kirche und Großstadt im 19. und beginnenden 20. Jahrhundert*. New York: Walter de Gruyter, 1990.

Encyklopedie dějin města Brna. Online: http://encyklopedie.brna.cz/home-mmb/?acc=profil_osobnosti& load=345 (15. 9. 2009)

Engels, Bedřich. *O rozkladu feudalismu a rozvoji buržoazie.* Prague, 1951.

Englová, Jana. "August Bebel a severní Čechy." In *Semper idem: Jiřímu Tůmovi k pětasedmdesátinám,* edited by Zdeněk Radvanovský. Ústí nad Labem: Univezita Jana Evangelisty Purkyně, 2003.

Escher, Felix. "Pfarrgemeinden und Gemeindeorganisation der katholischen Kirche in Berlin bis zur Gründung des Bistums Berlin." In *Seelsorge und Diakonie in Berlin: Beiträge zum Verhältnis von Kirche und Großstadt im 19. und beginnenden 20. Jahrhundert,* edited by Kaspar Elm and Hans-Dietrich Loock, 265–92. Berlin, New York: Walter de Gruyter, 1990.

Evans, Richard J. *Kneipengespräche im Kaiserreich: Die Stimmungsberichte der Hamburger Politischen Polizei 1892–1914.* Reinbek: Rowohlt, 1989.

Faber, Richard, and Frithjof Hager. *Rückkehr der Religion oder sekuläre Kultur?* Würzburg: Königshausen & Neumann, 2008.

Fasora, Lukáš: "Sekularizace a 'klerikální bašty' na Brněnsku a Vyškovsku." In *Sekularizace venkovského prostoru v 19. století,* edited by Lukáš Fasora and Jiří Hanuš and Jiří Malíř, 253–66. Brno: Matice Moravská, 2009.

Fasora, Lukáš, Jiří Hanuš and Jiří Malíř. *Sekularizace českých zemí v letech 1848–1914.* Brno: CDK, 2007.

———. *Sekularizace venkovského prostoru v 19. století.* Brno: Matice moravská, 2009.

Fiala, Petr, et al. *Český politický katolicismus 1848–2005.* Brno: CDK, 2008.

Filipinský, Jan. "Vzpomínky." In *Pamětní list československé sociálně demokratické strany dělnické, 1872–1922,* 127–28. Praha: Redakcí Dr. Františka Soukupa, 1922.

Fischer, Richard. *Pokroková Morava 1893–1918.* Vol. 2. Prague: Cesta, 1937.

Franěk, Otakar. "Josef Hybeš—život a dílo." In *Ideologická konference ke 125. výročí narození Josefa Hybeše,* 9–53. Brno: Městský výbor Komunistické strany Československa, 1975.

———. *Pankrác Krkoška, první redaktor Rovnosti.* Brno: Rovnost, 1975.

———. *Rebel a básník.* Hradec Králové: Kruh, 1982.

Fromm, Erich. *Obraz člověka u Marxe.* Brno: L. Marek, 2004.

Fuchs, Albert. *Geistige Strömungen in Österreich 1867–1918.* Vienna: Löcker, 1984.

Führer durch das nordwestböhmische Braunkohlenrevier. Brüx 1908.

Fürstenberg, Friedrich. *Religionssoziologie.* Neuwied, Berlin: Luchterhand,1964.

Gabriel, Jiří, and Jiří Svoboda. *Náboženství v českém myšlení.* Brno: Ústav etiky a religionistiky, 1993.

Gabriel, Jiří, et al. *Slovník českých filozofů.* Brno, 1998.

Galandauer, Jan. "Die Relation der Bildungspolitik der tschechoslawischen Sozialdemokraten zur Religionsfrage: Šmerals Versuch einer Prözision des Standpunktes." In *Internationale Tagung der Historiker der Arbeiterbewegung: XIII. Linzer Konferenz 1977: Geschichte der Arbeiterbewegung,* 295–302. Vienna 1981.

———. "Poměr Bohumíra Šmerala k náboženské otázce, klerikalismu a husitství." *Husitský tábor* 4 (1981) 215–20.

Gärdner, Christel, Detlev Pollack and Monika Wohlrab-Sahr. *Atheismus und religiöse Indifferenz.* Opladen: Leske, 2003.

Garver, Bruce M: *The Young Czech Party, 1874–1901, and the Emergence of a Multi-party System.* New Haven: Yale University Press, 1976.

Gatz, Erwin. "Katholische Großstadtseelsorge im 19. und 20. Jahrhundert: Grundzüge ihrer Entwicklung." In *Seelsorge und Diakonie in Berlin: Beiträge zum Verhältnis von Kirche und Großstadt im 19. und beginnenden 20. Jahrhundert,* edited by Kaspar Elm and Hans-Dietrich Loock, 23–28. New York: Walter de Gruyter, 1990.

Gauchet, Marcel. *Odkouzlení světa: Dějiny náboženství jako věci veřejné.* Brno: CDK, 2004.

Gawrecki, Dan. "Německá dělnická strana 1904–1918." *Slezský sborník* 71 (1973) 29–41, 81–90.

———. "Německá dělnická strana a její trutnovský program." *Sborník prací východočeských archivů* 3 (1975) 123–37.

Gawrecki, Dan, and Jana Machačová. *Dělnické hnutí v severozápadních Čechách do r. 1918.* Opava: Slezský ústav ČSAV, 1978.

Gelmi, Josef. *Papežové.* Prague: Mladá fronta, 1994.

Gentile, Emilio. *Politická náboženství: Mezi demokracií a totalitarismem.* Brno: CDK, 2008.

Bibliography

Georgiev, Jiří. "Mezi svéprávností a poručnictvím: K postavení církví v habsburské monarchii druhé poloviny 19. století." In *Bůh a bohové: Církve, náboženství a spiritualita v českém 19. století*, edited by Zdeněk Hojda and Roman Prahl, 169–185. Prague: Koniasch Latin Press, 2003.

Göhre, Paul. *Lebensgang eines deutsch-tschechischen Handarbeiters.* Jena, 1909.

———. *Vom Handarbeiter zum Jugenderzieher.* Jena, 1921.

Götz von Olenhausen, Irmtraud. "Die Feminisierung der Religion und Kirche im 19. und 20. Jahrhundert: Forschungsstand und Forschungsperspektiven." In *Frauen unter dem Patriarchat der Kirche: Katholikinnen und Protestantinnen im 19. und 20. Jahrhundert*, 9–21. Stuttgart: Kohlhammer, 1995.

Graf, Friedrich Wilhelm. "Dechristianisierung: Zur Problemgeschichte eines kulturpolitischen Topos." In *Säkularisierung, Dechristianisierung, Rechristianisierung im neuzeitlichen Europa: Bilanz und Perspektiven der Forschung*, edited by Hartmut Lehmann, 32–66. Göttingen: Vandenhoeck and Ruprecht, 1997.

———. *Die Wiederkehr der Gotter: Religion in moderner Kultur.* Munich: Beck, 2007.

Graf, Friedrich Wilhelm, and Klaus Grosse-Kracht. *Religion und Gesellschaft. Europa im 20. Jahrhundert.* Vienna: Böhlau 2007.

Gregorová, Hana. *Spomienky.* Bratislava: Tatran 1979.

Greyerz, Kaspar von, and Kin Siebenhüner. *Religion und Gewalt: Konflikte Rituale, Deutungen (1500–1800).* Göttingen: Vandenhoeck & Ruprecht, 2006.

Gröger, Florian. "Von unten auf." In *Arbeiterleben. Autobiographien zur Alltags- und Sozialgeschichte Österreichs 1867–1914*, edited by Stefan Riesenfellner, 157–61. Graz: Leykam, 1989.

Grote, Heiner. *Sozialdemokratie und Religion: Eine Dokumentation für die Jahre 1863 bis 1875.* Tübingen: Mohr/Siebeck, 1968.

Grunberger, Richard. *A Social History of the Third Reich.* London: Penguin, 1991.

Grunzel, Joseph. *Die Reichenberger Tuchindustrie in ihrer Entwicklung vom zünftigen Handwerk zur modernen Großindustrie.* Beiträge zur Geschichte der deutschen Industrie in Böhmen 5. Prague: Selbstverlag des Vereins für Geschichte der Deutschen in Böhmen, 1898.

Habermas, Jürgen, "Glauben und Wissen. Friedenspreisrede 2001." In Jürgen Habermas. *Zeitdiagnosen: Zwölf Essays*, 249–62. Frankfurt: Suhrkamp, 2003.

———. *Strukturální přeměna veřejnosti: zkoumání jedné kategorie občanské společnosti.* Prague: Filosofia, 2000.

———. *Zwischen Naturalismus und Religion.* Frankfurt/M: Suhrkamp, 2005.

Halas, František. *Kemka: Vzpomínky bývalého textilního dělníka.* Prague: Práce, 1950.

Hallwich, Hermann. *Reichenberg und Umgebung: Eine Ortsgeschichte mit spezieller Rücksicht auf gewerbliche Entwicklung.* Reichenberg: Franz Jannasch, 1874, supplement 6.

Hannich, Josef. *Ein Beitrag zur Geschichte der österreichischen Arbeiterbewegung.* Warnsdorf, [1910].

———. *Erinnerungen: Ein Beitrag zu der Geschichte der österreichischen Arbeiterbewegung.* Warnsdorf, [1910].

Hanuš, Jiří: "Kněz a politik: případ Jana Šrámka." In *Jan Šrámek: Kněz—státník—politik*, edited by Pavel Marek, 42–54. Olomouc: Univerzita Palackého and Moneta-FM, 2004.

Harna, Josef. *Politické programy českého národního socialismu.* Prague: Historický ústav, 1998.

Havelka, Miloš. "Byl Herbart filosofem biedermeieru?!: Herbartův pokus o realistickou akceptaci rozdvojenosti člověka a světa." In *Biedermeier v českých zemích*, edited by Helena Lorenzová and Taťána Petrasová, 25–38. Praha: Koniasch Latin Press, 2004.

Havíř, František. *Epištoly k rolnictvu a k pracovníkům, utiskovaným třídám vůbec.* Vyškov, 1904.

Havránek, Jan. "Příprava Husových oslav a antiklerikalismus českých studentů v předvečer první světové války." In *Bůh a bohové: Církve, náboženství a spiritualita v českém 19. století*, edited by Zdeněk Hojda and Roman Prahl, 235–44. Prague: Koniasch Latin Press, 2003.

Heerma van Voss, Lex. *Between Cross and Class: Comparative Histories of Christian Labour in Europe 1840–2000.* Bern: Lang, 2005.

Hegel, Georg Wilhelm Friedrich. *Vorlesungen über die Philosophie der Geschichte.* Leipzig: Reclam, 1924.

Helle, Hans-Jürgen. *Religionssoziologie: Entwicklung der Vostellungen vom Heiligen.* Munich, Vienna: Oldenburg, 1997.

Henrich, Dieter. "Die Grundstruktur der modernen Philosophie." In *Selbstverhältnise*, 83–109. Stuttgart: Ph. Reclam jun, 1982.

Hering, Rainer. "Säkularisierung, Entkirchlichung, Dechristianisierung und Formen der Rechristianisierung bzw. Resakralisierung in Deutschland." In *Völkische Religion und Krisen der Moderne: Entwürfe „arteigener" Glaubenssysteme seit der Jahrhundertwende,* edited by Stephanie von Schnurbein and Justus H. Ulbricht, 120–164. Würzburg: Königshausen and Neumann, 2001.

Heumos, Peter. "Hussitische Tradition und Volkskultur in Böhmen im 19. Jahrhundert." In *Jan Hus und die Hussiten in europäischen Aspekten,* 75–91. Trier: Karl-Marx-Haus, 1978.

Hiepel, Claudia. *Arbeiterkatholizismus an der Ruhr: August Brust und der Gewerkverein christlicher Bergarbeiter.* Stuttgart, Berlin, Cologne: Kohlhammer, 1999.

Hiepel, Claudia, and Mark Ruff. *Christliche Arbeiterbewegung in Europa 1850–1950.* Stuttgart, Berlin, Cologne: Kohlhammer, 2003.

Hildebrandt, Mathias, Manfred Brocker, and Hartmut Behr. *Säkularisierung und Resakralisierung in westlichen Gesellschaften: Ideengeschichtliche und theoretische Perspektiven.* Wiesbaden: Westdeutscher, 2001.

Hitz, Hafale, and Hugo Huber. *Geschichte der Österreichischen Tabakregie 1784–1835.* Vienna: Verlag der Österreichischen Akademie der Wissenschaften, 1975.

Hofer, Josef. *Pokrokáři, agrárníci, sociální demokraté, národní socialisté a náboženství.* Prostějov, 1910.

Hojda, Zdeněk, and Roman Prahl. *Bůh a bohové: Církve, náboženství a spiritualita v českém 19. století.* Prague: Koniasch Latin Press, 2003.

Holec, Roman. "Úloha katolíckej cirkvi pri formovaní občianskej spoločnosti na Slovensku." *Česko-slovenská historická ročenka* 11 (2006) 155–73.

Holek, Heinrich. *Unterwegs. Eine Selbstbiographie.* Vienna: Bugra, 1927.

Hölscher, Lucian. *Atlas zur religiösen Geographie im protestantischen Deutschland zwischen der Mitte des 19. Jahrhunderts und dem Zweiten Weltkrieg.* Vol. 4. Berlin: Walter de Gruyter, 2001.

———. "Möglichkeiten und Grenzen der statistischen Erfassung kirchlicher Bindungen." In *Seelsorge und Diakonie in Berlin: Beiträge zum Verhältnis von Kirche und Großstadt im 19. und beginnenden 20. Jahrhundert,* edited by Kaspar Elm and Hans-Dietrich Loock, 35–59. New York: Walter de Gruyter, 1990.

———. "Säkularisierungsprozesse im deutschen Protestantismus des 19. Jahrhunderts: Ein Vergleich zwischen Bürgertum und Arbeiterschaft." In *Bürger in der Gesellschaft der Neuzeit: Wirtschaft—Politik—Kultur,* edited by Hans-Jürgen Puhle, 238–58. Göttingen: Vandenhoeck and Ruprecht, 1991.

———. "Secularisation and Urbanisation in the Nineteenth Century: An Interpretative Model." In *European Religion in the Age of Great Cities, 1830–1930,* edited by Hugh McLeod, 263–88. New York: Routledge, 1995.

———. *Weltgericht oder Revolution: Protestantische und sozialistische Zukunftsvorstellungen im deutschen Kaiserreich.* Industrielle Welt: Schriftenreihe des Arbeitskreises für moderne Sozialgeschichte 46. Stuttgart: Klett-Cotta, 1989.

Horkheimer, Max, and Theodor W. Adorno. *Dialektik der Aufklärung.* Frankfurt: Suhrkamp, 1969.

Houfek, Václav. "Nacionalizace společnosti a dělnictvo na Ústecku do roku 1918." In *Nacionalizace společnosti v Čechách 1848–1914.* Acta Universitatis Purkynianae 142, Studia Slavogermanica 1. Ústí nad Labem: Univerzita J. E. Purkyně, 2008.

Houžvová, Jaroslava. "V naší havířské rodině v životě nepadlo sprosté slovo." In *Lidé z kolonií vyprávějí své dějiny,* edited by Martin Jemelka. Ostrava: University of Ostrava, Faculty of Arts, 2009.

Hoyer, Hans. "Die altkatholische Kirche." In *Die Habsburgermonarchie 1848–1918.* Vol. 4, edited by Adam Wandruszka and Peter Urbanitách, 616–32. Vienna: Verlag der Österreichischen Akademie der Wisswenschaften, 1985.

Hroch, Miroslav, et al. *Encyklopedie novověku: 1492–1815.* Prague: Libri, 2005.

Hromádka, Josef Lukl. *Masaryk mezi včerejškem a zítřkem: Československý boj o novou evropu.* Chicago: Jednota českých evangelíků v Americe, 1940.

Hrubý, Karel. "Kirche und Arbeiter." In *Bohemia Sacra: Das Christentum in Böhmen 873–1973,* edited by Ferdinand Seibt, 258–68. Düsseldorf: Pädagogischer Verlag Schann, 1974.

Huber, Kurt A. "Der Josephinismus und die staats-kirchliche Reformprogramm und die böhmische Länder." *Zeitschrift für Ostforschung* 31 (982) 223–30.

———. "Die Enzyklika 'Rerum novarum' und die Genesis der christlichsozialen Volksparteien der Tschechoslowakei." In *Die Erste Tschechoslowakische Republik als multinationaler Parteienstaat,* edited by Karl Bosl, 241–59. Munich: R. Oldenbourg, 1979.

————. "Nation und Kirche 1848–1918." In *Bohemia Sacra: Das Christentum in Böhmen 873–1973*, edited by Ferdinand Seibt, 246–257. Düsseldorf: Pädagogischer Verlag Schann, 1974.

Hübner, Ludwig. *Geschichte der Reichenberger Tuchmacherzunft*. Reichenberg: Tuchmachergenossenschaft, 1879.

Hybeš, Josef. *Práce a vzpomínky*. Vol. 1, edited by Otakar Franěk. Brno: Blok, 1976.

Jakubowski-Tiessen, Manfred. "Einleitung." In *Religion zwischen Kunst und Politik: Aspekte der Säkularisierung im 19. Jahrhundert*, edited by Manfred Jakubowski-Tiessen, 7–11. Göttingen: Wallstein, 2004.

————. "Pastor Förster und die Eisenbahner: Sonntagsheiligung im Maschinenzeitalter." In *Religion zwischen Kunst und Politik: Aspekte der Säkularisierung im 19. Jahrhundert*, 12–25. Göttingen: Wallstein, 2004.

————. *Religion zwischen Kunst und Politik: Aspekte der Säkularisierung im 19. Jahrhundert*. Göttingen: Wallstein, 2004.

Janšák, Štefan. *Život dr. Pavla Blahu*. I. Trnava: Spolok sv. Vojtecha, 1947.

Jaworski, Rudolf. "Konfession als Faktor nationaler Identifikationsprozesse in Ostmitteleuropa im 19. und zu Beginn des 20. Jahrhunderts." In *Pluralitäten, Religionen und kulturelle Codes*, edited by Moritz Csáky and Klaus Zeyringer, 131–47. Innsbruck: Studien Verlag, 2001.

Jehlicska, Ferenc. *A marxista vállásbölcsélet forrása és lényege*. Budapest, 1908.

————. *Társadalmi kérdés és etika: A marxista irány és a modern szociáletikai irány*. Budapest, 1908.

Jemelka, Martin. "K náboženskému životu v Moravské Ostravě (1854–1920)." *Acta Facultatis philosophicae Universitas Ostraviensis*, Historica 15. Ostrava: University of Ostrava, Fakulty of Arts, 2008.

Jiřík, Karel. "Čurda-Lipovský, Bedřich." In *Biografický slovník Slezska a Severní Moravy*. Vol. 4, edited by Lumír Dokoupil and Milan Myška. Ostrava: University of Ostrava, Fakulty of Arts, 1995.

Jiroušek, Tomáš. *Dějiny sociálního hnutí v zemích Koruny české*. Praha 1909.

Jordán, František. *Sjezd dělnictva českoslovanského v Brně. Lužánky 25. a 26. prosince 1887*. Brno: Museum dělnického hnutí, 1957.

Judův případ. Prostějov 1906.

Kadlec, Jaroslav. *Přehled církevních českých dějin 2*. Rome: Christian Academy, 1987.

Kaiser, Jochen-Christoph. "Sozialdemokratie und 'praktische' Religionskritik. Das Beispiel der Kirchenaustrittsbewegung 1878–1914." *Archiv für Sozialgeschichte* 22 (1982) 263–98.

Kaiser, Jochen-Christoph. *Arbeiterbewegung und organisierte Religionskritik: Proletarische Freidenkerverbände in Kaiserreich und Weimarer Republik*. Stuttgart: Klett-Cotta, 1981.

Kaiserová, Kristina. "Katolická církev, politika a sociální otázka v německojazyčných oblastech litoměřické diecéze." In *Sekularizace venkovského prostoru v 19. století*, edited by Lukáš Fasora and Jiří Hanuš and Jiří Malíř, 217–24. Brno: Matice Moravská, 2009.

————. *Konfesní myšlení českých Němců v 19. a počátkem 20. století*. Úvaly u Prahy: Nakladatelství Ve Stráni, 2003.

Kaiserová, Kristina, Jiří Mikulec, and Jaroslav Šebek. *Srdce Ježíšovo: Teologie—symbol—dějiny: Pocta Jeho Eminenci Tomáši kardinálu Špidlíkovi*. Ústí n. L.: Historický ústav AV ČR, Centrum pro výzkum církevních dějin ČBK, Centro Alletti Velehrad-Roma, 2005.

Kaiserová, Kristina, and Martin Veselý. *Národ místo boha v 19. a první polovině 20. století*. Ústí nad Labem: Ústav slovansko-germánských studií, 2006.

Karbusický, Vladimír. "Idea vlasti v nejstarších dělnických písních." *Hudební rozhledy* 5 (1952) 5–9.

Karbusický, Vladimír, and Jaroslav Vanický. *Český revoluční zpěvník*. Prague: SNKLHU, 1953.

————. *Český revoluční zpěvník*. Prague: SNKLHU, 1953.

Karbusický, Vladimír, and Václav Pletka. *Dělnické balady*. Prague: Nakladatelství politické literatury, 1962.

————. "Soupis českých a slovenských dělnických písní." Vol. 1, 2. Unpublished manuscript, Ústav pro etnografii a folkloristiku ČSAV, 1966.

Kautský, Karel. *Původ křesťanství: Historická studie*. Strakonice, n.d.

Kautsky, Karl and Luise. *Briefwechsel mit der Tschechoslowakei 1879–1939*, edited by Zdeněk Šolle and Jan Gielkens. Quellen und Studien zur Sozialgeschichte 11. New York: Campus, 1993.

Kepel, Gilles. *Boží pomsta: Křesťané, Židé a Muslimové znovu dobývají svět*. Brno: Atlantis, 1996.

Keplinger, Brigitte. "Lassaleanismus in der österreichischen Arbeiterbewegung bis 1914." In *Arbeiterbewegung in Österreich und Ungarn bis 1914. Referate des österreichisch-ungarischen Historikersymposiums in Graz vom 5. bis 9. September 1986*, 147–46. Vienna, 1986.

Klöker, Michael. "Das katholische Milieu." *Zeitschrift für Religions und Geschichte* 44 (1992) 241–47.

Klostermann, Karel. *V ráji šumavském.* Praha: Československý spisovatel, 1969.

Knoblauch, Hubert. *Reigionssoziologie.* New York: Walter de Gruyter, 1999.

Knoll, Reinhold. *Zur Tradition der Christlich-soziale Partei.* Vienna: Böhlau, 1973.

———. *Zur Tradition der christlichsozialen Partei: Ihre Früh- und Entwicklungsgeschichte bis zu den Reichsratswahlen 1907.* Vienna: Böhlau, 1973.

Kocka, Jürgen. "Arbeiterbewegung in der Bürgergesellschaft: Überlegungen zum deutschen Fall." *Geschichte und Gesellschaft* 20 (1994) 487–96.

Kolejka, Josef. "Cyrilometodějská tradice v druhé polovině 19. století." In *Velká Morava: Tisíciletá tradice státu a kultury,* 97–112. Prague: Nakladatelství Československé akademie věd, 1963.

Kondylis, Panajotis. *Die Aufklärung im Rahmen des neuzeitlichen Racionalismus.* Munich: DTV, 1986.

Kopecký, Jan. *Sto let tabákového průmyslu ve Svitavách.* Svitavy: Československý tabákový průmysl, n. p., 1974.

Kořalka, Jiří. "Ateismus průkopníků socialismu v Čechách." In *Církve v našich dějinách,* edited by Bohumil Černý et al., 22–43. Prague: Československá společnost pro šíření politických a vědeckých znalostí, 1960.

———. "Československá sociálně demokratická strana dělnická." In *Politické strany: Vývoj politických stran a hnutí v českých zemích a Československu 1861–2004. 1: 1861–1938,* edited by Jiří Malíř and Pavel Marek et al., 213–39. Brno: Doplněk, 2005.

———. *Češi v habsburské říši a v Evropě 1815–1914: Sociálněhistorické souvislosti vytváření novodobého národa a národnostní otázky v českých zemích.* Prague: Argo, 1996.

———. "František Palacký a čeští bolzanisté." In *Modernismus: Historie nebo výzva?,* 23–47. Brno: L. Marek, 2002.

———. *Severočeští socialisté v čele dělnického hnutí českých a rakouských zemí.* Liberec: Severočeské nakladatelství, 1963.

———. *Vznik socialistického dělnického hnutí na Liberecku.* Liberec: Krajské nakladatelství, 1956.

Kosseleck, Reinhart. "Einleitung." In *Geschichtliche Grundbegriffe.* Vol. 1, edited by Otto Brunner et al., XIII–XXII. Stuttgart: Klett-Cotta, 1972.

Kotek, Josef. "Městská lidová zpěvnost a dělnická píseň". In *Dějiny české populární hudby a zpěvu,* 117–32. Vol. 1. Prague: Academia, 1994.

Kotous, Jan. *Portréty vyšehradské kapituly.* Kostelní Vydří: Karmelitánské nakladatelství, 2007.

Kovács, Elisabeth. "Die katholische Kirche im Spannungsfeld von Nationalismus und Patriotismus zwischen 1848 und 1918." In *Chance der Verständigung: Absichten und Ansätze zu übernationaler Zusammenarbeit in den böhmischen Ländern 1848–1918,* edited by Ferdinand Seibt, 49–62. Munich: R. Oldenbourg 1987.

———. *Katholische Aufklärung und Josephinismus.* Munich: R. Oldenbourg, 1979.

Kraváček, František. "Katolická církev a dělnické hnutí na Moravě před první světovou válkou." *Sborník prací pedagogické fakulty Univerzity Palackého v Olomouci,* Historie 5 (1979) 93–115.

Krejč, F. V. *Dělnický kalendář českoslovanské strany sociálně demokratické v Rakousku 1907.* Prague: Printing department of the Czechoslovak Social Democratic Party (Zář magazine), 1906.

Kryštůfek, František Xaver. *Dějiny církve katolické ve státech rakousko-uherských s obzvláštním zřetelem k zemím koruny české: 1740–1898.* Vol. 2. Prague: Václav Kotrba, 1898.

Kudláč, Antonín K. K. *Příběh(y) Volné myšlenky.* Prague: Nakladatelství Lidové noviny, 2005.

Kudlich, Hans. *Rückblicke und Erinnerungen.* Budweis, n. d.

Kuhn, Elmar L. "Rückständig und glücklich?: Die Säkularisierung Oberschwabens." In *Die Säkularisation im Prozess der Säkularisierung Europas,* edited by Peter Blickle and Rudolf Schlögl, 484–516. Epfendorf: bibliotheca academica, 2005.

Kunte, Ladislav. *Cesty, kterými jsem šel . . .* Prague: Čas, 1907.

———. *Socializace. Základy reálného socialismu.* Prague: Gustav Dubský edition, 1919.

Kürbisch, Friedrich G., and Richard Klucsarits, editors. *Arbeiterinnen kämpfen um ihr Recht: Autobiographische Texte zum Kampf rechtloser und entrechteter "Frauenspersonen" in Deutschland, Österreich und der Schweiz des 19. Jahrhunderts.* Wuppertal: Hammer 1981.

Kutnar, František. *Přehledné dějiny českého a slovenského dějepisectví.* Vol. 1: *Od počátků národní kultury až po vyznění obrodného úkolu dějepisectví ve druhé polovině 19. století.* Prague: Státní pedagogické nakladatelství, 1973.

Kutnar, František. *Sociálně myšlenková tvářnost obrozenského lidu.* Prague: Academia, 1948.

Kutnar, František, and Jaroslav Marek. *Přehledné dějiny českého a slovenského dějepisectví: Od počátků národní kultury až do sklonku třicátých let 20. století.* Prague: Nakladatelství Lidové noviny, 1997.

Landtagsblatt über die Sitzungen des mährischen Landtags. 2. Session 1907/10, 1126–27.

Langewiesche, Dieter. "Die neue Religion des Sozialismus: Tat-Religion ohne Religionsstifter." In *Religionsstifter der Moderne: Von Karl Marx bis Johannes Paul II,* edited by Alf Christophersen and Friedmann Voigt, 83–93, 291. Munich: Beck, 2009.

Lehmann, Hartmut. "Von der Erforschung der Säkularisierung zur Erforschung von Prozessen der Dechristianisierung und der Rechristianisierung im neuzeitlichen Europa: Einleitung." In *Säkularisierung, Dechristianisierung, Rechristianisierung im neuzeitlichen Europa: Bilanz und Perspektiven der Forschung,* 9–16. Göttingen: Vandenhoeck and Ruprecht, 1997.

———. *Säkularisierung, Dechristianisierung, Rechristianisierung im neuzeitlichen Europa: Bilanz und Perspektiven der Forschung.* Göttingen: Vandenhoeck and Ruprecht, 1997.

Leisching, Peter. "Die römisch-katholische Kirche in Cisleithanien." In *Die Habsburgermonarchie 1848–1918.* Vol. 4, edited by Adam Wandruszka and Peter Urbanitsch, 1–247. Vienna: Verlag der Österreichischen Akademie der Wisswenschaften, 1985.

Lenz, Antonín. *Apologie sněmu kostnického v příčině odsouzení 45 vět Jana Viklifa.* 1896.

———. *Byly články, jež svým časem podrýval kněz Jan Viklif, a po něm kněz Jan Hus, jak se po theologicku říká, dobou tou quaestiones liberae, čili skromná odpověď na poučování pana docenta Václava Novotného.* 1899.

———. *Filosofie Jana Brázdy ze Zlámané Lhoty o nesmrtelnosti duše lidské, čili první výstřel Brázdův proti náboženému spisu Alfonse Šťastného o spasení po smrti.* 1874.

———. *Hus a svoboda.* 1890.

———. *Jan Brázda, sedlák ze Zlámané Lhoty, v půtce se sedlákem Alfonsem Šťastným, čili kratochvilné a velmi poučlivé dopisy o přeukrutné učenosti kandidáta filosofie Alfonse Šťastného, sedláka v Padařově, uložené v jeho nejnovějším spisu: „Ježíš a jeho poměr ke křesťanství".* 1873.

———. *Je pravdou nepochybnou, že Mistr Jan Hus umřel za své přesvědčení a že jest mučedníkem za pravdu?* 1898.

———. *P. Chelčického učení o sedmeře svátostí a poměr učení tohoto k Janu Viklifovi.* 1889.

———. *Pan dr. Eduard Grégr, liberalismus jeho a horování za poctu Husovu.* 1890.

———. *Pohroma principu mravnosti Padařovské, kterouž s velkým žalem popisuje Jan Brázda, ze Zlámané Lhoty.* 1875.

———. *Slušno-li zváti M. Jana Husa mučedníkem za pravdu.* 1890.

———. *Socialismus v dějinách lidstva, jeho povaha a církev katolická jedině schopná k řešení sociální otázky.* Prague: Cyrilo-metodějské knihkupectví. 1893.

———. *Soustava učení M. Jana Viklifa na základě pramenů.* 1898.

———. *Syllabus Jeho Svatosti Pia IX., jejž vykládá s povinným zřetelem k Syllabu náčelníka svobodných myslitelů, Alfonse Padařovského, Jan Brázda, sedlák ze Zlámané Lhoty.* 1878.

———. *Učená rozprava Jana Brázdy, sedláka ze Zlámané Lhoty, o jsoucnosti boží, čili druhý výstřel proti náboženému spisu Alfonse Šťastného o spasení po smrti.* 1874.

———. *Učení Mistra Jana Husi na základě latinských i českých spisů jeho, jakož i odsouzení Husovo na sněmu kostnickém.* 1875.

———. *Učení Petra Chelčického o Eucharistii.* 1884.

———. *Vzájemný poměr učení P. Chelčického, starší Jednoty Českých Bratří a Táborů k nauce Valdenských, Jana Husi a Jana Viklifa.* 1895.

Leyburn, James G. "Sumner, William Graham." In *International Encyclopedia of the Social Sciences,* edited by David L. Sills and Robert K. Merton, 407. New York: Macmillan, 1968.

Lidtke, Vernon. "August Bebel and German Social Democracy's Relation to the Christian Churches." *Journal of the History of Ideas* 27 (1966) 245–64.

———. "Social Class and Secularisation in Imperial Germany: The Working Classes." *Leo Baeck Institute Yearbook* 25 (1980) 21–40.

Liedhegener, Antonius. *Christentum und Urbanisierung: Katholiken und Protestanten in Münster und Bochum 1830–1933.* Paderborn: Schöningh, 1997.

Lieske, Adina. *Arbeiterkultur und bürgerliche Kultur in Pilsen und Leipzig.* Bonn: Dietz Verlag, 2007.

Lippert, Julius. *Allgemeine Geschichte des Priestertums.* Vol. 1–2. Berlin: Hofmann, 1883, 1884.

Listy: Príbeh manželstva Jozefa Gregora Tajovského a Hany Gregorovej. Bratislava: Archa 1996.

Loewenstein, Bedřich: *Víra v pokrok. Dějiny jedné evropské ideje.* Prague: Oikúmené 2009.

Luckmann, Thomas. *Invisible Religion: The Problem of Religion in Modern Society.* New York: Macmilllan, 1967.

Luhmann, Niklas. *Die Religion der Gesellschaft.* Frankfurt: Suhrkamp, 2000.

Machačová, Jana. *Mzdové a stávkové hnutí dělnictva v průmyslových oblastech českých zemí 1848–1914.* Opava: Slezský ústav Československé akademie věd, 1990.

———. "Prostředí drobného řemeslnictva v českých zemích druhé poloviny 19. století." In *K novodobým sociálním dějinám českých zemí, II: Z dob rakouských a předlitavských (1848–1918),* edited by Zdeněk Kárník, 101–14. Praha 1998.

———. "Prostředí továrního dělnictva ke konci 19. století: Analýza vzpomínek Františka Halase staršího z let 1885–1913." *Studie k sociálním dějinám 19. století* 6 (1996) 63–100.

———. "Tendence vývoje mezd dělnictva 1848–1914: Srovnání tzv. starých a nových průmyslových oblastí českých zemí." In *K hospodářským a sociálním dějinám 19. a 20. století,* 146–319. 1. Opava: Slezský ústav ČSAV, 1991.

———. "Výzkum stávek z 19. a 20. století v československé historiografii: Přístupy českých a slovenských historiků." *Studie k sociálním dějinám* 9, 139–51. Opava: Slezské muzeum Opava, 1998.

Machačová, Jana, and Jiří Matějček. "'Kdo jediné zná, co něho vůkol jest, zůstává vždy dítětem nevědomým.'" *Sborník prací Filozofické fakulty Ostravské univerzity* 219 (2005) 141–52.

———. "Náboženství, církev, sekularizace v českých zemích 1781–1945." *Slezský sborník* (2008) 1–13.

———. *Nástin sociálního vývoje českých zemí 1781–1914.* Opava: Slezský ústav ČSAV, 2002. 2nd ed. Prague: Karolinum, 2010.

———. *O středních vrstvách v českých zemích 1750–1950.* Opava: Slezský ústav AV ČR, 2002.

———. *Problémy obecné kultury.* Opava: Slezské muzeum v Opavě, 2008.

———. "Vzory chování v českých zemích v 19. století." *Studie k sociálním dějinám 19. století* 7 (1997) 399–482.

Machálek, Franz. "Velehrad ist uns Programm: Zur Bedeutung der Kyrill-Method-Idee und der Velehradbewegung für den Katholizismus in Mähren im 19. und 20. Jahrhundert." *Bohemia* 45 (2005) 353–95.

———. "Velehrad und die Cyril-Method-Idee im 19. und 20. Jahrhundert." *Archiv für Kirchengeschichte von Böhmen, Mähren und Schlesien* 6 (1982) 156–83.

Macková, Marie. "Lékaři v rakouské státní tabákové režii." In *Nardi aristae,* edited by Kristina Kaiserová, 131–49. Plzeň: Albis international, 2007.

———. "Penzisté a penzistky rakouské státní tabákové režie." In *Vetché stáří, nebo zralý věk rozumu?,* edited by Zdeněk Hojda and Marta Ottlová and Roman Prahl, 170–78. Prague: Akademia, 2009.

———. "Projevy nacionalizace společnosti v prostředí státní tabákové režie." In *Nacionalizace společnosti v Čechách 1848–1914,* edited by Kristina Kaiserová and Jiří Rak, 200–228. Ústí nad Labem: Univerzita J. E. Purkyně, 2008.

———. *Tabáková továrna v Lanškrouně jako součást státní tabákové režie.* Lanškroun: Městské muzeum Lanškroun, 2007.

Magris, Claudio. *Habsburský mýtus v moderní rakouské literatuře.* Brno: Barrister & Principal, 2002.

Maier, Hans. *Politická náboženství: Totalitární režimy a křesťanství.* Brno: CDK, 1999.

Malíř, Jiří, and Pavel Marek, et al. *Politické strany: Vývoj politických stran a hnutí v českých zemích a Československu 1861–2004.* Vol. 1. Brno: Doplněk, 2005.

———. "Die Parteien in Mähren und Schlesien und ihre Vereine." In *Die Habsburgermonarchie 1848–1918.* Vol. 8: *Politische Öffentlichkeit und Zivilgesellschaft.* 1: *Vereine, Parteien und Interessenverbände als Träger der politischen Partizipation,* edited by Helmut Rumpler and Peter Urbanitsch, 705–803. Vienna: Österreichische Akademie der Wissenschaften, 2006.

———. "Moravské rolnictvo mezi liberalismem a politickým katolicismem." In *Sekularizace venkovského prostoru v 19. století,* edited by Lukáš Fasora and Jiří Hanuš and Jiří Malíř, 47–68. Brno: Matice moravská, 2009.

———. *Od spolků k moderním politickým stranám.* Brno: Masarykova univerzita, 1996.

———. "Sekularizace a politika v 'dlouhém' 19. století." In *Sekularizace českých zemí v letech 1848–1914,* edited by Lukáš Fasora and Jiří Hanuš and Jiří Malíř, 11–24. Brno: CDK, 2007.

Bibliography

————. *Vývoj liberálního proudu české politiky na Moravě: Lidová strana na Moravě do roku 1909*. Brno: Univerzita J. E. Purkyně, 1985.

Malý, Karel. *Policejní a soudní perzekuce dělnické třídy v druhé polovině 19. století v Čechách*. Prague: Nakladatelství Československé akademie věd, 1967.

Maňák, Jaroslav. "Početnost a struktura české inteligence v letech 1945–1948." *Sociologický časopis* (1967), 398–409.

Marbach, Rainer. *Säkularisierung und sozialer Wandel im 19. Jahrhundert: Die Stellung von Geistlichen zu Entkirchlichung und Entchristlichung in einem Bezirk der hannoverschen Landeskirche*. Göttingen: Vandenhoeck and Ruprecht, 1978.

Marek, Jaroslav: *Šedesát let programové výstavby sociálně demokratické strany dělnické*. Prague: Nákladem Ústředního dělnického knihkupectví a nakladatelství (Ant. Svěcený), 1927.

Marek, Pavel. "Antonín Lenz." In *Cestami křesťanské politiky*, edited by Michal Pehr et al. Prague: Akropolis, 2007.

————. "Biskup Eduard J. N. Brynych: Praha nebo Vídeň? Vlastenectví nebo loajalita? Malý příspěvek k velkému tématu formování národního vědomí českého katolického lidu." In *Církvi a národy strednej Európy (1800–1950)*, edited by Peter Švorc and Ľubica Harbuľová and Karl Schwarz, 248–60. Prešov: Universum, 2008.

————. *Apologetové nebo kacíři?: Studie a materiály k dějinám české katolické moderny*. Rosice u Brna: Gloria, 1999.

————. *Česká katolická moderna*. Rosice u Brna: Gloria, 2000.

————. *Český katolicismus 1890–1914: Kapitoly z dějin českého katolického tábora na přelomu 19. a 20. století*. Olomouc: Gloria, 2003.

————. "Český politický katolicismus a politické strany." In *Politické strany*. Vol. 1, edited by Jiří Malíř and Pavel Marek et al., 255–311. Brno: Doplněk, 2005.

————. "Církev a česká společnost v 19. a na počátku 20. století." In *Česko-slovenská historická ročenka* (2006), 143–54. Brno: Masaryk University, 2006.

————. "Josef Hofer-Rectus: Předběžný náčrt portrétu osobnosti."" In *Acta Universitatis Reginahradecensis, Facultas Paedagogica*, 71–106. Humanistica 1. Hradec Králové, 2008.

————. "K Judově aféře z roku 1906." *Časopis Matice moravské* 113 (1994) 293–311.

————. "K náboženskému profilu Alfonse Šťastného." In *Sekularizace venkovského prostoru v 19. století*, edited by Lukáš Fasora and Jiří Hanuš and Jiří Malíř, 135–60. Brno: Matice moravská 2009.

————. "K problematice církevního rozkolu v Československu v roce 1920." *Český časopis historický* 99 (2001) 1, 87–88.

————. "Počátky českého politického katolicismu v letech 1848–1918." In *Český politický katolicismus 1848–2005*, edited by Petr Fiala et al., 8–170. Brno: CDK, 2008.

————. *Prof. ThDr. Theodor Kohn*. Kroměříž: Muzeum Kroměřížska, 1994.

————. *Teorie a praxe politického katolicismu 1870–2007*. CDK, 2008.

————. "T. G. Masaryk a Wahrmundova aféra." In *T. G. Masaryk a sociální otázka*, 145–57. Hodonín: Masarykovo muzeum v Hodoníně, 2002.

————. "Tisk českého katolického tábora před 1. světovou válkou." In *Tisk a politické strany*, edited by Pavel Marek, 53–88. Olomouc: Univerzita Palackého and Moneta F-M, 2001.

Margin [Jehlička, František]. *Nováveká filosofia a Slováci*. Turčiansky Sv. Martin, 1903.

Markl, Jaroslav. *Nejstarší sbírky českých lidových písní (Kolovratský rukopis, Rittersberkovy České národní písně, Sbírka ze Sadské a jiné)*. Prague: Editio Supraphon, 1987.

Marquard, Odo. "Lob des Polytheismus: Über Monomythie und Polymythie." In *Abschied vom Prinzipiellen, Philosophische Studien*, 91–117. Stuttgart: Ph. Reclam jun., 1981.

Marx, Julius. *Die wirtschaftlichen Ursachen der Revolution von 1848 in Österreich*. Veröffentlichungen der Kommission für Neuere Geschichte Österreichs 51. Graz, Cologne, H. Bohlaus Nachf, 1965.

Masaryk, Tomáš Garrigue. *Sebevražda hromadným jevem společenským moderní osvěty*. Prague: Ústav TGM, 1999.

————. *Světová revoluce: Za války a ve válce, 1914–1918*. Praha: Čin and Orbis, 1925.

————. *V boji o náboženství*. Prague: Čin, 1947.

Matějček, Jiří. "Český dělnický spolek Volnost ve Falknově 1897–1908." *Minulostí Západočeského kraje* 3 (1964) 95–116.

————. "Reálné mzdy horníků uhelných dolů v českých zemích do roku 1914." *Hospodářské dějiny— Economic History* 14 (1986) 217–324.

Matthes, Joachim. *Einführung in Die Religionssoziologie*. Vol. 1: *Religion und Gesellschaft*. Vol. 2: *Kirche und Gesellschaft*. Reinbeck bei Hamburg: Rowohlt, 1967.

McLeod, Hugh. "Berlin, London and New York in the Late Nineteenth and Early Twentieth Centuries." In *Religion and Modernisation: Sociologists and Historians Debate the Secularization Thesis*, edited by Steve Bruce, 59–89. Oxford: Clarendon, 1992.

————. *European Religion in the Age of Great Cities, 1830–1930*. London, New York: Routledge, 1995.

————. *Náboženství a lidé západní Evropy, 1789–1989*. Brno: CDK, 2007.

————. "Protestantism and the Working Class in Imperial Germany." *European Studies Review* 12 (1982) 323–34.

————. *Secularisation in Western Europe 1848-1914*. London: Macmillan, 2000.

Měchýř, Jan. *Bouřlivý kraj*. Ústí nad Labem, 1983.

Meiern, Johann Gottfried von. "Acta Pacis Westphalicae publica." Vol. 2, 15, paragraph 14. In *Die Religion in Geschichte und Gegenwart: Handbuch für Theologie und Religionswissenschaft*, 1280. 2. elektronische Ausgabe der Dritten Aufgabe. Berlin: Direktmedia, 2004.

Melmuková, Eva. *Patent zvaný toleranční*. Prague: Mladá fronta, 1999.

Mill, John St. *Autobiography*. New York: Columbia University Press, 1960.

Modráček, František. *Mistr Jan Hus a jeho doba*. Prague: Published by the printing cooperative of the Czechoslovak Social Democratic Party, 1903.

Molnár, Amadeo, and Josef Smolík. *Čeští evangelíci a toleranční patent*. Prague: Kalich, 1982.

Mommsen, Hans. "Arbeiterbewegung in Deutschland und Österreich." In *Deutschland und Österreich*, edited by Robert Kann and Friedrich Prinz, 424–49. Vienna: Jugend und Volk, 1980.

————. *Die Sozialdemokratie und die Nationalitätenfrage im habsburgischen Vielvölkerstaat. 1: Das Ringen um die supranationale Integration in der zisleithanischen Arbeiterbewegung (1867–1907)*. Vienna: Europa, 1963.

Mooser, Josef. "Volk, Arbeiter und Bürger in der katholischen Öffentlichkeit: Zur Sozial- und Funktions-geschichte der deutschen Katholikentage 1871–1913." In *Bürger in der Gesellschaft der Neuzeit: Wirtschaft—Politik—Kultur*, edited by Hans-Jürgen Puhle, 259–73. Göttingen: Vandenhoeck and Ruprecht, 1991.

Morava, Jiří. *C. k. disident Karel Havlíček*. Prague: Panorama, 1991.

Musilová, Milada. "Konfiskace Rovnosti v letech 1885–1905." *Sborník Matice moravské* 84 (1965) 278–99.

Náboženství, církve, klerikalismus a naše dějiny. Prague: Nakladatelství politické literatury, 1962.

Neruda, Jan. *Nechť nový cíl dá nový den*. Prague: Melantrich, 1973.

Nešpor, Zdeněk R. *Náboženství na prahu nové doby: Česká lidová zbožnost 18. a 19. století*. Ústí n. L.: Albis international, 2006.

Nipperdey, Thomas. *Deutsche Geschichte 1866–1918*. Vol. 1: *Arbeitswelt und Bürgergeist*. Munich: Beck 1998.

Nipperdey, Thomas. *Religion im Umbruch: Deutschland 1870–1918*. Munich: Beck, 1988.

Nolte, Paul. *Religion und Bürgergesellschaft: Brauchen wir einen religionsfreundlichen Staat?* Berlin: Berlin University Press, 2009.

Nový, Lubomír. "Masaryk volnomyšlenkář?" In *Náboženství v českém myšlení*, edited by Jiří Gabriel and Jiří Svoboda, 11–16. Brno: Ústav etiky a religionistiky, 1993.

Organische Bestimmungen und Verhaltungsregeln für die Arbeiter der k. k. Tabakfabriken. Vienna, 1877.

Osterhammel, Jürgren. *Die Verwandlung der Welt: Eine Geschichte des 19. Jahrhunderts*. Munich: C. H. Beck, 2009.

Österreichisches biographisches Lexikon 1815–1950. Vol. 5. Vienna: Verlag der Österr. Akad. der Wiss., 1972.

Pater Salesius [Jehlička, František]. *Sociáldemokracia a náboženstvo*. Trnava, 1912.

Patočka, Jan. *Péče o duši*. Vol. 1. Prague: Oikoymenh, 1997.

Pepřík, Erich. *Neboj se a pojď!: Rozhovory s Mons. Erichem Pepříkem o jeho kněžském povolání i některých aktuálních otázkách dnešní doby*. Vsetín: Jiří Míček, 1999.

Pepper, Hugo. "Die frühe österreichische Sozialdemokratie und die Anfänge der Arbeiterkultur." In *Sozialdemokratie und Habsburgerstaat*, edited by Wolfgang Maderthaner. Vienna: Löcker, 1988.

Bibliography

Petrmichl, Jan. *Bičem a Rašplí: Satira a humor v dělnickém tisku 1870–1918*. Prague: Státní nakladatelství politické literatury, 1959.

Peukert, Josef. *Erinnerungen eines Proletariers aus der revolutionären Arbeiterbewegung*. Berlin: Verlag des Sozialistischen Bundes, 1913.

Pitronová, Blanka. *Haličské migrace na Ostravsku*. Opava: Slezský ústav ČSAV, 1979.

Pokorný, Jiří. "Vereine und Parteien in Böhmen." In *Die Habsburgermonarchie 1848–1918*, vol. 8: *Politische Öffentlichkeit und Zivilgesellschaft*, part 1: *Vereine, Parteien und Interessenverbände als Träger der politischen Partizipation*, edited by Helmut Rumpler and Peter Urbanitsch, 609–703. Vienna: Österreichische Akademie der Wissenschaften, 2006.

Pollack, Detlef. "Religion und Moderne: Zur Gegenwart der Säkularisierung in Europa." In *Religion und Gesellschaft: Europa im 20. Jahrhundert*, edited by Friedrich Wilhelm Graf und Klaus Grosse-Kracht, 73–103.Cologne, Weimar, Vienna: Böhlau, 2007.

Popp, Adelheid. *Jugend einer Arbeiterin: Herausgegeben und eingeleitet von Hans J. Schütz*. Munich: Reinhardt, 1909. Reprint, Berlin: Dietz, 1978.

Potemra, Michal. "Rozvoj spoločenského myslenia na Slovensku na začiatku 20. storočia." *Historický časopis* 29 (1981) no. 3, 329–72.

———. *Bibliografia článkov zo slovenských periodík 1901–1918*. Vol. 3: *Robotnícke hnutie na Slovensku v rokoch 1901–1918*. Martin: Matica slovenská, 1969.

Prokš, Petr. *Politické programy Českoslovanské a Československé sociálně demokratické strany dělnické 1878–1948*. Prague: Historický ústav AV ČR, 1999.

Protokol čtvrtého řádného sjezdu Českoslovanské strany sociálně demokratické konaného ve dnech 8., 9., a 10. září 1900 v Českých Budějovicích zároveň s programem a všemi organisačními a tiskovými řády strany, edited by Fr. Soukup. Prague: Nákladem časopisu Zář, 1900.

Protokol o jednání společného sjezdu sociálně demokratické strany dělnické v Rakousku konaném ve Vídni 2.– 6. listopadu 1901. Prague: Published by the printing cooperative of the Czechoslovak Social Democratic Party (Zář magazine), 1901.

Protokol VI. sjezdu českoslovanské sociálně demokratické strany dělnické dne 30., 31. října a 1. listopadu 1904 v Prostějově. Prague, 1904.

Protokol X. sjezdu českoslovanské sociálně demokratické strany dělnické ve dnech 23. až 27. prosince 1911 v Národním domě na Smíchově. Prague, 1911.

Protokol XI. řádného sjezdu českoslovanské sociálně demokratické strany dělnické konaného ve dnech 7., 8. a 9. prosince 1913 na Žofíně v Praze. Prague 1913, 45.

Prüfer, Sebastian. *Sozialismus statt Religion: Die deutsche Sozialdemokratie vor der religösen Frage 1863–1890*. Kritische Studien zur Geschichtswissenschaft 152. Göttingen: Vandenhoeck und Ruprecht, 2002.

Puhle, Hans-Jürgen. *Bürger in der Gesellschaft der Neuzeit: Wirtschaft—Politik—Kultur*. Göttingen: Vandenhoeck & Ruprecht, 1991.

Purš, Jaroslav. "Tábory v českých zemích v letech 1868–1871." *Československý časopis historický* 6 (1958) 234–66, 446–70, 661–90.

Putna, Martin C. *Česká katolická literatura 1848–1918*. Prague: Torst 1998.

Rak, Jiří. *Bývali Čechové*. Prague: H&H, 1994.

———. "Dělníci na vinici Páně nebo na roli národní?" In *Bůh a bohové: Církve, náboženství a spiritualita v českém 19. století*, edited by Zdeněk Hojda and Roman Prahl, 128–38. Prague: Koniasch Latin Press, 2003.

———. "Exotismus doma aneb Venkov versus město." In *Cizí, jiné, exotické v české kultuře 19. století*, edited by Kateřina Bláhová, 221–27. Prague: Academia, 2008.

Randák, Jan. "Z apoštola se stal mučedník...": Robert Blum jako 'oběť' německé revoluce 1848–1849." In *Národ místo boha v 19. a první polovině 20. století*, edited by Kateřina Kaiserová and Martin Veselý, 34–52. Ústí nad Labem: Ústav slovansko-germánských studií, 2006.

"Rau, Heribert." In *Allgemeine Deutsche Biographie*. Vol. 27 (1888) 376. Online: http://de.wikisource.org/w/index.php?title=ADB:Rau,_Heribert&oldid=681972 (19.7.2009).

Rehbein, Franz. *Das Leben eines Landarbeiters: With an Epilogue by Urs J. Diederichs and Holger Rüdel*. Jena: Diederichs, 1911. Reprint, Hamburg: Christians, 1985.

Religion in Geschichte und Gegenwart. Vol. 5. Tübingen: Mohr/Siebeck, 1957–1963.

Rémond, René. *Náboženství a společnost v Evropě*. Praha: Nakladatelství Lidové noviny, 2003.

Ribbe, Wolfgang. "Zur Entwicklung und Funktion der Pfarrgemeinden in der evangelischen Kirche Berlins bis zum Ende der Monarchie." In *Seelsorge und Diakonie in Berlin: Beiträge zum Verhältnis von Kirche und Großstadt im 19. und beginnenden 20. Jahrhundert,* edited by Kaspar Elm and Hans-Dietrich Loock, 233–263. Berlin, New York: Walter de Gruyter, 1990.

Rieger, Eduard. "Nordböhmische Reminiszenzen." In *Der Kampf.* Vol. 2. Vienna, 1908/09.

Ritter, Gerhard A., and Klaus Tenfelde. *Arbeiter im Deutschen Kaiserreich 1871 bis 1914.* Bonn: J. H. W. Dietz, 1992.

Rohel, Jan. "Život dělnické rodiny v kolonii na Ostravsku." *Radostná země* (1954) 7–8.

Rückblick auf die Verwaltung und Tätigkeit des Industriellen Bildungsvereins in Reichenberg während seines zehnjährigen Bestandes vom 14. September 1863 bis 15. September 1873. Reichenberg: Selbstverlag, 1873.

Rychlík, Jan. *Korespondence T. G. Masaryk—slovenští veřejní činitelé (do r. 1918).* Praha: Masarykův ústav a Archiv AV ČR, 2008.

Řepa, Milan. "'Rušení náboženství' na Jižní Moravě: Sekularizace ve světle protokolů Krajského trestního soudu v Brně z let 1859–1914." In *Sekularizace venkovského prostoru v 19. století,* edited by Lukáš Fasora and Jiří Hanuš and Jiří Malíř, 125–34. Brno: Matice Moravská, 2009.

———. "Sekularizace českého národního hnutí na Moravě." In *Sekularizace českých zemí v letech 1848–1914,* edited by Lukáš Fasora and Jiří Hanuš and Jiří Malíř, 67–75. Brno: CDK, 2007.

Saldern, Adelheid von. "Latent Reformism and Socialist Utopia. The SPD in Göttingen, 1890 to 1920." In *Between Reformism and Revolution: Studies in the History of German Socialism and Communism from 1840 to 1990,* edited by David E. Barclay and Eric D. Weitz, 195–221. New York: Berghahn, 1998.

Saldern, Adelheid von. *Vom Einwohner zum Berger: Zur Emantipation der städtischen Unterschicht Göttingens 1890–1920: Eine sozial- und kommunalhistorische Untersuchung.* Berlin: Duncker&Humblot, 1973.

Salichová, Helena. *Ze starých časů: Kronika slezského kraje.* Prague, 1947.

Sauter, Gerhard. "Die Sorge um den Menschen in der evangelischen Theologie des 19. und 20. Jahrhunderts." In *Seelsorge und Diakonie in Berlin: Beiträge zum Verhältnis von Kirche und Großstadt im 19. und beginnenden 20. Jahrhundert,* edited by Kaspar Elm and Hans-Dietrich Loock, 3–21. Berlin, New York: Walter de Gruyter, 1990.

Sewering-Wollanek, Marlis. *Brot oder Nationalität?: Nordwestböhmische Arbeiterbewegung im Brennpunkt der Nationalitätenkobflikte (1889–1911).* Marburg 1994.

Schiller, Seff. *Gesammelte Werke.* Reichenberg: Verlag Ronge, 1928.

Schlögl, Rudolf. "Rationalisierung als Entsinnlichung religiöser Praxis?: Zur sozialen und medialen Form von Religion in der Neuzeit." In *Die Säkularisation im Prozess der Säkularisierung Europas,* edited by Peter Blickle and Rudolf Schlögl, 37–64. Epfendorf: bibliotheca academica, 2005.

Schmid-Egger, Barbara. *Klerus und Politik in Böhmen um 1900.* Munich: Robert Lerche, 1974.

Schmidlin, Josef. *Papstgeschichte der Neuesten Zeit.* Vol. 3. Munich: Kösel & Pustet 1936.

Schmidt, Jürgen. *Begrenzte Spielräume: Eine Beziehungsgeschichte von Arbeiterschaft und Bürgertum am Beispiel Erfurts.* Göttingen: Vandenhoeck and Ruprecht, 2005.

Schmitt, Carl. "Das Zeitalter der Neutralisierungen und Entpolitisierungen." In *Positionen und Begriffe,* 120–33. Hamburg: Hanseatische Verlaganstalt, 1940.

Schnadelbach, Herbert. *Philosophie in Deutschland 1831–1933.* Frankfurt: Suhrkamp, 1983.

Scholz, Franz. "Die Reichenberger Tuchknappenbruderschaft: Der Kampf um ihren Bestand und ihr Ende." *Mitteilungen des Vereines für Heimatkunde des Jeschken-Isergaues* 30 (1936) 145–61.

Schulze Wessel, Martin. "Tschechische Nation und katholische Konfession vor und nach der Gründung des tschechoslowakischen Nationalstaats." *Bohemia* 38 (1997) 311–27.

———. "Vyznání a národ v českých zemích." In *Češi a Němci: Dějiny—kultura—politika,* edited by Walter Koschmal and Martin Nekula and Joachim Rogall, 126–31. Prague, Litomyšl: Paseka, 2002.

Schulze Wessel, Martin, and Martin Zückert. *Handbuch der Religions- und Kirchengeschichte der böhmischen Länder und Tschechiens im 20. Jahrhundert.* Munich: R. Oldenbourg, 2009.

Schwaiger, Georg. *Papstum und Päpste im 20. Jahrhundert.* Munich: Beck, 1999.

Schwella, Eduard. *Geschichte der Glaubens-Mythen: Hilfsbuch zum Religionsunterrichte der konfessionslosen Schulkinder in der freien Kirche der Vernunft.* Vienna: Selbstverlag, 1881.

Skalák, Joža: *Ježíš-bůh a ne člověk.* Prague: Published by the press committee of the Czechoslovak Social Democratic Workers' Party (Zář magazine), 1910.

Bibliography

Skalníková, Olga. "Problém Ostravska jako etnografické oblasti: příspěvek ke studiu vytváření novodobé etnografické oblasti." *Český lid* 60 (1973) 362.

Sked, Alan. *Úpadek a pád habsburské říše.* Prague: Panevropa, 1995.

Smutný, Martin. "Srovnání činnosti Ladislava Kunta a Františka Loskota." Master's thesis. Masaryk University, Arts Faculty, 2004.

Sommer, Jiří. "Československý tabákový průmysl v letech 1918–1938." Master's thesis, Charles University, 1973.

Sommerlad, Philipp. *Vom „Hessebub" zum „Bochumer Jungen": 70 Jahre sozialistische Bewegung in Bochum (1878–1948).* Edited by Peter Friedemann. Essen: Klartext, 1990.

Soukup, František. *Bezvěrci dle práva rakouského: Vývoj, právní poměry a jich reformy.* Prague: Published by the press committee of the Czechoslovak Social Democratic Workers' Party (Zář magazine), 1904.

Soyka, Karl. *Der Fortbildungs- und Geselligkeitsklub in Reichenberg: Die Geschichte seiner Tätigkeit in den Jahren 1846–1896.* Reichenberg: Selbstverlag des Vereins, 1896.

Spohn, Wilfried. "Religion and Working Class Formation in Imperial Germany 1871–1914." *Politics and Society* 19 (1991) 109–32.

Stambolis, Barbara. *Religiöse Festkultur: Tradition und Neuformierung katholischer Frömmigkeit im 19. und 20. Jahrhundert: Das Liborifest in Paderborn und das Kilianifest in Würzburg im Vergleich.* Paderborn: Schöningh, 2000.

Staněk, František. *700 let kláštera v Nové Říši a útěk preláta Drápalka: Odpověď na jubilejní spis vydaný k 700-letému trvání jeho prelátem Norbertem Drápalíkem.* Brno 1912.

Stašek, Antal. "Hrst úvah, chumáč vzpomínek". In *Založení Národního divadla 1868,* 61–76. Prague: Slavnostní výbor pro jubileum Národního divadla, 1918.

Steenson, Gary. *After Marx, Before Lenin: Marxism and Socialist Working-Class Parties in Europe 1884–1914.* Pittsburgh: University of Pittsburgh Press, 1991.

Stenographische Berichte über die Verhandlungen des Deutschen Reichstages. 1. Legislaturperiode, III. Session 1872. Vol. 2. Berlin 1872. Online: http://www.payer.de/religionskritik/bebel01.htm.

Sto let jihlavské tabákovky. Jihlava: Československý tabákový průmysl, 1951.

Strauss, Emil. *Die Entstehung der deutschböhmischen Arbeiterbewegung.* Prague, 1925.

Svobodová, Blanka. "Nástin dějin kalendářové literatury Českoslovanské sociálně demokratické strany dělnické v letech 1878–1918." *Český lid* 76 (1989) 239–43.

Šamalík, Josef. *Hnutí katolických zemědělců v národě československém.* Brno: Czechoslovak People´s Party publication, 1931.

Šebek, Jaroslav. *Mezi křížem a národem: Politické prostředí sudetoněmeckého katolicismu v meziválečném Československu.* Brno: CDK, 2006.

Šebesta, Josef. "Pivo jako inspirační zdroj v českých národních písních aneb Život v písni od Rittersberga (1825) po sbírku Dítě vlasti (1895)." In *Pivo lepších časů,* edited by Martin Veselý and Kristina Kaiserová. Ústí nad Labem: Univerzita J. E. Purkyně, 2007.

Šindelář, Bedřich. "Přehled dějin dělnického hnutí na Moravě od hainfeldského sjezdu." *Časopis Matice moravské* 73 (1954) 1, 3–57.

Šlesinger, Václav. *Z bojů o pokrokovou Moravu 1890–1918.* Brno: Novela 1947.

Šmeral, Bohumír. *Klerikálové a oprava manželského práva: Sociálně-demokratická odpověď ke kněžské lži.* Prague: Published by the press committee of the Czechoslovak Social Democratic Workers' Party (Zář magazine) in Prague, 1906.

Šnebergová, Irena. *Augustin Smetana: Příběh jedné exkomunikace a doprovodné texty: Autobiografie, zápisky z pozůstalosti a korespondence Augustina Smetany.* Prague: Filosofia, 2008.

Šolle, Zdeněk. *Dělnické hnutí v českých zemích koncem minulého století (1887–1897).* Prague: Rovnost, 1954.

Šolle, Zdeněk. *Karel Kautsky a Československo.* Práce z dějin České akademie věd B 8. Prague: Archiv AV ČR and Masarykova dělnická akademie, 1995.

Šolle, Zdeněk. *Vojta Náprstek a jeho doba.* Prague: Felis, 1994.

Španodolinec [Kmeť, Štefan]. *Sociálny demokratismus a kresťanské náboženstvo.* Banská Bystrica, 1913.

Špera, Alois M. *Jak povstalo křesťanství.* Brno: In an edition of the magazine Červánky, 1906.

———. *Kdo stvořil člověka: Úvod do theorie Darvinovy.* Brno: In an edition of the magazine Červánky, 1906.

———. *O vývinu tvorstva a člověka: Tresť učení Darvinova.* Brno: In an edition of the magazine Červánky, 1892.

————. *Stručná pohlavní zdravověda*. Brno: In an edition of the magazine Červánky, 1914.

————. *Z dejín cirkve*. Chicago: Slovenské socialistické nakladateľské družstvo v Chicago, 1910.

————. *Z dějin církve: Vypsání všech důležitějších událostí od počátku křesťanství až do dnešní doby*. Brno: In an edition of the magazine Červánky, 1908.

Šrobár, Vavro. *Z môjho života*. Praha 1946.

Štaif, Jiří. *František Palacký: Život, dílo, mýtus*. Prague: Vyšehrad, 2009.

Tabellen zur Statistik des österreichischen Tabak- Monopoles der im Reichsrathe vertretenen Königreiche und Länder. Vienna 1880.

Taylor, Charles. *A Secular Age*. Cambridge, Mass.: Belknap, 2007.

Těhle, Jaroslav. *Přehled dějin československého odborového hnutí*. Prague: Práce, 1984.

Tenfelde, Klaus, and Bernard Ritter. *Arbeiter im Deutschen Kaiserreich 1871 bis 1914*. Bonn: Dietz, 1992.

Teuteberg, Hans-Jürgen. "Moderne Verstädterung und kirchliches Leben in Berlin: Forschungsergebnisse und Forschungsprobleme." In *Seelsorge und Diakonie in Berlin: Beiträge zum Verhältnis von Kirche und Großstadt im 19. und beginnenden 20. Jahrhundert*, edited by Kaspar Elm and Hans-Dietrich Loock, 161–200. New York: Walter de Gruyter, 1990.

The End of Ideology: On the Exhaustion of Political Ideas in the Fifties. Glencoe, IL: Free Press, 1960.

Tinková, Daniela. "Profanace posvátna a odkouzlení světa: Rouhačství a svatokrádež mezi magickým světem tradiční Evropy a na prahu občanské společnosti." *Lidé města. Revue pro etnologii, antropologii a etologii komunikace* 12 (2003) 13–49.

Tippelt, Rudolf, et al. *Handbuch Erwachsenenbildung: Weiterbildung*. 2nd ed. Opladen: Leske und Budrich, 1999.

Tobolka, Zdeněk V. *Politické dějiny československého národa od r. 1848 až do dnešní doby*. Vol. 2. Prague: Československý kompas, 1933.

Tocqueville, Alexis de. *Starý režim a revoluce*. Prague: Academia, 2003.

Trapl, Miloš. *Politický katolicismus a Československá strana lidová v Československu v letech 1918–1938*. Prague: Státní pedagogické nakladatelství, 1990.

Tumpach, Josef, and Antonín Podlaha. *Bibliografie české katolické literatury náboženské od roku 1828 až do konce roku 1913*. Prague: Dědictví sv. Prokopa, 1923.

Urban, Otto. "Bohumír Šmeral a František Modráček jako představitelé dvou ideologických linií v české sociální demokracii před první světovou válkou." *Československý časopis historický* 11 (1963) 432–44.

Urban, Otto. *Kapitalismus a česká společnost: K otázkám formování české společnosti v XIX. století*. Prague: Lidové noviny, 2006.

Vaněk, Karel. *Co dělat ?: Několik kapitol o nás pro nás*. Brno: Czechoslovak Social Democratic Worker´s Party publication, 1911.

Veber, Tomáš. "J. V. Jirsík a jeho kruh: Církevně-společenské aktivity biskupa Jana Valeriána Jirsíka a jeho spolupracovníků." In *Duchovní a myšlenkové proměny druhé poloviny 19. století*, edited by Rudolf Svoboda and Martin Weis and Peter Zubko, 98–108. České Budějovice: Jihočeská univerzita, 2006.

Ventura, František. *Dějiny c. k. továrny na tabák v Sedleci*. Kutná Hora, 1912.

Veverková, Kamila. "K problematice studia osvícenství u nás a pramenů, týkajících se některých Bolzanových žáků." In *Duchovní a myšlenkové proměny druhé poloviny 19. století*, edited by Rudolf Svoboda and Martin Weis and Peter Zubko, 25–47. České Budějovice: Jihočeská univerzita, 2006.

Vocelka, Karl. "Staat und Kirche in der Periode der deutschliberalen Herrschaft." In *Studien zum Deutschliberalismus in Zisleithanien 1873-1879*, edited by Leopold Kammerhofer, 74–90. Vienna: Verlag der Österreichischen Akademie der Wissenschaften, 1992.

Vocelka, Karl. *Verfassung oder Konkordat?: Der publizistische und politische Kampf der österreichischen Liberalen um die Religionsgesetze des Jahres 1868*. Studien zur Geschichte der österreichisch-ungarischen Monarchie 17. Vienna: Verlag der Österreichischen Akademie der Wisswenschaften, 1978.

Vojtěch, Tomáš. *Mladočeši a boj o politickou moc v Čechách*. Prague: Academia, 1980.

Vošahlíková, Pavla, and Milan Řepa. *Bratři Grégrové a česká společnost v druhé polovině 19. století*. Prague: Eduard Grégr and Son, 1997.

Vzájemnost. IX. Zpráva účetní za rok 1906.

Vzdělávejme se!, Hlas lidu 3.6. 1908, year 23, no. 44.

Wandruszka, Adam, and Peter Urbanitsch. *Die Habsburgermonarchie 1848-1918*. Vienna: Verlag der Österreichischen Akademie der Wissenschaften, 1985; 2nd ed. 2003.

Bibliography

Weber, Heiko, and Maurizio Di Bartolo. *Monismus um 1900—Organisation und Weltanschauung.* Jahrbuch für Europäische Wissenschaftskultur / Yearbook for European Culture of Science. Vol. 3 (2007), edited by Olaf Breidbach and Stefano Poggi. Stuttgart: Franz Steiner, 2008.

Weber, Max. *Gesammelte Aufsätze zur Wissenschaftslehre.* Tübingen: Mohr/Siebeck,1922.

Weber, Max. *Metodologie, sociologie, politika.* Praha: Oikoymenh, 1998.

Weber, Max. "Věda jako povolání." In *Metodologie, sociologie, politika,* 109–34. Prague: Oikumenh, 1998.

Weber, Max. *Wirtschaft und Gesellschaft: Grundriss der verstehenden Sociologie.* Tübingen: Mohr/Siebeck, 1921.

Wegner, Gerhard. *Alltägliche Distanz: Zum Verhältnis von Arbeitern und Kirche.* Hannover: Luthersches Verlagshaus, 1988.

Wehler, Hans-Ulrich. *Deutsche Gesellschaftsgeschichte.* Vol. 3: *"Von der 'Deutschen Doppelrevolution' bis zum Beginn des Ersten Weltkrieges 1849-1914."* Munich: Beck, 1995.

———. *Nationalismus: Geschichte, Formen, Folgen.* Munich: Beck, 2001.

Weis, Martin. "Osvícenští panovníci habsbursko-lotrinské dynastie." In *Osvícenství a katolická církev,* edited by Rudolf Svoboda and Martin Weis and Peter Zubko, 5–21. České Budějovice: Jihočeská univerzita, 2005.

Weis, Martin. "Proměny vztahů mezi církví a habsbursko-lotrinskou dynastií v druhé polovině 19. století." In *Duchovní a myšlenkové proměny druhé poloviny 19. století,* edited by Rudolf Svoboda and Martin Weis and Peter Zubko, 8–24. České Budějovice: Jihočeská univerzita, 2006.

Weitlauff, Martin. "'Modernismus' als Forschungsproblem." *Zeitschrift für Kirchengeschichte* 93 (1982).

Weitlauff, Martin. *Kirche zwischen Aufbruch und Verweigerung.* Stuttgart: Kohlhammer, 2001.

Welskopp, Thomas. "Die 'Generation Bebel.'" In *Generationen in der Arbeiterbewegung,* edited by Klaus Schönhoven and Bernd Braun, 51–68. Munich: Oldenbourg Wissenschaftsverlag, 2005.

Werner, Lothar. *Der Alldeutsche Verband 1890-1918: Ein Beitrag zur Geschichte der öffentlichen Meinung in Deutschland in den Jahren vor und währends des Weltkrieges.* Berlin, 1935; 2nd ed. Vadenz, 1965.

Winter, Eduard. *Der Josefinismus und seine Geschichte: Beiträge zur Geistesgeschichte Österreichs 1740-1848.* Munich, Vienna: R. M. Rohrer, 1943.

Wintzer, Friedrich. "Evangelische Predigt seit dem ersten Drittel des 19. Jahrhunderts." In *Seelsorge und Diakonie in Berlin: Beiträge zum Verhältnis von Kirche und Großstadt im 19. und beginnenden 20. Jahrhundert,* edited by Kaspar Elm and Hans-Dietrich Loock, 293–328. Berlin, New York: Walter de Gruyter, 1990.

Wladika, Michael. *Hitlers Vätergeneration: Die Ursprünge des Nationalismus in der k. u. k. Monarchie.* Vinna, Cologne, Weimar: Böhlau, 2005.

Wolker, Jiří. "Svatý Kopeček." In *Dílo Jiřího Wolkera, Básně, Prósy, Dramata,* 55. Prague: Václav Petr, 1926.

Xaver Rozkošný [Borek, Edmund] *Sociálna demokracia a náboženstvo.* Bratislava, 1913.

XVI. Ročenka Dělnického potravního spolku Vzájemnost 1913.

Z dějin hutnictví 11 (1982) and 12 (1984).

Zita, Stanislav. *Alfons Šťastný—sedlák a filozof.* Jistebnice: Obecní úřad, 2003.

Znoj, Milan, et al. *Český liberalismus: Texty a osobnosti.* Prague: Torst, 1995.

Zpěvník českých dělnických písní. Chicago: published by Josef Boleslav Pecka, 1887.

Zubek, Milan. *Tradice protináboženského a protiklerikálního boje v našich zemích (Volná myšlenka).* Prague, 1961.

Zuber, Rudolf. *Osudy moravské církve v 18. století (1695–1777).* Vol. 2. Olomouc, 2003.

Zumr, Josef. "The actions of Mr Masaryk are not viewed by Catholics as being unfriendly in nature: The Church and TGM 1880-1900." In *Bůh a bohové: Církve, náboženství a spiritualita v českém 19. století,* edited by Zdeněk Hojda and Roman Prahl, 46–54. Prague: Koniasch Latin Press, 2003.

UNPUBLISHED WORKS

Archiv města Brna [Brno City Archives]

Archiv města Ostravy [Ostrava City Archives]

Archív literatúry a umenia Slovenskej národnej knižnice [The Literature and Art Archives of the Slovak National Library] in Martin

Archív Spolku sv. Vojtecha [The Society of St. Adalbert's Archives] in Trnava

Moravský zemský archiv [Moravian Provincial Archives] in Brno
Moravské zemské muzeum [Moravian Museum] in Brno
Národní archiv [National Archives] in Prague
Sächsisches Hauptstaatsarchiv [The Saxon Central State Archives] in Dresden
Slovenský národný archív [Slovak National Archives] in Bratislava
Státní oblastní archiv [State Regional Archives] in Prague
Státní okresní archiv [State District Archives] in Liberec
Státní okresní archiv [State District Archives] in Prostějov
Státní okresní archiv [State Distrikt Archives] in Ústí nad Orlicí
Zemský archiv Opava [Opava provincial archives]

NEWSPAPERS AND PERIODICALS

Akademie
Arbeiterfreund
Arbeiterstimme
Červánky
Das Kuhländchen
Dělnické listy
Dělník v tabákové továrně
Der Tabakarbeiter
Hlas
Hlas lidu
Ječmínek
Kovodělník
Křik lidu
Naše listy
Nordböhmischer Volksbote
Nordböhmische Volksstimme
Odborný list dělnictva textilního v Rakousku
Právo lidu
Rašple
Reichenberger Zeitung
Robotnícke noviny
Rovnost
Slezský sborník
Slovenské ľudové noviny
Sozialpolitische Rundschau
Stráž Vysočiny
Svépomoc
Tribüne
Volksfreund
Volkspresse
Volksrecht
Volksstaat
Volksstaat-Erzähler
Volné slovo
Vorwärts
Wahrheit
Zájmy textilníka/Textilník

Index*

* terms in *italics* denote literary works

Index

Union of Social Democratic Atheists, 175–86
USSM, 184–86

Vaněk, Karel, 134
Vatican Council
  industrial society, Church response to, 116
  papal infallibility and, 92, 93–94, 164
Verband der deutschen Gehilfen und
  Arbeitervereinigungen [The Union
  of German Auxiliary and Workers'
  Association], 146
Verein der Konfessionslosen [The
  Association of Non-Believers], 170–71
Veselovský, František, 63, 64
Veselý, Antonin, 96–97
Virgin Mary, cult of, 33, 39
Voice, 62, 64–67, 69
Voice of the People, 100
Volná myšlenka, 96
Volná myšlenka [Free Thought]
  atheism as, 12
  Catholic Church, rival to, 174
  as core of Czech atheist movement, 96
  federation of atheists (Brussels) 1880, 94
  freethinking literature, Schwarz and, 171
  Myslík and, 96–97
  Ostravsko meeting (1919), 176–77
  press and, 155–56
  priests on, 152–53
  Šťasný and, 92
  World Congress, XIV (1907), 96, 153
  World Congress, XVIII, 178
  World Congress of Free Thought (1904), 96
Volné sdruženi sociálnedemokratických
  bezverců [The Free Union of Social
  Democratic Atheists], 178
Volné slovo, 175–79, 181, 182–83
Volnost [Freedom], miners' association, 29–30
Voltaire, on integration concept, 20
Vrchlický, Jaroslav, 80
Vzájemnost, 136
Vznik kresťanstva (Jehlička), 66–67

Wagner, Jan A., 75
Wahrmund, Ludwig, 107
Weber, Bedřich Dionys, 201

Weber, Max
  on de-religiousification, 12–14
  disenchantment of the world, 5, 12, 22, 40
  on magic, rejection of, 13–14
  objectivity of modern science, principles of, 9
  Occidental rationalization of the world, 12
  on Protestant ethics and capitalism, 6
  on rationality of behavior and decision-making, 15–16
  on science and religion, comparison of, 14–15
  "Science as a Vocation" lecture, 14
  "the iron cage of submission," 12–13
Weitling, Wilhelm, 54
White Flat, The, 158
Wichern, Johann Hinrich, 56
Wojtyla, Karol, 3
Wolker, Jiří
  Svatý Kopeček [The Holy Hill], 204
Woman and Socialism, The (Bebel), 56, xiii
women. *See* females
Workers' Academy, 179
workers' associations. *See* individual association names
Workers' Educational Association, 163
Workers' Hymn to the First of May 1890
  (Krapka-Náchodský), 205
workers' movements
  Catholic, 52
  Christian, 39–40
  in Liberec, 164
  Protestant, 40
  Social Democratic, 39–45
Worker's Newspaper, The, 71, 73, 80
Worker's Physical Education Unit, 179
workers' songs
  Byl prvni máj 1890 [The First of May 1890] (Neruda), 205
  as cultural category, 200–208
  Dělnická hymna k1.máji 1890 [Workers' Hymn to the First of May 1890] (Krapka-Náchodský), 205
  Hej, Slované [Hey, Slavs] (Pecka), 204
  manuscript of, 201
  Nová píseň [New Song], 202–3
  Pokrokářská [Progressive], 205
working class
  antiauthoritarian, 35, 36
  anti-clericalism, 28–29

www.ingramcontent.com/pod-product-compliance
Lightning Source LLC
Chambersburg PA
CBHW080234270326
41926CB00020B/4233